Women in American History

Series Editors

Mari Jo Buhle

Nancy A. Hewitt

Anne Firor Scott

A list of books in the series appears at the end of this book.

Mistresses and Slaves

Mistresses and Slaves

Plantation Women in South Carolina, 1830–80

Marli F. Weiner

University of Illinois Press

Urbana and Chicago

1 2 3 4 5 C P 5 4 3 2 1

This book is printed on acid-free paper.

Library of Congress Cataloging-in-Publication Data
Weiner, Marli Frances, 1953–
Mistresses and slaves : plantation women in South Carolina,
1830–80 / Marli F. Weiner.
p.   cm. — (Women in American history)
Includes bibliographical references and index.
ISBN 0-252-02322-6 (alk. paper). —
ISBN 0-252-06623-5 (pbk. : alk. paper)
1. Women slaves—South Carolina—Social conditions.
2. Plantation owners' spouses—South Carolina—Social conditions.
3. Plantation life—South Carolina—History—19th century.
4. South Carolina—Race relations. 5. Sex role—South Carolina—
History—19th century. I. Title. II. Series.
E445.S7W45   1998
305.48'8960757—dc21   96-45830
CIP

For Dale

Contents

Acknowledgments

Many people have helped me in the process of transforming my dissertation into this book. Suzanne Lebsock, Jerry Nadelhaft, David Smith, and Mazie Hough read all or most of the manuscript; I have benefited dramatically from their suggestions. Colleagues at the University of Maine have been supportive of all aspects of completing the manuscript and of me during a difficult period. Students, both graduate and undergraduate, have been enthusiastic about discussing gender and race and gracious about hearing more about South Carolina than most of them ever thought possible. I wrote my dissertation at the University of Rochester, where I benefited from the direction of Eugene Genovese, Christopher Lasch, and Stanley Engerman. Other teachers also influenced my thinking: I first learned to pay attention to southern women from Anne Firor Scott when she spent a year at Johns Hopkins University. Gerda Lerner, Ann J. Lane, and Alice Kessler-Harris continued my education in women's history at Sarah Lawrence College and provided important examples of scholarship.

Cathryn Adamsky, Susan Franzosa, Liz Whaley, and Barbara White of the University of New Hampshire's "Women in Nineteenth-Century American Culture: An Institute in the Humanities for High School English and Social Studies Teachers" (funded by the National Endowment for the Humanities) helped me to better understand every aspect of nineteenth-century women's experiences and to share what I know more effectively. I have learned far more than I can express about feminist scholarship from working with them.

A number of friends and family members also influenced my thinking and were helpful in the process of writing this book. Gail Seneca, Ayala Gabriel, Lucie Arbuthnot, and Colleen Keenan of the writing group were helpful in the early stages, as were Gail Alter Sacco and Cathy Tumber. My parents and late grandmother have been proud and confident in my abilities, if a bit impatient. My four-legged critters kept me company during long days at my desk.

Librarians at many institutions have made the task of studying southern history at a distance easier. The staffs of the interlibrary loan departments at the University of Rochester, Grinnell College, and the University of Maine filled seemingly endless requests with great patience. My work has also been made possible by the superb collections and helpful staffs at the Southern Historical Collection, University of North Carolina at Chapel Hill; the South Caroliniana Library at the University of South Carolina; the Manuscript Division of the William R. Perkins Library at Duke University; the South Carolina Department of History and Archives; and the Library of Congress.

The staff at the University of Illinois Press has been helpful and patient beyond measure. I am grateful to Carole Appel and Karen Hewitt for their faith in this project. I am also grateful to Anne Scott for pushing me to sharpen my ideas.

This book could not have been written without Dale Engel. Only she knows all of the difficulties she has helped me to transcend.

Mistresses and Slaves

Introduction

In the antebellum South, gender and race were the two most significant shapers of individual experiences. Other factors such as class, region, religion, family, skill, personality, even appearance, were also important, of course, but being born free or enslaved, male or female determined the possibilities and limitations for each individual. Although the presence of free blacks in small but significant numbers blurred the distinctions somewhat, race determined whether an individual was free or enslaved. As an institution, slavery was more than simply the absence of freedom; it carried with it a set of behaviors required of slaves and slaveholders. Although these behaviors were a matter of constant negotiation between individual slaves and slaveholders, their presence, like the violence that kept them in place, defined the experience of slavery. Similarly, gender expectations were based on a complex set of assumptions and rules about appropriate behavior. Men and women believed that their biological differences encompassed differences in personality and behavior that extended to every aspect of life.

Gender and race defined individual characteristics and behaviors expected of slave and free men and women. These simple bifurcations also defined social interactions, shaping the ways in which slave men, slave women, white men, and white women thought about, talked with, and acted toward one another. The expectations associated with gender and race created powerful ideologies that intersected in the lives of individuals and shaped their relationships in the complex society of antebellum plantations, farms, and cities.

Gender and race ideologies had particularly telling consequences for plantation women because they contained contradictory messages. As whites and as slaveholders, mistresses were told they were superior in every respect to slaves and that slaves were at once their responsibility and necessary for their livelihood. They were taught to believe that slaves were lazy and unwilling to work without violence or the threat of violence. At the same time they were taught to see themselves as devoted wives and mothers whose benevolent nurturing and caring were supposed to extend to those in need—including slaves. Inevitably, black women viewed whites and themselves in rather ambivalent and contradictory terms. As slaves, they were expected by whites to work as long and as hard as men. Their womanhood was not respected by whites, and they were vulnerable to physical, emotional, and sexual violence, as well as to separation from their families. Within the slave quarters, however, gender differences were accorded more validity, and women were expected to conform to notions of appropriate behavior in the slave culture.

Both groups of women took gender and race expectations seriously, in spite of the difficulties they could sometimes cause. When black and white women came together, as they did every day on most antebellum plantations, their interactions, influenced by their experiences and expectations as women and as slaves or slaveholders, were fraught with ambivalence. Such ambivalence, born of gender and race ideologies, helped to shape plantation women's lives as well as the nature of antebellum society.

Gender and race expectations had several kinds of consequences for plantation women. They determined the work each woman did and the circumstances in which she did it. They shaped how she saw herself and how others saw her. They influenced how she interacted with others. All of these consequences affected women differently. Some believed their similarities as women transcended racial differences, although in the South race could never be forgotten. Others perceived race as overriding gender. Most sought a middle ground between the two extremes, a juggling of similarities and differences that could add to—or ease—the tensions of everyday life.

The polarizing impact of race could be exaggerated when women used gender and race expectations to their own advantage. Ideology could justify behavior by white women that reinforced the institution of slavery. Ideology and oppression could also limit the ways in which black women understood themselves as women, with different experiences from black men. In this sense, gender and race ideologies and their interpretation by women in their daily lives can be said to have had conservative implications. At the same time, women's potential to identify common ground across racial lines offered them the possibility of transcending slavery and viewing one another as individuals. Their ability to do so, limited as it was by the circumstances of their lives, could have subversive, even radical implications for plantation women. That these possibilities could exist simultaneously should come as no surprise, given the complexities of southern society. They reflected the power of the ideologies of race and gender and the efforts women made to live up to what was expected of them as women and as slaveholders or slaves.

Patterns of race and gender relations were not abruptly transformed when the firing began on Fort Sumter. At least in South Carolina, most of which remained free of northern troops until the end of the war, the four years of fighting brought only slow changes to ideologies of race and gender and the patterns of behavior they helped to shape. With the end of slavery and the emergence of a new pattern of race relations, gender expectations were modified along with the ways in which black and white women thought of themselves and interacted with one another.

This study of plantation women focuses on South Carolina because the state offers several advantages, not the least of which is the richness of the documentary material available.[1] More important, the state's coastal area was lined with large and profitable rice and sea island cotton-growing plantations worked by a large slave population. Most of the up country was well within the "black belt" of extensive cotton production that stretched far to the south and west. The state's advantages for study are enhanced by its leadership in southern radical politics. White South Carolinians were more committed to the defense of slavery than any other group, as witnessed by their efforts to nullify the so-called "tariff of abominations," their leadership in the secession crisis, and the vehement rhetoric of their fire-eating, slavery-defending politicians. Slaveholding South Carolinians were self-conscious about slavery and its defense; they believed they had created an institution beneficial to all it touched. In the practice and defense of slavery, South Carolina led the way along a road it expected the rest of the South to follow. Occasionally, evidence from rice-growing areas of Georgia and contiguous areas of eastern North Carolina, where inhabitants largely shared the perspectives and experiences of South Carolinians, has reinforced the argument.

This study focuses on large plantations because they offer both more evidence and the best opportunity to test the interactions of race and gender. Large plantations are usually defined as those with twenty or more slaves, although some of the wealthiest slaveholders in the coastal areas of the state had far more than twenty. Large planters enforced gender expectations in ways smaller planters could not, if only because of the size of the work force. The presence of many slaves made assigning work according to assumptions about appropriate behavior for men and women, rather than according to physical abilities or immediate need, easy. Large planters in South Carolina were the acknowledged leaders of their communities. Smaller planters often shared their values, imitated their methods, emulated their style, and aspired to their successes.

Race and gender relations, like the connections between the ideology and behavior of southern women, have been widely debated by historians in recent years. Julia Cherry Spruill, Guion Griffis Johnson, and Mary Elizabeth Massey first began to ask the questions that Anne Firor Scott, Catherine Clinton, and Suzanne Lebsock have continued to refine. Since then, Jacqueline Jones, Jean Friedman, Deborah Gray White, and Elizabeth Fox-Genovese, among others, have added their voices to the debate.[2] Collectively, these historians and others like them have added to knowledge about gender, slavery, and race relations in the South. This book contributes to this discussion by focusing directly on women's day-to-day interactions on plantations and by examining the resonances between those interactions and the ideologies that pervaded southern society.

Any study of southern women's history is limited by the sources available, and this one is no exception. Inevitably, the sources reveal more about elite women than they do about slaves or nonelite whites. I rely heavily on the narrative oral histories of former slaves collected by the Federal Writers' Project of the Works Progress Administration in the late 1930s, an invaluable but imperfect resource.[3] One limitation is its use of language shaped as much by the interviewers' perceptions of what they heard as by what the black men and women actually said. Their language appears here precisely as written. White women often were inadequately educated and wrote their letters and diaries quickly; their errors have, for the most part, been reproduced without correction.

Part 1: *Women's Work*

Hard work was a part of life for all women living on South Carolina's plantations. Without women's work food would not be prepared, homes cleaned, or clothing laundered. Women made cloth and clothing, candles and soap, bread and sausage, medicine and blankets. They nursed the sick, cared for children, and attended to emotional needs. They were also expected to make sure all of these tasks were completed, although this requirement was rarely acknowledged.

The actual tasks assigned to women depended, of course, on whether they were slaves or mistresses. Much of their work was similar to men's work and thus divided by race. Black women labored in the fields alongside black men just as they did in the house alongside their mistresses while white women supervised and managed their slaves in addition to their domestic responsibilities. But when it came to women's work, a degree of overlap was inevitable. Not only did women of each race do work intended for the benefit of the other but each also sometimes did tasks typically assigned to the other. Their work brought slaves and mistresses into frequent contact in the dairy and garden, loomhouse and smokehouse, nursery and hospital. Their work interactions shaped the quality of plantation life as well as their ways of thinking about themselves and one another, thereby shaping race relations in the antebellum South.

I

The Work Lives of
Plantation Slave Women

Slave women did almost every type of work required on antebellum South Carolina farms to produce rice, sea island cotton, upland cotton, foodstuffs, and various other crops. Their work was the foundation of daily life for white families and the entire plantation community; they also cared for their own households. On the surface, slave men and women appear to have labored similarly. Both worked in the fields and in the Big House; both could be found in the barns, dairies, and gardens. They were assigned to the same gangs and were subject to the same authority. Because work tasks and quotas were allocated on the basis of ability, not gender, many women were counted as full hands in plantation record books. In spite of these apparent similarities, black women and men experienced their work quite differently.

Gender was a primary organizing characteristic of labor in African society, so slaves encouraged these familiar differences when they came to the South. White culture offered a powerful example and imposed its own assumptions about gender differences on slaves.[1] As a result, blacks together with whites created work lives for male and female slaves that reflected the gender divisions of the larger social order. Because all slave women's work experiences periodically brought them into close contact with mistresses as well as with the white men who routinely provided supervision, slave women must have developed an understanding of the impact of gender as well as of slavery on their experience. Since overseers and drivers were always male, most women spent most of their working lives in the fields under the direct authority of men. When working closer to the house, however, female slaves were directed by white or sometimes black women. These lessons of gender resonated not only in their own daily lives but also in the race and gender dynamics of the plantation.

Until the age of five, male and female slaves did little that can easily be called work. When they could take care of themselves without constant supervision, they were likely to help adults by completing such simple tasks as carrying water to the hands in the fields, assisting in the care of animals, and carrying baskets of rice or other crops from one place to another. Such children were often referred to as the "trash gang." Young boys and girls chased birds off the crops, a particularly important duty in rice-growing areas, and waited on tables in the Big House. A few helped their mothers make clothing. Many did odd jobs around the Big House or for the overseer's wife, even if they were expected to be field hands when they were old enough.[2] An elderly former slave, Ella Kelly, recalled her childhood experiences: "I was too little to work in slavery time, just hang 'round kitchen wid mammy, tote water and pick up chips, is all de work I done I 'members."[3] Until about age five, boys and girls performed similar tasks and had similar experiences.[4]

Between the ages of five and seven, slave girls' lives began to diverge from those of boys. Most boys continued with their odd jobs until they were ten or twelve, when they started as quarter hands in the fields. Few were expected to help their mothers or work in the Big House. Girls, however, were supposed to mind younger children, a task not usually required of their brothers. Sometimes they helped their mothers or the plantation granny assigned to supervise children whose parents were in the fields. Girls were also expected to help their mothers cook, clean, and do the wash in the slave quarters. These activities resembled the work done by young white girls throughout the United States as informal apprentices to their mothers in daily domestic tasks.

Young slave girls also cared for white children, often just a little younger than themselves. These significant responsibilities frequently presented girls such as Genia Woodbury with the first opportunity for recognizing the meaning of slavery and punishment. Woodbury recalled herself as a young girl who wanted to be with her mother in the quarters rather than watching white children: "Den I wuz de nu'se dere fa dem chillun. Ne'er lak it but I ha'e it to do. Hadder stay right dere to de big house aw de time. Miss Susan ne'er wouldn't 'low me take dem chillun 'way offen no whey en eve'ybody hadder be mindful uv wha' dey say 'fore dem chillun too."[5] Girls were occasionally given as gifts to very young white girls and served as their maids.

Another type of work bridged childhood and adult responsibilities for young slave girls. Allowed access to the Big House from an early age, they were expected to wait on white women. They helped white women dress and comb their hair and sometimes slept in their rooms to provide any assistance that might be required during the night. Mary Woodward remembered the services she provided her mistress: "Bout all I had to do in slavery time was to comb her hair, lace her corset, pull de hem over her hoop, and say 'you is served, mistress!' Her lak them little words at de last."[6] A newspaper account of former Virginia slave Adeline Henderson's early life reported: "Her earliest work was to wait on the table in her mistress' home. She was so small then that she had to stand on a little bench in order to reach the top of the table. Later, she did housework, serving and cooking, and acted as nurse to the children in the plantation family. She also did a little work in the fields."[7] Girls whose work satisfied their mistresses might be kept on as house servants; others were gradually initiated into field labor.[8] Not all girls experienced this gradual introduction to the world of work, or at least they did not remember experiencing it. A few elderly ex-slaves interviewed by those affiliated with the Federal Writers' Project of the Works Progress Administration (WPA) said they began their working lives in the fields, usually at about age twelve. Lucy Gallman said: "I was a girl in slavery, worked in the fields from the time I could work at all, and was whipped if I didn't work. I worked hard."[9]

Beginning at age eight or nine and continuing into their early teens, girls were taught another kind of domestic work by their white mistresses. The domestic economy of the plantation depended upon the centralized production of such essentials as food and clothing, which were partially the mistress's responsibility. Domestic production on most of the large plantations in South Carolina included tending the garden and the barnyard animals; cooking for the slaves, the children, and the unmarried men; making soap; and preserving food at harvest and animal killing time. Black as well as white women spent a good deal of time cutting out and sewing or knitting clothing and blankets and sometimes spinning and weaving the cloth as well. Although by the late antebellum period most plantation owners were prosperous enough to purchase the cloth that was being manufactured ever more cheaply by northern textile mills, some could not or preferred not to do so. Almost no clothing was available ready-made because the sewing machine was not yet in widespread use. Only white men's outer garments were likely to be made by a tailor; white women sometimes were able to hire seamstresses or the more fashionable mantua makers to produce dresses for special occasions. The manufacture of all other clothing was the responsibility of the mistress. As a result, one of the primary functions of the domestic economy of the plantation was to transform inexpensive "negro cloth" into summer and winter garments and bedding for every slave. These activities were clearly beyond the province of the house slaves, and few permanent house slaves on large plantations spent much time on domestic production.

Instead, a varying group of black women carried out such tasks under the direction of the white mistress. Domestic producers included girls not destined to be house servants but too young to be sent to the fields, women who were about to give birth or who had just done so, and women who were invalids, recuperating from illness, or elderly. In general, the group might include any woman on the plantation who was not a permanent house slave and who either could not perform ordinary field work or whose labor was considered more useful at domestic production than in the fields. In addition, able-bodied women could be set to domestic production during inclement weather; conversely, when the pressure of field work mounted, most of the domestic producers were sent to the fields. Thus, their number varied considerably over the course of the year.

Ex-slaves frequently described such work. Mary Johnson reported that her mistress "learned me to card and spin, and to weave when I was a child. When I was old enough, dey put me in de field to work, hoe and pick cotton." Jane Hollins boasted of her ability to card, spin, and cut out clothing. She also presented a litany of activities that might well have been typical of a young woman's introduction to field labor: "What I do?—I milk cows. . . . I do outside work wid de hoe—plant corn, potato, peas, rice! . . . Help fix the hogs, you know, make lard and cracklings to put in bread." Josephine Bristow, who was born during the war near Marion, South Carolina, told a WPA interviewer: "De people used to spin en weave, my Lord! Like today, it cloudy en rainy, dey couldn' work in de field en would have to spin dat day." Gracie Gibson, who lived in Richland County as a slave, remembered that on her plantation "some of de old women, and women bearin' chillun not yet born, did cardin' wid hand-cards; then some would get at de spinnin' wheel and spin thread, three cuts to make a hank. Other women weave cloth and every woman had to learn to make clothes for the family, and they had to knit coarse socks and stockin's." Adeline Jackson reported that "women in family way worked up to near de time, but guess Doctor Gibson knowed his business. Just befo' de time, they was took out and put in de cardin' and spinnin' rooms." Some women worked as domestic producers as well as in the fields, although this was not the usual pattern on large plantations. Margaret Hughes told her WPA interviewer: "The grown-up slaves had to work in de field all day and then at night they spin cloth and make their clothes."[10]

Plantation mistresses, and even masters, also frequently described the process of domestic production. Sophia Watson reported to her absent husband: "I did not make Ellen come in the house today—but gave her some sewing in order that she might keep quiet." In September, she wrote him that field slaves "Lucinda and Peggy are getting on famously now with their sewing—I sent down by Bill the last of the winter clothes to be made excepting the children's."[11] Gertrude Thomas noted in her diary that her slave woman Henrietta had been brought up from the plantation: "Henrietta knows nothing of sewing altho she appears to be a good disposed servant, never has been accustomed to anything except field [work]." Catherine Edmondston cynically charged all slave women over forty with deliberate ill health: "To be 'poorly' is their aim & object, as it ends in the house & spinning."[12]

On the plantation where Margaret Devereux made her home as a young bride, African-American women who had many children did not do field work but "had their regular tasks of spinning allotted to them." Younger women who disliked field work could also usually contrive "to be classed among the spinners." While Devereux's autobiography may be partly romanticized recollection, there was undoubtedly a varying group of spinners on the plantation who worked in the loomhouse. Elizabeth Allston Pringle, related by birth and marriage to two of South Carolina's most elite families, remembered how the head nurse "Maum Phibby trained the children big enough to learn, teaching them to run up a seam and hem, in the way of sewing, and to knit first squares for washcloths, and then stockings, and then to spin. When the war came there was not a grown woman on the plantation who could not knit stockings or spin yarn." Early in 1862, Kate Stone recorded in her diary that the house servants, assisted by "a contingent from the quarters," were killing hogs and making lard, sausage, and souse. In February she wrote: "Mamma had several of the women from the quarters sewing. Nothing to be done in the fields—too muddy." The war had not yet reached the large cotton plantation in northeastern Louisiana where Stone lived with her widowed mother, siblings, and 150 slaves.[13]

Henry William Ravenel, a member of another of South Carolina's elite planter families, remembered "the spinning of yarn was done mostly by invalids who could not work out, and by the women with young children." Frederick Law Olmsted, describing a visit to a large cotton plantation near the Mississippi River, saw a "loom-house, in which a dozen Negroes were at work making shoes, and manufacturing coarse cotton stuff for Negro clothing. One of the hands so employed was insane, and most of the others were cripples, invalids with chronic complaints or unfitted by age, or some infirmity, for fieldwork." Even writers of advice for slaveholders recognized the importance of domestic production: "Patching may be done by the women on wet days when they are compelled to be in the house. Or when a breeding woman gets too heavy to go to the field, she may be made to do a general patching for all the hands."[14]

Most women began their formal working lives as domestic producers, and most could expect to do such work periodically throughout their lives. Because preserving food, sewing, spinning, and the like were defined as women's work, only women worked as domestic producers. Men, for the most part, labored primarily as field hands, mechanics and other skilled artisans, or as house servants; only the latter worked closely with their white mistresses. Only women routinely moved back and forth between the field and the house and in general their work lives were more varied than were men's. Slave women as a rule spent considerable time with mistresses; for slave men such association was much more limited.

In spite of intervals of domestic production work, the vast majority of women spent most of their working lives in the fields.[15] No matter what the staple and supplemental crops were on individual plantations, women participated in all aspects of cultivation from preparing the fields to harvesting. Unless they were late in a pregnancy, had just given birth, or had many children, they were expected to work as hard, as long, and under the same conditions as men.[16] Some women reported working unusually hard; sometimes they said they worked as hard as men.[17] Lists of slaves categorize them as full, half, or quarter hands on the basis of physical ability, not gender, but plantation daybooks and diaries, overseers' reports, and other detailed accounts of daily plantation activities suggest that men and women often did different work. Although slaveholders rarely had scruples about charging black women with physically demanding tasks, their assumptions about gender often influenced the assignments they made.

Some tasks were delegated according to perceptions of physical ability or propriety. On rice plantations, men ditched, broke new ground, and chopped wood, all back-breaking jobs; they rarely dropped seed. Masters considered women better at hoeing and raking trash, men at plowing, and work assignments took this into consideration when possible, although men could be seen hoeing and women plowing. Other tasks also became associated with either men or women.[18] On Duncan Heyward's plantation, for example, men worked at ditching and women sowed: "Women always did this work, for the men used to say that this was 'woman's wuck,' and I do not recall seeing one of the men attempt it." David Doar, like Heyward owner of a rice growing plantation, described a similar division of labor: "In Winter threshing of the crop took up most of the time of every hand on the place but as Spring came on the men were employed cleaning ditches, repairing banks and trunks and women were busy digging land that the plows could not turn and doing other necessary work as required."[19]

In addition to routinely delegating specific tasks to men or women, masters frequently divided slaves into work groups, called gangs, according to gender, although sometimes both groups performed the same activity. Most likely, white slaveholders and overseers were influenced by stereotypes and assumptions when they designated men and women to work in sex-segregated gangs. In general white men believed that men and women who worked together were likely to flirt with one another and thus disrupt the routine. They were also afraid that husbands might try to help their wives meet work quotas or protect them in other ways. By avoiding opportunities for interaction between men and women, white men hoped to create a labor force more intent on its work than it otherwise might have been. Of course, on many occasions men and women were assigned to work at the same task in the same location. Even so, as domestic producers and field hands, female slaves spent much of their working time with other women, separate from men.

&

Just as some field work was routinely prescribed to women, the activities of slaves in the Big House were divided according to conventional nineteenth-century notions of male and female roles. Female house slaves worked as cooks and mammies, nurses and maids, while the men were butlers, valets, messengers, and coachmen. Men occasionally did work ordinarily assigned to women—wealthy planters sometimes had highly trained male cooks. Women, however, never did men's work in the Big House.[20]

Instead, women worked at the tasks necessary to keep a large group of people clean and fed. They combed and laced, washed and ironed, cooked and cleaned, churned and scoured. Since only the simplest technology was available, these were difficult, time-consuming tasks, as slaves, northern white women, and domestic servants all testified.[21] The tasks were made more difficult by the varying and sometimes arbitrary standards applied to them. A dinner cooked successfully or a shirt starched properly on one occasion might not be considered satisfactory the next time. Although southern whites sometimes viewed house slaves as an elite group among slaves, their work was not easy.

On large plantations, duties were highly demarcated. African-American cooks provided food for the white family and the guests who frequently appeared, using kitchens often ill-equipped even by nineteenth-century standards and at a distance from the Big House because of the heat and the danger of fire. Maids attended to the personal needs of the mistresses and completed daily housecleaning, laundry, and the more rigorous fall and spring cleanings. Nurses tended small white children and supervised older ones, providing both daily care and special care during illnesses. Mammies, elevated by postwar myth to a legendary status, provided many of these personal services in addition to psychological support.[22] A very small number of house slaves were trained to do highly skilled work, such as making elegant dresses or fine pastry. Usually these few worked for the most elite South Carolina families, who could afford such luxuries.[23]

Although house slaves' work was specialized, most learned at least the rudiments of all types of work so they could substitute for one another when necessary. For example, in Grace Brown Elmore's family, each person had a maid, all of whom were taught to cook "so if the cook proper is sick, there is the washwoman who cooks finely, and if she is unable, any of the maids take the place. . . . The only trouble was an inequality in the cooking, but most of them know enough to give us a tolerable dinner; and then too, a novice is always put in with one who knows so the work was light to both."[24] Illness of a slave could disrupt the smooth workings of domestic life, as Eliza Ann DeRosset knew when she wrote to her sister Mary DeRosset Curtis in 1841: "Betty has commenced your work but we can't keep her sewing steadily—ever since Fanny has been sick she has had to do the washing and ironing either the whole or in part every week. And to-day she has had to cook and wash too—Juliet being taken sick last night and Fanny not sufficiently strong to undertake either yet—her baby is four weeks old to-day." Nine years later, DeRosset and Curtis's recently married niece wrote to her absent mother about domestic life at home: "Maria Mc. has been quite sick all this week—suffering with violent head-ache. . . . Lavinia has supplied her place very satisfactorily, and I had to keep Sophy home two days to wash."[25] This cross-training both increased the burden on house slaves and made them more valuable to their white owners; certainly it had the potential to add to domestic harmony in the Big House, where whites and blacks lived intimately with one another's demands, expectations, and personalities.[26]

In spite of house slaves' ability to substitute for one another, white women sometimes found themselves in need of extra help during periods of illness, preparations for travel, or various other disruptions and turned to domestic producers. Mistresses either taught them some form of housework or arranged for an experienced and trusted house slave to teach them. In this way, the mistress could both ensure that the necessary work was done and assess the potential of an individual black woman for work in the Big House without committing herself to keeping her there. Because domestic production represented an intermediate category between housework and field work, women could be shifted from one kind of work to another with relative ease and without much risk of wasted investments in time or training.[27]

In Grace Brown Elmore's family the "supervisor of indoor" work was Cynthia, who Elmore reported "was brought from the plantation, where she has been reared, as we had tried many before her but none suited the position. She planted herself firmly from the first and she stuck." When faced with the prospect of having six boys at home for the summer, Meta Morris Grimball vowed to "take a hand off somewhere and relieve myself of the housekeeping." Mary Raines, an elderly ex-slave interviewed by the WPA, attributed her rise in status and better than usual rations while a slave to her lack of fear of cows. Because of that, she said, "they set me to milkin' and churnin'" and eventually to helping with the white children in the Big House.[28]

Occasionally a woman would be brought to the Big House for more unusual reasons. When several of Gertrude Thomas's children were born, her father lent her a plantation slave as a wet nurse. She was careful to send one of her own slaves in return.[29] Thomas occasionally brought other women from the fields to test their propensity for domestic work, although she said she wished to buy "a good steady woman."[30] Each of these women had the chance to switch from ordinary field labor to work in the Big House. For the most part, mistresses chose them because their skills and personalities were familiar, a familiarity born of the contact they had when the slaves worked as domestic producers.

Just as mistresses tested potential house slaves by observing them as domestic producers, they could also demote unsatisfactory house slaves by assigning them to part-time domestic production. Such part-time work acclimated African-American women to life in the fields. This intermediate period was not likely to last long, but it did present white women with a chance to make other domestic arrangements and black women with the possibility of changing their new assignments.[31] Although work in the Big House was generally considered desirable by both blacks and whites, not all slave women who worked there wanted or were allowed to stay.[32] Reporting on a large and successful rice plantation, Frederick Law Olmsted observed that such changes in assignments were often a form of punishment: "Slaves brought up to house-work dread to be employed at field-labour; and those accustomed to the comparatively unconstrained life of the negro-settlement, detest the close control and careful movements required of the house-servants. It is a punishment for a lazy field-hand to employ him at menial duties at the house . . . and it is equally a punishment to a neglected house-servant, to banish him to the field-gangs."[33]

Gertrude Thomas brought a woman up from the plantation and sent Isabella down because she found it "impossible to break her of stealing" and because Isabella "represented herself as being sick." Only two months after the beginning of the Civil War, Kate Stone noted in her diary: "The house servants have been giving a lot of trouble lately—lazy and disobedient. Will have to send one or two to the field and replace them from the quarters if they do not settle down."[34]

Reassignments may have been common approaches to disciplining slaves but they could unexpectedly improve conditions at the plantation, at least according to whites. Louis Manigault wrote to his father often about difficulties on Gowrie, his plantation on Argyle Island. On one occasion, he complained that Jane "did not attend to the sick at all, so Caramba! I put her on the field, and I tell you what it is one of the best changes ever made."[35]

Occasionally work shufflings were merely conveniences to masters and mistresses. When John Berkley Grimball planned to go to Virginia Springs for the summer of 1835, he recorded his difficulties in making satisfactory arrangements for his household slaves. He concluded he would send some of them to the country: "Patty will work in the field—doing however only so much as she can with ease—Just enough to benefit her health and keep her out of mischief—Eve, who is quite young, will run about, or perhaps be taken into the overseer's house."[36]

Some whites took the feelings and health of blacks into consideration when modifying their duties. Sophia Watson, in a series of letters to her absent husband, asked his opinion of her plan to bring the slave woman Margaret up from their plantation and to send Lucinda down. She hesitated, she said, only because she feared Lucinda might be physically harmed by more difficult work, although she was "convinced she is not kind to the baby—and cannot feel satisfied to have her nurse him—besides I am ashamed to have her about." While awaiting word from Henry about the new arrangements, Sophia kept Lucinda engaged in sewing. Once sent to the plantation, Lucinda continued to stitch for the slaves, for Sophia feared more rigorous work would make Lucinda ill.[37] Charles Manigault advised his son about a young black woman: "If you don't think she will be useful in yours, or the overseers house, then the best thing is to inniciate her into plantation work as soon as possible, but not to expose her during this winter to any rainy weather, or cold as she is not accustomed to outdoor work. And order her in, should it prevail, and only give her half task, should she not be employed at indoor plantation work (at the Thresher, Ec.) and by all means keep her under the care of Maum 'Bina.'"[38]

Caroline Merrick went beyond changing the duties of Julia, an African American who nursed Merrick's infant daughter. When Merrick caught Julia slapping the baby, she told Julia she could no longer touch the baby: she was free. According to Merrick, after two weeks Julia was so unnerved by her enforced idleness that she "threw herself at my feet in a deluge of tears begging to be forgiven and to be allowed to nurse her baby again."[39] Few mistresses were willing to follow Merrick's lead and risk losing a valuable slave by offering freedom; most were wise enough not to consider freedom a punishment and so sent those they considered unsuitable for domestic labor to the fields.

Most house slaves banished to the fields remained there, except perhaps for occasional stints as domestic producers during subsequent illnesses or pregnancies. However, in rare instances house slaves were expected to labor temporarily in the fields while retaining their house servant designation. Catherine Edmondston assigned her house slave Viney to sort seed corn during the corn harvest and found her "under heavy complaint as usual." In 1860, Keziah Brevard noted in her diary that she had sent two male house slaves to pick cotton for three days. She noted that she did "not like to make them do such hard work—they are house boys and can not stand the sun as the field hands do." In his plantation diary from Beaufort District Alexander J. Lawton separated the number of acres planted and amount of cotton produced by house servants from that produced by field hands for most of the years between 1816 and 1828. Lawton planted in conjunction with his widowed mother and his wife, and the contribution of each woman's house slaves was carefully listed.[40]

Slaveholders' willingness to take advantage of house slaves' abilities or to merely act on their own desires exacerbated the insecurity of slave life. In spite of the disruption to both black and white households, trusted house slaves and those with particular skills were not only moved from the house to the field and back but were also shared among the plantations or households of close relatives and neighbors.[41] These women were not hired out, nor were they hiring their own time; rather, they were borrowed from their owners by family members or others with close ties to aid during illness among the usual domestic staff, illness in the white family, the birth of a child to a young white woman, an extended period of travel, or even an unusual press of work. More often than not, older and more established households loaned slaves to younger, still forming ones. These loans were temporary and generally lasted a matter of months, seldom a year. Even the most generous of parents were rarely willing to allow their households to be inconvenienced by the too-long absence of a skilled slave. These loans added to the diversity and mobility of slave women's work, but disrupted their own domestic lives.

For white women, borrowing slaves provided an opportunity to accomplish specific tasks or weather a crisis. Trusted, well-trained, and highly skilled black women were sent from one family to another so that mistresses need not be concerned with teaching inexperienced slaves, getting new workers accustomed to household routines, or relying unduly on their domestic producers. Instead, the slaves sent to young women in crisis were likely to be older women whom they had known all their lives and whose presence was intended to be comforting. For the black women, however, temporary assignment to another household, no matter how short, meant separation from family, friends, and community and disruption of their personal lives.

Fortunately, these valued women were often familiar with slaves in the household to which they were sent and had mistresses who were willing to act as conduits for messages. The various households of the DeRosset family in North Carolina frequently shared slaves. When Mary DeRosset Curtis's children were born, her unmarried sisters obtained their father's permission to send Mom Bella to her to help with her daily responsibilities. In a letter to her sister Catherine, Mary reported Mom Bella's safe arrival and added "she seemed ready and anxious to go to work. . . . I have let her attend [the cooking] for the last two days. . . . My regular cook is to come to me, perhaps the first of next week—but as she is rather young, I am glad Mom Bella is here to direct a little in case of need—she is an excellent hand; seems to understand every thing about it." Several months later Mary wrote to her sister Magdalen that she intended to send Mom Bella home, but instead took advantage of the slave's offer to stay until her mistress was completely recovered from her illness. Many of the family's letters to Mary include messages to Mom Bella about her children; after her return, Mary's include greetings as well.[42]

The DeRossets were not unique in this practice. When Susan McDowell's baby was born, her mother sent the family nurse to stay "until you get able to take care of your children and family." Elizabeth Ervin of Darlington District included in her will the provision for one of her slave women to be shared by her daughter and daughter-in-law. The slave woman was "to work as a seamstress month about with each of them." Occasionally this sharing proved detrimental to the operation of the plantations. When Charles Manigault installed his son Louis at Gowrie Plantation in the Savannah River, a steady stream of slaves moved between Gowrie and the senior Manigault's other plantations. Sometimes sickly African Americans were sent to Charles's plantations to recruit new slaves to Gowrie, but Louis put a stop to the practice, saying: "I begin to think that it has a bad effect moving them back to recruit to Silk Hope. It makes them think this is a very unhealthy place."[43]

Black women with the skills and trust to be shared among family members experienced much more diversified work lives than did the average female slave. Not only did their work include a variety of tasks but they were also performed in more than one setting, and usually with the confidence of the white family. These exceptional women were granted an unusual amount of privilege and mobility.

Other women on large plantations similarly benefited from their peculiar status. Elderly women unable to work as domestic producers or field hands were often appointed plantation "grannies."[44] Most grannies worked as field hands until age and physical infirmity made their caring for children more useful than field work, although the same infirmities undoubtedly limited their ability to fulfill these demands. Trusted elderly house slaves also worked as grannies, although such women were more likely simply allowed to cut back the extent of their responsibilities until their deaths. Working as a granny represented a kind of retirement for elderly women, even though caring for large numbers of children could not be easy in spite of the help from older children. Grannies supervised the activities of young children whose parents were at work, fed them, nursed them during minor illnesses, and directed the slightly older children who aided in providing care.

Mary Howard Schoolcraft described the responsibilities of the woman in charge of the nursery for slave children: "An old, black, medical crone is at the head of this establishment, and she is required to keep up large fires, to feed, watch over, and report any sickness or accident to her young charges, while their mothers are absent in the fields." Maria Jenkins remembered the plantation granny who cared for her: "Rachel cook in de big pot for we chillun, and he dip um out. . . . Yes, Ma'am, he name Rachel, and he lick we. We haffa love um or she lick we. . . . [Rachel] teach me to wash de baby, clean and put on de dipa, and if I ain't do um good he konk my head."[45] Grannies were granted their status primarily because of their unsuitability for any other type of work and their skill and experience with children. Duncan Heyward remembered Abby Manigault, who had been a field hand for his grandfather Nathaniel: "When I planted rice, Abby, for years was my 'foreman' of the children. No one could equal her in managing them, especially when it came to making them load a schooner."[46]

Women who were particularly skilled at tending the sick could be designated nurses, either permanently or when necessary.[47] When John Edwin

Fripp's slaves were ill, they were usually tended by members of their own families unless seriously ill. In that case, they were cared for by the plantation nurse, Miley. Sophia Watson assigned her slave Ellen to care for the sick children and wrote her husband of her satisfaction with Ellen's behavior: "There is nothing more trying than to nurse a sick child—I think she deserves credit for her care of them—but Jen's mother would have been as kind—I mean among the Negroes." Eliza Mims assigned two slave women to care for her mother after she apparently had a stroke, as she reported in a letter to Emily Jordan: "Margaret and Louisa does little else but attend to her[.] one attends to her one day and the other the next[.] she is never left alone not even for a few minutes."[48]

These black women did not even have the primitive arsenal of contemporary medicine at their disposal, which may have contributed to their success. Instead, they relied on a combination of folk knowledge, instinct, and more or less worthless advice from whites in combating disease. Lina Anne Pendergrass remembered her early days as a nurse in Chester County: "My ma made me make teas to cure folks' colds and ailments. She made me fetch her water and towels and other things while she wait on de sick folks. Dat's de way I was broke into nussing." Gus Feaster remembered the presence of old women, "too old to do any work and dey would take and study what to do fer de ailments of grown folks and lil' chilluns." Thanks to their skill, these women were afforded respect that most slaves did not garner. According to Columbia physician Robert Gibbes, "the sick nurse, or doctor woman, is usually the most intelligent female on the place; and she has full authority under the physician, over the sick." Women also worked as midwives to other slave women, and sometimes to whites as well.[49]

The women who cared for the sick were not considered house servants or full-fledged domestic producers by whites, although they usually spent their spare time sewing or completing other domestic tasks. When Ellen was not tending the sick children, Sophia Watson "require[d] nothing of her but the cooking and washing for their small household." Susan Witherspoon's nurse made mattresses when no one in the extended family required her care.[50] Unlike other slaves, nurses and grannies were sometimes exempt from serving whites or producing crops; instead they ministered to the needs of other blacks.

Whites granted a few black women on a handful of large plantations even more exceptional work responsibilities. In addition to performing their usual assigned tasks, they directed the domestic producers. Louis Hughes, who in 1897 wrote a book-length narrative of his experiences as a slave in Mississippi and Tennessee, recalled "a forewoman, who . . . had charge of the female slaves, and also the boys and girls from twelve to sixteen years of age, and all the old people that were feeble." Although they were somewhat analogous to black male drivers, doing the bidding of their white owners while retaining slave status, these black women usually did not have the authority to punish slaves as many drivers did. Throughout the South variously called the forewoman, the manager, the head weaver, or the black overseer, they worked mostly under the jurisdiction of the white mistress. They made sure that her orders about domestic production were carried out; they also taught inexperienced slaves the skills necessary for domestic production. Ned Walker of Berkeley County remembered: "Dere was a big hall wid spinnin' wheels in it, where thread was spin. . . . Mammy was head of de weave house force and see to de cloth."[51]

Many of these women became truly autonomous. On Burleigh, a large cotton plantation in Mississippi, Susan Dabney Smedes remembered field slaves being brought to the Big House to sew during rainy weather: "Then Mammy Maria, who was in her way a field-marshall on such occasions, gave out the work and taught them to sew. By word and action she stimulated and urged them on. . . . From being a confidential servant, she grew into being a kind of prime minister." Grace Brown Elmore remembered a woman who did similar work in South Carolina: "As Dick is the head of all out door work, so Cynthia is supervisor of indoor. She is so smart and strong that she can be a hewer of wood and cook, seamstress, and director of everything. The servants call her 'Lawyer' for they say she always gives a reason for everything."[52] Undoubtedly, few plantations in South Carolina or elsewhere had a formally designated "director of everything," but some African-American women were expected to direct the work of others, occasionally without specific recognition of the supervisory nature of their duties. Some women may simply have assumed responsibility without overt acknowledgment. No matter what title or formal recognition they received, a small number of women were granted the authority to direct the activities of other women.

Domestic work within the slave quarters was similarly structured according to gender, but it could commence only when work for the master and mistress was finished.[53] Adeline Jackson remembered how the women cared for their homes whenever they could: "When farm work was not pressing, we got all of Saturday to clean up 'round de houses and wash and iron our clothes." On the plantation where Jane Johnson lived "most of de grown slave women knocked off from field work at dinner time on Saturdays and done de washin' for de rest of de slaves." Fred James's mother was not so fortunate. Their master did not allow Saturday afternoons off, so "my mammy had to wash clothes on Saturday nights for us to wear on Sundays." Other masters made distinctions based on the number of children a woman had. One advice writer suggested "women with six children alive at any *one* time, are allowed all Saturday to themselves." On the Allston plantations, "three days in each year are set apart for cleaning their houses," one in May, one in October or November, and one during the Christmas holidays.[54]

Like women, men labored in the quarters. According to an overseer, "women are expected to scour the houses, wash up every thing etc. while the men are (according to season) either planting, working, or harvesting their own little crops, or laying in a supply of fuel."[55] When their husbands were "abroad," which meant that they lived on another plantation, wives often had to do the men's work as well. Black men did as much as they could whenever they were able to visit their wives. Some tried to bring food with them; many more used the limited time with their families to provide firewood.

Even work-related social occasions such as cornshuckings, rice whippings (to separate out the grains) and quilting bees were not exempt from gender restrictions. Sometimes these were held simultaneously, with men shucking corn or beating rice while women either sewed or prepared food. These events were important social occasions for slaves as well as opportunities to accomplish specific tasks, as Houston Holloway remembered: "The ladys wore all Seated a round the quilt stiching away the Boys was Standing a round threeding there needles. . . . I Stood a round and lookt on at the nimble fingers as they stiched away. . . . Shortly after that the quilt was done and then the Supper witch was all ways a good one. Then untill a late hour Dancing was the order of the night."[56]

Even beyond the hours of direct supervision by whites, black women and men labored differently. Although work for their own families had a very different social meaning from that done for slaveholders, it still resonated with the implications of gender.

2

The Work Lives of
Plantation Mistresses

The cavalier tradition of white southern society portrayed the mistresses of large South Carolina plantations as refined and virtuous ladies who reflected the gentility of their class and gender. They were assumed to be more moral, more pure, and more religious than men, who placed them on a pedestal and sought to shelter them from the unpleasantness of life. White women were to enjoy all of the benefits that plenty of servants and a comfortable style of living could provide. At the same time, however, they were responsible for the smooth functioning of the domestic side of plantation life. While the presence of slaves meant that white women did relatively little of the actual physical work themselves, they had to ensure that this work was done efficiently and unobtrusively. White women were responsible for providing adequate supplies of clothing for everyone on the plantation; they shared responsibility for supplies of food with their husbands. They cared for their families and slaves by tending the sick and teaching religion, morals, and domestic skills. Although expected by their husbands and their society to appear refined and genteel, plantation mistresses in fact worked quite hard at fulfilling their domestic obligations. However, the magnitude and meaning of their work were quite different from those of black women, whose coerced labors were the foundation for the less rigorous and generally more varied work of plantation mistresses.[1]

The importance of plantation mistresses' domestic responsibilities was not lost on white southerners. Louisa Cheves Stoney, a descendent of several important antebellum families, claimed "their women were as distinctive as their men. Necessarily individual, isolated, independent thinkers, their duty was to provide food, warmth, clothing, medical treatment, part of the discipline and most of the religion for their own families and for two or three hundred Africans. . . . The conscientious mistress, and she was in the vast majority, had no opportunity for laziness, little for rest."[2] A female character in Mary E. Herndon's 1852 novel *Louise Elton; or, Things Seen and Heard* voiced similar sentiments in praising another woman: "She is one of the finest managers I ever saw. . . . About the management of her household matters, her garden, dairy, the scissors, needle, loom, and spinning wheels, she is a capital hand. She never does a stitch of work herself; but she knows how work ought to be done."[3]

Mistresses recognized the importance of their labors and sometimes regretted both their inability to be better housekeepers and the lack of time domestic cares left for anything else. Lucilla McCorkle frequently confided both her cares and her frustrations to the diary she kept in the late 1840s:

> My domestic cares engross my mind to the exclusion of all religious and social duties.

> My heart has been heavy with domestic care this week.

> It is no easy task to control servants and superintend matters with an eye to every thing.

She frequently prayed for guidance in performing domestic duties: "May I see and know those things which will render me an efficient and systematic housekeeper."[4] The importance of women's activities was also noted in the advice older women gave to younger ones, as in this record by Elizabeth Allston Pringle of the advice given to her mother by her mother's aunt: " 'To be the wife of a rice-planter is no place for a pleasure-loving, indolent woman, but for an earnest, true-hearted woman it is a great opportunity, a great education. To train others one must first train oneself; it requires method, power of organization, grasp of detail, perception of character, power of speech, above all, endless self-control.' "[5]

Women such as Eliza Ann DeRosset knew their work had to be done despite their physical health or personal inclination but acknowledged that obligation only to one another or in the privacy of their diaries. DeRosset wrote to her sister in 1837: "I shall have but little time left I fear for writing to my dear Mary as I have suffered one little thing after another to take up my attention till it is eleven o'clock." Even women who enjoyed the challenges of domestic responsibility could feel them to be burdensome at times, as did Catherine Edmondston: "I like housekeeping and housewifery cares, tho today they sit uneasily on me as I am far from well." Meta Morris Grimball knew there was no alternative to hard work: "In the years that have passed of my married life I have when ill dragged round after my duties with weak wretched feelings."[6]

The round of obligations that absorbed women's days was long, varied, and arduous, as Grimball knew: "A plantation life is a very active one. This morning I got up late having been disturbed in the night, hurried down to have some thing arranged for breakfast, Ham and eggs; wrote a letter to Charles. . . . Had prayers, got off the boys to town. . . . Had work cut out, gave orders about dinner, had the horse feed fixed in hot water, had the bin filled with corn:—went to see about the carpenters working . . . and now I have to cut out flannel, jackets, and alter some work." Similarly, Grace Brown Elmore remembered the clutter of her mother's daily activities:

> A mistress of such a household as our's must be Argus eyed and many handed. It seems to me Mother's whole life is taken up in small duties. She begins the day with prayers, at which all the servants must be present. . . . Then comes breakfast. . . . That over, she saunters to the stables with the smallest of her maidens, "Little Mary" and the key basket close behind. She and Dick talk over many matters. . . . The poultry yard comes next, and Cynthia's notched stick is seen to tally with the number of chickens, turkeys and ducks killed since last inspected, for our poultry is raised at the plantation and eaten here. Next the servants' houses are visited, the sick looked after, and cleanliness insisted upon, then Mother seems to be all eyes. . . . Last of all Mother reaches the vegetable garden which takes up at least three acres at the back of the house. . . . After this tour over her own domain, Mother takes her chair in her own corner by the dining room fire, and then starts Alfred rubbing off the table legs and long mahogany desk, doors of the sideboard, etc., Scipio has the large table and whatever Alfred can't reach, whilst Mother's maidens, Jane, Venus, and "Little Mary" stitch, overseam and hem . . . often lectured by Mother for some daily pecadillo.[7]

Mistresses knew that their husbands expected the day-to-day life of the extended household to proceed smoothly. Women understood the standards by which they were to measure their housekeeping and hospitality and worked hard to live up to them. However, with few conveniences and with all of the perceived difficulties of directing a slave labor force, to live up to those definitions proved a challenge for even the wealthiest and most efficient of mistresses. Men were sometimes direct in proclaiming their expectations of women. One father published his advice to his recently married daughter in the *Southern Literary Messenger*, presumably because he thought it useful for all women: "In the management of your domestic concerns, let prudence and wise economy prevail. Let neatness, order and judgement be seen in all your different departments. Unite liberality with a just frugality." James Louis Petigru offered his sister similar advice on the occasion of her marriage: "But a woman, if she has a sense of virtue and honor, is to show it, like Solomon's good wife, in rising betimes and setting her maidens to work."[8] Charles Colcock Jones also extolled the characteristics of a good wife, this time in a letter to his recently married son in which he described his wife's qualities: "Her industry, her economy, her prudence, her foresight, her resolution, her intelligence are uncommon. . . . And how she manages her household, and how she discharges her duties therein . . . [show] how my esteem and admiration and affection for her continues and grows."[9] Men such as J. Motte Alston acknowledged how much they owed to women's domestic activities. Alston recalled the grandmother by whom he was raised before the Civil War: "My grandmother having listened to all complaints and given her orders as to the course to be pursued in each, and having visited the sick, etc., we return home. My grandfather has nothing to do with all these matters. . . . Her duties are never ending—day by day she learns all that is going on and her presence is everywhere." Duncan Heyward was also well aware of mistresses' duties: "It was the rule to leave largely to the women of the planter's family the supervision of all welfare work. So much was this done that the charge has been made that the wives of Southern slaveholders, in seeking to meet the responsibility which they felt slavery devolved upon them, neglected their own children, leaving them too much to the care of Negro house servants, while they themselves looked after the condition of the children of their slaves; and there may be some foundation of truth in this charge."[10]

Men were rarely reluctant to make their expectations known to their wives. Henry Cumming wrote his wife more than a page of advice regarding her domestic servants, then told her: "But now that I have said all I think on the subject let me repeat that I shall most willingly acquiesce in any arrangement you think proper to make; for I am sensible that the temper and deportment of the servants will always affect your peace and comfort more than mine." In spite of this apparent generosity, he concluded his letter with nearly another page in which he told her what decisions he wanted her to make.[11] More often, men indirectly, but no less effectively, pressured women to conform to their expectations. Women were upset by their inability to live up to their husbands' wishes, even when badly prepared dinners and other domestic disasters could be blamed on slaves. In January 1844, Chevillette Simms, wife of South Carolina writer William Gilmore Simms, wrote a friend in New York that her husband "is constantly provoking my envy, by telling me what a fine housekeeper you are. . . . You must know that at this time of the year, at the South, housekeepers are always expected to have *nice things* on table."[12] Like their friends in the North, financially comfortable southern white women faced extensive domestic obligations that filled their days with a variety of tasks.[13]

Even visitors to the South recognized the value and extent of plantation mistresses' domestic responsibilities. Fredrika Bremer, a Swedish traveler whose letters offered careful observations about the people and places she visited, described the Charleston home of Mrs. W. Holbrook in 1850. Bremer commented that within her own home, her hostess was

> more like a Swedish lady than any woman I have met with in this country, for she had that quiet, attentive, affectionate, motherly demeanor; always finding something to do, and not being above doing it with her own hands. . . . Thus, I see her quietly busied from morning till evening; now with the children, now with meals, when she assists her servants to arrange the table, or when meals are over and removed, and all is in order which needs looking after (for the Negroes are naturally careless,) she will be busy cutting out and making clothes for them, or in dressing and smartening up the little Negroes of the house; then she is in the garden, . . . or she is receiving guests . . . and all this with that calm comprehension, with that dignity which, at the same time, is so full of kindness, and which is so beautiful in the mistress of a family, which makes her bear the whole house, and be its stay as well as its ornament.[14]

Although plantation mistresses, their husbands, and guests recognized the importance of white women's contributions to the health and comfort of everyone on large plantations, their work was made possible only by the labor of their slaves. Plantation mistresses worked hard and for long hours, but few were willing to acknowledge that slave women worked harder and longer. In fact, mistresses were more likely to criticize slaves for the work they created or did not do than they were to praise them for the escape from drudgery or the luxuries their labors made possible. Some white women such as Caroline Rush denied the work of black women so deeply as to describe themselves using the language of slavery. Author of *The North and South; or, Slavery and Its Contrasts*, Rush claimed "as a general thing, the greatest slave on a plantation is the mistress. She is like the mother of an immense family, of some fifty up to five or six hundred children."[15] Caroline Howard Gilman expressed similar sentiments in a novel serialized in the *Southern Rose Bud*, a children's (later women's) magazine published in Charleston: "However well educated and disciplined in domestic duties housekeepers may be, they are still slaves to the ignorance and caprice of others."[16] Other women used related language to describe themselves and their duties. Mary Jones, wife of Charles Colcock Jones, apologized to a relative for not writing sooner: "I am evidently one of the working class. . . . Yesterday and today I have been as busy as I well could be."[17] Plantation mistresses, when considering their own activities, were quite sure they worked as long and as hard as it was possible to do.

Daughters of plantation owners began their working lives at a much later age than slave women did. As girls, their primary responsibility was preparing themselves for their adult lives. In keeping with this goal, formal education, while considered important by some families, was secondary to the intricacies of domestic life.[18] Young white women were expected to concentrate on learning the various duties they would have as mistresses; they were not expected to make significant contributions toward accomplishing their mothers' work. Letitia Burwell's recollections of her early life in Virginia could easily have been echoed by South Carolina women: "At that period a girl was expected not only to be an ornament to the drawing-room, but to be also equipped for taking charge of an establishment and superintending every detail of domestic employment on a plantation—the weaving, knitting, sewing, etc.—for the comfort of the negro servants to be some day under her care." A writer for the *Gospel Messenger* warned women not to use the period between school and marriage for frivolity; instead, that time should be used "for the study of *their professions.*" Many women apparently took such advice seriously. Elizabeth Allen Coxe recalled visiting, as a young woman, the DeVeaux sisters on their family's large plantation on the Santee River: "The four girls each had her own maid, whose manners and morals she was supposed to take charge of, as well as cutting out their clothes, etc., and tending them when sick. . . . Nannie, the oldest of the sisters, . . . supervise[d] personally the skimming and churning, the making of the butter into large moulds for the table, sending fresh milk for the Negro children and clabber for the pigs. At the same time she arranged the trays for the guests' early treats."[19] As daughters approached marriageable age, they assisted their mothers quite extensively, particularly if there were many younger children.

Daughters did not always enjoy learning or performing these tasks. Kate Stone complained to her diary in 1861: "There seemed so much to do today with Mamma sick that I felt overwhelmed so compromised and let the servants do the best they could and I did what I pleased—a little reading, sewing, and talking with Mamma." Several months later Stone's aunt began making a silk quilt: "I am so afraid Mamma will commence work on it herself, and if she does I shall feel in duty bound to put up my linen embroidery and help her. And I simply detest making and quilting quilts. Precious little of it have I ever done. . . . After quilting, one rises from the chair with such a backache, headache, and bleeding pricked fingers." A month later when the quilt was finished Stone confessed: "I helped three days and then begged off. Quilting is a fearsome job."[20]

Not all daughters shared Stone's reluctance to work—or her honesty. Most of them anticipated marriage and the duties it brought and so recognized the necessity of learning domestic skills. Franklin Elmore explicitly told his eleven-year-old daughter Ellen to find happiness in obeying her mother: "If she requests you to attend to & perform any of the duties of Housekeeping for her, it too is that you may learn what will be useful to you." Susan Dabney Smedes remembered the period after her mother's death as "days of trial and perplexity to the young mistresses. The old house-servants, though having at heart an affection for them, considered or pretended to consider them too young to know what they wanted." Finally she and her sisters were able to demonstrate to the servants "that there was to be a head to the house even though that head was set on young shoulders." Women who did not learn domestic skills suffered the consequences. Married just a few months, young Katherine Meares took charge of her mother's household while her mother went away in the fall of 1850. She wrote to her mother: "There is a quantity of work to be done, and if only I knew what it was, and how to set about it, or had got directions from you before you left, a good deal might have been accomplished, during your absence."[21]

Plantation daughters' primary duty, however, was to attract husbands with suitable wealth, status, and breeding. That quest necessitated an active round of social activities. Mary Howard Schoolcraft claimed "the miss in her teens does no work in South Carolina, except in her flower-garden, in reading, or perfecting her education, and doing amateur fine needle-work; for she *always* has a maid of her own to attend to her chamber, to sew, and to dress her, etc.; so that a young lady's life there is one of great personal liberty, and all sorts of recreation."[22] The daughter of a well-to-do planter probably enjoyed more leisure than any other person in the antebellum South, but once married and installed in her own home, she began her work life in earnest.[23] Schoolcraft acknowledged the transformation: "But the moment she becomes a planter's wife, her domestic talents grow by the square-yard every year; for by a quick transformation, she is changed from a laughing, thoughtless flirt, seeking only to make herself beautiful and admired," into a hard-working mistress.[24] She did not mention the children most women began to have shortly after marriage, adding considerably to the demands on their time and energies.

Young Mary Mallard was aware of her lack of preparation for housekeeping, as she wrote to a friend: "Mary, can you realize that I am a minister's wife and am actually keeping house and trying to feel the importance of my station? . . . I am quite a novice in the housekeeping art."[25] Many years later Margaret Devereux recalled: "I was so young a bride, only seventeen, when I was taken to our winter home, and so inexperienced, that I felt no dread whatever of my new duties as mistress. The household comforts of my childhood home had seemed to come so spontaneously that I never thought of *processes*, and naturally felt rather nonplussed when brought into contact with realities." Like most young brides, Devereux managed to gain control of her domestic affairs, an effort that required patience and perseverance and that cost, in her case, a ruined carpet and the exchange of several house and field slaves.[26]

Such extreme insecurities and difficulties rarely lasted long, as Devereux's sister-in-law Catherine Edmondston discovered in 1863 when reading a diary she had kept fifteen years earlier as a young bride: "My housekeeping [now] gives me but little trouble & that of a pleasurable nature. . . . I can do more work in one day now than I could in three in those days, so I suppose knowing what I ought to accomplish & then not doing it fretted me & I had not so good servants then as I have now & so had more to see after. Now the idea of sitting down & apportioning my time as I did in 1848 is not only horrible to me but simply impossible." Edmondston described herself as "willing enough and happy in attending to domestic duties. You were too well brought up by your mother either to undervalue or feel them a burden to you."[27] Edmondston's positive assessment of her domestic abilities was relatively unusual. The majority of mistresses found the duties required of them so extensive and the difficulties of directing slave labor so pervasive, that domestic work seemed at best a never-ending series of challenges and at worst an overwhelming nightmare.

Mistresses of large South Carolina plantations performed four distinct but closely related kinds of work. First, they arranged everything for the day-to-day and season to season continuation of domestic health and comfort. This housekeeping work included everything from creating adequate supplies of food and clothing for whites and blacks to distributing those supplies. Second, women supervised the activities of their house slaves and domestic producers. Third, all women performed a measure of domestic work themselves, and except when entertaining male guests, were rarely found without some sort of needlework in hand. Finally, women cared for family members and for slaves. They tended the sick, provided religious and other forms of training, and raised children. Together, these activities made mistresses' days an endless stream of work.

As housekeepers, white women shared with their husbands responsibility for utilizing the material resources of the plantation. Only white men dealt
with the outside world by corresponding with factors, arranging for credit
and shipment of goods, and keeping financial records for the household.[28]
They also took responsibility for supervising every aspect of the large-scale
agricultural production on which their economic well-being rested. However, they expected their wives to attend to what might be called the domestic
side of plantation life and to provide the most comfortable life possible for
all members of the household. Although women's direct purchases were limited to clothing, small luxuries, and gifts, indirectly they arranged for adequate supplies of essentials and luxury goods by requesting from their husbands what could not be produced on the plantation. They worked alongside
their husbands to maintain the financial health of the plantation and economized when necessary for survival.

Although neither white women nor men fully acknowledged the importance of women's housekeeping contributions to the plantation, many wom-
en recognized how time-consuming their activities were. They often apologized for their inability to write more frequently to one another because
they were too busy. Catherine Kennedy wrote to her sisters in November
1837: "This you know is every where a busy season. . . . I have scarcely been
seated ten minutes unless when at meals."[29] The burdens on women's time
never ceased, as Susan Witherspoon wrote to her daughter in March 1840:
"I take my pen my dear Susan when I can to scribble you a line—my time is
so completely occupied as spring approaches that you must never be uneasy
at not hearing from me." Catherine Hammond made similar excuses to her
husband's brother: "But though my duties are very different from yours I
can yet, like you, plead them as an excuse for my apparent neglect. My little
family engages every moment of my time and every thought."[30]

Fredrika Bremer acknowledged this housekeeping role as well, stating that
southern mistresses had "much to look after and to provide for, so that house
and home may be supplied with not merely the material things, but with
those that shall beautify it." In Elizabeth Allston Pringle's recollections of her
mother, she remembered: "It took all her own precious time to direct and
plan and carry out the work. The calls to do something which seemed important and necessary were incessant." Recently married Mary Mallard had
no doubts about the importance of what she did: "I keep my own house and
visit the smoke house *occasionally;* also make my fingers acquainted with the
ingredients of loaf bread, undertake to whip eggs, wash cups, see that the
servants thrust their brooms into dusty corners, buy beef, pickle cabbage and
other vegetables, besides many other fascinating amusements connected with

this wonderful science called housekeeping."[31] Plantation mistresses were convinced that housekeeping was a serious undertaking that occupied considerable amounts of time and was vital to the well-being of their families.

Women's primary housekeeping responsibilities required organizing domestic production and arranging for the distribution of available supplies. In the best of circumstances this took considerable skill, but maintaining a high standard of living in rural areas required plantation mistresses to be especially resourceful, flexible, and proficient at long-range planning. Women were mindful of their growing families and kept careful count of how many slaves were under their care. Only through meticulous preparation could the plantation run smoothly. Early in the fall and spring each year mistresses began organizing the production of clothing and blankets for the white family and the slaves. Using plantation records that listed slaves by sex and age, mistresses determined how many garments of each particular style and size needed to be made. Generally using purchased cloth, they cut out the necessary clothing and arranged for it to be sewn by domestic producers. Once this was finished they distributed the clothing in the quarters, making sure each slave received his or her due. The work required was enormous, even on plantations of relatively small size and with many domestic producers to accomplish the bulk of the actual physical labor; it usually demanded a concerted effort that lasted several months each time. Hester Hunter, who had been a slave on a rice plantation, remembered the work her mistress did to clothe the slaves and to ensure "dat we is hab nice clean place to sleep. De Misus never 'low none uv us to lay down in rags. She see 'bout aw dis she self." Similarly, Nancy Settles recalled that on her plantation "de cloth fur de slave close wuz all made on the place and Missis see to mekkin' all de close we wear."[32]

When the arduous process was completed, mistresses and slaves celebrated. Sophia Watson described this day of rejoicing to her absent husband: "That the Negroes might lose as little time as possible we waited until they came to dinner and then proceeded to distribute the clothes—The men were first served, then the women and lastly the children[.] [A]ll looked well and were perfectly delighted with their new clothes—and danced hopped—seemed scarcely to know what to do with themselves."[33] Sophia journeyed several hours from her home to be present at the distribution. Women who could not be present gave explicit instructions as to how this could best be accomplished. Harriott Pinckney wrote the overseer of her Pinckney Island plantation that she would "thank you to set in the house and call out the names while the clothes and sugar were distributed by the drivers."[34]

Women's duties as housekeepers included seeing that adequate supplies of some kinds of food were grown and preserved. Although men took charge of raising corn, hogs, and other food crops, women supervised the production of all other domestic foodstuffs in the gardens, barnyard, dairy, smokehouse, and orchards, although they were sometimes aided by men. Women also managed the storage and preservation of all food and usually saw to it that given supplies lasted. They made decisions about daily food preparation for their own families and guests, a not inconsiderable challenge given the standards of hospitality among wealthy plantation owners.

Plantation mistresses also played an important part in the distribution of food to slaves. Although on many large plantations the physical distribution of food was performed each week by overseers, white women took an active interest in the way this was done and sometimes participated in the process. The amount of pork, corn, molasses, and other staple foods that each slave received was fixed by custom and rarely changed, but mistresses took responsibility for creating, preserving, and distributing dietary "extras": fresh and dried fruits, garden produce, salted meat and fish, white bread, and the like. Since blacks were sometimes seriously underfed and normally did not have much variety in their diets, white women had to take measures to prevent foodstuffs from being appropriated. Emily Burke, a northern schoolteacher who lived on a large plantation in Georgia in the 1830s and 1840s, remarked that the mistress of the family "is obliged to weigh and measure everything that passes into the hands of the cook. In a large family, this duty is so arduous that I have often thought the mistress was the greatest slave." Women also often determined who should be handed the food allotment for which slaves, thus claiming for themselves a direct role in defining the composition of slave household groupings. In addition, on those occasions when food was prepared communally, mistresses decided what and how much would be cooked. When the slaves worked to build a dam against a rising river, Catherine Edmondston "hurried home to have a supper cooked for the hands. Had a bushel of Beans made into soup and five or six quarts of Coffee parched & a large wash pot of Coffee made, besides bacon, Potatoes, etc, & bread of course."[35]

Unlike arranging for adequate supplies of clothing, food preparation and preservation tasks were usually repeated daily or weekly throughout the year. Grace Brown Elmore mentioned that her mother visited the poultry yard, vegetable garden, and orchards each day. Meta Morris Grimball attended to meals, filling the corn bin, and feeding the horses daily. Natalie de DeLage Sumter's accounts of her day-to-day activities also reflect her concern for provisioning slaves with food and clothing. Her diary is filled with comments like the following from the summer of 1840:

4th July	had the allowance given to all the Negroes
5th July	gave dinner to all the black children. . . . In the evening . . . arrange[d] the affairs of the house
7 July	began to count all the clothes. . . . Took an acct of every thing in the kitchen cellar provisions closets etc etc
3d Aug	the wagon came to day with my supplies from town I have been all the morning on my feet seeing the sugar put away and the closets got ready. . . . Spent the afternoon in fixing again all the closets I have not done I'll be at it all day tomorrow
4th Aug	having sugar put in jars and the dairy fixed to put in the lamp oil the candles and the soap
8th Aug	saw about the beef and every thing and the garden.[36]

While few mistresses wrote of their activities as elaborately as Sumter, they all shared her preoccupations with ensuring adequate provisions.

Plantation mistresses' housekeeping tasks stretched beyond ordinary supplies of food and clothing to the maintenance of high standards of domestic life. This required not only keeping their homes in order and their larders stocked but also being ready to provide the lavish hospitality that southern planters prided themselves on offering even at a moment's notice. Kate Stone remembered an occasion when her mother gave the house servants a holiday and worked with some domestic producers making sausage, lard, and souse from freshly killed hogs. Unexpected company was announced, "and in ten minutes everything was changed. Everybody was in a stir, the servants sent for, dressing, making fires, preparing for dinner, and just as everything was ready and we were sitting comfortably in the parlor, the company arrived."[37] An important aspect of a wife's success as defined by her husband and community was her ability to manage domestic responsibilities invisibly.

Women with limited economic resources found housekeeping especially burdensome. For them, housekeeping demanded not only keeping up appearances but also economizing and even engaging in limited commodity production for sale. For members of elite families in the antebellum years these were potentially humiliating tasks, sometimes undertaken to avoid the sale of land or slaves.[38] For example, Meta Morris Grimball claimed she refused to stop her domestic duties or hire a nurse when she was ill or pregnant. She complained to her diary in 1861 about the "dreary details of expenditure discussed at my bed side" and cataloged her experiences: "For the 12 confinements I had:—Motives of economy induced me to only 4 times have a regular nurse, and only twice for a whole Month, the other I had what I could get at home, and the regular nurse here was with me 2 weeks. . . . I believe now this was a mistake, . . . [but] I made a sacrifice to what I considered necessary economy." Susan Witherspoon was similarly aware of the necessity for economizing in 1840. She found work for one of her house slaves making mattresses, and she herself attempted to raise silkworms for profit with the assistance of several young black women. Occasionally an African-American woman was willing to come to the rescue of embarrassed whites. Elizabeth Avery Meriwether reported that after the deaths of her parents, her brother's efforts to support his sisters were sometimes inadequate. "On such days Charlotte, our negro woman, came to the rescue" by hiring herself out to sew and bringing her wages back to help the family.[39] Of course, by providing such aid Charlotte also helped to preserve her own position.

Chevillette Simms decided that the best way for her to cut down on expenses was to manufacture her own "Negro cloth," for which she had a loom and loom house built. She wrote a friend: "so you see we have regularly turned into economizing, in every way, now that the raising of cotton yields us so little."[40] Eliza Mims also turned her female slaves to producing cloth for sale: "They do a good deal [of] spining and weaving[.] Josephine is knitting away now while I am writing on a very nice piece of janes of 45 yards that she Rachel and Henrietta has spun between them to sell. . . . I had to put them to the wheel and loom and I find it very profitable and saves a great deal of buying they have wove a great many hamsome bedcovers."[41] Each of these women stepped beyond what she would have considered necessary housekeeping duties in more fortunate economic circumstances.

In certain situations, women's housekeeping duties were extended until they were essentially running plantations themselves. Occasionally a single women would inherit property and choose to take an active part in its operation. More often, women whose husbands were absent through illness, death, or business found themselves surrogate masters. While empowered to act for their husbands in day-to-day decision-making, they derived their authority from men and usually relied on them for advice and direction. One of the best surviving records is a series of letters exchanged by Sophia Peck Watson and Henry Watson during the nine months he was away from their home in Alabama settling his father's estate and making arrangements for his mother and eleven younger siblings. She wrote him detailed letters filled with requests for advice about those activities not normally part of her domestic responsibilities. Henry's letters to her provided that advice and frequently contained instructions and messages for her to pass along to the overseer and slaves.[42] Shortly after Henry left Sophia reported: "My fears with regard to the servants are going to prove *groundless* I believe." As the weeks passed, she continued to be satisfied: "The boys work better now than they did the week after you left." Eventually, however, she became less confident of her ability to make decisions and longed for Henry's return: "I thought you might be at home in the course of a week or ten days or at least in that time I would know when to expect you." Three months after her first letter was written, Sophia's confidence was shaken, although she remained optimistic about her ability to manage the slaves: "They are certainly doing much better than I expected when you left—in one or two instances they have given me some trouble—but seem to feel sorry for it as soon as it is over and strive the more to please me after it—on the whole I have no reason to complain. I only fear that their having so little to do will result in their becoming very lazy and difficult to accomplish their duties when of necessity they have more to do." Some weeks later she could only complain: "Things are so much exaggerated when reported by negroes—that I sometimes think I will believe nothing they tell me."[43]

Henry's letters in return provided support and advice. Early in his absence, he inquired about "the servants" and indicated he knew her authority derived from his: "Tell them that I bear them in mind & inquire about them— It will have a tendency to induce them to study your comfort & save you trouble." He asked whether "the servants stay at home nights" and worried that they would go into town, "which I can by no manner of means permit and trust that you will look to this part of our domestic economy." He warned her he had "no confidence in *Spencer's* Honesty" and advised her, "when you leave the House, while he is about, not to leave matters *too much* exposed. . . . He is a *sly* rogue however & will not steal when he thinks he runs a risk of detection." Henry advised Sophia on work assignments for slaves and gave her instructions for the overseer.[44]

The Watsons were not the only family in which plantation management became women's work in men's absence. Mary Strother Means described her mother's efforts to run the plantation while her father and brother were away: "We miss them a great deal, but get on pretty well, Mother attends to the plantation in Father's absence."[45] Emily Jordan ran her absent husband's turpentine business with the aid of a manager, reporting: "As for myself I am up to my eyebrows in work and have not even time to feel lonely."[46]

Most women who ran large plantations relied on both overseers and drivers. Harriott Pinckney, the daughter of Charles Cotesworth Pinckney, remained unmarried and inherited several plantations from her wealthy father. She supervised from afar several drivers and an overseer who ran her holdings. Even as an elderly woman she remained active in the management of her plantations. Ada Bacot, a young widow who lived near Darlington with her father, inherited a plantation some distance away just prior to the Civil War. She wrote in her diary about her decision to leave her father even though "no one will do for him as I do" and to go live alone in her own home because "every thing [there] requires my presence." She managed the plantation with an overseer until she left to nurse soldiers in Virginia.[47]

After she was widowed Keziah Brevard inherited property from her father and managed it alone for forty years. Unlike many women who relied on overseers, she spent most of her time on her plantations, occupying herself with both traditionally female tasks and those normally reserved for men.[48] Perhaps the most remarkable of these women was Natalie de DeLage Sumter, who ran her plantation alone for about a year and a half after she was widowed, without even an overseer. Her detailed diary is filled with references to work normally defined as men's as well as more familiar domestic concerns. Sumter ran the plantation by referring to the authority of her dead husband. She replaced her driver with another because the first "disobeyed me having made the Negroes work in the heat of the day though I had told him it was his master's last orders they should not work when it was hot."[49] Sumter's friends did not consider dealing with drivers and riding over the plantation to check on the progress of the crops and the behavior of slaves appropriate activities for a woman, and South Carolina law made employing a white overseer mandatory.[50] She mentioned in her diary several instances when friends kept her up late, trying to convince her to hire an overseer.[51]

For each of these women, housekeeping was extended far beyond its usual boundaries to include work typically done by men. Even so, they did not "become" men or assume their social role; rather they were women whose housekeeping responsibilities had expanded far beyond the usual limits because of unusual circumstances. The duties expected of housekeepers grew as a result of the temporary or permanent absence of men; the options available to these women did not.

Plantation mistresses' ability and success in creating a comfortable home depended in part on their adeptness at supervising house slaves and domestic producers. White women made sure black women were taught the necessary skills and saw that the work was done properly—tasks that were especially difficult in the case of domestic producers, who were frequently rotated. They also had to motivate slaves to work, when possible without recourse to physical punishment. Mistresses knew that they were judged by the performance of domestic producers and house slaves, and so were especially anxious to have these slaves well trained and proficient at their tasks. These goals were made particularly difficult by the resistance of black women and by the tendency of white men to commandeer laborers whenever the demands of the crop were pressing.

Mistresses knew well the responsibilities and burdens associated with supervising slaves and spoke often of the inherent difficulties. They wrote frequently in their diaries and to one another of their efforts to train their slaves and to improve their own supervising abilities. Emily Hammond's letter to her mother, written after a visit from her brother-in-law and his family, is typical: "My servants are so young, and flighty, that company in the house, and kitchen, upsets them completely, and much of the time I would like to devote to my guests, is spent in seeing that one little job after another is performed without an interval of more than an hour between each. I feel more and more each day, that I am no manager at all, and that all my attempts at becoming one, only serve to infuse my temper." Other women recorded similar emotions and obligations even without the guests. Lucilla McCorkle filled her diary with pleas for divine guidance for her work as supervisor of slaves and frustration with what she saw as their difficult behavior. The following comments are typical of those throughout the diary she kept from 1846 to 1858:

> Our servants are a source of discomfort. There is a lack of confidence so necessary to the comfort of that relation. O for more forbearance. Will it not be better to seem not to suspect them of meanness than to be too strict? I pray to be divinely directed.

> I fear I have not made due allowance for native depravity—nor for real bodily ailments. Business negligently done and much altogether neglected—slovenliness—rudeness. . . . Used the rod for first time with Lizzy—for disobedience and inattention to duty!![52]

Several endpapers in the hand-bound volumes in which she wrote listed the duties she expected of her house slaves.

Susan Cornwall turned instead to anger, complaining about "many petty trials to which my temper gives way" and wishing she had "a huge pair of scissors to cut everything in my way." When two young slaves were careless in their work, she "made them do all over again.—had to scold a little as usual. I dare say thay would have done as well or better without the scolding, if I had been positive in my manner, but I've got into the habit and must try to quit it." She vowed to "mend my ways," become more cheerful and systematic, and pay more attention to duty. McCorkle and Cornwall's concerns were echoed in the advice given by Caroline Howard Gilman, who was born in Massachusetts but moved to Charleston as a bride and who spent much of her life writing advice for women: "Let the first walk of the housewife after breakfast be—not to her boudoir or to her library, but—to the *kitchen.* The certain recurrence of this visit, will stimulate her cook to neatness and activity. She must look under dressers, into closets, overhaul soiled towels, enter into the mysteries of wash-tubs and the gloomy caverns of iron pots and kettles. . . . At the South, it requires great energy, . . . but the southern lady who would be sure that all is well, must not shrink from this duty." Gilman herself was aware that her advice could be difficult or impossible to follow, but thought that not to follow it was worse: "She knows that, unless she *manages,* all will go wrong: and she knows as surely, that, if she *seems to manage,* all will not go right."[53]

Women unable to follow Gilman's advice, or unsuccessful at doing so, sometimes believed their difficulties in supervising slaves stemmed from the frustrations of teaching them. Mary Curtis complained to one of her sisters early in 1842: "The girl whom I have, is the most awkward creature I ever met with, has everything to learn, and is *so ugly.* . . . Having never been about the house before, it is very troublesome to teach her her business." In 1844 she complained again to another sister, although determining whether she wrote about the same slave is impossible: "My maid seems to show some disposition to do better—but she can't be relied on a moment—She is excessively heedless, you know and resents being told of it. . . . But I am pretty well resolved not to let her worry me again as she has done—I will try to bear with a good deal first." Apparently, the situation was not satisfactorily resolved, for in the spring of 1846, Mary's sister Eliza Ann DeRosset wrote regarding arrangements for another servant: "Mary Ann we think will make a good servant if well trained—but she does not know much. . . . We will teach her all we can before you get her." She warned her sister: "It requires patience and steadiness to train a young servant—don't expect too much of her at first dear Min you know it will take some little time to become accustomed to new ways."[54] The letters do not indicate whether Mary Curtis found Mary Ann a satisfactory servant.

Sophia Watson wrote her husband about a slave recently brought from the plantation: "Margaret is very awkward—and judging from her appearance I should say she was stupid. . . . I hope when her plantation manners wear off she will appear to better advantage." Flora Adams Darling, a northern woman who married a Louisiana man, reported another kind of difficulty teaching slaves: "I only attempted one innovation, which was immediately abandoned. I proposed a cooking stove—it seemed antidiluvian to me having our

dinners cooked on spits, and in tin ovens, before an open fire—but my prop-
osition was emphatically rejected by 'Ole Miss,' and the cook said she 'had seen
one of those internal shells, and never wanted to see another; would rather
use the debbil for a spit than blow herself up with young Misses invention.' I
was satisfied if the others were, and abandoned improvements."[55] However,
like all plantation mistresses, these women knew that supervising domestic
producers and house slaves required vast commitments of time and energy.

White women who spent long periods of time away from home found
their slaves particularly difficult to manage when they returned. Catherine
Kennedy refused her nephew's invitation to spend August and September
with him, claiming "it takes me all winter to get them any thing like trained,
after having their own way all summer."[56] Catherine Edmondston bemoaned
the effects of "continued leaving & coming back home" on her servants:
"They get out of the way of their duties, neglect, forget them. This causes
me to carry a double portion of . . . Household cares." Supervising slaves who
had not had a mistress for some time was no simpler. Henry Cumming wrote
his wife a gossipy letter about his brother's second wife, who he said "no
doubt suffers occasionally from being mother to another's children, and
mistress of servants who have had none for a long time past. Caty has behaved so badly to her . . . that Brother has determined to put her out of his
family." The second Mrs. Joseph Cumming was not the only mistress who
found assuming authority over her slaves difficult. Susan Dabney Smedes's
father was a widower for three years before he married her mother, who
found their Virginia home "full of her husband's servants, who had been
accustomed to take care of him during his life as a widower. She felt shy about
taking things into her own hands, fearing to excite their jealousy, and she
took no voice in the housekeeping for two years."[57] Later, when Sophia
Dabney died, young Susan and her sisters struggled to develop their authority over the household slaves their mother had trained. Virginia Clay-Clopton's memoir quotes a letter from her newly married cousin: " 'For a long
time after coming I felt I was not exactly admitted by the different servants
as "one ob de family." In fact, it was plain I was on trial, being "weighed in
the balance!" ' "[58] While absent from home, Mary Jones warned her sons: "Do
be sure and make the servants provide for your wants. They are so much
accustomed to my direction I fear you may want many comforts."[59]

⌖

Male and female slaveholders routinely complained about the arduousness
of getting slaves to obey them, relying on everything from incentives to the
lash to inspire, command, or coerce compliance. Mistresses' own subordi-

nate position in southern society compounded their difficulties. Enforcing their authority was challenging because they were trained to be deferent and often found it difficult to wield their own power, especially when their husbands criticized their decisions. Their private papers record their frustration with recalcitrant slaves as well as their struggles to maintain control.

House servants and domestic producers presented two different sets of problems. The work of both had to be assigned, evaluated, and monitored, and house slaves had to be cross-trained as well. Any recalcitrant slave was punished, sometimes physically, a task some mistresses chose to perform themselves and others transferred to husbands or overseers. However, because house servants and domestic producers understood their work differently, their interactions with the white women who supervised them were different. While the range of personalities and circumstances within each group make pointing to exceptions easy, some generalizations can be made about the nature of supervision.

Supervising domestic producers was intensely complex.[60] Domestic producers knew most of their working lives would be spent in the fields, where they would be supervised by men. As a result, they were likely to view an interlude in the house as an opportunity to take full advantage of illness or pregnancy, by forcing a relaxation of the usual standards of labor and discipline. Black women were also very much aware of the dynamics of gender relations among whites and so tried to play on the sympathies of mistresses.[61] No matter their sympathies, plantation mistresses knew the work of domestic producers had to be done, and while some might have wished to lessen the work discipline, they rarely could. As a result, they usually found it necessary to supervise domestic producers closely, often by remaining in the same room with them whenever possible.

Elizabeth Allen Coxe remembered living on a large plantation in Eutaw, where "Aunt Anna used to spend the entire morning sometimes, laughing and talking with seven or eight seamstresses who sat flat on the floor sewing, while she too stitched away at a fine linen cuff." Kate Stone "used to be sorry for Mamma in the spring and fall when the time would come to have everything cut out; a room would be cleared out and the great bolts . . . would be rolled in and the women with great shears would commence their work." While on a visit to Virginia in 1837, Virginia Campbell wrote her uncle: "Aunt has been very busy attending to the garden—she keeps Aunt Lethe, Lucy, Eliza, and David constantly working there." Slaves were cognizant of the close supervision mistresses gave domestic producers. Former slave Hester Hunter remembered: "My Missus see to it she self dat de plantation peoples clothes been make right." While Hunter, a girl during slavery, saw this as an indication of her mistress's benevolence, the mistress was obviously keeping an eye on those who were making the clothing. Similarly, George Fleming, who had been a slave in Laurens County, remembered: "Missus was in charge de big garden, but cose she didn't have to do no work. She sho seed atter us too."[62]

Then there were the ubiquitous house slaves upon whom so much of the mistresses' success depended. Duncan Heyward said he did "not see how the mistress of the house ever kept up with them all." While few mistresses considered themselves overstaffed, the irregular rhythms of domestic work made vigilance daunting. Keziah Brevard frequently noted the transgressions of her house slaves and their costs in both financial and personal terms:

> I have put up four bottles of the juice of the wild plum today. Yesterday Mary spoiled six lb of loaf sugar in failing to make jelly.

> [guests for dinner—]two fowls and vegetables for dinner all done up in the very worst order—the soup passable—I am mortified every time I have a dining.[63]

Mistresses struggled to cultivate good working relationships with their house slaves. Sometimes they allowed these slaves to work relatively independently, knowing that those who were watched too closely or criticized too freely could easily break a favorite object or ruin a dinner.[64] However, they also knew that careful attention to the work done by even the most trusted of slaves was usually required. Always, they were aware of their own accountability. As Lucilla McCorkle put it:

> At times the responsibility of training my son and daughter and the servants, to regular and industrious habits—good dispositions, and respectful manners, presses like a mountain upon my spirit.

> At times again, the ambition of having a well conducted house—despatch and neatness in sewing—cutting—and keeping the distinct wardrobes in good order this presses on me.

Training house slaves and keeping their work at acceptable levels of performance required patience and persistence, as Eliza Ann DeRosset warned one of her sisters: "We must not expect perfection in any one—particularly in the young and ignorant—we must make allowances for thoughtlessness, ignorance, inadvertence and even more serious faults—and the consciousness of our own infirmities should dispose us the more readily to bear with those of others."[65] While most plantation mistresses would have recognized the usefulness of her advice, few were able to put it into practice as successfully as they wished.

Mistresses' supervisory responsibility extended to deciding which slaves would work in the Big House, although they often had to take their husband's ideas into account.[66] Women determined which domestic producers should be brought into the house and which house slaves should be assigned elsewhere, arrangements that necessitated familiarity with the work and personalities of the particular slaves. Supervising both groups of slaves required plantation mistresses to use all of their abilities.

~

The third type of work plantation mistresses did was domestic tasks. Even very wealthy white women with a great many house slaves and domestic producers did a certain amount of household work, primarily those skilled jobs they could not entrust to slaves. The most important of these was cutting out the garments to be sewn together by domestic producers. Mistresses rarely asked slaves to do this, for cloth was expensive and cutting it into the pieces necessary to make even ill-fitting clothing required considerable expertise in an era long before standard-sized patterns were available. They also feared slaves would be too generous in the amount of cloth they allotted per garment. The work and time demands of this biannual activity were enormous, as every plantation mistress, including Natalie de Delage Sumter, was willing to testify. In spite of her preoccupation with running her plantation, Sumter almost always mentioned some sort of sewing in her diary. These entries from 1840 are typical:

> After dinner I cut out cloths for the Negroes [and] fixed those for my sons & brasilia.

> Remained till 1/2 12 cutting out work for adeline & Sary. . . . Had hampton's coat cut out & pantaloons Adeline is making it.

Catherine Kennedy acknowledged her frustration with the time-consuming work: "In providing winter supplies for my children and servants I am more than sufficiently occupied. Yesterday and to-day have been spent in cutting out."[67]

Charles Colcock Jones described his wife's labors in a letter to his daughter-in-law: "Mother has been busy all day both without and within the house, and is now measuring off clothing for the plantation." His married daughter reported being similarly busy in a letter to a friend in 1860: "I have had a quantity of sewing work to do of late, so that I have scarcely been able to do anything else. I do not know how I would accomplish the work of the family if I did not have a Grover & Baker machine. Sewing machines are great inventions."[68]

Women made occasional efforts to lighten the burden of sewing, as Anna King reported to her sister: "I must not forget to tell you of our 'Sewing Society'—It meets once a week at each house in sucession—we sew for the benefit of the lady of the house at [which] we meet—It is to promote sociability—The 3 & a half hours of sewing is diversified by a pleasant book being selected. . . . Thus the ladies of the place are drawn together. Is it not pleasant?"[69] In addition to preparing cloth for domestic producers to stitch, mistresses constructed a great deal of their own and their families' clothing, also a never-ending task. If that were not enough, women mended, quilted, embroidered, and did other types of practical and decorative sewing as well.

Plantation mistresses' own housework spread beyond sewing. White women were likely to do any household task that required specific skills, including preparing special meals, preserving food, and handling prized, scarce, or fragile objects. For example, they often made jam, sausage, and other preserved foods themselves. They decorated or even baked cakes, and many set the table and arranged flowers when expecting guests. Women took on these jobs because they considered slaves incapable of delicate work or because they took pride in their own skills. Lucilla McCorkle found doing domestic work on occasion to be helpful in managing slaves: "Each servant should have a definite round of duties, for which she must be made to feel responsible—the mistress should herself know how to perform these and if she occasionally *chooses* to do it *her* self *cheerfully* it will have an excellent effect. This will obviate the necessity of daily *chiding, chafing* and chaffering of mind soul and body and temper and waste of time and breath."[70]

White women were not always able to choose their work cheerfully. Housework took on unaccustomed proportions whenever illness, pregnancy, or absence made it impossible for black women to continue their work, which happened regularly.[71] While prudent mistresses cross-trained their slaves so that they did not have to absorb full responsibility for the work of their missing slaves, a portion of the labor did inevitably fall to mistresses. This could cause considerable inconvenience, as Meta Morris Grimball found when her family moved from their plantation to Charleston in the spring of 1861: "We came down on the 10th. . . . Since that time, the servants have been sick one after another, and I have been quite ailing, the house had to be rearranged to accommodate the family." On several occasions during Henry Watson's absence, his wife Sophia had to take over the duties of sick blacks. Once she apologized for a late letter, explaining, "this morning I got through cleaning—(for you must know I am still housemaid as Eveline is sick. . . .)" Natalie de DeLage Sumter complained bluntly to her diary: "Prescilla is sick I am all up and down." Even Mary Chesnut occasionally found herself doing the work of slaves, as she noted in her diary for 1861: "While out of sight today I made a pudding and put the finishing touches to a jar of pickles. Then Molly's baby is ill. Nancy's died last week. So we have a kind of baby epidemic. I had to see the cows fed in Molly's place."[72] Despite taking on additional burdens, white women were unlikely to perform any of the physically rigorous labor expected of black women under any circumstances. Mistresses, for example, did not do laundry, one of the most physically demanding of domestic tasks, no matter how limited their access to slave labor.

The final type of work done by plantation mistresses was caring for their dependents, which they routinely considered their own family members and their slaves. They nursed the sick, tended children, provided religious training and prayers, and taught domestic skills. These nurturing activities best fit nineteenth-century definitions of appropriate behavior for white women and were those most likely to be recognized by white men. Nurturing and nursing slave families in addition to their own required considerable time and attention, especially for those plantation mistresses who saw these tasks as the core of their identities as women. Both slaves and mistresses recognized these important contributions to plantation life. Sam Mitchell, who had been a slave near Beaufort, remembered: "If a 'ooman slave sick, Big Missus would go and see dem." Natalie de DeLage Sumter described her own actions: "Went to the plantation to see about the sick women." Elizabeth Allston Pringle elaborated from her experience as the child of slaveholders: "Mamma walked out often to the sick-house to see the patients and taste the soup and other nourishment, and then on to the 'chillun's house' to see how their food was prepared, and whether they were all kept clean and healthy." Like most plantation mistresses, Pringle's mother was concerned with more than just the physical well-being of slaves and slave children; she also "taught them what she could of the great mercy of God and what he expected of his children." The weekly lesson was sweetened by the cake served afterwards.[73] Further, mistresses went beyond religion and attempted to instill manners and the rudiments of morality as they saw it; they also claimed responsibility for teaching slaves domestic skills and eagerly claimed credit for raising the children. In all of these activities mistresses' training and expectations overlapped those of slave children's own families, who sometimes viewed mistresses' efforts as interference. But whatever the view from the quarters, mistresses believed that extending their care and concern to slaves was appropriate and necessary.

More necessary, however, was attending to their own families, which plantation mistresses considered their primary nurturing role. Sally McMillen claims motherhood was central to white women: "No other experience had such significant effect on the way married women in the South conducted their daily lives."[74] White women were taught to see in child-rearing and husband-tending the central core of their existence, but no matter how important nurturing was emotionally, men considered it expendable. Most of women's domestic work was necessary to the survival of the plantation, and if wives were unavailable or unable to perform these duties, substitutes, either slave or hired, had to be arranged. Overseers' wives, who were the only possible substitute white nurturers for slaves, had no particular motivation to accept the role; they certainly were not viewed as capable of nurturing a planter's children. Thus men with no relatives to perform nurturing work did without.[75]

Perhaps the clearest picture of the complexity and importance to the plantation economy of all four types of activities occupying white women can be found in a letter Catherine Kennedy wrote in July 1837. Detailing the minutiae of daily existence, the letter is worth quoting at length because it suggests the variety of tasks mistresses did on large plantations and the often difficult conditions under which they did them:

> Aggy was very sick for a day or two in the same way she was last summer, only we got the Doctor in time to prevent the worst consequences and now that she is up again we have to keep her from any hard work—Peggy is now cooking and as she is but a learner it is but poorly and slowly done, and Charlotte has to wash and wait in the house—Maria, my only help in sewing has to attend to the children, so that work is not so speedily done as before. The children's summer clothes are done and now I am just about to begin their shirts and their Father's besides having servants clothes to make. Mr. Kennedy has been called away on business and I had to hurry with his clothes—Maria and myself made a pair of pantaloon on Monday—but the work was too hard and made me sick as is always the case when I sew steadily in warm weather.[76]

⤜

The labors of white women varied with the size of the establishment. Although the working lives of white women on small plantations and farms remain difficult to assess, some tentative comments about their differences from those on large plantations are possible.[77] First, small farms did not have the resources for the job specialization common among slaves on large plantations, and such specialization was not necessary. Instead of three overlapping categories of black female workers—field hand, domestic producer, and house servant—there were two, with probably less movement between them.[78] Because of the much smaller amounts of clothing and food needed, domestic production could be accomplished by mistresses and their house servants, with perhaps occasional help from pregnant and nursing women or other field hands. Among field hands there also may not have been the gender division of tasks possible on large plantations. Instead, jobs were probably assigned according to the physical abilities of individual slaves, although most slaves did most kinds of work.

Similarly, the work expected of white women was simpler on small plantations and farms, since with smaller establishments and fewer slaves their housekeeping and supervisory tasks were lessened. However, these women undoubtedly did a greater proportion of the physical labor themselves, since all available hands would be used for income-producing agricultural work. A farm might have only one slave regularly assigned to domestic work, assisted perhaps by children or elderly slaves, leaving a good deal of the labor in the hands of the mistress. Alexander Lawton's mother had no slaves assigned exclusively to domestic work, although she owned the equivalent of nine full hands in 1819. Under such circumstances, white women would clearly be responsible for more physical labor than their more affluent neighbors. David Gavin remembered his mother "spun, wove cloth, cooked and occasionally went to cow pen to milk the cows. . . . My mother always seed to her cooking and did a good deal of it, had her spinning and weaving all done for the whole plantation white and black, no cloth or Negro shoes were bought whilst father and mother lived, father made his own Negro shoes and mother the clothing."[79]

Although white men with few slaves frequently aspired to planter status and had some economic basis for their goals, their wives clearly did more physical work to maintain their families' standard of living. As we move down the economic ladder to those households with only one or two slaves, the work required of white and black women changed again. On these farms, the key difference in labor was that black women worked in the fields while white women did not. Except under the most unusual circumstances, slaveholding white women were protected from field labor.

Although their lives were still affected by their economic status, those women in South Carolina's cities worked differently from those who lived on plantations.[80] Black urban women were almost always house slaves, since there was little need for field hands. Some engaged in petty production for market, selling cooked food, garden produce, or other products of their skill. Depending on the circumstances and personalities of their owners, who frequently had homes in the city and plantations in the country, urban house slaves were likely to be somewhat more privileged than plantation house slaves. Letitia Burwell described an urban black woman known as Aunt Fanny, whose owners "stood in awe of [her], and yet could not do without her, for she made unapproachable light-bread and conducted the affairs of the place with distinguished ability." Burwell explained: "Aunt Fanny kept herself liberally supplied with pocket-money, one of her chief sources of revenue being soap, which she made in large quantities and sold at high prices; especially what she called her 'butter soap,' which was in great demand, and which was made from all the butter which she did not consider fresh enough for the delicate appetites of her mistress and master."[81] Urban slaves were less likely to be sent to the fields if their wealthy mistresses were dissatisfied, since this move took considerable time and expense, and there were more conveniences available to them. While their owners' extensive social life in the city meant African-American women often worked quite hard on domestic tasks, they also had access to the urban black community, which allowed them a far greater flexibility in their personal relationships and free time than did plantation social life.[82]

White women similarly benefited. For elite women who spent part of the year in the city and the rest on plantations, time in the city represented a break from their usual routine. With smaller houses and no cash crops, housekeeping was easier in urban areas and there were fewer slaves to supervise. The bulk of their obligations were in abeyance, and the presence of only highly skilled and presumably trustworthy house slaves made domestic tasks seem easy.[83]

Less well-to-do mistresses living in cities year round obviously could not view urban life as a well-deserved break in routine. They were subject to the same pressures and expectations as their counterparts in rural areas. Depending on their economic status, they did much of their own domestic work; some of the very poorest even engaged in the limited production of household commodities for market.

For women of both races, work in Charleston, Columbia, and smaller cities reflected economic position, just as the size and prosperity of the plantation determined women's work patterns in rural areas. Women throughout the state and in all economic circumstances, regardless of race, did work that was defined at least partly by their gender. The centrality of gender in shaping work meant that women in South Carolina shared important experiences across the line that separated free white women from enslaved black women.

The patterns of work common on large South Carolina plantations had important consequences for the ways in which mistresses and slaves thought about themselves and one another. Mistresses worked closely not only with house slaves but also with ordinary field hands in their roles as supervisors of domestic producers. Thus, mistresses could interact directly with all of the female slaves on the plantation during their lives. Similarly, all black women, not just those who normally worked in the Big House, had to work closely with their mistresses. Work with black women enabled white women to learn about slavery directly, instead of through white men's intervention, and it provided them a convenient mechanism for intervening in slaves' lives. At the same time, work with mistresses enabled slave women to observe firsthand gender relations among free people and to have their own womanhood affirmed. Both sets of consequences of women's work helped to define relations between slaveholding and slave women in antebellum South Carolina.

Part 2: Expectations and Interactions

Working closely together in an environment that defined gender distinctions as almost as significant as racial ones, mistresses and slaves were constantly forced to confront both their similarities and their differences. Although white and black southerners understood that gender created fundamental distinctions between men and women, not only in work but in every aspect of life, the social meanings of gender and race were quite complex. Assumptions about gender and appropriate behaviors did not transcend racial differences but still influenced the behavior of everyone on the plantation.

The story of gender assumptions is, by now, familiar to women's historians. Even though the impact of those assumptions on actual behavior has been a matter of debate and controversy, there is little doubt that many nineteenth-century women, black and white, tried to live up to expectations of proper female behavior. Women of both races used their understanding of gender assumptions to try to improve their position within the complex society of the plantation while still filling the role of ideal woman. Mistresses were deeply influenced by the expectations that white women should treat slaves with kindness and benevolence, thus ameliorating some of the harshness of slavery. Black women shared some of these assumptions and used their understanding of gender to influence their mistresses' behavior and shape interactions with them.

In practice, of course, one woman's improved quality of life was created by another woman's work. Even women who tried to live up to the ideal were not always able to transcend the strong antagonisms caused by slavery. Nor could the behaviors expected of women transcend the tensions created by the sexual conduct of white men, whose violations of slave women created hostility, jealousy, and rage in both groups of women. Individually, women of both races could, and did, sympathize with one another and try to minimize the daily indignities of slavery. More often, women interacted with one another according to gender expectations when it was not difficult or suited their purposes to do so; sometimes they ignored gender expectations completely. The consequences of women's efforts to conform to gender expectations helped to define the complexity and contradictions of plantation life.

3

Expectations for White Womanhood

White women brought a particular view of womanhood to their interactions with black women. Like other nineteenth-century Americans, their understanding of themselves was shaped by definitions of acceptable sex roles and gender relations during the time. The expectations for white women in the antebellum United States have been examined in some detail by feminist historians. In an important article Barbara Welter argued that nineteenth-century society expected "true women" to be pious, pure, submissive, and domestic. Subsequent historians have refined her ideas and elaborated on definitions of what Nancy Cott refers to as the canon of domesticity. Welter, Cott, and numerous other historians maintain that nineteenth-century Americans viewed women and men as very different, so different that each sex should inhabit a separate sphere. The ideology of domesticity dictated that men should command the realms of education, business, industry, law, politics, science, medicine, philosophy—in short, the entire domain defined as "public." Women, on the other hand, were assigned responsibility for the home. The ideal nineteenth-century white woman was therefore defined as a devoted mother, loving wife, and guardian of moral virtue. She was to be submissive to her husband, pious and pure, an example of virtue to her children, and a soother of her husband's cares. She was to be an angel in the house: selfless, virtuous, and good—all of which meant, of course, that she was never to get her hands dirty in the masculine public world.[1]

Historians contend that the ideology of domesticity, with its strict division of public and private spheres for men and women, developed out of the social and economic changes of the late eighteenth century and the first twenty-five or so years of the nineteenth. As the consequences of independence and republican ideology unfolded, the lives of white middle-class

Americans became increasingly complex. With greater economic diversification, men followed their work away from the home and farm and into the factories and businesses of the growing cities of the Northeast. Yet the same forces that drew men out of the home simultaneously robbed the women who remained there of much of the work they had previously done. Women no longer needed to spin thread and weave cloth, make candles or soap, or produce any of a multitude of other things for which they had once been responsible because these items were increasingly manufactured in the marketplace. Although women's domestic responsibilities remained considerable, especially for those outside the orbit of the market economy, the focus gradually shifted from production to consumption. Women who had been active partners in the family economy became passive consumers of the goods men purchased with the money they earned outside the home. They were left to create an uplifting environment—a haven to which their men could return. Men, who needed a refuge from the competitiveness of the marketplace, and women, who resented the relative decline in their status, elaborated the ideology of domesticity both to justify keeping women at home and to enhance the status of what they did there.

A cardinal tenet of the ideology of domesticity—and what made it attractive to so many white middle-class women—held that women were morally superior to men. Finding themselves increasingly superfluous in the world of economic production and excluded from a public voice, middle-class women discovered in the notion of moral superiority not only a source of self-esteem but also a means of affecting the world at large, albeit from the sidelines. By setting women up as an example of Christian piety and virtuous conduct, the proponents of the ideology of domesticity offered the nineteenth-century woman the opportunity to believe herself capable of exerting influence over her husband and children. A beacon of morality in a world run amok, her very existence embodied the Christian ideal. And women could at least hope that their piety and purity would have an elevating effect on male callousness and brutality.

Even though masculine morality never attained the hoped-for standards, the ideology of domesticity did have other equally profound consequences for American middle-class culture. Not only did it justify the exclusion of women from the public world in terms acceptable to most women and men but, more importantly, it also cultivated common bonds among women. Relegated to a separate sphere, women found they had far more in common with one another than they had with men. They shared the biological experiences central to their definition as women and spoke the same language of virtue and piety. In short, the ideology of domesticity instilled an awareness among women of a set of common experiences and values specific to women and distinct from those of men. Key to this distinctly female culture were the extensive networks of female friends and relatives that women developed.

Since women were separate from and better than men, it was relatively easy to believe that women were obliged and privileged to work together to aid other women who were, for whatever reason, unable to put the ideology of domesticity into practice in their lives—"fallen" women, widows, poor women, orphan girls, abused women, and the wives of alcoholics. Many white middle-class women in the Northeast used the rhetoric of domesticity to explain their participation in a wide range of reform movements. By extending the sphere of their moral influence beyond the walls of their homes, they hoped to create a direct change in the world in which they lived. Not coincidentally, they also managed to create important work and a significant social role for themselves.

Historians who draw this picture of nineteenth-century womanhood almost invariably find the evidence for it in the northeastern part of the country; those who venture outside that region still focus on areas within its economic and cultural orbit. Industrialization, urbanization, and immigration had proceeded further in the Northeast than anywhere else, and the ideology of domesticity helped to assuage the anxieties these transformations produced in both men and women. The Northeast was the region most characterized by social dislocation and the corresponding need to try to establish or reestablish a sense of order. The majority of the most vocal proponents of the ideology of domesticity—women such as Sarah Josepha Hale of *Godey's Ladies Book* and Catharine Beecher as well as male ministers, doctors, publishers, and writers—lived and worked primarily in the Northeast. While they sought to bring their values to other regions of the country, they, like the historians who have written about them, assumed their most receptive audience was to be found in the Northeast.

Southern white women, however, were similarly acutely aware of the ideology of domesticity and tried to implement its teachings in their lives.[2] Expectations of white womanhood were frequently articulated in the South; their content was quite similar to those in the North, even though few of the factors historians have identified as encouraging domesticity existed in the South.[3] There was little industrialization, little urbanization, little immigration, and therefore little of the resulting social dislocation and sense of anxiety found in the North. With the important exception of slavery, southern anxieties were rooted in external threats—abolitionism and other challenges to the southern way of life—and not by changes within their society. Why, then, did white southern men and women advocate female moral superiority and the separation of spheres as central to definitions of appropriate behavior for women?

To some extent, southerners did so as a result of the cultural domination of northeasterners. The nation's largest and most influential publishers were located there, as were many of the popular writers who helped to shape public opinion for the nation. However, these ideas took root and flourished luxuriously in southern soil, suggesting that the ideology of domesticity resonated with social meaning there as well. For white southerners, increasingly on the defensive in the antebellum years, an articulated ideology of domesticity for white women helped to confirm both their regional superiority and the virtues of their racial beliefs and institutions. These ideas are illustrated by their pronouncements on the ideology of domesticity.

Southern proponents of domesticity drew on many of the same sources as those in other regions and came to many of the same conclusions. Of course, they defined domesticity in exclusively white terms; they considered the differences between blacks and whites as even more profound than those between white men and white women and certainly did not consider the possibility of any similarity among women. Southern writers had no doubts about the importance of what they considered fundamental differences between white men and women or about their meaning. Their primary concern, in numerous articles and books, was to elaborate the causes and implications of those differences. As a writer proclaimed in *DeBow's Review:* "That woman is better than man, no true and brave and generous man will deny. She is of more delicate and refined fibre, more sensitive, more alive to impressions from without, more sympathetic, more benevolent; better, therefore, by nature. She is less exposed to temptation, less indurated by contact, competition and collision with the world; and, therefore, she is better by education."[4] Southern writers, like their northern counterparts, attributed such differences either to nature and biology or to various human influences such as Christianity, education, republican government, or even civilization. While few writers adopted one set of explanations to the complete exclusion of another, most identified a characteristic explanation. In doing so, they also reflected their own society in a way that illuminated differences between northern and southern versions of the ideology of domesticity and shed light on unique aspects of the meaning of southern white womanhood.

According to many of the southern proponents of the ideology of domesticity, differences between white men and women were best explained by references to the natural world and to women's biological role in childbearing. Thomas R. Dew, the author of "Dissertation on the Characteristic Differences between the Sexes, and on the Position and Influence of Woman in Society," defined his purpose as explaining "the constitutional differences between the sexes—to point out the effects which those differences have produced upon their moral, social and political characters—to show that the position of woman in society is not an accidental one, but results from the law of nature."[5] He argued that the greater physical strength of man led him to be "the shield" of woman, "destined by nature to guard and protect her." By contrast, woman's "inferior strength and sedentary habits confine her within the domestic circle; . . . she must rely on the strength of others." Woman's dependence and weakness, fortunately, were also the source of her "irresistible power" and allowed her to "perfect all those feminine graces, all those fascinating attributes, which render her the centre of attraction. . . . By her very meekness and beauty does she subdue all around her." He then used these differences to explain various characteristics of women, such as affection, sympathy, virtue, and tact, and to conclude that "a woman's whole life is the history of the affections. The heart is her world."[6]

Such sentiments were common in the South and quite similar to those penned in the North. However, southern writers had a more complex intellectual task than simply identifying women's physical inferiority and men's superiority as the source of women's domestic and men's public responsibilities. They had to convince readers both that white women were physically inferior to men but that superior strength did not automatically convey public superiority. Otherwise, they risked implying the unthinkable notion that the physical strength of male or female slaves gave them superiority over whites. Of course, no white southern writer seriously considered the possibility that blacks could in any way be superior to whites. However, to prove their arguments about the implications of gender, the more thoughtful of them had little choice but to find a way to demonstrate both white women's inferiority (in terms of gender) and their superiority (in terms of race). Their often convoluted efforts to resolve this dilemma reflect a uniquely southern ideology of domesticity.

One writer accepted the notion that women were physically weaker than men, but did not consider that this implied their minds were weaker: "If the relative strength of mind must depend upon the greater or less development of muscular power, how much superior the minds of the ploughman and of the common laborer must be to those of the inhabitant of the cloister." He did believe, however, that women were "physically unable to tax their mental organs as severely, and as continuously as men," and as a result, could not attain the knowledge necessary to be legislators, lawyers, judges, or soldiers.

Some authors, with perhaps more interest in a consistent argument, claimed white women's physical weakness did not imply social inferiority, merely a different set of acceptable behaviors. A. G. M., author of "The Condition of Woman," identified one of the "distinctive characters of the female organization [as] a feebleness of muscle." As a result of this "muscular debility," woman was thrown into dependence on man, which in turn "inspires her with a strong desire to please." Woman, he claimed, was deficient "in those great attributes of mind by which man rules the masses." Like other authors, he extrapolated from women's physical weakness to definitions of their characteristics and proper sphere. He resolved the dilemma of white women's simultaneous inferiority and the need to recognize their superiority by claiming women were both powerful and powerless, weak and strong: "If she is to possess power, (and who shall gainsay her claim to the possession?) it must be the power of her weakness." Another writer claimed simply that woman's physical weakness and dependence meant she "feels greater veneration for the great and the powerful, and acquiesces much more readily in the tyranny and oppression of rulers. Even women of the very first order of intellect feel this reliance and trust on the greater powers around them."[7]

The difficulty of reconciling differences based on gender with those based on race and class led some white male authors to examine the nature of inequality and to define a physical and social hierarchy. To prove that natural inequalities exist, the author of "An Essay on the Moral and Political Effect of the Relation between the Caucasian Master and the African Slave" relied on differences between white men and women, which he identified in familiar terms. He explained that the "diversities between the male and female character [were] contrived with a view to the happiness and to the moral and intellectual excellence of both." He then compared these differences to those between masters and slaves, claiming that in both instances "the very antagonism of tastes, capacities and powers is made reciprocally a source of happiness to all concerned."[8] Another author dismissed the significance of intellectual differences in similar fashion: "The lowest standard of the white intellect is not the measure for the white race, nor the highest, of the black. We may sometimes admit that Sukey or Sally is quite as sensible as her mistress, yet concede nothing of any importance in the discussion of the question." Proslavery ideologue George Fitzhugh chose a more eloquent solution to this dilemma. He argued that inequality was not at issue because all white women and all blacks were weak and in need of protection: "The duty of protecting the weak involves the necessity of enslaving them—hence, in all countries, women and children, wards and apprentices, have been essentially slaves, controlled, not by law, but by the will of a superior."[9] According to this logic, slavery was the only institution able to provide protection for the weak, the poor, and the ignorant, including white women; as such, it was among the most fundamental of human institutions. In *Sociology for the South*, Fitzhugh argued that the emancipation of white women and slaves would be equally destructive of what he considered admirable in society: "Be she white, or be she black, she is treated with kindness and humanity in the slaveholding South." Only slavery provided the weak with adequate protection against selfishness and competition: "A state of dependence is the only condition in which reciprocal affection can exist among human beings—the only situation in which the war of competition ceases, and peace, amity and good will arise. A state of independence always begets more or less of jealous rivalry and hostility."[10] White men's superiority was the result of both race *and* gender; the combination obligated them to protect the weak, their dependents.

Each of these authors recognized the difficulties of defining white women as physically inferior and therefore ill prepared to participate in the public world. Each sought to qualify the consequences of physical characteristics. Each tried to find a middle ground between attributing white men's position to their superior strength and identifying strength as the primary source of social authority, and thus contributed to developing a uniquely southern ideology of domesticity.

Perhaps in an effort to avoid this dilemma, other white southern writers defined the position of white women in society as the result of a complex mixture of human factors: civilization, religion, education, or republican government. Here too, echoing northern arguments was easy, although the more thoughtful once again found it necessary to add a peculiarly southern twist to the argument to avoid contradicting their beliefs about race and slavery. Authors who attributed the ideology of domesticity's expectations to human factors claimed that cultural progress allowed for the elevation of women to a privileged position in society—within the domestic sphere. Earlier societies had not allowed women to attain such a lofty status; only with the beneficial influence of Christianity or education or republican government were women liberated from servitude or debasement. For example, one author claimed: "In this enlightened age woman has, at length, asserted her true dignity, and occupied that station in society from which, in ruder periods, she was excluded by the selfishness and tyranny of uncultivated man." The male editors of the *Southern Ladies' Book* were even more explicit: "Christianity has brought up the female character from the drudgery and oppression of barbarian bondage to a moral elevation accordant with the grace and loveliness of her person—has warmed into beauteous life the bland virtues of her heart, and made her home a charmed circle, within whose magic lines vice has no possession, and where purity dwells a guardian and an ornament."[11]

Such ideas, however, had to be modified to suit the southern context. After all, civilization, religion, education, and republican government had elevated only white women to such lofty heights. J. L. M. maintained: "It is an undisputed fact, that the social position and relative importance of woman, have undergone a remarkable modification since the birth of modern civilization." This could perhaps be attributed to "the ancient manners of the German race" and to "the softening and benevolent spirit of Christianity." However, the most convincing explanation was "the influence of feudalism or chivalry." J. L. M. recognized "the age of chivalry has long since departed," but maintained, "it has left many of its traces impressed upon the face of modern society, and its vocabulary of love and honor is still in vogue. The spirit of knight-errantry may have vanished, indeed, with all its romantic enterprises, yet the change which it effected in the position and estimation of woman has fortunately survived."[12] Southern readers were unlikely to miss his point.

Other writers were less subtle about defining southern society as the location of the greatest progress for women. Maria McIntosh claimed that southern homes resulted in the "attainment of high cultivation" and were responsible for "the formation of a character uniting, in a rare degree, refinement and simplicity." The combination led southern women to "that charm so generally attributed to their manner—a charm which is never felt so fully as in their own homes."[13] The anonymous author of "A Few Thoughts on Slavery" was even more direct, attributing the superior position of women not simply to southern society, but to slavery itself: "If the institution of slavery has supplied a school of moral discipline to the men of the South, we believe it has had a direct agency in preserving to us the noblest, loveliest and purest race of women ever sent by Heaven to comfort and adorn humanity." Just as this writer left slave women out of this formulation, omitted too were poor white women, who certainly did not conform to these assumptions about women or enjoy the supposed benefits of slavery. Slavery, the author maintained, kept women from menial duties, and thus they were "exempted from those contaminating examples and debasing influences to which women are exposed, where a rash equality puts the servant on a level with the mistress." Furthermore, southern society kept women from "the frivolity, blasphemy and licentiousness of circulating libraries," which might expose them to such evil influences as Lucy Stone, Fanny Wright, or "a female Atheist." Southern society was best for women because "southern women have been taught, and are happy in the belief, that their rights are best maintained in the performance of their duties."[14] One northern writer saw relative advantages for women in living in the South compared with the North: "I do not know how you southern husbands treat your wives and children, but I presume that, having other slaves, you allow them the more ease and freedom. Then, while they as well as you are served by slaves, I think there must be more of equality amongst you." This writer claimed "man is by nature a despot" and that the wives and children of northern men, including "our crying abolitionists" were "in a state of slavery." Northern women were abolitionists not only to protest slavery in the South but also their own "tyrannical husbands and fathers."[15] Slave women may well have borne the brunt of the master's rage, thus inadvertently protecting white women from their husbands' violence.

A few writers proclaimed that southern society produced women who were superior to northern women, although their comments are sometimes overly defensive. In the novel Mary Eastman wrote to refute *Uncle Tom's Cabin*, she told her northern readers: "Our women can bear to be compared with yours in every respect, in their intellect, and refinement of manners and conversation."[16] Another writer attempting to refute the novel's message claimed Stowe did not understand southern women, who were clearly superior to their northern counterparts. The author urged Stowe to study the history of southern women for "examples of genuine character, and the most enduring strength and resolve." Others argued southern women were superior because they were not interested in the unacceptable ideas common in the North: "Our ordinary women much prefer to follow the example of genuinely womanly feeling, set them by the ladies around them, than that set by northern ladies."[17] Only a character in Sue Petigru Bowen's story "Old Maidism versus Marriage" believed northern women made better wives than southern women, who, she said, "are apt to be either slaves or tyrants; and themselves aid in making their husbands despots or jerry sneaks."[18] Otherwise, southern writers agreed that southern civilization and institutions were beneficial for the white women who lived there. Southern society proclaimed white women's moral superiority even as it imposed physical and social restrictions upon them.

The ideology of domesticity articulated in the South confirmed for white southerners their regional superiority and the virtues of their racial beliefs and institutions. This ideology also helped them to articulate the characteristics of the ideal woman. If southern society was beneficial for women, it also set high standards of behavior for them to follow. Once again, these standards echoed those articulated by northerners, but with a peculiarly southern perspective. Those shapers of southern public opinion who wrote about education, marriage, family life, women's rights, and individual behavior all defined expectations for white women distinctly. Together, their writings formed a guidebook of appropriate behavior and a powerful mechanism for reinforcing southern views about gender and race.

Proponents of the ideology of domesticity believed wholeheartedly in the importance of intellectual development for women, although none expected that education to have the same content as did men's or insisted that it be widely available: "Whatever contributes to elevate and ennoble the mind of woman, has a direct influence upon the character of society and the progress of the age. . . . It is high time, now that Christianity has elevated woman to her proper sphere in the scale of society—in an age of light and in a free country, that the education of woman should receive greater attention, and should awaken a more solicitous interest, than it has hitherto done."[19] Educating women offered a variety of advantages. Perhaps most important, it would create women who were suited for motherhood and able to raise virtuous and responsible children. G. W. argued: "It is highly important that she should be well instructed, to enable her to infuse into the minds of her offspring an early love of knowledge and the principles of virtue. . . . The well educated mother, has it in her power to raise up citizens, who may be a blessing and ornament to their country . . . for the impressions which she makes upon the plastic minds of her offspring, are never eradicated, and seldom fail to influence their future conduct in life."[20]

Oliver Oldschool agreed, warning of the consequences of not educating women with sufficient care: "*Our matrons,* our *mistresses of families* . . . contribute . . . more than all other causes put together, to form the national taste, opinions, principles and morals; how vitally essential then is it that all possible attention should be paid to *their* education. Our children derive from them their *first lessons in every thing.* Should they be incapable of giving them to good purpose, all their pupils will probably become instruments of evil rather than of good, and curses instead of blessings to society." He urged that women be taught "skill in *housewifery*" and "to become real *helpmates* to their husbands" and deplored the "hundreds and thousands of dollars [that] are worse than thrown away" in vain attempts to teach them "*accomplishments.*"[21] A writer in *DeBow's Review* assured the audience that attention to female education had not been harmful: "The effect has been to improve their minds and manners without robbing them of the extreme delicacy and refinement for which they have always been distinguished."[22] According to another author, women's education "increases the pleasures of society by multiplying the topics upon which the two sexes take a common interest; and makes marriage an intercourse of understanding as well as of affection."[23]

On a larger scale, educating women would improve national prosperity and enhance the workings of government and society. One writer was convinced *"From woman is the character of a nation formed."* Eugenius Nisbet urged that women be educated "that the rulers of the realm may learn wisdom; that our inappreciably free and just system of government may endure." Another writer claimed educating women was necessary to "aggrandize our country in a rational way" and would contribute as much "towards forwarding the great end of 'Internal Improvement' as you could were you a life-member of the annual Commercial Convention, or a director of a railroad bank."[24] Southern writers were convinced that education did not contradict expectations of appropriate behavior for women, a notion made explicit by Alexander Sands in his commencement address at Hollins Female Institute in 1859: "Least of all should this instruction be imagined to exempt one from the ordinary routine of household duty. It begets a contempt for learning when it contents itself with moping over books and dreaming of sentiment, when the objects and occasions of duty are all around us neglected and unimproved."[25]

Southern writers also agreed that only a particular sort of education offered all of these advantages: only a southern education would do. Parents who sent their children, particularly their daughters, to the North to be educated were widely criticized. The evils associated with a northern education were carefully described in an 1840 article in the *Southern Ladies' Book*. Northern education would "tend directly to discourage a taste for the solid information and learning, and to increase the love of the imaginative and frivolous." Northern schools produced haughtiness and pride in young girls, causing "them to feel when they return home that they are superior to others." They created "a spirit of egotism, self-conceit, and love of distinctions in society; an evil of which those in the South are entirely free." Furthermore, northern education would give rise "to opinions in relation to morality . . . as will reconcile them . . . to vice, and incapacitate them for judging of moral right and wrong."[26] Additional criticisms of northern teachers were possible. Many southern parents objected to importing governesses from the North because northern society was "more or less infected with a fanaticism, which is at war with our peculiar institutions, upon which depend . . . nearly all that is distinctive in our habits, our manners, and our governmental policy."[27]

The evils of northern education only became more apparent to southern writers as time passed. In the fall of 1861, *DeBow's Review* included an essay that defined the "great and prevailing vice" in southern education as "*Yankeeism.* . . . Our schools—especially the female schools—have been based on northern models . . . officered by Yankee teachers, who introduced Yankee books. . . . The system of education which has been introduced by them is very faulty."[28] These faults could easily be remedied by offering girls a proper southern education, which would not only leave women "better prepared to discharge the high and weighty offices of their station, but the whole South will experience from it beneficial effects."[29]

One of the chief advantages of southern schools was their location: "In most cases, daughters may be sent to school without boarding them out." Parents in close proximity could supervise their daughters to be sure they did not spend time or money in frivolous pursuits and could ensure they would devote themselves to serious study. Those daughters who did go away to school could return home frequently, so "mothers can have opportunity to instruct them in domestic management, and in all those private matters which are needful to them. . . . There can be no doubt that daughters, when growing up, should be much in the company of their mothers."[30] Parents agreed, even when their daughters wished otherwise, as Mary Robarts confided in a letter: "Ellen says she wishes to be a very intelligent young lady; that she is studying very hard . . . and that I had better send her to Mount Holyoke. I tell her she must make the best use of the opportunities she has and learn domestic duties at home."[31] Southern writers reinforced the importance of southern education by endorsing specific schools and urging parents and legislatures to support them.[32] They did so out of the conviction that only southern schools could provide their daughters with proper training and cultural values.

Similarly, those who wrote about marriage and the family strove to tell white women how to behave and meet the standards for the ideal woman. Many of their pronouncements would be familiar to readers of northern literature; few of their ideas were original. But as before, the areas in which they did diverge from northern views were profoundly significant for understanding southern white womanhood.

Southern writers told women over and over again how to behave to guarantee a happy marriage. Women not only were expected to be good wives but they were also responsible for making men into good husbands. One author listed a series of maxims for women to follow, the first of which was "to be good yourselves. To avoid all thoughts of managing a husband. Never try to deceive or impose upon his understanding, nor give him uneasiness, but treat him with affection, sincerity, and respect. Remember that husbands, at best, are only men, subject, like yourselves, to error and frailty."[33] Many writers warned women not to expect happiness from marriage: "Think not, that you are entering into a state of perpetual love, and joy, and peace. . . . It will produce new uneasiness, of various kinds, and will fill you with numberless fears, and disquiets, which, in a single state, might probably have been avoided."[34]

Writers warned women to avoid conflict with their husbands and to submit to them: "Oh, young and lovely bride, watch well the first moments when your will conflicts with his, to whom God and society have given the control. Reverence his *wishes* even when you do not his *opinions*." Mothers such as A. W. Habersham echoed this advice to their daughters, often in remarkably similar language. Habersham warned her daughter Fannie, recently married to Louis Manigault, "I wish you to feel happy all the time. try to make your-self pleasant to your *Husband*. do as far as you can, as he wishes."[35] Southern writers recognized that such submission was not simple: "To repress a harsh answer, to confess a fault, and to stop (right or wrong) in the midst of self-defense, in gentle submission, sometimes requires a struggle like life and death. . . . Woman loses by petulance and recrimination! Her first study must be self-control almost to hypocrisy."[36] Although hypocrisy was apparently acceptable, the failure of self-control was dangerous: "The contest for power is always a losing one for woman." Instead of striving for power, the ideal wife was "a being who can comfort and counsel [her husband]; one who can reason and reflect, and feel, and judge, and discourse, and discriminate; one who can assist him in his offices, lighten his cares, soothe his sorrows, purify his joys, strengthen his principles, and educate his children."[37] Women, in short, were responsible for the quality of marriage; they were to view self-effacement as strength, compromise as success.

Like the ideal wife, the ideal mother was devoted and selfless. The best home was one in which "the pious, gentle mother, exercising her maternal rule in the fear and love of God, teaches obedience, virtue and self-restraint."[38] The good mother needed "a patient temper, a cheerful spirit, and a good judgement" and should expect to find her work "laborious." Such a noble mother was one who "will tenderly chide and carefully correct; who will lift the ambition by gradual exercises; who will subdue the passions without outraging the nature; who will control the will without vexing the spirit; who will inform the moral, by daily habitual duties."[39] The responsibilities associated with this work were extensive, as were the rewards: "From the travail of birth to the benches of the school, is the child in the lap of the mother. Her plastic hand moulds him, forms him, finishes him, and, when he goes forth into the little world of his school-fellows, he bears the impress of his mother's signet upon his character. . . . A thousand blessings will de-scend upon the head of that woman whose child does her honor, for thereby he seals the good deeds of his mother to him, when helpless, and his name will never perish from the face of the earth!"[40] Mothers, like wives, were expected to devote themselves selflessly to the needs of others and were constantly exhorted to carry out this crucial job with ever more care.

Southern writers recognized that the responsibilities of wives and mothers took on different meanings in the South than elsewhere and were quick to warn southern women not to stray from what was expected of them. Mary Howard Schoolcraft claimed that, in South Carolina at least, women accepted their role without question: "South Carolina is such an 'old fogy,' that all the ladies *there* are brought up to be obedient to their husbands; who are regarded so much the *head* of the house, that every temporality, even the purse, is under their direction; and never, since that State was settled by the chivalrous cavaliers of England, has such a progressiveness been thought of as 'Woman's Rights Conventions.'" However, southern writers recognized the difficulty that the women's rights movement among northern women presented for their region and tried to forestall even the appearance of challenges to southern beliefs about gender. Southern women were alternately praised for rejecting anything with the faintest tinge of women's rights ideology and exhorted about the dangers of not doing so. According to one writer, "You do not see them fidgetting and fretting about women's rights—they are cautious first to approve themselves true women—and as such always get their rights, and cannot help but get them. . . . Heaven forbid that our women should ever put off the armour of modesty, which has always made them invincible, to become the poor, puny, pitiful prattlers—debating and disputing about claims and rights for the sex, which the sex must establish in action, before they seek to assert in words." Another writer was more direct: "There has been instances where woman has dared to assert her rights, but how has she been derided and ridiculed—how has the finger of scorn been pointed at the unfortunate, who strove to assert the dignity of her sex."[41]

Some southern writers offered women the opportunity to participate indirectly in political life, at least in periods of political crisis, and celebrated the patriotic activities of women during the American Revolution: "The mother of the household has been no indifferent or insensible spectator of public affairs. . . . She has an interest which is sleepless and unceasing in whatever concerns her family; and she watches, with increasing anxiety, those growing specks of danger which gather on the horizon of her country, to which the fingers of masculine apprehension point with indignation and misgiving. Silently and gradually she prepares against their approach. Sterner cares attend her in her domestic duties." A woman was not to be mistaken for a political being by such activities. Instead, by them she "proves the ministering angel of the household, and exhibits a strength, a courage and a variety of resource, which no one had deemed her to possess, and of which she herself had never conjectured the possession until the day of unknown exigency and trial."[42] Such statements would become more common during the secession winter and the early months of the war, when the meaning of female patriotism was transformed.[43] Only a political emergency that threatened domestic life could justify explicit attention to public affairs, and even that attention was defined in exclusively domestic terms. Otherwise, southern women were expected to be oblivious to political considerations, and especially to discussions of women's rights.

Women writers, northern and southern, were subject to particular scrutiny for their views about women's sphere and rights. No writer was more soundly criticized than Harriet Beecher Stowe, one of whose many sins in southern eyes was her unladylike behavior.[44] At the beginning of a review of *Uncle Tom's Cabin*, George Frederick Holmes claimed that while women's "natural position entitles them to all forbearance and courtesy," such considerations did not apply in this case: "If she deliberately steps beyond the hallowed precints—the hallowed circle—which encompass her as with the halo of divinity, she has wantonly forfeited her privilege of immunity as she has irretrievable lost our regard, and the harshness which she may provoke is invited by her own folly and impropriety."[45] He explicitly warned southern women not to read Stowe's work: "It is intolerable that Southern women should defile themselves by bringing the putrid waters to their lips." Stowe and other women writers, along with women's rights conventions, had "unsexed in great measure the female mind, and shattered the temple of feminine delicacy and moral graces. . . . If the annals of prostitution are to be raked over and republished, they should find no students or lecturers among women of refined feelings or respectable character." Holmes warned all those who lived "where female purity is sincerely prized" about the dangers of those who tried to redress "grievances which exist chiefly in imagination, by means of social revolution and servile war."[46]

Another reviewer claimed American women—Stowe excepted—were not susceptible to such dangers, at least not compared with English women. English women were tainted by their commitment to abolitionism; southern women, like all true American women, were not: "Fortunate it is for America, that she has succeeded so much better than the mother country in not only enlightening her daughters regarding her institutions, but in teaching them so successfully woman's mission; and the enlightened women of

America can turn a pitying eye upon the misdirected sympathies of their English sisters." The "wisdom-imbued mothers of America" were not only to pity the English but they were to pity Stowe as well. Stowe should "remember that forever more she is an American woman whose name the pure-minded women of her own country hold in pitying contempt."[47] Southern writers not only did not want women to engage in any activities that challenged definitions of appropriate behavior, they did not want them even to read about them. Stowe and the women's rights movement were considered so unacceptable partly because of their connection in the public mind with abolitionism. Women's political knowledge and activity, especially women's rights activity, threatened the sexual and racial position of white men, and southern men were determined to resist such challenges in any manner necessary.

Although southern men wanted to forbid women access to unacceptable ideas, they allowed, even encouraged under carefully controlled circumstances, women to extend the range of their interests beyond their homes and families. The southern ideology of domesticity, like its northern counterpart, offered women a model of behavior that could include extending charity and benevolence to those outside the family. In the North, women moved through benevolence to participation in a wide variety of reform movements. Such activity was not widely encouraged nor widely practiced in the rural South, but public benevolence was discussed in positive terms frequently enough to be considered an unquestioned part of the meaning of southern womanhood. The editor of the *Gospel Messenger* praised "ladies in the higher walks of life, eminent for their piety, and benevolence, uniting together more effectually to diffuse the blessings of religion and charity, among their suffering fellow-creatures" and urged others to follow their example.[48] He specifically mentioned the Ladies' Benevolent Society and Female Domestic Missionary Societies as organizations doing God's work.[49] Others urged individual rather than collective benevolence. Alexander Sands believed that society "needs the reforming touch of woman's genius," while the poet Mrs. S. A. Dinkins saw benevolent activity as the cure for the boredom of a recently married woman:

> Minister to those whom God has plac'd within your reach,
> And lessons of philanthrophy and charity thus teach!
> I've read your heart, I knew it well, its latent powers, too,
> Oh! do not let them dormant lie, while there's so much to do!
> Brood not in idleness, but let your sympathies extend,
> To those who need a kindly voice, a sister or a friend.[50]

Unmarried women were also urged to engage in benevolent activity and praised for their efforts, albeit in rather sarcastic tones: "The old maids whose knight I now constitute myself . . . are *silent* and *active* doers of good. . . . Is a poor woman sick? They visit her, with medicines and food suitable to her case. . . . Is a poor boy or man in want of clothes? They make him new ones, or prevail upon their fathers or brothers to supply him from their superfluities."[51] Every woman would be honored if she "seeks out sorrow to mitigate it; administering to the sick; bestowing the precious balm of sympathy on the sorrowing; and relieving pain and misery wherever it is to be found."[52]

Benevolence and charity were the responsibility of all women, but southern women were particularly urged to turn their benevolent impulses in the direction of their slaves. One father publicly advised his newly married daughter how to arrange domestic concerns effectively: "Unite liberality with a just frugality; always reserve something for the hand of charity; and never let your door be closed to the voice of suffering humanity. Your servants, in particular, will have the strongest claim upon your charity;—let them be well fed, well clothed, nursed in sickness, and lever let them be unjustly treated." Another writer urged a more indirect approach to the same end: "Under the elevating and benign influences of christianity, she proceeds to subdue, to reform, to elevate, to ennoble, and to perfect every thing around her; and by this supernatural power, she so softens the affections and refines the feelings of the lords of creation, as to dispose them to ameliorate the condition of classes of his fellow beings still more abject."[53]

Southern women writers were especially likely to encourage white women to behave charitably toward blacks. Maria McIntosh made the connection between the ideology of domesticity and benevolence toward slaves quite explicit in her directions to southern women: "Especially should the gentle care of woman not be withdrawn from the home of the slave. She should be there to interpose the shield of her charity between the weak and the strong, to watch beside the sick, to soothe the sorrowing, to teach the ignorant, to soften by her influence the haughty master, and to elevate the debased slave."[54] McIntosh refused to comment on the morality of slavery, considering that the responsibility of men because only they could make laws. Even so, she believed women's "benevolence and charity should be a law unto themselves, softening the pressure of the fetters which they cannot break, and lightening the darkness which they may not wholly dispel." Even writers of didactic fiction urged southern women to think of the needs of slaves, as did Anna's mother in a story called "The Selfish Girl": "Do you think servants are so destitute of feeling, that you have so little consideration for them? Remember that although they belong to you, and you can do as you please with them, you will hereafter have to give an account of your conduct to them. . . . Believe me, my child, if we do not think of the comforts of others, we shall neither be respected nor valued ourselves, and shall find few friends."[55]

A character in *Aunt Phillis's Cabin* made the connection directly: A planter's wife "must care for the health and comfort of her family, and of her servants. After all, a hundred servants are like so many children to look after." Mary Howard Schoolcraft advised women to "stay at home, love our husbands, love our children, govern our servants in righteousness, and bring up our sons and daughters with . . . reverence for the Bible and the civil law."[56]

This message of benevolence was echoed by the lessons of paternalism taught by southern men. Southern rhetoric viewed slaves as dependents who needed the same protection and guidance white children did. Like children, slaves were considered unable to care for themselves, so it was the responsibility of slaveholders to provide for them physically, morally, and spiritually. This line of reasoning was developed by southern men partly to defend the institution of slavery from growing challenges by the northern antislavery movement. However, white men were rarely able to offer slaves the protection, care, and guidance required by paternalism; they were too busy with the demands of supervising their labor. They found it easier to delegate to white women the daily responsibility of caring for slaves, especially since women had already assumed concern for white dependents and moral issues.

Similarly, religious teachings in the white South offered plantation mistresses explicit instructions reinforcing the ideology of domesticity. According to Anne Firor Scott, "The image of the ideal Christian woman was very close to the image of the ideal southern lady so that religion strongly reinforced the patriarchal culture."[57] Southern Christianity defined masters as morally obligated to care for their slaves and mistresses as the moral agents responsible for enacting that care. Together, these teachings ensured that mistresses would feel both a sense of responsibility toward slaves and empowered to act upon it.

White southern women were inundated from all directions with messages about what was considered appropriate behavior. The ideology of domesticity shaped the content of their educations, defined their roles as wives and mothers, and dictated a set of beliefs and practices regarding the society in which they lived. Like women in other regions of the country, plantation mistresses were expected to be benevolent and kind, moral and religious, and yielding to their husbands' authority. The reasons they were to behave in this fashion were familiar, but the institution of slavery gave a uniquely southern twist to the argument. The presence of slaves added a racial dimension to justifications for white women's proper place. The presence of slaves also made the threat of white women stepping out of their place quite alarming, because it was linked to the external threat of abolitionism. In addition, the presence of slaves forced a refinement of the ideology of domesticity that encouraged mistresses to see themselves as materially and morally responsible for those slaves. The ideology of domesticity in the South was a mechanism for defining and controlling race as well as gender differences.

The characteristics and expectations of southern white womanhood that emerged from the didactic literature suggest the importance the white South placed on beliefs about gender, race, and its own uniqueness. Influenced by these cultural messages and committed to the society that created them, slaveholding women were faced with the complex task of turning the expectations of the South's ideology of domesticity into a daily reality.

4

Plantation Mistresses' Behavior toward Slave Women

The women of South Carolina's plantation elite were not merely aware of the ideology of domesticity, they were highly motivated to put it into practice. According to Anne Firor Scott, who was the first to raise these issues in her analysis of the image and the reality of elite women's lives, "Southern women sought diligently to live up to the prescriptions, to attain the perfection and the submissiveness demanded of them by God and man."[1] Although a direct link between ideology and behavior cannot be assumed, in this case there can be little doubt that the ideology of domesticity was a powerful influence on white women's lives. This ideology marked the only acceptable route to personal satisfaction or success, and certainly these elite women faced few practical impediments to keep them from achieving what was expected of them. Because they were married to wealthy planters, they could implement the ideology of domesticity in their daily lives, and because they had slaves they were free from the demands of directly productive work.

Plantation mistresses' private papers reveal their efforts to devote themselves to their families, homes, and religion. For example, from 1846 to 1858 Lucilla McCorkle filled a combined diary and commonplace book with material quoted and clipped from newspapers and periodicals that defined the virtues to which women should aspire; the material includes quotes from Catherine Maria Sedgwick, a northerner whose writings were widely reprinted in southern periodicals, and other important champions of the ideology of domesticity. McCorkle frequently assessed her progress in living up to her ideal; usually she found herself falling far short of her goal. Although born into a comfortable Virginia family, she complained that "not having been formed and established early in life a lady-like deportment & habits of dignity & self profession—will be a sore impediment to me in my intercourse with society." This was true, she said, even though "my sympathies are with the refined." She was aware that "housekeeper, wife—Mother—Mistress—Claims of society—all constitute a complicated machinery of duties." She turned to God and advice from others for guidance.[2]

In her strivings, McCorkle was like many white southern women. Mary Hort berated herself for behaving contrary to Christian charity, as did Keziah Brevard; and Natalie de DeLage Sumter recorded her reading in the literature of domesticity. Gertrude Thomas, Kate Stone, Catherine Edmondston, and Mary Chesnut read classics as well as contemporary books and magazines, and each used her quick intelligence to evaluate her culture even while accepting many of its pronouncements about women.[3] Thomas wrote approvingly of Lydia Sigourney, another northerner whose widely reprinted writings defined women's acceptance of the ideology of domesticity. In 1855, Thomas thanked God for her husband "combining such moral qualitys, such an affectionate heart, with just such a master will as suits my woman's nature, for true to my sex, I delight *in looking up* and love to feel my woman's weakness protected by man's superior strength."[4] Catherine Edmondston occasionally chafed under the restrictions she faced as a woman, but chided herself for stepping out of her sphere. When a poem she had written was rejected by a newspaper, she refused to apologize for writing it, "as I neglect no duty by it," but warned herself: "But beware. O! beware of stepping out of your sphere & publishing them. Then indeed you would forget a woman's first ornament, modesty. Women have no business to rush into print; so wide an arena does not become them." On another occasion she reminded herself: "Well obedience is a wife's first duty," and on yet another attributed her present happiness to recognizing that her "husband was right; that a well ordered table, well cooked, well prepared food was the keynote to health, happiness, and usefulness."[5]

Occasionally, however, her efforts to submit failed, and she found meeting the demands of ideal womanhood overwhelming and contradictory:

> This teaching of negroes is a sore problem to me. It ought to be done & I ought to do it. I am afraid I magnify the Lions in the Path because it is disagreeable. . . . My difficulties I am convinced beset many a well intentioned mistress who like me because she cannot do what she feels she *ought* does *nothing*. It is not right. I ought to do something, but I do not know what. . . . We are put here with a heavy responsibility on our shoulders which we do not discharge aright. One duty I am sure of—I am put here to be Patrick's companion & help meet, & I cannot spend all Sunday preaching, teaching, & "missionizing" without an evident neglect of my plain duty.

Edmondston found acquiescing painful, but had no doubt that she should do so. Even old Aunt Polly, a South Carolina slave in Mary Eastman's novel *Aunt Phillis's Cabin*, offered advice directly from the ideology of domesticity when her mistress bemoaned the hardship of obeying her husband's wishes: "Men's mighty onreasonable, the best of 'em, but when a woman is married she ought to do all she can for the sake of peace."[6] These writers may have been more sophisticated than most South Carolina plantation mistresses, but they were typical in their awareness of what was expected of them and in their belief that they should live up to those expectations.

By attempting to become ideal women, mistresses performed a vital role in slaveholding society. Inspired by their duty to care for dependents, they performed a number of important services for African Americans. The time they spent with the black women they supervised helped plantation mistresses to know—or try to know—what slaves needed; their efforts to fulfill the expectations of southern womanhood encouraged them to respond.

∽

Assistance to slaves often took the form of providing extra material goods for those deemed worthy.[7] In addition to regular supplies, mistresses provided additional food and clothing to slaves with special needs, to children, and for special occasions such as weddings, funerals, and holidays. Natalie Sumter, for example, provided needy slaves with extra food, luxuries for weddings, and clothing beyond the usual allotment.[8] When Sophia Watson's slave Patience was ill, her mistress feared for her ability to survive but comforted herself by telling her husband, "Whatever she fancies to eat I get for her if I can—Eveline attends to her and room—keeps things clean and nice about her."[9] During the cold winter of 1860, Keziah Brevard made sure all of her slaves had sufficient clothing and blankets; when a slave child died she gave its mother a new sheet to use as a shroud.[10] During the war, Catherine Edmondston provided blankets and clothing for a black family whose cabin burned, even though she feared she would need them for her own family and knew she could not get more.[11] Constance Cary, Susan Dabney Smedes, D. E. H. Smith, Robert F. W. Allston, Katherine Meares, and Sarah Putnam all provided slaves with supplementary clothing or remembered female members of their families doing so.[12]

African Americans such as Gus Feaster also frequently recalled the gifts their mistresses provided in times of need: "Missus 'low her niggers to git buttermilk and clabber, when de cows in full" and work days were long. Sarah Poindexter remembered her mistress bringing her mother a basket of food when her mother was too ill to work. Genia Woodbury's mistress also "carr[ied] em nice basket uv t'ing eve'y time dey wuz sick," in addition to the medicine she mixed herself from ingredients gathered in the woods. Walter Long reported he felt obliged to love his mistress for her goodness: "Many was de blessings dat fell from her hands for de sick and 'flicted."[13]

Furnishing additional provisions was a logical extension of white women's responsibilities as housekeepers. Far more than their husbands, whose primary concern was for corn and pork supplies, mistresses knew what luxuries and extras were available for distribution to slaves: thus Gus Feaster's mistress made milk products available to slaves "when de cows in full." Providing aid to blacks in need was an extension of white women's housekeeping obligations from the immediate family to the entire plantation "family"; it was also a direct and logical application of the ideology of domesticity. Mistresses eager to fulfill their society's expectations felt obliged to help.

Many white women went beyond simply providing material goods to more complex forms of assistance. Mistresses sometimes intervened on behalf of slaves, either individually or collectively, to mitigate what they perceived as abuse. Intervention depended directly upon the inclination of the mistresses toward the particular slave in need; they were only willing to intervene when they considered the slave worthy of care. Usually, this meant white women were willing to aid only those slaves whom they knew personally, did not consider excessively troublesome, and believed would be appreciative. Intervention also depended upon mistresses' ability to perceive abuse. Their sympathies and imaginations were evoked more readily by black women, encountered regularly as domestic producers, than by black men. The ideology of domesticity also encouraged white women to recognize common experiences with other women. Circumstance and inclination led mistresses to intervene disproportionately on behalf of slave women.

White women's willingness to intervene also depended on the quality of their relationships with their husbands. Women who were intimidated by their husbands or who believed appeals on behalf of slaves would be useless were unlikely to be willing to risk disrupting their own domestic harmony to offer help. Those who thought their husbands were attracted to a particular slave were often too threatened to intervene, even if they did not blame the slave. When a slave named Diana asked her mistress to protect her from being raped by her master, former slave Virginia Hayes Shepherd reported the results: "The mistress sympathized with the girl, but couldn't help her, because she was afraid of her own husband. He would beat her if she tried to meddle. Indeed he would pull her hair out."[14] Mistresses who offered aid could easily find themselves threatened with violence from husbands who did not share their sympathies. When one slaveholder became so angry he vowed to kill a slave named Leonard, Miss Sally ran to his aid:

> She run up to Marse Jordan an' caught his arm. Old Marse flung her off an' took de gun from Pappy. He leveled it on Leonard an' tole him to pull his shirt open. Leonard opened his shirt an' stood dare big as er black giant sneerin' at Ole Marse.
>   Den Mis' Sally run up again an' stood 'tween dat gun an' Leonard.
>   Ole Marse yell to Pappy an' tole him to take dat woman out of de way, but nobody ain't moved to touch Mis' Sally, an' she didn' move neither; she jus stood there facin Ole Marse. Then Ole Marse let down the gun. He reached over an' slapped Mis' Sally down, den picked up de gun an' shot er hole in Leonard's ches' big as yo' fis'. Den he took up Mis' Sally an' toted her in de house.[15]

Clearly, although white men held the ultimate authority in the South, even over their wives, mistresses were sometimes willing to brave their wrath to aid slaves.

The most common intervention attempted, like that of Miss Sally, was to prevent the physical punishment of blacks. Ben Horry vividly remembered his mistress' efforts to prevent slaves from being beaten: "Anybody steal rice and they beat them, Miss Bessie cry and say, 'Let 'em have rice! My rice— my nigger!'"[16] Her logic closely resembled that of slaves, who argued that because they were property, they could not be accused of stealing from their masters what was, after all, only another form of property. Nelson Cameron's mistress also stood up to her husband to protect slaves from punishment: "Her mighty good to de slaves. Take deir part 'ginst de marster sometime, when him want to whup them."[17] We can only speculate what this meant for the dynamics of their marriage. George McAlilley's mistress intervened to save his "hide" when the overseer "ketched me in de watermelon patch."[18] In Adeline Hall's white family it was the three daughters who ended her only beating after "three licks."[19] Even didactic fiction could describe such incidents. The female narrator of the fictional memoir *Recollections of a Southern Matron* described a meeting with a slave man who had run away: "He looked haggard, and approaching with a humble air confessed his fault, and begged my intercession with his master to allow him to return once more to his duties. I undertook the office, and the next day he was permitted to go into the field."[20]

Although mistresses certainly could not prevent all physical punishment, Hester Hunter's mistress reportedly came close: "My Missus wouldn' allow no slashing round bout whe' she was. I remember my boss had one of my old Missus niggers up dere in de yard one morning en say he was gwine whip

him en my Missus say, 'John C., you let my nigger alone.' " Hunter explained
the mistress's assertiveness as one result of her father's will, which suppos-
edly granted her the slaves "so long as dey would look after dem en treat
dem good." Otherwise, the will stipulated the slaves were to be taken "right
back to dey old Massa home." Hunter reported the results: "Dere been two
long row of nigger hous up in de quarter en de Bethea niggers been stay in
de row on one side en de Davis niggers been stay in de row on de other side.
En, honey, dere been so much difference in de row on dis side en de row on
dat side. My God, child, you could go through dere en spot de Sara Davis
niggers from de Bethea niggers time you see dem. Won' no trouble no time."
She went on to describe the domestic comforts and moral training Sara Davis
provided her slaves.[21] Not many white women were able to maintain such
firm authority over their slaves while their husbands were alive, nor did many
white fathers make wills giving their daughters legal control.[22]

Plantation mistresses intervened on behalf of slaves in other circumstances
as well. In an 1863 interview with the American Freedman's Inquiry Commission, Harry McMillan commented on the work expected of pregnant
women: "Sometimes the wife of the planter learned the condition of the
woman and said to her husband you must cut down her day's work."[23] When
Junius Quattlebaum's master joined his slaves at a corn shucking and passed
the jug of apple brandy a few times too many for everyone, his mistress decided to take matters into her own hands. As Quattlebaum remembered: "De
next mornin, after dis night I's talkin' 'bout, Miss Martha, our good missus
come 'round to de slave houses and 'quire how they all felt. She say: 'You all
can rest today and do what you want to do, 'cause Marster Jim ain't feelin'
so well dis mornin'.' She knowed what was gwine on at de corn shuckin' de
night befo' but she ain't sain nothin' 'bout it." The wealthy slaveholder John
Berkley Grimball reported in his diary that the free black woman he had
hired as a baby nurse had requested a raise in her monthly salary. Instead of
applying directly to him, however, she asked his wife to arrange it for her,
and all negotiations took place through her.[24]

Sometimes white women could dramatically change slaves' lives. On two
separate occasions, in 1838 and 1841, the DeRosset sisters persuaded their
father to purchase a woman's husband to avoid breaking up the marriage.
In one instance Catherine DeRosset Kennedy delayed returning to her family after her husband died until the owner of her slave's husband agreed to
sell him at what was acknowledged to be an exorbitant price.[25] Letitia Burwell claimed her "mother would as soon think of selling her children as her
servants." When Lucy Gallman was "put up on the block and sold when a
girl," she cried "and held tight to my mistress's dress, who felt sorry for me

and took me back with her." Gallman thought her mistress "as fine a woman as ever lived." Some blacks, however, did not rely solely on their mistresses' consciences to prevail. A. E. Davis's family bought one slave and reluctantly sold another to preserve slave marriages; both transactions were requested by the slaves themselves. Another slave woman appealed to Maria Bryan Harford to prevent separation from her husband, but with less success. As Harford explained to her sister: "I would make any sacrifice of interest to duty—but Dinah has a husband every few months, and I conceive it far more for her good to bring her back than to leave her to the uncertainty she would always be in there from changing owners." In spite of Harford's refusal to intervene and her belief that she knew what was best for Dinah, she prided herself on the assumption made by her husband and by Dinah that the plea would be effectual, "touching me upon my religious scruples [and] assailing me at my weakest point . . .—I hope *that* is my weakest point, or rather I hope it is my strong one."[26]

Slaves and slaveholders alike recognized that intervention such as Dinah requested had financial consequences that forced confrontation between economic and moral motivations. Anne Broome's mistress regretted the sale and separation of slaves: "My old mistress cry 'bout dat but tears didn't count wid old marster, as long as de money come a runnin' in and de rations stayed in de smoke house." Susannah Sutton imposed a financial burden on her heirs when she stipulated in her will that her slaves should not be separated but "kept as much together as possible or conveniently can." Sutton's will sought to ensure the integrity not only of slave marriages but of a mother-daughter bond as well. In the autobiography Houston Holloway wrote early in the twentieth century, he recounts the story of his aunt Suasan, who was bought back from the slave trader to whom she had been sold. According to Holloway's account, Suasan's original master suffered several sleepless nights during which he could not erase the images of Suasan leaving her husband and of his own wife's broken heart.[27]

On occasion, plantation mistresses revealed a fundamental measure of respect for the physical integrity of slave women. When Gus Feaster's mother and another woman were sexually accosted by the overseer and threatened with whipping when they refused to comply, they pushed him into some blackberry bushes and "put out fer de 'big house' fas' as our legs could carry us." Once there, the mistress was called. "She come and ax what ailing us and why we is so ashy looking. Well, my Mammy and old lady Lucy tell de whole story of dey humiliations down on de creek." Feaster's mistress dismissed the overseer on the spot, even though her husband was away and the overseer questioned her authority to do so. Andy Marion's mistress also dismissed overseers hired by her husband on two occasions: "They was poor white trash, not as good as de niggers. Miss Mary run them both off and told Marster what she couldn't see to when he was away, she'd pick out one of de slaves to see after." Apparently she shared Marion's opinion that "all de overseer done was to wake us up, see to feeding stock and act biggity."[28]

Most of the time white women did not intervene on behalf of African Americans to this extent. Far more common were simple situations representing less of a challenge to the authority of white men. While no mistress was willing to intercede for all slaves or in all situations, many did so often and successfully enough to justify the confidence slaves felt in asking.[29] Intervention to prevent slaves from being abused, like provision of material assistance, represented an important mechanism by which white women applied the ideology of domesticity to their daily lives.

Plantation mistresses also interpreted the ideology of domesticity as justifying concern for the personal lives of slaves. Although many African Americans undoubtedly resented attempts to intrude upon their private lives, some blacks and white women considered it a means of personalizing their associations with one another. Such concern on the part of a white woman could range from trivial courtesy to profound influence. For example, white women who brought food or medicine to sick African Americans were likely to express genuine caring, no matter how it was interpreted by the recipient. The DeRosset sisters frequently inquired about the health of individual slaves in their letters to one another; their indications of sympathy and concern were usually shared with the slaves, who often replied in kind.[30]

Their sister-in-law, Eliza Jane Lord DeRosset, was so concerned about the difficult childbirth of her slave Emily that she sent for the doctor to supplement the midwife and wrote a detailed account to her daughter, continuing, "I will go to see her as I go to ride and leave my letter open until I return when I will give you an account." She did as promised, adding in the margin: "It is almost dark but I write again to say Emily is doing very well the Dr. relieved her—I will see her every day or two." Such apparent regard for the well-being of African Americans beyond the simple provision of medical care was common among plantation mistresses. Ada Bacot spent at least one afternoon reading to an old slave woman who was dying, and in her diary expressed apprehension for Hannah, who had just had twins: "H. had been delivered of a child & she was going to have another, poor thing I thought, tis bad enough to have one & you are going to have two . . . after the Dr. left I went to see the twins, they are two boys, fine healthy looking fellows. The mother doesn't complain of being very bad off, as they say." In addition to providing food and care to the dying slave Patience, Sophia

Watson endeavored "to do all we can for her comfort." She consoled herself with the knowledge that "she is much better attended to [here at the Big House] than she possibly could be at the plantation," for which kindness Patience and the other slaves were apparently grateful.[31]

Mary Ross Banks's mother frequently read and prayed with a paralyzed black woman unable to do more than knit. When Susan Witherspoon's slave Patty was about to have a baby on Christmas Eve, Witherspoon, at great inconvenience to herself, mobilized four or five slaves to provide assistance and go for the midwife. Like Eliza Jane DeRosset, she wrote a detailed account to her daughter that reflected the personal interest she had in the woman, a concern both women assumed their daughters shared. Mary Mallard wished to visit her mother, but believed that until one of her slaves "passes through her trouble I feel that I ought not to be long from home."[32] Caring at this level was not motivated primarily by the desire to protect a financial investment, although that may well have been a factor. Instead, it stemmed from white women's genuine feelings for slaves: comforting the dying and easing the pains of childbirth are not pecuniary. White women's thoughtfulness about slaves' comfort also stemmed from their desire to see themselves as good mistresses who fulfilled the obligations of ideal womanhood.

Another responsibility was the religious training of their families, and mistresses frequently took it upon themselves to teach slaves to pray, lead them in prayer, and bring them to white churches. In a letter about slave life in South Carolina written to Governor Robert Allston, Columbia physician Robert Gibbes claimed: "It is very common for the young ladies of the household to have classes on Sunday of the children as well as grown negroes, to whom they give oral instruction, texts of scripture, and hymns."[33] Mary Jones, wife of the author of several works on the religious instruction of blacks, made her arriving guests wait until she concluded Sunday school. She wrote her daughter: "I have always delighted in the work of teaching the Negroes."[34] That slaves had their own religious beliefs mattered little to mistresses, who were convinced that their missionary activity was necessary and appropriate for the standard bearers of Christ. While masters were interested in their slaves' religious lives and often led prayers, most were willing to leave missionary work to their wives.

Some missionary activity seemed to be welcomed by slaves. Constance Cary recalled with pleasure and amazement the emotional reactions of blacks to whom she read the Bible. Fairy Elkins, a small child during slavery, recalled: "Sometimes missus would take me to church with her, and when she kneeled down to pray, I would kneel down, too." Nancy Settles also went to church and camp meeting before the war, sometimes riding "in de white foke's kerrage."[35] Walter Long told his WPA interviewer: "Mistress was mighty 'ticular 'bout our 'ligion, 'cause she knowed dere was no nigger any too good nohow. Us slaves 'sorbed all de good us had in us from our mistress, I really believes." This "kind and gentle" mistress and her daughter-in-law "teached us how to read, write and figure," enough to help them in small businesses after the war.[36] While Long's testimony has an element of dissembling about it, his mistress's concern for the religious lives of her slaves is apparent.

Some mistresses, like Long's, were willing to go far beyond teaching religion to provide basic literacy for slaves. Fredrika Bremer discovered in Charleston and elsewhere "some young girls, the daughters and sisters of planters, who are not ashamed of keeping schools themselves for the children of the slaves on the plantation, and of teaching them to pray, to think, and work. They speak highly of the powers of mind, and the willingness to learn, of the Negro children, especially when knowledge is presented to them in a living and pleasing form by means of narratives and pictures."[37] Former slave John N. Davenport reported that his sister, who was a housemaid, was taught to read and write by white women; Houston H. Holloway's father may have been too.[38] Harriet Miller, born about 1837 to a Cherokee father and a white mother and given by her mother to a white overseer at age three, remembered: "My whitefolks tried to send me to school but de whitefolks wouldn't receive me in deir school on account of I was mixed, and dere warn't no colored school a t'all, nowhere. Some of de white ladies taught deir slaves. Yes'm some of 'em did." That "some" included women in her owner's family.[39]

Other plantation mistresses went so far as to intrude on slaves' interactions with one another. Although Letitia Burwell claimed that "model women . . . were uniformly kind to, but never familiar with, their servants," in practice the distinction was quite hazy. White women, particularly the young daughters of planters, enjoyed sharing the romantic adventures of black women, attempting to teach them in the process the conventions of genteel nineteenth-century female behavior. In a 1938 interview, ninety-year-old Sarah Fitzpatrick recalled: "White fo'ks ax us, 'What do yo' al say when ya court? We tell 'em we jes' laff an talk. Dey ax' us ef de boys ever ax us to kiss 'em an' marry dem. We sey, 'No Ma'am.' Dey say 'Yo'al don't know how to court', den dey tell us how to court." Maria Bryan Harford wrote to her sister about her slave Henny, who had "as many compliments to tell me of, as Sophia used to." Although Harford complained that Henny's "head is nearly turned with flatteries," she apparently found them amusing, for she wrote of Henny's romantic entanglements at length. Black women similarly enjoyed gossiping with white women. Emma Holmes noted in her diary that a friend "told me one of her maids asked her if I was not engaged to W. Heyward." Eliza Andrews acknowledged "Mammy" as an important source of gossip near the end of the war, and Elizabeth Coxe learned the rudiments of community etiquette from house servants.[40]

Once the details of courtship were resolved, white women often ensured that the resulting weddings were memorable. Natalie de DeLage Sumter took pride in giving her slave Venus "a fine wedding" that lasted until one o'clock in the morning. Susan Dabney Smedes's memorial volume about her father included a chapter called "Mammy Harriet's Recollections," in which Smedes describes Harriet's wedding in what purport to be her own words: "I had on your pa's wife's weddin' gloves and slippers an' veil. De slippers was too small, but I put my toes in. . . . De whole day 'fore I was to be married Miss Mary—dat was your pa fust wife—kep' me shut up in a room. 'A bride must not be seen,' she said. An' she wouldn't lemme come out to dinner, but she sent my dinner in to me on a plate."[41] Mary Mallard reported herself busily readying a dress for a slave's hastily arranged wedding: "She has been a good, faithful servant to me and always a kind nurse to my children, so I felt she was entitled to a nice dress."[42] Such mistresses assumed, usually correctly, that slave women were eager for the finery and delicacies they could provide. White women also assumed that, like them, black women considered weddings important and thus were only indulging their wishes. Given the fragility of slave marriages, since they were not legally recognized and could be broken up with a simple financial transaction, mistresses' assumptions could mask slaves' very different experiences.

White mistresses also demonstrated their emotional identification with black women by their attentions to slave children, an activity that probably inspired the fond comments of many elderly former slaves interviewed by the WPA. The attentions white women paid to black children ranged from kissing babies as spontaneous gestures of affection to providing extensive care. It may have been relatively common for white women to raise black children whose own mothers were prevented from doing so. Frankie Goole, a young slave girl, was raised by her mistress after her mother was sold. After the war, twelve-year-old Goole did not recognize the mother who came to claim her. Sylvia Cannon hid under the bed when her parents came for her after the war and remained with her mistress another eight years because "Miss Hatchel been so good to me." Slaveholders generally acknowledged their obligation to care for motherless slave children, although they rarely recognized the additional care other black women undoubtedly provided. When Jimmie Johnson's mother died, his mistress stepped in to take her place. Abbey Mishow's mother also died when she was a baby, and Mishow recalled: "De missus promise my ma to tek care of me, and she sho' did. I was raise just like a pet. . . . I hardly miss my ma, no mudder couldn't treat me better dan I treat."[43] Charles Colcock Jones Jr. wrote a letter consoling his mother for the death of a slave woman: "The death of Sina is indeed sad—especially so in view of the family now motherless, and the fact of Eva's recent demise. There is this to be said, however: that with kind masters the orphans are always cared for, which is more than can be affirmed of many poor persons not occupying a similar relation in life. Their children are left to public charity, which is too often meager and beggarly." The deaths of the two women left Mary Jones responsible for nine slave children. In an 1840 letter to the owner from whom he had escaped, Joseph Taper sent "my respects to Mrs. Stevens. I thank her for her kind usage to me in time of sickness. She acted more like a mother than a mistress." Blacks whose mothers were alive and present also acknowledged mistresses who treated them as if they were their own children. Melvin Smith reported: "My old Miss, I called her Miss Mary, took care of me 'till I was eight year old. Then she give me back to my ma. . . . Old Miss jest wanted me to be in th' room with her an' I slep' on a pallet right near her bed."[44] He did not mention what his mother thought of this arrangement.

Mistresses' concern for slaves reflected the sense of personal responsibility they felt for them. Susan Dabney Smedes described an incident in which "a great lubberly, stupid Negro woman stalked" into her mother's room and demanded a dress. According to Smedes, who was a girl at the time,

> the woman was uncouth and rude. The little girl sitting with her mother saw her get up at once and hand a pretty woolen dress to the woman. "She did not even thank you," the child objected, when the Negro had gone out. "And don't it teach her to beg to give her the dress when she asks for it?" Time has not obliterated the memory of the gentle rebuke. "Poor thing, she has no one to teach her manners, and she has so little sense, and no one to ask for anything but me. I was very glad, indeed, that she came and asked me for something."

Smedes used the voice of the slave in relating an incident with a young woman who worked in the house: "'I asked missis to button my dress for me one mornin'. I didn't know no better. An' missis buttoned it up for me.'"[45] Smedes's mother presumably believed giving blacks clothing and attending to their personal needs demonstrated her generosity and concern. She did not interpret their actions as challenging her authority; rather, she saw herself as a good mistress dispensing favors and offering kindnesses.

But that kindness sometimes had ulterior motives. One new mistress found the distribution of "a black silk dress to one servant and a morning robe to another" a useful method "to hasten an expression of their good-will." Another mistress wrote to her daughter: "Your maid has improved so much that I have not had occasion to reprove her for nodding since you left; the promise of that new dress stimulates her to overcome the habit."[46] Others ensured good service while visiting by offering presents to the slaves, who saw "the neglect of this rite . . . as a breach of politeness."[47]

More often, however, mistresses' actions were motivated by genuine goodwill. Gertrude Thomas noted in her journal that a friend invited to a party did not come because she wanted to attend a sick slave boy herself.[48] The importance of this type of personal attention was not lost on Robert F. W. Allston. According to his daughter, his very young wife was reluctant to visit a sick slave: "'I know nothing about sickness, and there is no earthly use for me to go with you. I have been having the soup made and sending it to him regularly, but I cannot go to see him, for I can do him no good.'" Again according to her daughter, Adele Allston later came "to love the plantation life, with its duties and its power to help the sick, to have the girls taught to sew and cut out simple garments, to supply proper and plentiful nourishment for the hospital—all this came to be a joy to her."[49]

Adele Allston was not the only plantation mistress who found pleasure in plantation life or developed strong bonds of affection for slaves. Mary Curtis wrote her sister about a young black woman who had recently left: "I felt very badly for several days after she left, and could think of little else— The child had been with me so long, attending the children, that it seemed as though I had parted with something I loved when she left me."[50] Gertrude Thomas also acknowledged her affection for a slave, although she was so frustrated by the woman's habit of stealing that she considered selling her: "Isabella is not suited for field work and yet she can not be a good house servant while she will impose upon ones confidence by taking any and every thing and yet it is strange—that to this girl I have a feeling amounting nearer to attachment than to any servant I ever met with in my life."[51] Eliza Clitherall, writing about herself as a young woman, remarked: "I found great scope for my affections, and my happiest hours then at the Hermitage were those past with the loving Negresses."[52]

~

Despite their best intentions, not all white women were able to live up to society's expectations for them. Some were unable to view their slaves as anything but property. When an unnamed former slave woman from Texas was forced by her master to spend a night with a slave man against her will, she unsuccessfully applied to the mistress for assistance: "Missy say dat am massa's wishes. She say, 'Yous am de portly gal and Rufus am de portly man. De massa wants you-uns fer to bring forth portly chillen.'" Benjamin Russell, who had been enslaved in Chester, South Carolina, suggested whites' intervention into blacks' lives was not always motivated by benevolence: "The master and mistress were very particular about the slave girls. For instance, they would be driving along and pass a girl walking with a boy. When she came to the house she would be sent for and questioned something like this: 'Who was that young man? How come you with him? Don't you ever let me see you with that ape again. If you cannot pick a mate better than that I'll do the picking for you.' The explanation: The girl must breed good strong serviceable children."[53]

Subject to the stresses that cause everyone's behavior to fluctuate, even the most well-intentioned mistresses occasionally resorted to the whip to enforce their wishes; the potential for violence lay beneath even the most harmonious of surfaces. Although mistresses preferred to think of themselves as benevolent and kindly mothers to weak and dependent slaves, the difficulty of daily life on the plantation often led them to vent their frustrations on blacks. Most also undoubtedly overestimated their own benevolence, and few were aware of the complex reactions of slaves to their ministrations.[54] For some, interacting with slaves did not arouse the parentlike and charitable impulses supposed to be characteristic of women; instead, they found African Americans an unrelenting source of irritation that had been inflicted upon them.

For obvious reasons, only slaves and former slaves talked willingly about mistresses' violence.[55] Few mistresses confessed cruel or arbitrary behavior, although many prayed for divine assistance in improving their rapport with blacks. Lucilla McCorkle's insight into her own behavior was rare:

I find myself—and so does my dear husband find, that I am getting too hard in my manner toward her foibles. God forgive me.

I have to confess a want of patience & forbearance towards forward & slothful servants—

I felt a good deal irritated at Laura's disobedience. . . . I often get out of patience but I know it is wrong.

Catherine Edmondston ruminated on similar matters after reading an essay called "Things Slowly Learnt": "Would that I could accept the fact once for all that my servants are careless & negligent, as it advises, and have *one worry* at it and not let each successive instance fret me any more—take them only as proof of a known fact. But I cannot. Each successive proof only brings the fact home to me & I am fretted all the same. If I could, as he says, admit that some people are dull, unamiable & obstinate & never look for any thing but distress, ill temper, & obstinacy from them, it would perhaps be better."[56]

Not surprisingly, in view of the expectations for white women in southern culture, most mistresses preferred to remember their successes in dealing with slaves, not their failures. Even so, white women rarely hesitated to chastise blacks they considered in need of discipline and suffered no loss of self-respect for doing so. Emma Holmes was shocked and surprised when her sister's slave Margaret drowned herself rather than submit to punishment because such action was not unusual. Holmes reported that Margaret was "often sullen when scolded or punished," although she also had "often taken whippings with utmost indifference, either physically or mentally, then gone back quietly to her work." Margaret's final punishment was attempted because she became "excessively negligent & indifferent to her duties & withal so impertinent." Holmes's sister was not willing to administer the whipping herself, however; she asked her husband to do it for her.[57]

White women found disciplining blacks difficult, as Ada Bacot noted when several of her slaves behaved unacceptably: "I had a most unpleasant duty to perform. . . . I had to go this morning & see them punished. My very soul revolted at the very idea, but I knew if I let it pass I would have more trouble so I thought the best way was to have a stop put to it at once. I hope I shall have nothing more of it." On another occasion, Bacot found one of her slave women idle with nothing but a sullen look for explanation: "I could have had her well whiped . . . but I commanded my self . . . to order her to get to work instantly." Keziah Brevard was also frustrated by slaves she considered insolent and lazy but was uncertain of the best remedy. Sometimes she found herself "compelled to speak harshly to them." She claimed she was never "cross . . . without cause" and had taken "gross impudence hundreds of times & let it pass unpunished." However, Brevard believed that discipline was sometimes necessary and apparently did not hesitate to use it: "I have slaves under my care—some are very good—never give the least trouble—but I have a few terrible spirits to keep in order. Some we manage by kindness, some nothing but the fear of punishment will restrain in the least." Her slave Sylvia was one of those she thought needed frequent punishment. Brevard complained often about Sylvia's slow and careless work and about her own inability to elicit obedience: "Nothing on this earth can change [Sylvia's] heart—it is a bad one." Sylvia and her three sisters were "just as impudent as they desire to be, whipping did very little good and good treatment made them think themselves better than white people."[58] Like most white women, Brevard considered herself a kind mistress, although her catalog of grievances and punishments lasted as long as she kept her diary. Violence was regarded by Brevard and others like her as necessary; they apparently failed to ask themselves why slaves sometimes behaved in ways they found unsatisfactory and troubling.

Plantation mistresses' violence toward slaves, like all white violence, was most likely tempered by fear. Whites were notoriously reluctant to confront this anxiety and only rarely acknowledged it. In the first year of the Civil War, a cousin of Mary Chesnut's was murdered on her plantation by one of her slaves. Chesnut, who lived in town at the time, reacted in a manner typical of many in her situation: "Hitherto I have never thought of being afraid of Negroes. I had never injured any of them. Why should they want to hurt me? Two-thirds of my religion consists in trying to be good to Negroes because they are so in my power, and it would be so easy to be the other thing. Somehow today I feel that the ground is cut away from under my feet. Why should they treat me any better than they have done Cousin Betsey Witherspoon?" Frances Kemble also believed whites had reason to be fearful, although only women would admit to it: "I know that the Southern men are apt to deny the fact that they do live under a habitual sense of danger; but a slave population, coerced into obedience, though unarmed and half-fed, *is* a threatening source of constant insecurity, and every Southern *woman* to whom I have spoken on the subject has admitted to me that they live in terror of their slaves."[59] Fear was not enough to stop violence; indeed, it could even be a cause of violence. But given the opportunity or the temperament to choose between benevolence and terror, prudent mistresses curbed their tempers whenever possible.

๛

Mistresses who successfully curbed their tempers humanized an inhuman institution. By providing material goods and a measure of respect for slaves, white women softened some of the indignities of slavery. Joint work and the ideology of domesticity, which encouraged white women to emphasize what they shared with black women—biology, home, family, children, nurturing, domestic work—also encouraged them to identify emotionally with them.

At the same time, mistresses beset by fear, violence against them, and the frustrations of daily life could not shake off the racist assumptions of their culture. The care they offered their slaves was thus contingent upon what they considered an appropriate degree of subordination. White women were never able to forget the superior position their culture offered them and recognized that they could compel obedience by force. At best, emotional identification and brutality coexisted in plantation mistresses' behavior toward slaves.

White women, subordinate to their husbands yet having power over their slave women, were able to influence the quality of life on the plantation from a position between white men and slaves. White men entrusted them with responsibility for the private side of life, recognizing both that women possessed superior skills for addressing such concerns and that their own position of authority precluded them from doing so. Similarly, blacks recognized that white women were better able to improve their quality of life in at least some circumstances, while white men were rarely so inclined.[60] Men created paternalism as a mechanism of social control; women put it into practice by their efforts to fulfill the expectations of the ideology of domesticity. By thus ameliorating some of the physical and emotional hardships experienced by slaves, women were the inadvertent agents of paternalism. Taught the importance of fulfilling their responsibilities to white men and to slaves, mistresses mediated between them. This role made them contributors to their husbands' desire for a stable labor force. Mistresses' efforts to mediate slavery and make life a little more tolerable for slaves helped to defuse discontent. Ironically, then, one result of the ideology of domesticity and of white women's mediation may have been to enable slavery to continue.

5

Plantation Mistresses' Attitudes toward Slavery

The ideology of domesticity as well as the daily challenges of interacting with slaves influenced the way white women thought about slavery. Their attitudes ranged from full acceptance to mild or moderate criticism to questioning to condemning its evil consequences. Well aware of the South's official position regarding its peculiar institution, plantation mistresses struggled to define their understanding of the consequences of slavery in the privacy of their journals and in correspondence with one another. They complained about the constant burdens of living with slaves and deplored the immoral consequences of slavery on family life. A few defended the institution publicly, particularly in a rash of novels refuting the portrait of the South and slavery in *Uncle Tom's Cabin*.[1] Attitudes at the critical end of the spectrum may well have been common among women, but were never expressed publicly in South Carolina. (Sarah and Angelina Grimké spoke out, but only after they left the state.[2]) Plantation mistresses' beliefs about slavery were a complex mix of mostly unexamined assumptions about race, gender, and class.

The strongest defenders of slavery developed their ideas primarily in the suitably genteel form of the novel. Conventions of nineteenth-century southern society limited women's political expression, but the novel lent itself to domestic settings and values and was adopted by those eager to express themselves in the debates of the day. Most of the writers, like Mary Howard Schoolcraft and Mary Eastman, were quite self-conscious about their reasons for writing and their defense of slavery. Some agreed with the widespread southern belief that slavery was divinely ordained. Mary Herndon put her beliefs into the mouth of Mr. Manville: "'I believe that the white race are special favorites with our Heavenly Father; that he made the negro for their benefit, just as much as I believe that he made for our use the horse, the cow, or the sheep, only He favored us more in the mental structure of the negro, for He gave them power to think, to understand, what we desire them to do, and to converse with us in an intelligible manner.'" Herndon believed "African slavery will exist, as long as there is a white man on the earth," in part because "freedom, amongst negroes, is just as useless as razors amongst children."[3]

Proslavery women like Caroline Lee Hentz asserted that slaves were well treated. Hentz, who was born in the North but lived in various parts of the South after her marriage, claimed she had "never *witnessed* one scene of cruelty or oppression, never beheld a chain or a manacle, or the infliction of a punishment more severe than parental authority would be justified in applying to filial disobedience or transgression. . . . On the contrary, we have been touched and gratified by the exhibition of affectionate kindness and care on one side, and loyal and devoted attachment on the other." Like many of her contemporaries, Hentz believed that slaves were better cared for and happier than other laboring groups, particularly northern and English industrial workers and servants.[4] Martha Haines Butt was convinced "there is not a place on earth where servants are treated more kindly, or have better care taken of them." She offered an ultimatum to northerners: "If the Northern people have any sympathy to spare, let them give it to their poor white servants, for our slaves do not stand in any need of it at all."[5] Mary Eastman was particularly critical of northerners' racism: "I know 'lots' of good men there, but none good enough to befriend colored people. They seem to me to have an unconquerable antipathy to them."[6] By contrast, Eastman and others believed that slaveholders were kind and generous toward slaves.

As defenders of slavery white women were publicly united in their belief that, as Eastman put it, "most of our Southern slaves are happy, and kindly cared for; and for those who are not, there is hope for the better." Mary Howard Schoolcraft knew that society would take care of slaves in such a position: "Public opinion in South Carolina so scorns a master that is unjust or cruel to those that God has placed entirely in his power, that such a monster would not be tolerated for a moment. Indeed his neighbors would publicly prosecute him, if he overworked or was cruel to his slaves." One of Hentz's characters concurred: "'I know of some bad masters, and, what is still worse, bad mistresses; but public opinion brands them with its curse. Their character is considered as unnatural and execrable as the cruel and tyrannical parent of the North.'" Herndon, however, was not so optimistic, recognizing that laws were necessary to hold men accountable for their treatment of slaves: "The laws of the country must force people to do their duty to their slaves, and punish them if they do not do it. It is the cruelty of a few, who have been permitted to escape the penalty of the law, that has disgraced the reputation of the many, who own slaves, and who treat them with humanity."[7]

According to most defenders of slavery, the majority of slaveholders were not only aware of their obligations to slaves; the best also sought "'improvement in their modes of living—improvement in our systems of government—above all, [improvement] by earnest and persevering efforts to communicate to them sound moral and religious instruction.'"[8] Even local slave trading, although shunned by some, was harmless according to Martha Haines Butt: "It is not at all probable that a Southerner of refined and delicate feelings, and such are wealthy Southerners generally, would sell a much-valued slave."[9] Novelists went to great lengths to demonstrate the benevolence of slavery: virtually every slave character in each of the novels is happy, devoted to the white family, and, by the end of the novel at least, reconciled to being a slave. In several of the novels, slaves offered freedom either reject it outright or come to regret having accepted it.[10] The title character of *Aunt Phillis's Cabin* confessed on her deathbed that she thought for a time

> that God did not mean one of his creatures to be a slave . . . [and] would often be put out, and discontented. It was wicked, I know, but I could not help it for a while. When my children was born, I would think "what comfort is it to give birth to a child when I know it's a slave." I struggled hard though, with these feelings, sir, and God gave me grace to get the better of them, for I could not read my Bible without seeing there was nothing agin slavery there; and that God had told the master his duty, and the slave his duty.[11]

Aunt Phillis, of course, was a figment of a white person's imagination.

But even the most ardent defenders of slavery could not avoid some reservations. One of Eastman's white proslavery characters claimed he would "'like to see every man and woman that God has made, free, could it be accomplished to their advantage. I see the evils of slavery, it is sometimes a curse on the master as well as the slave.'"[12] Several of the proslavery women writers criticized the domestic slave trade, particularly the separation of slave families. Slave traders who sought "the glory of earthly grandeur" were "an infringement upon the moral law," according to Herndon, but she did not object to planters making purchases for their own plantations: "Our Southern planters generally prefer purchasing whole families at once. And should they even separate some, humanity should prevail, and they should have a family by law, and observe it, that these slaves shall hear from their friends and commune with them by letter." McIntosh proclaimed: "Yet it cannot be denied, . . . that no step was so unpopular at the South, when voluntary, or considered so indicative of utter ruin, when involuntary, as the sale of slaves."[13] Despite these doubts, the novelists made quite clear their defense of slavery as institution and as practice.

A somewhat different defense of slavery was proposed by an unidentified Georgia woman in an article in *DeBow's Review* about Stowe's *Key to Uncle Tom's Cabin*. This author argued that "slavery, even if it be an evil in the abstract, is not one in our case, because emancipation would lead to still greater evils." She credited God with creating slaves as "'nothing but niggers'" and asserted that "emancipation never can whiten those black skins, or elevate those weak intellects." In fact, slavery was the best condition for slaves because under it they did not suffer from the effects of racism as did free blacks in the North: "If the slave is anywhere to look for friends to improve his condition, certainly they are to be found among enlightened and liberal Southerners, in whom this prejudice is, as might naturally be imagined, mitigated, from having played with them, been nursed by them, and surrounded by them from childhood."[14] At the same time, she was willing to consider the possibility of "endeavoring to correct the abuses of the system, to Christianize and humanize it," a plan "every liberal, intelligent, humane southerner would give his support." However, humanizing slavery would be possible only if the abolitionists "cease the efforts which so stir up the masses, as to tie the hands of those who would act in this way."[15]

Few women elaborated such careful defenses of slavery in their letters, diaries, or other personal papers because they had little inclination or time for such sustained expression. Most simply jotted down their ideas, often in response to political events. Lucilla McCorkle feared the consequences of "Black republicanism" nearly a year before the outbreak of war but was not willing to compromise on slavery: "I should my self feel a natural repugnance toward slavery if I did not find it existing & myself an owner lawfully & scripturally." Susan Cornwall also rationalized the legitimacy of the institution shortly before the outbreak of war. She considered slavery "a condition highly honorable to both parties, when viewed in a proper light." She considered free blacks as "a tool without a workman, a machine without motive power" and believed that only after centuries of enslavement and hearing the gospel would God "lift the cloud" from their "understanding" and let their minds emerge from "twilight."[16]

The vast majority of plantation mistresses left no trace of their views before the institution was directly threatened by war; their silence most likely suggests acceptance of the prevailing assumptions of southern culture. Many, like Catherine Edmondston, found that the responsibilities and frustrations of daily interactions with slaves shaped their views of the institution itself.

When the slave woman assigned to supervise the slave children complained "its powerful hard on me" because the older children were sent to work in the fields just when they were old enough to watch the younger ones, Edmondston countered in her diary: "So it goes Cuffy. Your aim & I suppose the aim of the whole world is to keep things from getting 'powerful on yourself'!" She fumed about blacks' awkwardness, inefficiency, laziness, and incompetence, and did "not think negroes possess natural feeling. I see so many instances of neglect & insensibility to each other amongst them that I seriously doubt it."[17] Unwilling to defend slavery or to criticize it, Edmondston and women like her simply accepted its presence in their lives and society and dealt with it as best they could.

Women who expressed doubts about slavery generally confided their thoughts only to their diaries or close friends. These private acts offered no direct challenge to slavery as an institution, in contrast to the deliberately political acts of publishing novels and essays.[18] Yet even such private acts and beliefs affected southern society. Anne Firor Scott has argued that many white women saw slavery as evil. In addition to those former mistresses who, following the war, "recalled" their opposition to slavery although they had not articulated it, Scott categorizes mistresses' private complaints about slaves and the work they caused as opposition to slavery: "Most southern women who expressed themselves on the peculiar institution opposed slavery and were glad when it was ended."[19] Suzanne Lebsock reaches a similar conclusion, claiming that slaveholding women's complicity in slavery was "unsteady" because "there was in women's willingness to make the personal exception a quality of sabotage." She attributes women's "uneasiness with slavery" to their belief "that slavery was sinful because of what it did to the slave," to their self-interest, and to their religious and moral convictions.[20]

Many mistresses grounded their doubts about slavery on the threat it presented to the bonds of marriage and family among both blacks and whites. Regrets when separating slave families and complex reactions to miscegenation were for some a short step away from discomfort with the institution that caused these things. Charlotte Ann Allston let slip a degree of doubt about some of the harsher consequences of slavery while writing to her son about the division of her husband's estate: "The poor Negroes appear in dread I feel for them, but it is evident they all cannot belong to me." When Eliza Ann DeRosset confided in her sister Mary Curtis in 1838, she made more explicit the connection between her reluctance to separate black husbands and wives and the institution of slavery: "Poor Fanny is in trouble— her husband's master sent for him to Fayetteville about a fortnight ago and intends carrying him to the West. . . . It is really a sin to separate them they are so affectionate—is not it the most deplorable thing connected with slavery—I wish it were possible to prevent it."[21]

Doubts about slavery were not linked exclusively to convictions about the importance of family life. Amie Lumpkin reported that her mistress was favorably impressed by the attitude of a black man caught trying to stow away to Charleston in hopes of making his way to Massachusetts and from there to his home in Africa. According to Lumpkin the mistress said: "'Put yourself in this slave's shoes, and what would you do? Just as he has.'" Lumpkin reported that this man considered himself freed by the Emancipation Proclamation, but told the mistress he would stay and work for her until the end of the war. The white woman was apparently so moved that she paid his way to Boston and Africa.[22] Eliza Ann DeRosset, Lumpkin's mistress, and other women like them throughout the South disliked at least some of the consequences of the institution of slavery, largely because they empathized with individual slaves. Kate Stone linked empathy for slaves and doubts about slavery a bit more precisely:

> As far as Mamma could, the Negroes on our place were protected from cruelty and were well cared for; they were generally given Saturday evening and had plenty to eat and comfortable clothes. Still there were abuses impossible to prevent. And constantly there were tales circulated of cruelties on neighboring plantations, tales that would make one's blood run cold. And yet we were powerless to help. Always I felt the moral guilt of it, felt how impossible it must be for an owner of slaves to win his way into Heaven. Born and raised as we were, what would be our measure of responsibility?[23]

While Stone's comments clearly bear the stamp of hindsight, sympathy for slaves and the impulse to aid them were genuinely felt contemporaneously with ruling over them. Slaveholding presented a responsibility and a moral dilemma these women could not ignore.

Other women also challenged the South's unqualified acceptance of slavery because of the obligations and personal commitment it demanded. At least one woman, Elizabeth Allston Pringle's paternal aunt Elizabeth Blythe, apparently felt the responsibility so strongly that she chose to marry for her slaves' benefit. According to her niece, Blythe inherited a plantation and many slaves, which she felt were "a great trust and responsibility and most difficult to manage, for it was almost impossible to get an overseer who would treat the Negroes with gentleness and justice." Since she could not claim the authority to care for them alone, she married. "She was then able to live on her plantation and see that her Negroes were kindly and properly managed and looked after." H. R. Warren also felt the burdens imposed by slaveholding but chose a different solution, perhaps because of her greater age or lack of suitors. In 1849 she asked her attorney to sell her slaves or give them to relatives, claiming these were better solutions than hiring them out or moving them: "The Negroes suffer and God has given me these to take care of and I feel responsible to him to make them comfortable as far as I can some have Husband here that had rather stay than go back and I do not want to stay in the same place with them for I cant bear to see one dissatisfied."[24] Since she had no way to guarantee that new owners would respect slaves' family relationships or aim to satisfy them, Warren's decision was hardly ideal, but it enabled her to respect her religious and moral beliefs.

Most of the women who sympathized with slaves and were sensitive to the practical and moral responsibilities they represented did not want to abandon the institution of slavery. Most kept their doubts to themselves or articulated them in vague terms to female correspondents; they did not develop a program to end slavery nor could they imagine a world without it. A few, however, turned their sense of sympathy with the plight of slaves and their discomfort with slaveholding into questions about the institution. They expressed doubts about slavery on theoretical humanitarian grounds as well as on their personal awareness of its consequences. However, none of the few South Carolina women who expressed doubts about slavery was willing to act on her beliefs, and all stopped far short of pushing their thinking to its limits. Though they might have been critical of slavery, they acknowledged its legitimacy and did not wish to end it. Shortly before the outbreak of war, Keziah Brevard wrote in her diary about her doubts about slavery, or at least about fighting to defend it: "I think we all have some, the fewest in number, who would not butcher us—but I am sure the most of them would aim at freedom—tis natural they should and they will try for it. O that God would take them out of bondage in a peaceable way. Let no blood flow. We are attached to our slaves."[25]

The few white women who dared to develop their doubts about slavery based them on its moral and sexual consequences. Gertrude Thomas argued that slavery degraded women of both races. Ella Gertrude Clanton Thomas was a Georgia woman who used her long-term journal to record her ideas and thoughts regarding her world. Unusually well educated and well read for a woman in her culture, she was a careful and informed observer of political activities affecting her section of the country. She based her doubts about slavery on its implications for southern morality and her sympathy for the plight of light-skinned black women, who were "subject to be bought by men, with natures but one degree removed from the brute creation and with no more control over their passions—subjected to such a lot are they not to be pitied. I know that this is a view of the subject that it is thought best for women to ignore but when we see so many cases of mulattoes commanding higher prices, advertised as 'Fancy girls,' oh is it not enough to make us shudder for the standard of morality in our Southern homes?" Miscegenation destroyed family life, claimed Thomas, but unable to reject slavery, she despaired of finding a solution. She believed that she, like other southern women, was powerless to solve a problem she did not create: "There is an inborn earnestness in woman's nature to teach her to do right, but this is a mystery I find I can not solve—Southern women are I believe all at heart abolitionists but then I expect I have made a very broad assertion but I will stand to the opinion that the institution of slavery degrades the white man more than the Negro and oh exerts a most deleterious effect upon our children." Thomas criticized the sexual double standard prevalent in the South that condemned white women for transgressions that not only did not bring any criticism to white men but could elevate them in the eyes of other men. Thomas's ambivalent opposition to slavery may have been a result of her discomfort with the behavior of the men in her own family. Thomas's father, Turner Clanton, was also the father of several children by Lurania (Lurany) Clanton, a black woman. In fact, Thomas's outburst in her diary was inspired by seeing Lurany and her daughter Lulah, "a remarkably pretty child . . . and as white as any white child."[26] Nell Irvin Painter suggests Thomas's husband may also have fathered a slave child at about the same time her own first child was born.[27]

Thomas also objected to the treatment of pregnant black women, including those owned by family members. When two slave women were close to confinement, she wrote: "In that condition I think all women ought to be favoured. I know that had I the sole management of a plantation, pregnant women should be highly favored. A woman myself, I can sympathize with my sex, wether white or black." At the time, Thomas was the mother of one small child and had suffered a premature birth and a miscarriage. In spite of her professed sympathy for black women, Thomas's doubts did not lead her to contemplate a world without slavery. She was certainly unwilling to admit those of even partial African descent to positions of social equality. When the son of an acquaintance fled to the North with a mulatto slave and tried to marry her, Thomas was not surprised by the father's mortification and efforts to have the son declared insane: "I can well understand his horror of that kind of marriage." She was horrified herself when a man who appeared to be a mulatto "came in at the front gate" and accepted invitations to sit by the fire and to dinner. When asked by Thomas's husband, he willingly acknowledged that his father had been black. She admitted that if his mother had been black she would have been tempted to insult him, but she resisted in part because she "felt sorry for the poor fellow—He may indeed merit the expression of *base born*."[28]

Gertrude Thomas's objections to slavery and her inability to imagine a world without it were shared in large measure by Mary Chesnut, easily the most famous of southern women diarists.[29] The daughter of a nullification leader and wealthy South Carolina planter, Mary Boykin allied herself with another prominent South Carolina family when she married James Chesnut in 1840. The young couple lived in Camden until 1858, when James Chesnut's political career took him first to Washington, then to Richmond.[30] Intimately connected with the important families of South Carolina, Mary Chesnut was well aware of the norms of her society. Unlike many of her peers, she was an articulate and perceptive critic of the world in which she lived.

Like Gertrude Thomas, Mary Chesnut had real doubts about the morality of slavery. Although she enjoyed both its material benefits and the social world it created, she deplored the effects it had on women of both races, arguing that it was a curse because it degraded morals and encouraged the brutality of white men. She combined what have been termed feminist and antislavery arguments in her understanding of southern life, although both her feminist and antislavery ideas were muted by her reluctance to admit the possibility of social equality and her racism. Her ideas are worth quoting at length:

> I wonder if it be a sin to think slavery a curse to any land. . . . Men and women are punished when their masters and mistresses are brutes and not when they do wrong—and then we live surrounded by prostitutes. An abandoned woman is sent out of any decent house elsewhere. Who thinks any worse of a Negro or mulatto woman for being a thing we can't name? God forgive us, but ours is a *monstrous* system and wrong and iniquity. Perhaps the rest of the world is as bad—this *only* I see. Like the patriarchs of old our men live all in one house with their wives and their concubines, and the mulattoes one sees in every family exactly resemble the white children—and every lady tells you who is the father of all the mulatto children in everybody's household, but those in her own she seems to think drop from the clouds, or pretends so to think. Good women we have, *but* they talk of all *nastiness*—tho' they never do wrong, they talk day and night of [erasures illegible] my disgust sometimes is boiling over—but they are, I believe, in conduct the purest women God ever made. Thank God for my countrywomen—alas for the men! No worse than men everywhere, but the lower their mistresses, the more degraded they must be.[31]

While sharing the racist assumptions of her class, Chesnut was nevertheless able to imagine herself in the situation of individual slaves, a leap not encouraged by white southern society. She sympathized with the matrimonial difficulties of her maid and refused to condemn black women who had children without being married.[32] When she saw a woman sold in Montgomery, Alabama, she reported feeling faint and tried hard to explain the situation to herself: "I sat down on a stool in a shop. I disciplined my wild thoughts. You know how women sell themselves and are sold in marriage, from queens downward, eh? You know what the Bible says about slavery—and marriage. Poor women. Poor slaves."[33] She blamed the horrors of slavery on white men and applauded the efforts of white women to improve the quality of slaves' lives. She wrote about her own family members, who she said were doing their duty as they conceived it, and contrasted them with northern abolitionists:

> They do not preach and teach hate as a gospel and the sacred duty of murder and insurrection, but they strive to ameliorate the condition of these Africans in every particular. They set them the example of a perfect life—a life of utter self-abnegation. Think of these holy New Englanders, forced to have a Negro village walk through their houses whenever they saw fit—dirty, slatternly, idle, ill-smelling by nature (when otherwise, it is the exception). These women are more troubled by their duty to Negroes, have less chance to live their own lives in peace than if they were African missionaries. They have a swarm of blacks about them as children under their care—not as Mrs. Stowe's fancy paints them, but the hard, unpleasant, unromantic, undeveloped savage Africans. And they hate slavery worse than Mrs. Stowe.[34]

Others agreed that Chesnut's mother-in-law was one of these fervent haters. Chesnut had a conversation with James Team, the overseer on the senior Chesnuts' plantation, about her mother-in-law. According to Team, "In all my life I have only met one or two womenfolk who were not abolitionists in their hearts—and hot ones, too. Mrs. Chesnut is the worst. They have known that on her for years. Tom Haile said as soon as he married he found all the ladies of this family hated slavery." Undoubtedly, part of her hatred stemmed from the unavoidable daily contact with mulatto children fathered by her husband. But Mary Chesnut clearly admitted to hating slavery herself. Her angry response to a northern woman who, though married to a southerner and living in the South, refused to own slaves, was: "Who would, that was not born to it?" In the middle of the war she read Harriet Beecher Stowe's works and the abolitionist James Redpath's biography of John Brown and found herself

> utterly confounded at the atrocity of African slavery. We look upon the miserable black race as crushed to earth, habitually knocked down, as John Brown says

"by an iron shovel or anything that comes handy." At home we see them, the idlest, laziest, fattest, most comfortably contented peasantry that ever cumbered the earth—and forget there is any wrong in slavery at all.

I daresay the truth lies between the two extremes.[35]

During the last weeks of the war she continued to equivocate between these two views. She identified her landlady, Mrs. Munro, as "a violent abolitionist in the sense I am one," but qualified her statement by adding: "Mrs. Munro is a Yankee sympathizer, and that is one too much for us."[36]

Like a few other southern women, Mary Chesnut both hated slavery and yet could not imagine a world without it. She translated the teachings of nineteenth-century culture regarding women into a sophisticated understanding of her own position and into a critique of slavery, yet was unable to act on her beliefs. Gertrude Thomas bemoaned her own ineffectiveness: "The happiest of homes are destroyed but what is to be done. . . . This is a mystery I find I cannot solve."[37] Mary Chesnut implied that white women could do very little about slavery: "women were brought up not to judge their fathers or their husbands. They took them as the Lord provided—and were thankful." For Chesnut, in this helpless condition women were no better off than slaves. Late in the war, she recorded this conversation with the wife of General Johnston:

> Mrs. Johnston said she would never own slaves.
> "I might say the same thing. I never would. Mr. Chesnut does, but he hates all slavery, especially African slavery."
> "What do you mean by African?"
> "To distinguish that form from the inevitable slavery of the world. All married women, all children, and girls who live on in their father's houses are slaves."

Given their own difficulties, Chesnut could only try to reassure herself that women were not responsible for slavery: "As far as I can see, Southern women do all that missionaries could do to prevent and alleviate the evils."[38]

Unable to imagine a world without slavery in spite of their distaste for its consequences, Chesnut and other elite women in South Carolina who shared her views struggled with their own ineffectiveness but were essentially alone. Because South Carolina women whispered their distaste for the worst consequences of slavery only to their diaries or to one another they were forced to work individually to counteract it and could help only the black men and women on their own plantations. Influenced by the ideology of domesticity to behave sympathetically and benevolently, some mistresses worked hard to improve conditions for their slaves. But, taught to defer to men and unable to unite politically, they did not develop their dislike of slavery beyond the individual emotional level. Their complaints about slavery and their dismay at its consequences remained private and apolitical.

In the antebellum years, three South Carolina women defied the dictates of their culture to publish their ideas about gender, race, slavery, and other important topics of the day. As writers and intellectuals Caroline Howard Gilman, Louisa McCord, and Mary Howard Schoolcraft were exceptional for their time and place. These political women were simultaneously rigorous defenders and sharp critics of the separation of spheres, slavery, and race and gender relations. Like reformers elsewhere in the country, they believed that bringing the problems of their society to light would help to eliminate them. Yet for all three women, criticisms of southern society were tempered by genuine acceptance of its assumptions and institutions. An examination of their very different ideas offers the potential to develop the connection between ideology and behavior more closely, as well as to assess the complex attitudes and expectations defining the place of white women in slaveholding society.

Caroline Howard Gilman was born in 1794 in Boston; in 1819 she married a Harvard Divinity School graduate and moved to Charleston, where her husband was appointed minister of the Unitarian church.[39] Charleston remained her home for most of the rest of her life. Between 1820 and 1831 she gave birth to six children, two of whom, along with a seventh born in 1839, died in infancy. In 1832 she founded a magazine for children called the *Rose Bud, or Youth's Gazette;* she changed its name to the *Southern Rose* in 1835 because, she said, the buds had blossomed. The magazine ceased publication in 1839 but was followed by a series of annual gift books intended for women that were filled with advice, stories, and other material similar to that included in the magazine. Gilman also published two novels, *Recollections of a Housekeeper* (1834) and *Recollections of a Southern Matron* (1838), both of which had been serialized in the magazine. She claimed the novels were as true to life as possible and even solicited anecdotes from the readers of the magazine to weave into the stories if appropriate.[40]

In all of her writing, Caroline Howard Gilman defined and defended the ideology of domesticity, both as it applied in the North and in the form directed at plantation mistresses. She believed that white women had a special mission and that their domestic responsibilities were essential to the success of their families and the nation. She filled many pages of her magazine and annual registers with poems and stories, essays and quotations extolling the importance of women's activities, particularly as mothers and homemakers:

But never in her varied sphere
Is woman to the heart more dear,
Than when her homely task she plies,
With cheerful duty in her eyes,
And every *lowly* path well trod,
Looks meekly upward to her God.[41]

Mothers, she said, were to be always supportive of their sons: "Whilst his mother lives, he will have one friend on earth who will not listen when he is slandered, who will not desert him when he suffers, who will solace him in his sorrow, and speak to him of hope when he is ready to despair. Her affections know no ebbing tide. It flows on from a pure fountain, spreading happiness through all this vale of tears, and ceases only at the ocean of eternity." Gilman did not indicate that daughters should receive similar treatment.[42]

These nurturing activities were extremely important for Gilman, and she sometimes chided men, albeit indirectly, for their failure to appreciate women's significance. In the brief essay "The Wife" she celebrated women's ability to manage husbands, homes, children, and social obligations successfully and asked what would happen if a man were "only for one day, in their position? The servants would all be discharged, the children whipped and sent to bed, and himself, by nightfall, just fit for Bedlam." She offered advice to women as well: "The most busy housewife must find a little time to refresh her mind with reading and give it some new ideas to meditate upon. . . . Women must endeavor to keep up an interest in what is going on out of doors—it enables them to enjoy home better and join more readily in conversation, and it varies the routine of their household and more domestic duties."[43] By celebrating the importance of women's activities and offering advice both general and specific on how to accomplish them more effectively, Gilman presented herself as a powerful public champion of the ideology of domesticity and of women.[44]

Gilman had equally strong views about slavery and race relations. In spite of her northern upbringing, she considered herself a southerner after her marriage and remained loyal to the South during the war. She had few moral objections to the institution of slavery but advocated more considerate treatment of slaves. White women, she felt, had a particular responsibility to be considerate toward blacks and to teach their children to treat blacks with kindness. The narrator's grandmother in *Recollections of a Southern Matron* demonstrated Gilman's model of ideal behavior: "The influence of her manners was evident on the plantation, producing an air of courtesy even among the slaves. It was beautiful to witness the profound respect with which they regarded her." Gilman applauded the real contributions plantation mistresses made to the health and well-being of those in their care, in spite of the apparent indolence made possible by slavery:

> Many fair, and even aristocratic girls, if we may use this phrase in our republican country, who grace a ball room, or loll in a liveried carriage, may be seen with these steel talismans [keys], presiding over store houses, and measuring with the accuracy and conscientiousness of a shopsman, the daily allowance of the family; or cutting homespun suits, for days together, for the young and the old slaves under their charge; while matrons, who would ring a bell for their pocket handkerchief to be brought to them, will act the part of a surgeon or physician, with a promptitude and skill, which would excite astonishment in a stranger. Very frequently, slaves, like children, will only take medicine from their superiors, and in this case the planter's wife or daughter is admirably fitted to aid them.

Gilman assigned duties to men as well as women. The well-prepared slaveholder had to learn "personal discipline" and study medicine and mechanics. He had to be "aware that he controlled the happiness of a large family of his fellow creatures. He neither permitted himself to exercise oppression, nor tolerated it in others. . . . He felt how much a planter has to answer to man and to God in the patriarchal relation he holds, and he shrank not indolently from the arduous demand."[45] Under these circumstances, with both male and female slaveholders fulfilling their obligations to slaves, Gilman believed slavery was advantageous for everyone, including the slaves themselves.

Gilman devoted a great deal of attention to the difficulties women in both sections of the country faced in finding and retaining suitable domestic assistance. White domestic servants were unreliable and needed close and constant supervision; blacks were loyal but unskilled and demanding. At one point in *Recollections of a Southern Matron*, the narrator engaged a white woman as housekeeper and brought her to the South, an experiment illustrating Gilman's sensitivity to the class and race tensions of the region. The narrator did not know how to treat a white servant in the presence of slaves: "She was not actually graceful or elegant, but how could I think of ordering such a person? I was really embarassed, said *Ma'am* to her in my incertitude, and used as much form and perhaps more than I should to a distinguished stranger. Southerners must necessarily experience this awkwardness from the different mode in which servitude exists in other portions of the country." When the narrator overheard the servant discussing literature she asked herself: "How *can* I ask her to bring me a glass of water, thought I; and my difficulty in placing her in the right position at home, again occurred to me."

An acceptable solution eluded her: "She seemed to hang in an unbalanced sphere between me and the [black] servants of the household." The white woman also found her position in the South anomalous, bursting into tears when she discovered a newspaper reference to her arrival as a servant. Another white servant in the novel was homesick and afraid of blacks: "When I went to bed, it seemed to me as though I should see their faces peering through the doors and windows." The servant was also discomfited by the easy relationship between the white mistress and one of her slaves: "I had never seen but one negro before, and always had a dread of them; from early prejudice I could hardly believe my own eyes when I saw the confidence that was placed in Dinah." Each of the white servants in the novel either marries a respectable man of her class or returns to the North. Experiments with white servants pushed the narrator to a simple conclusion: "Experience seems to have decided that an attached, faithful negro, is a more suitable servant in our portion of the country than any other."[46]

Gilman's acceptance of slavery was expedient: the institution was desirable because it allowed white women to fulfill their domestic responsibilities effectively. She never considered the perspective of African Americans except to assume they accepted their place and their owners without question: "It would weary me were I to relate the instances which have fallen under my observation, of devoted kindness from this class of persons to those by whom they have been reared; their jealousy of the rights and reputation of their masters, their kindness in sickness, and the affectionate demonstrations of grief with which they follow them to the grave."[47] For Gilman, slavery was a positive institution for both whites and slaves because each group recognized and fulfilled its responsibilities to the other. White women had particular obligations of care and protection, which were repaid with reliable service and personal devotion from black women and men. Many of Gilman's readers must have been inspired by these ideas because she sympathized with their difficulties and offered them a vision and a prescription for success in coping with lovable but irritating husbands, complex households, and slaves who never behaved as they were expected to. Gilman's success as a writer of southern domesticity was her ability to acknowledge both the ideal to which women should aspire and the reality that made that ideal difficult—but not impossible—to achieve.

⟡

Unlike Gilman, Mary Howard Schoolcraft developed a rigorous defense of slavery based not only on its advantages for the domestic life of whites but also on its presumed beneficial effects for blacks. Born in the Beaufort District of South Carolina to a long-established and well-connected family, she moved to Washington sometime before 1851; in 1860 she said she no longer owned slaves nor did she expect to again. Around this time she published an essay in the form of a novel called *The Black Gauntlet* and claimed she wrote the book at the request of her husband: "God knows that I have no ambition to be an author;—and nothing but my romantic veneration, that makes your wishes my law, could have induced me to take up my pen, other than as your amanuensis." Schoolcraft's husband was paralyzed in 1848, after which she "felt no earthly aspiration beyond the honor of helping" him and became his "assiduous copyist and constant nurse" while he completed his voluminous history of Indians.[48]

Schoolcraft considered blacks inferior to whites and was "so satisfied that slavery is the school God has established for the conversion of barbarous nations, that were I an absolute Queen of these United States, my first missionary enterprise would be to send to Africa, to bring its heathen as *slaves* to this Christian land, and keep them in bondage until *compulsory* labor had tamed their beastliness, and civilization and Christianity had prepared them to return as missionaries of progress to their benighted black brethren." Although she could amuse herself by "imagining a millennial world, where all are born equal," to do so would "fritter away the mind, not strengthen it," because it would require blotting "out the history of the whole human race, whose glaring inequality of mind, body, and condition, has been manifest to every observer, from the time that God created it." If all were indeed equal "we must search at once for an anti-slavery Bible, and an Abolition God," since "slavery is God's ordinance for one set of His rebellious creatures." For Schoolcraft, all justifications for slavery were based on God's will in allowing it to exist, while the daily reality was tempered by the self-interest of the master and the maternal benevolence of the mistress.[49]

Schoolcraft did not absolve slaveholders from all responsibility. No one dared "assert that the degraded African heathen has not been benefitted, for time and eternity, by being brought even as a slave to this Christianized country." Although these supposed benefits were the result of the care whites provided for blacks, that care resulted from self-interest: "We may . . . be divested of every noble social virtue; but we have still remaining too much of the Yankee in us, to hurt our own property, by cruelty or hard work, or any tyrannical oppressions that destroy the health or curtail the lives of our slaves."[50] Uncaring masters were unimaginable because of the law of self-interest: "As long as negroes are *property*, no master, unless he was a lunatic, would ever hurt them. Shooting or beating a slave to death, would insure the perpetrators being sent to the asylum for the insane; for such an episode, in plantation policy, could not occur, unless the *reason*, and with it, the *self-love* of the master, was dethroned."[51]

Schoolcraft emphasized the parallels between slaveholders' self-interested protection of slaves and parents' care of children. She contrasted both with the poor conditions of free blacks in the North and Canada. There, a former slave "is alike despised and deserted, and left to famish, or exist in a place so small and filthy that our cows could not survive a winter in them. . . . Poor slave! you once had a master, whose interest and whose humanity protected you, and supplied your every want; who kept you from idleness and drunkenness, and from the indulgence of crime and fiendish passions." According to Schoolcraft, abolitionists caused much of the misery in the nation because they enticed slaves away from the benefits of life in the South and threatened to create insurrection and thus impoverish the South.[52]

Schoolcraft was so confident that slavery was beneficial for blacks because she was convinced that white women adequately provided for them. All slaveholders were motivated by self-interest, but a mistress had an even more direct responsibility: "She has not only every principle of self-interest to urge her to be up and doing at sunrise; but from her very nursery she is taught that the meanest creature on God's earth is a master or mistress who neglects those that Providence has made utterly dependent on them. Her conscience, educated to this self-denying nobility of action, would feel as wounded by the neglect of her helpless children as by disregard for her hard working slaves." Schoolcraft was contemptuous of northern women who condemned southern women for idleness: "Let a Yankee lady fancy herself surrounded by a family of two hundred persons (as is often the case with a Southern planter's wife), all dependent, more or less, on herself." A planter's wife was responsible for a wide variety of tasks; she was to be "a responsible, conscientious 'sister of charity' to her husband's numerous dependants."[53]

Indeed, Schoolcraft argued that white women suffered more than slaves: "I am certain that wives have suffered more intense, more hopeless anguish, from brutal, non-appreciative husbands, than any slave has ever experienced, since God first gave the command to his people to bring heathen nations into bondage to his Christian nations; for the slave being made, by the mercy of his Creator, property, secures a more undying interest, in a selfish master's heart, than a wife, who can be so easily replaced, particularly when her husband begins to get tired of her; which is so often the case." Schoolcraft believed self-interested masters showed they valued slaves more than their wives in very practical ways: "It is an undoubted fact, that a *bad* master will take more care of his slaves in sickness and in health, than he will of his wife; will sit up with him, administer every dose of medicine, and send for the doctor, and the parson, too, if the slave's mind is troubled so as to increase his fever; while his own poor wife may make her exodus to the other world as soon as she pleases, and her place can be easily, and perhaps profitably supplied, by his marrying a young heiress." Schoolcraft criticized white men who married flighty, irresponsible, beautiful girls, instead of women with enterprise, learning, thriftiness, or thought. In particular she reproached the man who chose a second wife without any "idea of marrying a sensible, experienced, managing, thrifty old maid, to take care of his household—not a bit of it; he instantly falls madly in love with some romping, unstereotyped, dashing, smart-spoken, coquettish little miss in her teens—who does not know how to work, or keep house, or to do a single practical thing—who has no knowledge of human nature, or even pondered much about philosophy; but who is instinctively appreciative of his (her husband's) perfections."[54] Men who married such women, Schoolcraft believed, were vain, irresponsible, and foolish.

No matter how inferior men were, Schoolcraft maintained women were "still required to bow as *inferiors*" to them because of Eve's transgressions. Although she condemned both men and women, the outcome was the same. Women who felt superior in "morals and practical sense" to "these boys in men's clothes that have been palmed on us, with few exceptions, for husbands, ever since Adam lost his godlike, manly dignity" nevertheless had to treat them with respect because of biblical command: "God orders the wife to be obedient to her own husband, to honor and love him." Women who thought they were "wiser than our Creator" and asserted their independence were the anomalous creatures of women's rights conventions: "Instead of ruling the men with our dimples, and our curls, and our smiles, and our moral loveliness, and refined dependence on them to vote for us, and work for us, and fight for us, and let us stay at home to enjoy the magnificent privilege of teaching the young idea how to shoot; instead of this sublime destiny for mothers and wives, we should have a race of coarse, ugly Amazons, scratching and biting all who oppose them." Women should not aspire to men's activities but should use their power over the human heart to create a more moral society. Even though "the husbands of to-day . . . are not such respectable, august fellows as Adam was before he was thrust out of Paradise," women's beauty, dependence, and moral fealty to them were "just as powerful to bring them chivalrously to our feet *now*."[55] Schoolcraft believed the surest way for women to improve their situation was to defer to men, even when those men were not worthy of deference. No matter how inferior men were, they were still superior to women, who had little choice but obedient acceptance of their destiny. The key for Schoolcraft was for women to bow gracefully, without sacrificing virtue or responsibility.

Schoolcraft believed she was accurately describing South Carolina women in her works. She knew they were not interested in women's rights conventions, nor were they "progressive enough to become public lecturers." She had nothing but praise for the women of her state: "No women on earth are more high-mettled and self-respecting, nor more honored by gentlemen, than they are; none are more frank and fearless in the expression of their feelings and opinions in the refined enclosure of the drawing-room." But, just as women in the Revolutionary War had behaved heroically and sent their men off to fight, "bidding them never to return except as triumphant victors from the conflict waged in defence of their just rights," their descendants "are ready now to exercise the same patriotism." If nothing else, South Carolina women were remarkable for their "chivalry of sentiment."[56]

Schoolcraft's vision of race and gender relations was complex and contradictory. Critical as she was of men and their actions, she was unwilling to consider any significant challenges to their authority; religion demanded submission even when men's behavior was unacceptable. Acceptance of male authority was the only path for white women to follow to a moral life, just as acceptance of white authority was the only possible path of improvement for slaves. Whether or not slaves and women liked their inferior condition was simply irrelevant because God had willed their subordination and their circumstances; she advised both groups not to challenge God's will.

Schoolcraft's arguments about race and gender were particularly appealing to female readers. She advocated a profoundly apolitical stance for women, sanctioned by God, suggesting that their only legitimate form of influence was in the domestic realm. While applauding their efforts to improve their society within the safety of socially accepted norms, she warned them of the dangers of violating those norms even in the name of improvement. But at the same time, by insisting on deference to men she offered an explanation for women's inability to be completely effective even there. She exhorted women about proper behavior but sympathized with the circumstances that prevented it from having the desired effect. Such reasoning reassured southern women who saw their country on the verge of war because it removed the necessity of taking action—which would have been impossible anyway—and absolved them of direct responsibility for virtually everything. Schoolcraft offered her readers a way to simultaneously support and criticize their society, which no doubt comforted many struggling plantation mistresses.

If Mary Howard Schoolcraft's work would allow white women the illusion of power through submission to men and acceptance of God's will, Louisa Cheves McCord's writing offered a more active version of the same advice. The only South Carolina woman who regularly published her essays in the *Southern Quarterly Review, DeBow's Review,* and other periodicals not aimed specifically at women, McCord became a leading theoretician of the ideology of domesticity and of proslavery thought. McCord was the Charleston-born daughter of Langdon Cheves, a wealthy lawyer and the president of the Bank of the United States. She was well educated and unusually independent for a woman of her culture. At age twenty she undertook the management of a cotton plantation near Columbia and two hundred slaves she had inherited. Like many plantation mistresses, McCord took it upon herself to provide clothing, medical care, and moral training for her slaves. In 1840, ten years after inheriting the plantation and slaves, she married a widower with ten children; they had three more within five years. McCord's husband was also a political essayist and plantation owner. After he died in 1855, McCord moved to Columbia, where she committed herself wholeheartedly to the war effort and ceased much of her writing.[57]

In her essays and poetry, written primarily in the early 1850s, McCord defended the view of womanhood defined by the southern ideology of domesticity from the heresies against God and nature committed by northern women's rights advocates. Unlike Schoolcraft, who saw women as inferior to men, McCord recognized women's inferiority in "corporeal strength" but argued that "each [person] is strong in his own nature. They are neither inferior, nor superior, nor equal. They are different." She defined woman's mission as

> even nobler than man's, and she is, in the true fulfillment of that mission, certainly the higher being. . . . Woman's duty, woman's nature, is to love, to sway by love; to govern by love, to teach by love, to civilize by love! . . . Pure and holy, self-devoted and suffering, woman's love is the breath of that God of love, who, loving and pitying, has bid *her* learn to love and to suffer, implanting in her bosom the one single comfort that she is the watching spirit, the guardian angel of those she loves. . . . Each can labour, each can strive, lovingly and earnestly, in her own sphere.

She warned women to reject the follies of those who wanted to vote: "Woman, *cherish thy mission.* Fling thyself not from the high pedestal whereon God has placed thee." She outlined women's mission in terms that would have been familiar to other advocates of domesticity: "The woman must *raise* the man, by helping, not by rivalling him. . . . She it is who softens; she it is who civilizes; and, although history acknowledges her not, she it is who, not in the meteoric brilliancy of warrior or monarch, but in the quiet, unwearied and unvarying path of duty, the home of the mother, the wife and the sister, teaching man his destiny, purifies, exalts, and guides him to his duty." She set what were essentially the same sentiments to verse in her poem "Woman's Progress":

> Her mission is
> to labour and to pray; to help, to heal,
> To soothe, to bear; patient, with smiles, to suffer;
> And with self-abnegation nobley lose
> Her private interest in the dearer weal
> Of those she loves and lives for. . . .
>   If her life be true
> And based upon the instincts of her being
> She is a living sermon of that truth
> Which ever through her gentle actions speaks,
> That life is given to labor and to love.[58]

McCord's verse tragedy *Caius Gracchus* also illustrates her commitment to domesticity as well as her limited skill as a poet. In the play, a woman advises her daughter-in-law not to go outdoors to greet her husband after a long absence: "Nay, stay within doors, daughter; 'tis the place / Most meet and fitting woman." When the daughter-in-law protests, the woman advises her on appropriate female behavior:

> 'Tis meek endurance, quiet fortitude
> That make her life and beauty. . . .
> But in our bosoms, if too fierce the flame
> That feeds such spirit-struggles, we must check,
> Or drive it back, at least, to seeming quiet.
> If hard the effort, it is woman's task.
> Her passions, if not smothered, must be hid,
> Till in their faintly-beating pulse, herself
> Will scarcely know her blood the same which bounds
> Through manlier veins unchecked.

Near the end of the play, the woman abandons her own advice and inter-
venes in her son's affairs, although she knows she is sending him to his death.
Her last words to him explain her unwomanly behavior: "These bursting
tears / Now come to show the woman's heart, whose boldness, / Your sickly
resolution to upbraid, Usurped the man."[59] Apparently McCord believed
that women driven to action by dramatic circumstances must at least apologize for their failure to smother their passions and their consequent viola-
tion of domesticity.[60] For McCord, adhering to the expectations of domesticity required constant efforts not only to quash rebellious thoughts but also
to live up to their rigorous demands. Women's physical inferiority defined
their place in society, but McCord insisted on the importance of that place
as defined by motherhood.

Louisa McCord also defended slavery in closely reasoned essays. She was
convinced that human society was "improving, improvable, ceaselessly and
boundlessly" and that slavery was inherent in human progress.[61] She argued
that the institution was a Christian system, beneficial to both slaves and slaveholders: "The master gives protection; the slave looks for it." She claimed
that slavery brought the greatest good to the greatest number, including
blacks, who were "Nature's outcast" and "unfit for all progress."[62] Although
slavery encompassed crime, sin, and abuse of power, abolition was not the
solution because it disrupted what would otherwise be harmonious relationships: "Our system of slavery, left to itself, would rapidly develop its higher
features, softening at once to servant and master." Abolition also was not best
for slaves: "The Negro, left to himself, does not dream of liberty. He cannot indeed grasp a conception which belongs so naturally to the brain of the
white man." The best solution was Christian slavery: "Make your laws to
interfere with the God-established system of slavery, which our Southern
states are beautifully developing to perfection, daily improving the condition of the slave, daily waking more and more the master to his high and
responsible position; make your laws, we say, to pervert this God-directed
course, and the world has yet to see the horrors which might ensue from it.
The natural order of things perverted, ill must follow."[63]

By defending slavery as beneficial to blacks, McCord joined a long intellectual tradition in the South. However, she added another dimension to the
argument when she wrote about women. In her review of *Uncle Tom's Cabin*, McCord criticized Stowe's portrait of the wife of a brutal slaveholder and
in the process illustrated her own expectations of plantation mistresses: "This
very sensible, moral and religious lady, when made acquainted with her
husband's brutal conduct, is very naturally distressed at it. But what remedy
does she find? Does she consult with him as a wife should consult? Does she

advise as a woman can advise? Does she suggest means and remedies for avoiding such a crisis? Does she endeavor to show her husband the folly and madness, as well as the wickedness of his course?" Stowe's heroine clearly did not live up to McCord's ideal southern woman. Another of Stowe's female characters also failed to earn McCord's approval, again illustrating her perceptions of appropriate behavior:

> The coarse indifference which this elegant lady constantly expresses for the feelings of her dependants, and particularly for those of "mammy," an old family servant, who has tended her from childhood, and whom she has separated from husband and children, can find its parallel in no rank of society. *Never*, we contend, was there the Southern woman, brought up in decent associations, at once so heartless and so foolish, that, supposing it possible for her to feel nothing in such a case, would not, for mere fashion and gentility sake, imitate those feelings of which she would know it to be her shame to be devoid. It is not the *fashion* with us to hang out the flag of hard-heartedness.[64]

Slavery, then, was an institution both beneficial to African Americans and carrying great responsibility for white women. Female slaveholders' unique obligations encouraged them to curb the abuses of their husbands and treat slaves humanely. McCord raised these issues indirectly in an 1852 essay, in which she defined the differences between men and women:

> Her mission is one of love and charity to all. It is the very essence of her being to raise and to purify wherever she touches. Where man's harder nature crushes, her's exaults. Where he wounds, she heals. . . . God, man and nature alike call upon her to subdue her passions, to suffer, to bear, to be meek and lowly of heart; while man, summoned by nature, and often by duty, to the whirl of strife, blinded in the struggle, forgets too often where wrath should cease and mercy rule. What, then, more beautiful than woman's task to arrest the up-lifted arm, and, in the name of an all-pardoning Heaven, to whisper to his angry passions—"Peace, be still!"[65]

While McCord was not specifically referring to behavior toward slaves, she may well have had slaves in mind when she wrote. Women reading her essay would very likely interpret her words as a suggestion to curb the tempers of men toward them.

Louisa McCord combined ideas about gender and race into a vision of southern society that defined white women and all blacks as inferior, but not doomed to passivity and insignificance: "Inferiority is not a curse. Every creature is suited for its position, and fulfilling that position can certainly not be called cursed. . . . As He has made you to be women and not men— mothers and sisters, and not (according to the modern improvement system), soldiers and legislators, so has He fitted the negro for his position and suited him to be happy and useful in it."[66] Both women and blacks needed the protection of white men, and both must pay for that protection "by the abandonment of privileges which otherwise might seem to be [their] right."[67] McCord relied on both physical and moral inferiority and a divine plan to justify the subordination of women and blacks. To challenge was impossible, and those antislavery and women's rights advocates who did so deserved stinging rebukes. Only by acceptance of the laws of God and nature could human society be improved and harmony and prosperity achieved. McCord believed that duty was white women's highest virtue, and, rather than seeking to imitate men in any way, they should strive only to be more womanly. Similarly, McCord believed that all people of African descent were suited by God and nature for slavery and insisted that it was a beneficent institution when southern whites were allowed to practice it according to their own traditions.

For each of these three South Carolina writers, justifying the subordination of white women was a primary intellectual task. Each recognized that subordination and each accepted it as part of God's plan for humanity. Similarly, each accepted slavery as beneficial for blacks and a responsibility for whites. Each established a connection between gender and race that placed special obligations for the well-being of slaves on the shoulders of white women. The survival and advancement of society required white women and slaves to accept subordination.

In many respects, the theories of these South Carolina intellectuals were little more than carefully articulated and developed versions of the views that shaped the daily activities and interactions of many of the plantation mistresses of the state. Mistresses who sought to understand themselves, their slaves, and their society as they fulfilled their domestic responsibilities struggled to come to terms with the implications of assumptions about gender and race. Unable to imagine the South without slavery, mistresses and intellectuals made a variety of efforts to justify its existence and improve its consequences by appealing to what they considered the fundamental characteristics of blacks and of white women. Only a very few white women interpreted those characteristics in ways that challenged domesticity or slavery, and they remained isolated and largely silent.

6

Slave Women Confront the Ideology of Domesticity

For slave women, work and womanhood had very different meanings than they did for plantation mistresses. The complex African-American culture developed in the quarters shaped their experiences, as did the assumptions of slaves and slaveholders about gender and race differences. Like whites, blacks developed a set of expectations defining appropriate behavior for men and women. Those expectations blended African practices, observations of white behavior, and, by the antebellum years, centuries of African-American cultural development. While the nature of the institution made it difficult for slaves to follow their beliefs regarding gender differences, they did the best they could. The degree to which slaves could act on their beliefs was partly determined by whites, who brought their gender assumptions to interactions with slaves but sought to minimize their significance. Slaves' beliefs about gender differences and their efforts to practice them marked important areas of resistance to white authority.

These beliefs were rooted in the rich heritage slaves brought from Africa, but unfortunately very little reliable information about sex roles in African society before the slave trade is available. Anthropologists who have studied African culture and society did so after significant European contact and brought their own biases to whatever observations they made; they have not been particularly helpful in suggesting where to look for gender-specific behavior among antebellum slaves. Historians using anthropological or folklore techniques also have not made gender distinctions the center of their analyses. What we do know about African societies suggests that gender was an important determinant of life experience.

After slaves were brought to the colonies, African traditions changed in response to new circumstances, particularly their work experiences. Whether in the fields and homes of whites or in their own communities, male and female slaves labored distinctly. Individual black women on large plantations, in general, performed a wider variety of work than black men did. Some tasks were defined as uniquely theirs, both in the fields and in the quarters, and women were sometimes assigned to single-sex work groups. Over the course of their lives female slaves on large plantations spent far more time than most men in close contact with whites, especially white women.

By the antebellum period, slaves' experiences and beliefs about gender differences encouraged a coherent yet flexible set of behaviors, always within the limits imposed by slavery. Women learned from one another and from men what was expected of them as women. Female family networks, female work gangs, groups of domestic producers, and all of the more informal interactions among female slaves allowed them to communicate their understanding of appropriate behavior. Slaves' religious beliefs also helped to encode and reinforce beliefs about gender differences. Women who violated these standards were often subject to censure by the slave community. While slaves admired a certain amount of defiance against white authority, they were far less willing to tolerate violations of their own norms, particularly those that defined the roles of women and men.

In its adaptation to its constantly changing surroundings, African-American culture sometimes mimicked white culture. Some black women reproduced aspects of clothing, appearance, courting behavior, and wedding rituals that they witnessed among whites. Former slave Maggie Black described in detail the clothing worn by white women at the time and remembered her own childhood efforts to imitate their wide skirts by using vines for hoops.[1] Mistresses often supported black women's efforts to adopt the external conventions of nineteenth-century white womanhood. Constance Cary, a white woman, recalled visiting a cotton plantation and being asked by a housemaid to write letters to her fiance: "In one of these epistles I was requested, with many giggles, to tell Tom 'yes, please, young mistis.' On beseeching her to supply words for this avowal, she threw her apron over her head and, tittering, observed: 'Why, don' you know, Miss? Jes' de way you does it yerself.'"[2]

Sarah Fitzpatrick, who was a slave in Alabama, learned directly from her mistress the secrets of female behavior, particularly while courting: "My Mistus use 'ta look at my dress an' tell me when hit wuz right. Sometime she make me go back an' put on 'nother one, tell us what to wear, tell us to go back an' com' our heads." An unidentified former slave also claimed that blacks learned to dress by imitating white fashion, even when it was uncomfortable: "We wore hoop skirts on Sunday, jest like the white folks. I never did like them things; if you didn't sit down this-a-way, that old hoop skirt would shoot up like this. I never had no use for them things. . . . Then, you know, the style come in of wearing these here long things that warn't 'xactly no drawers—come way down to yo' ankles, and we wore them, too, jest like the white folks."³ Her testimony suggests the ambivalence some black women felt about conforming to the expectations of their community, even in the midst of their compliance.

As Amanda Styles well knew, women's behavior was circumscribed in both significant and trivial ways by the expectations of the slave community: "A 'oman that whistled wuz marked to be a bad 'oman." Lucy McCullough also believed women had to watch their behavior: "Black folks wuz better folks den dey is now. Dey knowed dey hed ter be good er dey got beat. De gals dey diden't sho' dare laigs lak dey do now. Cloff hed ter be made den en hit wuz er heap mo' trouble ter mek er yah'd er cloff, den it is ter buy it now, but 'omans en gals, dey stayed kivvered up better den." The beatings Mc-Cullough spoke of were inflicted by family members. Not all women agreed that African-American women accepted such strict models of appropriate beauty, courting, and sexual rituals. In response to a question put by a WPA interviewer, Jane Johnson responded: "How old was I when I done my courtin'? What's dat? Dat courtin' stuff is what white folks does, no nigger knows what dat fancy thing is. . . . Colored people don't pay no 'tention to what white folks call love, they just 'sires de woman they wants, dat's all."⁴ In spite of her denial, Johnson was obviously cognizant of what whites considered appropriate behavior. Her comments suggest that slaves who adopted white conventions of appropriate behavior for women might do so without fully accepting their beliefs.

Remarks from black men provide more evidence that black women were expected to conform to the trappings of nineteenth-century white womanhood. Phil Towns, who was born a slave in Virginia in 1824, reported: " 'Gov.' Towns was interested in assisting any one wanting to learn. The little girls who expressed the desire to become 'ladies' were kept in the 'big house' and very carefully trained. The tastes of these few were developed to the extent that they excelled the ordinary 'quarter' children and were the envy of the group at social affairs." Gus Feaster keenly observed the efforts black girls made to adopt white conventions: "Young gals couldn't eat much in public, kaise it ain't stylish for young courting gals to let on like dey has any appetite to speak of. . . . Culler gals tried to do jes' like de young white missus would do." His perceptions of female modesty were echoed by W. M. Green: "When I was a boy, girls acted like de old folks and dey did not carry on. Nobody ever heard of a girl drinking and smoking den. If a girl made a mistake in de old days she was throwed overboard. Why when I was little, us boys went in a-washing wid de girls and never thought nothing 'bout it. We was most grown befo' we know'd a thing 'bout man and woman."[5]

In spite of Green's claims, slave girls smoked when they could, as did many southern women except those among the most elite planter families, and pre-marital pregnancy was hardly uncommon. One former slave reported: "If you fooled a girl up and got her with a arm full you had to take care of her." Frank Menefee remembered the restrictions on women's sexual behavior as quite severe: "Iffin a gal went wrong, dey beat her nearly to death."[6] While this was not always true in practice, both male and female slaves were well aware of the expectations of slave morality and tried to live up to them.[7] While blacks may have adopted some white conventions for women's behavior, they did not necessarily share white gender expectations. Slaves did not articulate a logic of female inferiority or superiority, nor did they insist upon women's subor-dination to their husbands. Their conventions may have appeared similar to those of whites, but the logic behind them was very different.

Mistresses, and to a lesser extent masters, failed to grasp the logic behind slaves' morality or conventions and tried to impose their own version of conventional behavior on black women. As domestic producers, African-American women spent a good deal of time with plantation mistresses who attempted to instruct them in appropriate female behavior. Because this time was usually at transitional points in slaves' lives—puberty, pregnancy, child-birth and lactation, miscarriage, menopause—mistresses looked on it as an opportunity to pass along the tenets of domesticity and share biological experiences. Even black women could find enough common ground with white women to feel comfortable sharing their fear of the dangers of child-birth, their pleasure in the activities of young children, and their grief at the illness or death of those children and other family members. Masters also expected conventional behavior of their female slaves, in spite of their as-sumptions about slave women's work abilities and sexuality. The rules of P. C. Weston's rice plantation, for example, included an injunction to the over-seer that "fighting, particularly amongst women, and obscene, or abusive language, is to be always rigorously punished."[8]

Slave women looked at plantation mistresses for an example of what the free expression of womanhood could mean and sometimes saw them as models of behavior to follow or avoid. Of course, black women were never uncritical imitators of white women. As Deborah Gray White acknowledges, slave women "stood beyond the boundaries of Victorian womanhood." But, she asks, "did they want the empty deference given to those within its bounds? . . . Did they want America's ideas about a woman's place to envelop them?"[9] Certainly black women were openly contemptuous of whites when the war and emancipation made it safer to be so; many had been privately contemptuous before. But plantation mistresses, particularly those who took the ideology of domesticity as a model for their own behavior, did serve as an important example of female behavior for slave women.

Despite these pressures African-American women made real efforts to follow their own community's expectations about womanhood. Slave marriages, for example, were not built upon the economic dependence of wives, which gave black women a degree of autonomy not possible for white women. At the same time, whites' lack of respect for slave marriages made them quite vulnerable, and African-American men and women sought to minimize damage to family life. Black husbands did what they could to protect their wives, whom they expected to defer to their authority even as they encouraged them to be independent. Likewise, slaves' beliefs about premarital pregnancy were similar to and different from those of whites. Although some former slaves insisted that women who became pregnant outside of marriage were condemned by other slaves, blacks generally refused to censure these women or to criticize those who voluntarily broke up their marriages. Perhaps in recognition of the realities of separation of families and sexual assault, slaves tolerated infidelity and promiscuity.

Slaves' beliefs about gender differences and expectations of moral behavior were complex, but generally consistent. Whites, particularly white men, unable to credit beliefs that differed from their own, were convinced that morality among blacks was limited or totally lacking. Judge Harper of South Carolina believed that a large "proportion of this class of females . . . set little value on chastity."[10] Edward Pringle recognized that part of the reason slaves did not have "a due regard to the conjugal relation" was "the necessarily uncertain life of the negro" and urged planters "to make some effort to render the marriage relation more sacred among them." His intentions were not strictly benevolent: "Nothing is so great a civilizer as the family education which results from a strict observance of the marriage tie. . . . His own position, and his master's interest and feelings, combine to give encouragement to matrimony." H. N. McTyeire told planters it was their duty "to promote virtuous and fixed attachments between the sexes, and, while encouraging marriage, to guard it with all the forms of consent, postponement, preparation, and solemn consummation."[11] One newspaper went so far as to urge serious consideration of a proposal to "render legal the institution of marriage among slaves" and claimed "the main features of the movement have been adopted in practice, or at least approved in theory, by nearly all our planters, so far as circumstances would allow."[12] Slaveholders wanted the

benefits of marriage among slaves, so long as their own interests did not dic-
tate the separation of spouses.

Beliefs among blacks about gender differences and women's proper role were
a complex mix of African cultures, European influence, and response to daily
life. Their efforts to develop a consistent set of beliefs about gender reflected the difficulties of slavery and their desire for independence. All of these
factors influenced their ability to practice their beliefs, as well as their views
of the society in which they lived and labored. In particular, these factors
influenced black women's views of white women, whose similarities and differences as women had to be managed and understood not in the realm of
ideology but in the everyday society of the plantation.

However much the ideology of domesticity helped to determine the ways
in which plantation mistresses behaved toward and thought about their
slaves, the benevolence and generosity expected of white women clearly
could not define the thoughts or actions of black women. Did slave women
simply view plantation mistresses as female versions of white authority? Or
did their notions of female behavior and their common experiences allow
black women to perceive a small measure of shared ground with white wom-
en? Answers to these questions can never be clear cut or definitive. There
was simply too much variation from individual to individual and plantation
to plantation. Even so, examining the limits of the interactions between
women of the two races should help to assess the range of possible attitudes
slave women held toward their mistresses.

Nearly all African-American women on large South Carolina plantations
worked closely with mistresses at a variety of points during their lives. Contact with white women offered advantages not routinely available to black
men. First, working with mistresses provided young women the chance to
enhance the domestic skills that made life in the quarters physically possible, such as sewing and cooking. Being taught to sew or cook under the direction of the mistress was advantageous not simply for the skill itself but
also for the needles, cloth, utensils, and other material goods that were often provided with the training.

Working closely with mistresses also offered female slaves personal attention and a chance to distinguish themselves as individuals. Delia Thompson remembered her pride in being chosen to be a housemaid for her young
mistress:

> 'Members how 'twas young missie say: "You come go in my room Delia, I wants
> to see if I can put up wid you". I goes in dat room. . . . Well, she allow to me,

"Delia, put kettle water on de fire". So I does in a jiffy. Her next command was: "Would you please be so kind as to sweep and tidy up de room"? . . . I do all dat, then she say: "You is goin' to make maid, a good one!" She give a silvery giggle and say: "I just had you put on dat water for to see if you was goin' to make any slop. No, No! you didn't spill a drop, you ain't goin' to make no sloppy maid, you just fine." Then her call her mother in. "See how pretty Delia's made dis room, look at them curtains, draw back just right, observe de pitcher, and de towels on de rack of de washstand, my I'm proud of her!" . . . De happiness of dat minute is on me to dis day.

Other slaves welcomed plantation mistresses' attention because they could escape the drudgery of the fields. Katie Sutton, a former slave from Indiana, sang a song for her WPA interviewer that included the following lines:

Yo daddy ploughs de massa's corn,
Yo mammy does the cooking;
She'll give dinner to her hungry chile
When nobody is a lookin.

Mary Raines was glad to get out of the fields: "House servants 'bove de field hands, them days. If you didn't git better rations and things to eat in de house, it was your own fault, I tells you!"[13]

Not all slaves were as happy as Thompson and Raines with the personal attention given them by white mistresses or their work in the Big House. Jessie Sparrow reported that her mother disliked both: "My mammy been de house girl in my white folks house. She marry when she ain' but 13 year old. Dat wha' she tell me. She say she marry to ge' outer de big house. Dat how come she to marry so soon. Say de white folks take she way from she mammy when she won' but uh little small girl en make she sleep right dere on uh pallet in de Missus room aw de time 'fore she marry. Coase a'ter she marry, she been de house girl right on but she never stay in de Missus house when night come."[14] An unidentified former slave was well aware of the disadvantages of recognition by white women. The other slaves "wouldn't say anything before me, 'cause I stayed in the house, and et in there, and slept in there. Yes they were 'fraid to say anything 'fore me."[15] Whether working full-time with mistresses was viewed positively or negatively depended very much on the individual.

For the majority of female slaves, however, the advantages of working occasionally with plantation mistresses as domestic producers clearly outweighed the disadvantages. In addition to the respite from field work it sometimes offered them an opportunity to serve the slave community as well. A domestic producer could most directly turn her work experience with white

women to her own and her community's advantage by picking up and sharing information. This was consistently an important source of information,
but it would be vital during the Civil War.[16]

Slaves gained knowledge about the world beyond the plantation primarily by listening to whites talk. Obviously house slaves had ample opportunity to eavesdrop, and whites usually tried to be suitably cautious in front
of them. But domestic producers were also able to overhear what whites had
to say and communicate what they learned to others. Mistresses may well
have been less cautious in front of domestic producers, assuming they would
not understand the significance of what was being said. Both groups kept
their ears open. Benjamin Russell recalled that slaves got news by remaining alert: "The sources were: Girls that waited on the tables, the ladies' maids
and the drivers; they would pick up everything they heard and pass it on to
the other slaves." Elizabeth Hyde Botume, a northerner who went to Beaufort to teach for the Freedman's Aid Society even before the war ended, noted
the experience of a woman who could not read, but who said her uncle could.
The woman said she "'used to help missis to dress in the morning. If massa
wanted to tell her something he didn't want me to know, he used to spell it
out. I could remember the letters, an' as soon as I got away I ran to uncle
an' spelled them over to him, an' he told me what they meant.'" Sometimes
slaves working in the house acquired knowledge with long-lasting value to
the slave community. Both Alice Green's mother and Tom Singleton's sister learned to read and write by watching the white children in their care,
which enabled both to become school teachers after the war.[17]

In addition to receiving information, African-American women working
as domestic producers or house servants conveyed information about the
slave community to white women. Aware that the material assistance provided by mistresses was vital to the slave community, these female slaves
proved a key link in communicating the needs of their people. If the ideology of domesticity encouraged plantation mistresses to ameliorate some of
the harshness of slavery, slave women provided the information that made
their intervention possible. The slaves on Pierce Butler's plantations in
Georgia, for example, were so mindful of Frances Kemble's sympathy for
them that they besieged her wherever she went with requests for cloth, soap,
food, and other goods: "No time, no place, affords me a respite from my in-
numerable petitioners; and whether I be asleep or awake, reading, eating,
or walking—in the kitchen, my bedroom, or the parlor—they flock in with
urgent entreaties and pitiful stories." These women clearly recognized the
opportunity to ameliorate their living conditions by appealing to Kemble's
sympathy for their situation. On one occasion, Kemble told several preg-

nant women they would have to make their request for a lighter work load to their master. Kemble reported "they said they had already begged 'massa,' and he had refused, and they thought, perhaps, if 'missis' begged 'massa' for them, he would lighten the task." Butler eventually forbade his wife to bring the slaves' concerns to him.[18]

Aware of the dynamic within white society that encouraged women to behave benevolently toward slaves, some black women appealed to their mistresses for help on disputes ranging from minor grievances to punishment to sale to rape. Although not every entreaty met with success, they did often enough for slaves to continue asking. Because house servants and domestic producers had more opportunities to interact with their mistresses, field hands could be frustrated by their inability to gain the ear of their mistresses. Mack Taylor, who had been a slave on a large Wateree River rice plantation, commented: "My mistress was a gentle lady, but field niggers never got to speak to her. All I can say is dat de house slaves say she was mighty good to them." Ben Horry, once a slave on a Waccamaw Neck rice plantation, also spoke of a brutal overseer and ordinary field slaves' inability to get help: "Just the house servant get Marse Josh' and Miss Bess' ear."[19] Sometimes, asking for assistance posed considerable risks. Frances Kemble reported being told by one of her slave women that the overseer "had flogged her that morning for having told me that the women had not time to keep their children clean."[20]

African-American women who were heard by their mistresses often based their appeals for assistance or intervention on a shared understanding of the female experience in the hope that mistresses would be moved to action out of sympathy. Slave women were particularly likely to appeal to mistresses' sympathy when they were threatened by an experience uniquely female: rape, childbirth, or even the death or sale of a child. Slaves' efforts to influence their situations in this way reflected their awareness of the ideology of domesticity, which emphasized common elements among female experiences. The DeRossets' slave woman Anna may well have been appealing to this common identity when she asked her absent mistress for the gift of "a *white* baby."[21]

Black women's effectiveness in using the ideology of domesticity for their own benefit is illustrated in white women's writings. Mary Eastman wrote of an African-American woman who offered her mistress solutions to the cooking problems resulting from her husband's adoption of temperance. The mistress did not want to do anything her husband would disapprove of, a position endorsed by the slave: "My old man's dust and ashes long ago, but I always done what I could to please him. . . . I don't see what a man has got to do interferin with the cookin, no how; a woman oughter 'tend to these matters." The two women solved the cooking dilemma by agreeing that the slave would take charge of the wine bottles.[22] Caroline Howard Gilman included a scene in a novel in which the narrator went to check on the activities of a black woman, whose "reception of me at the dairy was more that of a dignified hostess than a servile dependant, as with a low curtsey and a wave of the hand she pointed to a bench for me to be seated." Catherine Edmondston wrote in her diary of Gatty, a granny who "called up all hands to make their manners & tell Missus thanky for their dinner. She drew a harrowing picture as to what they would [be] if they didnt have no Master & Missus to give it to them. She knowed their daddies would not have it to give them."[23] Even as they enjoyed the flattery, white women could detect that they were being manipulated.

Blacks' knowledge of gender relations among whites could have other consequences as well. While many slaves responded to the authority plantation mistresses could wield on their behalf and the sympathetic understanding they could offer, others were sensitive to the subordinate position of white women. Instead of viewing plantation mistresses as sources of benevolence and protection, some slave women, such as Caroline Richardson, saw them as weak figures who, like themselves, were subject to white men's authority. Richardson, who had been a slave in North Carolina, remembered: "Mis' Adeline wus little an' puny an' Marse Ransome wus big an' stout, dat's why it am funny dat mammy won't let Mis' Adeline whup her but she don't say nothin' when de marster gits de whup." Lila Nichols, also from North Carolina, was even more blunt: "I know one time do' missus 'cides ter whup a 'oman fer somethin' an' de 'oman sez ter her, 'No sir, Missus, I ain't 'lowin' nobody what wa'r de same kind of skirt I does ter whup me.'" Vermeille Bradford complained about a similar reluctance on the part of two of her slave families to her attorney, who was apparently selling her husband or father's estate. The two families, she said, refused to work and "subsist by stealing from the neighbors and all seem to think you are the only one who has a right to interfere."[24] To gain a small measure of dignity and autonomy for themselves, these black women refused to recognize the authority of white women.

Other slave women sought to assert their autonomy by preventing mistresses from doing domestic work normally expected of slaves. Elizabeth Avery Meriwether claimed her slave Evelyn "would run up, take the broom or duster out of my hand and say: 'Laws a mussy, Miss Betty, dat ain't no work fer a lady. Dats nigger's work. Gib dat broom ter me.'" Caroline Merrick's cook reportedly chased her out of the kitchen, arguing, "'Yer ain't no manner er use heah only ter git yer face red wid de heat. I'll have dinner like yer wants it. Jes' read yer book an' res' easy till I sen's it ter de dining-room.'" Merrick's cook and Evelyn both used their knowledge of race and gender expectations to carve out an arena in which they could claim personal responsibility, implicitly rejecting white women's assumption that they held authority there.[25]

Whether they rejected white women's authority or appealed to them for assistance and intervention, slave women demonstrated their ability to turn the conventions of white society to their own advantage. In doing so, they effectively reinforced those conventions.

Slave women who accepted the ideology of domesticity sometimes reciprocated the affectionate feelings of mistresses. Women of both races testify to the sharing of warm personal emotions, which were nevertheless always tempered by the realities of slavery. For African-American women, expressing affection for the plantation mistresses who held them in bondage could be psychologically difficult, although the improvements mistresses provided in the quality of their lives were a powerful incentive. Many slaves, unconsciously echoing the rhetoric of paternalism, described their mistresses as substitute mothers. When Lydia Maria Child interviewed Charity Bowery for the *Emancipator* in 1848, Bowery said, "Oh, my old mistress was a kind woman. She was all the same as a mother to poor Charity." Abbey Mishow, who had been a slave on a rice plantation in Georgetown County, reported a similar relationship: "My mudder died w'en I was almost uh baby. . . . De missus promis my ma to tek care of me, and she sho' did. I was raise just like a pet. . . . I hardly miss my ma, no mudder couldn't treat me better dan I treat." Hester Hunter told her WPA interviewer: "I here to tell you my old Missus was a dear old soul en we chillun sho had a fine time comin up. . . . She was good to us en we stuck to her."[26] Granny Cain also wished to stay with her mistress: "I . . . waited on my mistress, Mrs. Lucy Kenner, who was the best white woman I know of—just like a mother to me, wish I was with her now."[27] Blacks who referred to their mistresses in familial terms echoed the language of whites, who often gave elderly trusted house slaves titles such as "mammy," "granny," "daddy," "aunt," and "uncle," terms also common among the slaves themselves.

Other black women spoke of their mistresses in positive terms without referring to family relationships. Benjamin Russell had been the slave of Rebecca Nance: "After eighty-eight years, I have a vivid recollection of her sympathy and the ideal relations she maintained with her slaves." Lethe

Jackson, who was a slave in Virginia, wrote to the daughter of her former owner: "And my Mistress too I am glad to hear she is getting better and that she has not forgotten lowly *me*. . . . Tell Mistress I hope I shall soon hear of her recovery and that we long for the time when she will be again here to give her directions and have every thing as it ought to be and as she wants it."[28] Walter Long viewed his mistress in very positive terms: "Us slaves 'sorbed all de good us had in us from our mistress, I really believes. She was so kind and gentle, she moved 'mong us a livin' benediction. . . . She got tired, but I has never seen her too weary to go to a cryin' child or a moanin' grown person on de place and 'quire what was de matter. Us was 'bliged to love her, 'cause she knowed us more better than us knowed ourselves." Andy Marion used similar language: "My mistress was a angel, good, and big heart-ed. I lay my head in her lap many a time." Samuel Boulware reported that his mistress "was a good woman and done things 'zactly right 'round de plantation. Us slaves loved her, 'cause she said kind and soft words to us." Although Boulware's mistress was kind, his master "had a bad temper" and "would say terrible cuss words. When de mistress heard them bad words, she would bow her pretty head and walk 'way kinda sad lak. It hurt us slaves to see de mistress sad, 'cause us wanted to see her smilin' and happy all de time." Sarah Poindexter's mother thought so highly of her mistress that she went back to work before she was really well, as a way of repaying the white woman's kindness in bringing her a basket of food: "All of us loved her, 'cause she was so kind and good to us."[29]

A few slaves, though generally positive about their mistresses, qualified their feelings in significant ways. Genia Woodbury was assigned to tend the white children, a job she disliked because she was separated from her own mother for much of the day. Even so, she did not criticize her mistress: "Dere ain' nobody ne'er been no better den Miss Susan wuz to me. It jes lak dis, I wuz jes uh child den en yuh know it uh child happiness to be raise up wid dey mammy." Mary Woodward attributed the good treatment she received as a girl to her owners' childlessness: "I 'spects if they had had chillun they wouldn't have been so good to me." Pauline Worth was able to rationalize being whipped by her mistress: "I was small den en she was trying to learn me." Emoline Glasgow claimed "Marse Pettus and Miss Harriet was good to us. I never got a whipping, except Misses whipped me once wid just one lick."[30]

All of these slaves appreciated the efforts of their mostly benevolent mis-tresses and were willing to repay their kindnesses with loyalty and affection. Just as some mistresses were able to identify with slaves, these slaves found something in common with their mistresses. Although the relation was in-herently unequal, African-American women nevertheless responded not only with occasional gratitude, which underlined their dependence but, more important, with a reciprocal measure of respect, which transcended it. Although men like Walter Long and Andy Marion enjoyed similar affinity with white women, the field hands who were unable to get the ear of their mistresses remained at a distance. The frequent interactions and shared concerns that developed close relationships were uncommon between white women and black men. The ideology of domesticity that divided women from men could also join women, albeit tentatively, across racial lines.

This was, however, only one of the possible patterns of interactions between slave women and mistresses. Some mistresses were considered oppressors, no different from masters. Susan Hamlin, who was born in the early 1830s and lived in Charleston, described a situation in which a slave woman publicly told her mistress why she hated her master. The mother "cursed de white woman fur all she could find. She said: 'dat damn white, pale-faced bastard sell my daughter who jus' married las' night,' an' other t'ings. The white 'oman threated' her to call de police if she didn't stop, but de collud woman said: 'Hit me or call de police. I redder die dan to stan' dis any longer.'" Hamlin did not know what happened after the police took the slave to the work house.[31] This black woman did not distinguish between the behavior of master and mistress and viewed both as equally responsible for the sale.

Susan Hamlin described another unpleasant incident between a female slave and her mistress. Hamlin's comments implied that she believed the black woman might have been partly at fault. She described Clory as "very high-tempered. She wus a mulatta with beautiful hair she could sit on; Clory didn't take foolishness frum anybody." One day when the mistress found fault with her work, "Clory didn't do a t'ing but pick her up bodily an' throw 'er out de door. Dey had to sen' fur a doctor 'cause she pregnant an' less than two hours de baby was bo'n. Afta dat she begged to be sold fur she didn't want to kill missus, but our master ain't nebber want to sell his slaves." Instead Clory was brutally whipped: "I t'ought she wus goin' to die, but she got well an' didn't get any better but meaner until our master decide it wus bes' to rent her out. She willingly agree' since she wusn't 'round missus. She hated and detest' both of them an' all de fambly."[32] Jennie Hill, who had been a slave in Missouri, was caught in a conflict between a man and his daughter over which of them had final authority over Hill. The daughter told Hill she could not go to a party, but afterwards the father told her: "Lawsy, Jen, who owns you anyway? Go on and go to the party." The next day, the daughter beat Hill for attending.[33] In each of these instances, the mistresses felt their rights as white women were being challenged and took advantage of the privilege afforded by their race to impose punishment.

Slaves sometimes attributed punishments or the cruelty of mistresses to their own behavior. Ninety-year-old Victoria Adams reported: "De massa and missus was good to me but sometime I was so bad they had to whip me. I 'members she used to whip me every time she tell me to do something and I take too long to move 'long and do it."[34] A Kentucky slave woman recalled: "What I got this whipping about, the mistress rang the bell and I didn't come, and I told her I come as quick as I could, and she whacked me across the head with a broomstick, and I whacked her back, and got a good whipping." Dinah Cunningham was beaten only once while a slave. She was assigned to tend the mistress's child: "I had de baby on de floor on a pallet and rolled over on it. Her make a squeal like she was much hurt and mistress come in a hurry." After comforting the baby, Cunningham's mistress cut a switch from a tree and beat her.[35] Black women who took responsibility for the cause of their beatings were not necessarily ceding authority to white women; they may have been claiming agency over their own actions.

Sometimes slaves saw their punishments as stemming from arbitrary expectations or unreasonable demands. This could also be a way of claiming agency. Jacob Branch described the punishments his mother received from their mistress: "Every washday old missy give her de beatin'. She couldn't keep de flies from speckin' de clothes overnight. Old missy git up soon in de mornin', 'fore mama have time [to] git dem specks off. She snort and say, 'Renee, I's gwinter teach you how to wash.' Den she beat mama with de cowhide." Rebecca Jane Grant's mistress beat her when she was still a young girl because she refused to address a baby as "Marse Henry."[36]

Most often, however, slaves attributed the violence they experienced to the unfounded brutality of mistresses. Fannie Moore claimed her master's mother "was a rip-jack. She say niggers didn't need nothin' to eat. Dey just like animals, not like other folks. She whip me, many time with a cowhide, till I was black and blue." Elizabeth Spacks, who had been a slave in Virginia, claimed that her Aunt Caroline's mistress was quite cruel: "She used to make my Aunt Caroline knit all day and when she get so tired after dark that she'd get sleepy, she'd make her stand up and knit. She work her so hard that she'd go to sleep standin' up and every time her head nod and her knees sag, the lady'd come down across her head with a switch." She regarded her own mistress, the daughter of the woman who beat Caroline, as "purty nice to me," if only by contrast: "She was a good woman. Course I mean she'd slap and beat you once in a while but she weren't no woman for fightin', fussin', and beatin' you all day like some I know." Susan Merritt made no apologies for the behavior of her mistress: "Lots of times she tie me to a stob in the yard and cowhide me till she give out, then she go and rest and come back and beat me some more. . . . She stomp and beat me nearly to death and they have to grease my back where she cowhide me and I'se sick with fever for a week. If I could have a dollar for every cowhidin' I get, I'se never have to work no more." Robert Falls knew why his mother was such a hard worker: "She had to be. Old Mistress see to that." Austin Steward was a slave in Virginia early in the century, but his assessment of his mistress's behavior was similar, if more detailed: "Mrs. Helms was a very industrious woman, and generally busy in her household affairs—sewing, knitting, and looking after the servants; but she was a great scold—continually finding fault with some of the servants, and frequently punishing the young slaves herself, by striking them over the head with a heavy iron key, until the blood ran, or else whipping them with a cowhide, which she always kept by her side when sitting in her room. . . . No slave could possibly escape being punished."[37]

John Boyd reported the evident satisfaction his mistress derived from punishing slaves: "Aunt Polly had no patrollers on her place. She would not allow one there, for she did her own patrolling with her own whip and two bull dogs. . . . Those two dogs held them and she did her own whipping."[38] Daily life on many plantations included such acts of violence against slaves by mistresses venting the frustration stemming from the stress of living with them. White women who spent their days in close proximity to black women and who had to compel their labor as well as depend on them for everyday needs found it easy to lose their tempers and reach for the lash. Slaves were vulnerable to the seemingly arbitrary behavior of mistresses, who could sometimes wear the garb of benevolence and at other times flourish a whip.

Although it was highly unusual, on a few plantations mistresses were more violent than masters. Fannie Griffin recalled: "My massa was good to all he slaves, but Missy Grace was mean to us. She whip us a heap of times when we ain't done nothing bad to be whip for." Peggy Grigsby had a similar experience: "I was a slave of Alec Grigsby. He was a fair marster, but his wife was awful mean to us. She poked my head in a rail fence once and whipped me hard with a whip." Isaiah Butler lived on a large rice and cotton plantation with owners who behaved in much the same way: "My ole boss, preacher Joe Bostick wuz one of de best of men. . . . But de ole lady, ole 'Miss Jenny', she wuz very rough. She hired all de overseers, and she do all. If'n anybody try to go to de old man wid anyt'ing, she'd talk to 'em herself an' not let 'em see de old man."[39] Slaves who lived on such plantations viewed women who had rejected the dictates of the ideology of domesticity as the primary agents of white authority.

Most slave women saw their mistresses neither as wholly benevolent nor as unrelievedly brutal. Instead, African-American women saw white women as dangerous and easily duped, powerful and unpredictable, lazy and quickly provoked. Mary Frances Brown thought her mistress had been "good to me, teach me ebbery ting, and take the Bible and learn me Christianified manners, charity, and behaviour. . . . She good an' kind an' I lub her yet, but don't you forgit to mind what she say." Josephine Bacchus believed whites were "glad to have a heap of colored people bout dem cause white folks couldn' work den no more den dey can work dese days like de colored people can. Reckon dey love to have dey niggers back yonder just like dey loves to have dem dese days to do what dey ain' been cut out to do." Slaves also acknowledged that some mistresses behaved differently from others. Louisa Gause reported her mother was whipped by a brutal mistress, but that those slaves "what lived on Miss Susan Stevenson's plantation, dey been fare good all de time."[40]

Instances of violence by plantation mistresses were expressions of the hostility that women of both groups could feel toward each other. Sometimes that antagonism was the result of the jealousy and rage white women felt when their husbands paid sexual attention to black women.[41] Sometimes it was a matter of personality. Sometimes slave women resented mistresses' efforts at benevolence, interpreting them as unacceptable interference. Sometimes competition between women caused tension. Whatever the cause of hostility, it made the expectations resulting from the ideology of domesticity burdensome. Although very few white women denied the influence of the ideology of domesticity in their lives, fewer still were able to put its expectations into practice successfully and consistently. Shattering easily in the stress of daily life, domesticity remained an ideal for white women; slaves bore witness to the limited extent to which mistresses were able to achieve it.

Although most black and white women shared views of appropriate behavior for women, the ideology of domesticity did not shape black women's perceptions of their mistresses to the extent it informed white women's perceptions of their slaves. Female slaves viewed plantation mistresses along a continuum from useful allies to powerful enemies, with their attitudes ultimately depending in some measure, although not exclusively, on the behavior of individual mistresses. Since mistresses were far more likely to be generous to slaves than their masters were, slaves often enough viewed them as the kindly mediators of slavery mistresses saw themselves to be. But black women could never forget they were slaves and so were well aware of the price of white women's benevolence. Grateful for the assistance mistresses could provide, black women nevertheless were reluctant to accept sympathy—or tolerate punishment—when it would damage their own dignity. They resisted white women's encroachments and their own subordination by every means they knew, from fighting back, like Clory the wash-erwoman who caused her mistress to have a miscarriage, to attempting to turn mistresses' sympathy for them to their own advantage. Because their deeply held fundamental assumptions about female behavior were similar to those of plantation mistresses but shaped by their experience of slavery, black women were able to exploit the ideology of domesticity even as they perpetuated it.

7

Slave Women and the Meaning of Womanhood

Slave women's understanding of gender differences shaped more than just their perceptions and interactions with their mistresses. Their assumptions about the proper behavior of women and men also shaped their beliefs about themselves. Influenced by their understanding of the ideology of domesticity and by the expectations of the quarters, African-American women battled mightily to conform to their own ideals. Just as black men longed to protect and provide for their wives and children, black women desired to devote time and attention to their families. Although African Americans recognized that the limits imposed by slavery prevented them from acting according to their own beliefs about gender differences in all circumstances, this still evoked constant tension with slaveholders. The efforts of slaveholders to impose their own views of gender relations on slaves coupled with their ability to compel slave labor proved a potent force. African-American women's efforts to define the meaning of womanhood for themselves took place in the context of white interference, which ranged from insistence on women's labor to separating slave families to rape. Nevertheless, black women were able to define a consistent pattern of behavior that minimized white influence over their lives.

Black women could not eliminate the impact of slavery but they could attempt to mitigate its destructive potential. African-American women knew that toiling under male and female slaveholders set them apart from white women and restricted them from behaving as they thought women should. Many would seek the first opportunity to withdraw from the labor force after the Civil War. Yet black women took pride in their ability to work as hard and as long as men even as they sought to separate their identities as women from the work they did. A former slave, identified only as Mrs. Sutton, commented: "I could cut wood. I have done anything any man ever done 'cept cut wheat; but then after they cut it I would gather it up. I am way up in 80 now; before the War I worked plenty, just like men. Could look up any day and see ten women up over dar on the hill plowing; and look over the other way and see ten more. . . . You would have to do everything, and some of them very same devils what made you do it are in hell burning now."[1] Clearly, Sutton was proud of her abilities even as she resented having to demonstrate them. Former Louisiana slave Sarah Benjamin defined the connection between women's work lives and their expectation of themselves as women more explicitly: "De women had to run de gin in de daytime and de men at night."[2] Although many black women enjoyed putting on the trappings of femininity, they took their productive work quite seriously and were proud of their abilities.

Family life provided another arena in which slaves sought to alleviate the impact of white intrusion. To the extent possible given the exigencies of slave life, black women sometimes deferred to their husbands in ways that resembled white women's behavior, thereby acknowledging the ideology of domesticity. At the same time, they recognized that the realities of slavery meant they could not rely on their husbands for protection and support for themselves and their children, so they often developed great personal strength. Dorcas Elmore, who had been sold in South Carolina to a man in Alabama, ran away and made her way back to her former home only to find that her husband had taken another wife. According to Elmore's son, "Jenny had cared so well for her children while she was off, that she liked her. They lived in the same house with pa till my mother died." Jenny continued to raise the children after Elmore ran away to the woods and later died.[3] The tension between Dorcas Elmore's desire to care for her husband and children and her affection for her husband's new wife made her life unusually difficult. Slaves' efforts to overcome the consequences of slavery required flexibility in their assumptions about gender behavior and family life.

In spite of the difficulties, many African-American women fully accepted the slaves' version of the ideology of domesticity and worked hard to implement it. An unidentified male ex-slave from South Carolina spoke about his parents: "He was a powerful man and my mother rejoiced in him so. She wouldn't do anything without first asking him. It was so joyful to see them together. . . . My mother just rejoiced in him. Whenever he sat down to talk she just sat and looked and listened. She would never cross him for anything. If they went to church together she always waited for him to interpret what the preacher had said or what he thought was the will of God." Another former slave commented on her efforts to please her husband: "As

I grew up I used to frolic a lot and was considered a good dancer but I never took much interest in such things. I just went many times to please my friends and, later on, my husband."[4] As Millie Barber recalled, one night the slave patrol caught her father hiding in the chimney at her mother's house: "They stripped him right befo' mammy and give him thirty-nine lashes, wid her cryin' and a hollerin' louder than he did." Men also suffered when their wives were punished. Sylvia Durant remembered being told that "dey take de wives en whip de blood out dem en de husband never didn' dare to say nothin."[5]

Men helped to shape gender expectations and expected their wives to conform to them. In what its unnamed white author claimed to be a true story, a driver named Stephen first adopted his wife's clothing and then committed suicide while still wearing it because she had not only refused to be whipped by him but had also "wrested his whip from him and in the fray had thrown him to the floor where she held him until he promised not to strike her again." The woman, who was younger and stronger than her husband, had "suffer[ed] his ill treatment patiently for some time" because of her "habitual subserviency to him," but when "the evil at last became intolerable," her master suggested she defend herself. According to the teller of the tale, "having been overpowered by a woman he declared himself unworthy the name and outward condition of a man" and so had surrendered "his masculine office" and asked "for women's clothes and woman's work."[6] While the story's truth is certainly open to question, it does suggest the impact gender expectations could have on both male and female slaves.

Despite the pressures African-American women worked hard to create dignified lives for themselves and their families. Fannie Moore spoke of her mother: "I never see how my mammy stan' sech ha'd work. She stan' up fo' her chillun tho'. De overseeah he hate my mammy, case she fight him for beatin' her chillun. Why she git more whuppin's for dat den anythin' else." Similarly, David Goodman Gullins's mother endeavored to care for her children the way she believed proper: "All through the cold, bitter winter nights, I remember my mother getting up often to see about us and to keep the cover tucked in. She thought us sound asleep, and I pretended I was asleep while listening to her prayers. She would bend down over the bed and stretching her arms so as to take us all in, she prayed with all her soul to God to help her bring up her children right." Charlie Pye's mother also struggled with the conflicting pressures of slavery and motherhood: "My mother resented being whipped and would run away to the woods and often remained as long as twelve months at a time. When the strain of staying away from her family became too great, she would return home. No sooner would she arrive than the old overseer would tie her to a peach tree and whip her again."[7] Against overwhelming odds and adversities, each of these women fought to behave according to her ideals.

The contradictions between black women's desire to practice domesticity and the realities of slavery were always present, especially for mothers. Black women struggled to protect their children from the harshness of slavery as well as to prepare them for its consequences, tasks made especially troublesome by the meddling of whites. One male ex-slave described his mother's efforts to instill in him both moral and practical knowledge: "As a boy I lived close to my mother and she taught me how to live and pray and how to take care of myself. She taught me how to wash my clothes because she was always afraid that I might be sold from her or that she might be sold and sent away from me." Ben Leitner's master made "mammy whup us chillun, when us need a whuppen," while Bill Young's mistress "wouldn't let his own mother whip him. She would say, 'Don't tech that boy, as he is my Nigger.'"[8] Black mothers resented the control whites claimed over child rearing and worked hard to minimize its impact.

African-American women knew that gender as much as slavery and race caused their difficulties. A former slave who had been sold at auction as a child commented to Fisk University interviewers: "Mammy finally died and left a little bit of a baby and do you [know] I had sense enough to be glad when the baby died too. Poor little thing would have to go through the world like I have come; all alone with no mother. Yes sir, I was a child, but I was really glad when the baby died. It was a girl, too. You see that made it even worse." Harriet Jacobs's baby did not die, but she too regretted giving birth to a daughter: "When they told me my new-born babe was a girl, my heart was heavier than it had ever been before. Slavery is terrible for men; but it is far more terrible for women. Superadded to the burden common to all, *they* have wrongs, and sufferings, and mortifications peculiarly their own."[9] Robert Smalls, born a slave in 1839, responded to a question put to him by the American Freedman's Inquiry Commission in South Carolina in 1863 in a manner that indirectly acknowledged another potential source of some of the sufferings of slave women: "I will tell you what made me get a wife. My idea was to have a wife to prevent me running around—to have somebody to do for me and to keep me. The colored men in taking wives always do so with reference to the service the women will render." When asked "Do the colored men fall in love very often?" Smalls's response was "No, Sir; I think not."[10] Smalls later served in the U.S. House of Representatives.

Both male and female slaves knew what was expected of them, and most tried to live up to those expectations. However, for some women, the ideals were simply too high to be met consistently. Some black women, like some white women, could not live harmoniously with their husbands, in spite of demands from whites and other blacks that they do so. Everett Ingram, a slave from Alabama, recalled: "I 'members dat de overseer use ta whip mammy an' pappy, 'ca'se dey fight so much."[11] A former slave woman reported: "My father was a Bailey, but mother and father separated before I was born. . . . No, they didn't sell him; he and mother just got mad in a quarrel and separated. He tried to get her back and the white folks tried to get her to take him back, but she wouldn't do it, 'cause he drawed back to hit her with a chair, and he'd never done that before. He woulda hit her too if her brother hadn't been there and stopped him."[12]

Women could invoke the censure of the slave community when they failed to meet commonly held standards of behavior. According to one former slave, "They taught us to be against one another and no matter where you would go you would always find one that would be tattling and would have the white folks pecking on you. They would be trying to make it soft for themselves. I had an aunt by marriage who would peep around and tell the women things." Mary Smith described "a terrible thing" that happened when she was a girl. In spite of prohibitions against stealing from other slaves even while stealing from whites was tolerated, a black woman from another plantation stole all of Smith's clothing as well as her mother's, which prevented them from going to church.[13] Although slaves were clear about the mode of behavior they expected from women, and women made real efforts to conform, all African Americans recognized that slavery—and human nature—sometimes made fulfilling those expectations impossible.

⌖

The net of race and gender relations was woven most tightly around the issue of coerced interracial sexual activity.[14] Everyone, enslaved and free, male and female, was aware that such things were common, but few acknowledged this openly. Coerced sex was the underside of the beliefs white southerners held about themselves. If masters were, as their paternalistic self-definition suggested, responsible for the physical and moral well-being of slaves, then forcing sex upon female slaves was the ultimate betrayal of responsibility. If the ideology of domesticity taught plantation mistresses to sympathize and recognize what they had in common with other women, then the sexual activities of their husbands extended their similarities to the most personal—and unacceptable—of levels. Blacks recognized rape as one of the mechanisms by which whites imposed their will, although obviously it was experienced and therefore perceived differently by men and women. For all groups in South Carolina society except the white men who originated it, coerced sex reinforced the authority of white men and challenged black women's efforts to maintain dignity in the face of that authority.[15]

Sexual relations between white men and black women ranged from rape to intimate and apparently loving relationships that lasted many years. Whatever the nature of the understanding—or lack of understanding—between the individual man and woman, such interactions were not likely to be viewed positively by the slave community or by white women. Interracial sexual activity of any kind reinforced the distinctions between men and women, enslaved and free, in southern society. As Sena Moore explained: "I see many good white men, more than I got fingers and toes, but a low down white man can git low downer than a nigger man. A good white lady told me one time, dat a bad white woman is a sight worser and more low downer than a bad nigger woman can ever git to be in dis world."[16]

Interracial sexual activity had two related social consequences. First, it reinforced white male domination over black men and women by separating slave women from slave men, which increased women's double burden of race- and gender-based oppression. At the same time, it prevented black men from fulfilling what whites considered the first expectation of nineteenth-century manhood, the protection of women. Second, interracial sexual activity reinforced the subordination of white women by demonstrating their inability to impose their own moral values on men. By transcending the boundaries of race and gender, sex with black women allowed white men to maintain their authority over all other groups in southern society.

The threat of rape constantly reminded slave women of their vulnerability as women and as slaves. While not all black women directly experienced advances from white men, African Americans were well aware that they occurred.[17] Carrie Mason, born during the Civil War, acknowledged the rumors: "I hyeard tell of er white man whut would tell his sons ter 'go down ter dem nigger quarters an' get me mo' slaves.'" Rev. Ishrael Massie, who had been a slave in Virginia, used blunt language: "Did de dirty suckers associate wid slave wimmen? I call 'em suckers—feel like saying something else but I'll 'spec ya, honey. Lord chile, dat wuz common. Marsters an' overseers use to make slaves dat wuz wid deir husbands git up, do as dey say. Send husbands out on de farm, milkin' cows or cuttin' wood. Den he gits in bed wid slave himself." As former Alabama slave Lizzie Williams acknowledged, it was impossible to remain blind to mulatto children: "Many de pore niggah women hab chillun for de massa, dat is iffen de massa a mean man. Dey jes tell de niggahs whut to do and dey know better den to fuss."[18]

Mrs. Sutton, another former slave, was aware of differences among whites regarding coerced sexual activity: "There was two classes of white folks, some who wouldn't bother with nigger women and others who would; but the ones who wouldn't wouldn't mix with those who would. They would make women do that. Some of them would treat these children better, and some of them wouldn't." Women's experience was the focus for another former slave: "Now, mind you, all of the colored women didn't have to have white men, some did it because they wanted to and some were forced. They had a horror of going to Mississippi and they would do anything to keep from it. A white woman would have a maid sometimes who was nice looking, and she would keep her and her son would have children by her." Robert Ellett described the same situation in stronger language: "In those days if you was a slave and had a good looking daughter, she was taken from you. They would put her in the big house where the young masters could have the run of her." Often enough, women recognized the futility of resistance. When Frances Kemble rather insensitively criticized a black woman for bearing a mulatto child, she responded: " 'We do anything to get our poor flesh some rest from de whip; when he made me follow him into de bush, what use me tell him no? He have strength to make me.' "[19]

Slaves such as Carrie Mason believed that white men slept with black women to increase the number and value of their slaves. Others thought whites arranged marriages for blacks for the same reason. Josephine Bacchus knew that whatever whites did, they "sho been mighty proud to see dey niggers spreadin out in dem days. . . . You see, dey would have two or three women on de plantation dat was good breeders en dey would have chillun pretty regular fore freedom come here." Nelson Cameron's owner did not have many slaves but learned how to get more by watching men who raised horses: "Have a whole lot of mares and 'pendin' on other men to have de stallion. Fust thing you know dere would be a whole lot of colts kickin' up deir heels on de place. Lakwise a white man start out wid a few women folk slaves, soon him have a plantation full of little niggers runnin' 'round in deir shirt-tails and a kickin' up deir heels, whilst deir mammies was in de field a hoeing and geeing at de plow handles, workin' lak a man." Being a "breed 'omans" was advantageous to Hector Godbold's Africa-born grandmother after the apparently frequent efforts she made to run away: "If dey catch her, dey didn' never do her no harm."[20] Not all "breeding women" were targets of the sexual advances of white men, nor were all forced to accept husbands of their owners' choice. But just as all black women recognized that they were vulnerable to the advances of white men, so they knew that they and their children were economic assets for slaveholders, who at best might express reluctance to sell them, but who would ultimately do so if necessary.

African-American women resisted the sexual advances of white men when their fear of the consequences did not get the better of them and when they thought they had a chance of success. Fannie Berry of Virginia took pride in her ability to resist: "I wuz one slave dat de poor white man had his match. . . . One tried to throw me, but he couldn't. We tusseled an' knocked over chairs an' when I got a grip I scratched his face all to pieces; an dar wuz no more bothering Fannie from him; but oh, honey, some slaves would be beat up so, when dey resisted, an' sometimes if you 'belled de overseer would kill yo'. Us colored women had to go through a plenty, I tell you." Harriet Jacobs relied on her own intelligence and her master's fear of gossip in their small town to resist his advances. Some African-American women resisted rape by seeking the assistance of sympathetic white men. Alabama slave Martha Bradley recalled her reaction to unwelcome advances from the overseer: "I took my hoe and knocked him plum down. I knowed I'se done sumpin' bad so I run to de bushes. Marster Lucas come and got me and started whoopin' me. I say to Marster Lucas whut dat overseer sez to me and Marster Lucas didn' hit me no more."[21]

More commonly, black women sought aid from plantation mistresses, hoping that they would offer sympathy as well as protection.[22] By recognizing mistresses as potential allies against male aggression, slave women demonstrated their belief in a shared female understanding and made a powerful leap across the gulf of race. Harriet Jacobs criticized her mistress for refusing to aid black women sexually threatened by her husband: "Mrs. Flint possessed the key to her husband's character before I was born. She might have used this knowledge to counsel and to screen the young and the innocent among her slaves; but for them she had no sympathy. They were the objects of her constant suspicion and malevolence." At the same time, Jacobs pitied her mistress's plight. "I was an object of her jealousy, and, consequently, of her hatred; and I knew I could not expect kindness or confidence from her under the circumstances in which I was placed. I could not blame her. Slaveholders' wives feel as other women would under similar circumstances. . . . Yet I, whom she detested so bitterly, had far more pity for her than he had, whose duty it was to make her life happy. I never wronged her, or wished to wrong her; and one word of kindness from her would have brought me to her feet." Jacobs applauded the behavior of those white women who could overcome their jealousy and live up to the ideals of womanhood: "I have myself known two southern wives who exhorted their husbands to free those slaves towards whom they stood in a 'parental relation' and their request was granted. These husbands blushed before the superior nobleness of their wives' natures. Though they had only counselled them to do that which it was their duty to do, it commanded their respect, and rendered their conduct more exemplary. Concealment was at an end, and confidence took the place of distrust." Another black woman reportedly refused to inform her mistress about the master's sexual advances because she was reluctant to make the white woman unhappy.[23]

At the other extreme were slave women who lived as what amounted to the wives of white men. Alice Marshall, daughter of a slave woman and a slaveholder in Virginia, made note of such a relationship: "Why on de 'jinin' plantation ole massa had a brother what had a grea' big fat colored 'oman for his house maid. She light too. 'Deed dem two lived together jes' same's dey's married. And ole fat Sophie had chillun right and left. . . . Sophie was treated very kind too. . . . Ole marse Oliver ain' want no nigger men hangin' roun' Sophie neither."[24] Too young to remember slavery but aware of its practices in South Carolina, Willie McCullough painted an exaggerated picture that contained a kernel of truth: "There was classes of slavery. Some of the half-white and beautiful young women who were used by the marster and his men friends or who was the sweetheart of the marster only, were given special privileges. Some of 'em worked very little. They had private quarters well fixed up and had a great influence over the marster. Some of these slave girls broke up families by getting the marster so enmeshed in their net that his wife, perhaps an older woman, was greatly neglected."[25] Such women evoked ambivalence and mistrust from other slaves.

Most black women reacted to interracial sexual activity in far less dramatic ways, neither physically assaulting their attackers nor enjoying privileged surroundings. Instead, most sought to make the best of a situation they could not change. Ishrael Massie reported what may have been a common experience:

I know our overseer we all thought wuz doin' wrong wid dis slave gal but we wuz feard to say hit. When de chile come, 'twas white. One day all de little chillun wuz in yard playing—running 'roun. An de gal's husband wuz settin' near de do' wid de baby in his arms—rockin' away—looking in child's face an' at de chillun playin' in de yard. Wife wuz tendin' to sumpin in de house. All at once he called her an' sed, "Ole lady, dis chile ain't like our other chillun." She say, "Ole man, er-er-stop stedin' so much foolishness." He dar rockin' de chile looking down at hit and says, "Dis chile is got blue eyes. Dis chile is got white fingernails. Dis chile is got blue eyes jes like our overseer." "Ole man, I don' tole ya, stop settin' dar stedin' so much foolishness! Ole man, you kno' jes as well as I kno', de mornin' I sent ya to Aint Manervia's to git dat buttermilk. Dat wuz six months gone—March an' setch, April an tetable, May an' dat"—Ha, ha, ha. Dats 3 months she count-

ed. Ha! Ha! Ha! Foolin' de ole man.—He sed, "Yas, dat is nine months." Den he
satisfied hit wuz his chile. De pint 'im at is, she wuz feared to tell on overseer den.[26]

This anecdote illustrates a number of aspects of slave women's experiences
of coerced sexual relations with white men. First, fear of the consequences
often kept women from defending themselves or seeking help. Second, coerced sex separated black women from black men, forcing at least this one
woman to deny that it had even occurred. Her response to her husband indicates some measure of the pain the experience caused her. Finally, Massie's telling of the story suggests that although slaves recognized women's
inability to prevent coerced sex, sometimes they were nevertheless aware of
a sense of fear, disgrace, and secrecy associated with it.

The shame associated with miscegenation could extend to mulatto children as well. Alabama ex-slave Lizzie Williams remembered the slave girl
she cared for as a child who looked white. In spite of good treatment, Williams remembered: "Emily have de saddes' look on her yaller face cas' de
other niggahs whisper 'bout her pappy." A former Texas slave spoke about
a slave woman who had at least five children by her owner and one by a slave
man: "When she was drunk or mad she'd say she thought more of her black
chile than all the others."[27] Whatever humiliation associated with being or
having mulatto children vanished when slaveholders tried to sell them. Many
slaves reserved their deepest outrage for men who would sell their own offspring. A woman who had been the slave of a Methodist preacher commented that her owner "would sell his own children by slave women just like he
would any others. Just since he was making money."[28]

Even in everyday matters, most slaves reported that mulatto children were
not favored by their white fathers. Lizzie Williams reported that Emily's "pappy pay no more 'tention to her den to de res' of de niggahs."[29] Occasionally
when slaveholders did favor their children by black women, it was understood
ambivalently by slaves. Martha Jackson reported: "Ev'y time hit come time
fer 'em yaller gals ter work in de fid', dey got sarnt Norf. I reckon 'case he
never wanted see his own blood git beat up, and dat Jim Barton was 'er cru'l
overseer, sho's yer bawn. 'Twas a heap of dem yaller gals got sarnt Norf from
'roun' here sho' was."[30] Even if white men did not feel the pain, miscegenation caused black women emotional anguish. Black women resisted the sexual advances of white men as well as they could, and most loved their children
no matter who their fathers were. Recognizing that resistance to coerced sex
could range from overt defiance to loving mulatto children, women maintained
a strong identity with the values of their community and a clear understanding of the behavior expected of them as women.

Black men shared their pain. Rev. Ishrael Massie undoubtedly spoke for many slave men when he commented years later: "What we saw, couldn't do nothing 'bout it. My blood is bilin' now [at the] thoughts of dem times. If dey told dey husbands he wuz powerless." Charles Grandy reported what happened when the overseer "started bothern" with a black woman in front of her husband: "De colored man made at him an' he shot him wid a gun. Den de colored man come at him wid a hoe. He kept shootin' 'till de man fell dead in his tracks."[31] Given a choice between powerlessness and death, most African-American men could only stand by while their women were raped. Both slave men and women knew that rape was one way white men asserted control over them; consequently, they resisted its occurrence and minimized its consequences however they could. Black men considered protecting their wives an important obligation, and at least on occasion some were willing to risk death trying. They also recognized that rejecting raped women or mulatto children enhanced the destructive power of white men, and that resistance could take many forms.

Few white men spoke publicly about their sexual activities with black women, although undoubtedly they boasted to one another. Judge Harper of South Carolina was one of the few who analyzed the subject in print. Harper argued that slave women "set little value on chastity" because of their "very loose" morals and acknowledged the evil that let "the passions of men of the superior caste, tempt and find gratification in the easy chastity of the females." However, he argued, a black woman in such circumstances was "a far less contaminated and depraved being" than a white prostitute; unlike the white woman she was "not a less useful member of society than before." In Harper's view, the black woman had done nothing wrong: "She has not impaired her means of support, not materially impaired her character, or lowered her station in society; she has done no great injury to herself, or any other human being. . . . The want of chastity . . . among slaves, hardly deserves a harsher term than that of weakness." Harper believed that white men's intercourse with slave women "is less depraving in its effects, than when it is carried on with females of their own caste." He claimed that no "Carolina woman of education and family, proved false to her conjugal faith," and did not doubt that "this purity is caused by, and is a compensation for the evils resulting from the existence of an enslaved class of more relaxed morals."[32] In addition to assuming that black women welcomed these sexual advances he did not consider the pain these white men caused all women.

Interracial sexual activity at once threatened and reinforced white women's female identity.[33] Like black women, white women usually believed they were powerless to prevent men's actions, although they were in a position to offer help. Plantation mistresses' notions of morality as well as their sympathy for slave women explain the willingness of some to help individual black women threatened with rape. Complicating these beliefs was jealousy. Mistresses were more likely to aid women when the attacker was the overseer or other nonelite white man than they were when he was their own husband or son. Mistresses, of course, blamed black women who drew the attention of their husbands or sons and hated the children they fathered.

Former slave Willie McCullough of South Carolina explained mistresses' hatred in terms of the relative status of women, claiming that masters' sweethearts were given special privileges while wives were neglected. An African-American woman who had been a slave warned of the consequences for family life: "If his wife find it out he would have to sell her (Negro concubine)." Another former slave believed mulatto children caused tension between women: "You know when a man would marry, his father would give him a woman for a cook and she would have children right in the house by him, and his wife would have children too. Sometimes the cook's children favored him so much that the wife would be mean to them and make him sell them. If they had nice long hair she would cut it off and wouldn't let them wear it long like the white children." Harriet Jacobs's mistress was extremely jealous of the attention her husband paid to black women and blamed them for his transgressions. Jacobs found the white woman's anger misplaced: "The mistress, who ought to protect the helpless victim, has no other feelings towards her but those of jealousy and rage. . . . She felt that her marriage vows were desecrated, her dignity insulted; but she had no compassion for the poor victim of her husband's perfidy. She pitied herself as a martyr; but she was incapable of feeling for the condition of shame and misery in which her unfortunate, helpless slave was placed."[34] Slave women considered mistresses who not only failed to protect them but who also blamed them for white men's attentions arbitrary and deceitful. These white women, unable to acknowledge the responsibility of white men, assumed black women were complicit in their own sexual abuse and so blamed them as much, if not more, than the men whose power and control it represented.

Clearly, white men's sexual activities exacerbated tensions between mistresses and slave women. Mistresses who found the rigors of daily life with slaves difficult at best found interacting with the women chosen by their husbands nearly impossible. Inspired by a tangle of sexual jealousy and powerlessness at their inability to curb white men's behavior, white women were easily provoked to violence. Delia Garlic enraged her mistress merely by imitating her appearance: "I seed his [master's] wife blackin' her eyebrows wid smut one day, so I thought I'd black mine jes' for fun. I rubbed some smut on my eyebrows an' forgot to rub it off, an' she kotched me." Garlic's mistress was angry and punished her for "mocking her betters." Henrietta King, who had been a slave in Virginia, easily explained the source of the ill feeling between her mistress and a slave woman: "Mary was what de slaves called a 'clabber-colored' gal wid long black hair. Neither Josephine nor Missus Octavia liked her 'cause she was better lookin' dan either of dem." King described an instance in which a suitor of Josephine's mistook Mary for "some white gal," which infuriated Josephine. "De nex' day she made Marsa take Mary to Richmond an' dey say he hired her out or sol' her." Not all mistresses eliminated the source of their jealousy as effectively as Josephine. A former North Carolina slave identified only as Granny claimed that her mistress "looked like a witch. She'd set dere an' dat look 'ud come into her eyes an' she'd study an' study what to whip me about. I 'members one mornin' she look at me an' she says to marster, 'dat nigger needs a whipping.' He don answer, but wen' out in de field." Granny's mistress did contrive to have her whipped on that occasion, but both women knew the whipping was as likely to have been inspired by the five children Granny bore her master as the butter she ostensibly spoiled.[35]

A few plantation mistresses transcended feelings of animosity for their husbands' slave mistresses and mulatto children. These women identified white men as the source of the problem, although they were likely to maintain a degree of bitterness toward the black women and seldom would provide assistance. A few may have been relieved; given the absence of reliable birth control and the dangers of childbirth, a husband's attention to black women could offer white women a respite from constant reproduction as well as demanding husbands. Jacob Manson, who had been a slave in North Carolina, reported: "One of de slave girls on a plantation near us went to her missus and tole her 'bout her marster forcing her to let him have sumthin to do wid her an her missus tole her, 'Well go on you. Belong to him.'" Savilla Burrell's former mistress recognized her husband's guilt and maintained a degree of sympathy for black women and their mulatto children: "Ole Marse was de daddy of some mulatto chillun. De 'lations wid de mothers of dese chillun is what give so much grief to Mistress. De neighbors would talk 'bout it and he would sell all dem chillun away from dey mothers to a trader. My Mistress would cry 'bout dat."[36] Gertrude Thomas's long-standing and personal criticism of white men's sexual transgressions, based partly on the behavior of the men of her own family, led her to expressions of sorrow and outrage as well as doubts about slavery.[37] Similarly, Mary Chesnut was sharply critical of the behavior of white men toward black women. Equating the plight of white and black women, both Chesnut and Thomas identified interracial sexual activity as the root of the evil in southern society.[38] White men were degraded by the baseness of their slave mistresses, Chesnut argued, and virtuous white women were forced to live surrounded by prostitutes and their mulatto children. Chesnut, like Thomas, had firsthand experience of this: her father-in-law had several children by one of his slaves.[39] By basing their opposition to slavery on interracial sexual activity, both women underscored the deep divisions it created in southern society.

Gertrude Thomas, Mary Chesnut, and other white women were conscious that interracial sex made their desire to live up to the ideology of domesticity nearly impossible: the presence of mulatto children provided irrefutable and constant proof that their efforts to raise men to their own moral level were unsuccessful. Although some plantation mistresses held white men accountable for their actions and consequently expressed sympathy for female slaves, mistresses' understanding of the proper interactions between women and men as well as their inherent racism prevented them from full identification with black women. Unable to transcend the values of nineteenth-century womanhood, plantation mistresses held attitudes toward interracial sexual activity that limited their understanding of themselves and their society. Although interracial sex had the potential to unite women of both races in a common perception of the immorality of white men and the evils of slavery, it failed to do so, leaving slaveholders and slaves, men and women ultimately divided.[40]

⌁

These disjunctions were duplicated elsewhere in South Carolina plantation life. Just as the conventions of nineteenth-century white society demanded different expectations and patterns of behavior for white women and men, so too did the conventions of the slave quarters separate the experiences of black women and men. Within the slave community and in the larger world of the plantation, female slaves filled a variety of social roles and helped to define the complex interactions in the South. The roles of black women, influenced as they were by the ideology of domesticity and the experience of slavery, help us to understand the intersections of race and gender.

The tasks performed by African-American women significantly shaped their unique perspective and experience. As slaves, their work was defined by the needs of the crop and the demands of the master. As women, their labor was defined by generally accepted notions of what was appropriate for women. As a result, work reinforced the ideology of domesticity that was largely responsible for shaping those aspects of their lives that set them apart from other groups in South Carolina society and that determined their place in it.

The labor of black women also played an important part in making possible the position of white women. On large plantations black women enabled their mistresses to avoid much routine work, which in turn permitted their adherence to the ideology of domesticity. In addition, slave women's work patterns allowed them to inform mistresses about the slave community's need for assistance and the conditions of slave life, thus encouraging mistresses' activities as mediators. Through their labor African-American women actively molded the meaning and experience of white womanhood.

Plantation mistresses such as Mary Curtis occasionally acknowledged the contributions slave women made to their lives. Accepting a trusted slave's offer of continued assistance, Curtis wrote her sister: "Perhaps it would have been better in me not to take advantage of her offer . . . but I am too glad to put off the evil day of parting with her." Another sister wrote Curtis about the problems frequent illnesses caused in accomplishing domestic responsibilities. Recognizing the need for increased effort, she wrote: "Peggy has just got out too & the prospect of help gives a fresh impulse to my diligence."[41] Maria Davis, a northern woman who claimed to be an abolitionist but who married a southern planter, was willing to visit her family in Massachusetts but preferred to live in South Carolina: "I have many things here I dislike very much to leave which I cannot carry to the North with me or have if I were there." Among these she listed chicken, meat, and fresh game, along with her ability to "have it cooked & brought to me & that is very comfortable you know—when any one does not feel in a mood to get it themselves."[42] Mistresses valued black women for more than just the duties they carried out. In an earlier letter addressed to a sister, Maria Davis also protested her antislavery sentiments but admitted her dependence on a female slave while her husband was away: "I am obliged to have her or stay alone & that I dare not do." Meta Morris Grimball recognized a friend's even greater dependence on slaves. She wrote in her diary about the friend's favorite maid, "Emma, a very light Mulatoe & her son, who tell her everything which goes on in her house," including some scandal about the governess, who promptly left. Eliza Simkins apparently thought so highly of her slave Malinda's fidelity and devotion to the white children that she stipulated in her will that Malinda should care for them while they remained minors.[43]

The important contributions made by slave women were also acknowledged by the slave community, sometimes to the chagrin of whites. A male slaveholder complained about a group of three slaves, two of whom confessed to stealing corn and other items. He identified the ringleader as the only woman of the three, Sally: "She has been sleeping in the house consequently had free access to my keys and would hand them to these negroes whenever they asked for them, permitting them to come into the house also." Slaves acknowledged the important role women who worked among whites played in transmitting information to and from the slave community.[44]

Perhaps black women's most important gender-specific activity was caring for their families. Their work for plantation mistresses made possible some types of contributions to life in the quarters, but their activities from sundown to sunup provided greater opportunities. Houston Holloway pointed to one such chance when he wrote in his autobiography about being sold at age thirteen. In his new home "Aunt Ellen who was the Milk Made and gardner [took] me for her boy and adopted me for her son[.] She washed and patched my clothes and was very good to me[.] She was [illegible] religious and she had much to [do] with [the] job of getting me into the Methodist Church." Henry Trentham also appreciated women's activities: "Some of de women plowed barefooted most all de time, an' had to carry dat row an' keep up wid de men, an' den do dere cookin' at night."[45] African-American women's practice of the black version of the ideology of domesticity, and their consequent valuing of home, children, family, and religion, helped make the quarters a bearable place to live. Their commitment to their marriages and relatives encouraged a stability and community that they passed on to their children. As Holloway suggested, their concern for those within and beyond their immediate nuclear family helped to create the network of social relationships so necessary to slave life. Former slave Ed McCrorey paid homage to this role of women: "My father was name Washington. . . . My mammy name Dolly. . . . You ask me why I say father and not say mother? Well boss, let me see; maybe I regard father, but I loves mammy. My white folks say father but I learnt on de breast and knees of mammy to say mammy, and dat's a sweet name to dis old nigger, which and how I ain't gonna change 'less her changes it when I git to heaven bye and bye."[46]

In all of their familial activities, African-American women used their understanding of the meaning of womanhood in nineteenth-century society to help make the slave quarters a better place to live. Their behavior contributed to the stability of their society and encouraged all slaves to put limits on unacceptable behavior. Because black women encouraged strength and perseverance they defused discontent to a certain extent. However, by adopting some of the dominant white culture's values regarding women and incorporating them with their own, slave women were by no means betraying the larger concerns of African-American life. Black women's behavior

was a means of fighting the dehumanization of slavery. The actions and attitudes of these women were an important mechanism by which slaves maintained a sense of their own humanity in the face of brutality.

The important similarities and the significant differences in the activities and
attitudes of female slaves and plantation mistresses in antebellum South
Carolina gave them complementary roles in southern culture. On the surface, those roles appear to be essentially conservative ones. As mediators
plantation mistresses perhaps helped to make slavery more tolerable for
individual blacks but presented no significant challenge to the institution.
Inspired by the ideology of domesticity, some white women were willing to
confront slavery, but only so far as to minimize some of its worst aspects.
Although these efforts were not insignificant in bettering slaves' lives, by
striving to make slavery more endurable white women perhaps inadvertently
became agents of paternalism, helping to advance the white South's goal of
a docile and dependent labor force. The interpretation of plantation mistresses' role as essentially conservative is reinforced by the inability of virtually all of them to go beyond providing immediate help to individual slaves.
Very few freed the slaves they owned during their lifetimes or in their wills
and even fewer could imagine a world without slavery.[47] Because they failed
to grapple with the larger issues of slavery and racism, plantation mistresses
could not transcend the racial assumptions of their culture to forge an identity of interests that was in any sense political.

Similarly, the social role of slave women can also be viewed as conservative. Black women rarely engaged in overt forms of rebellion against slavery.[48]
Women led no slave revolts. Most successful runaways were male or led by
men.[49] Slaveholders rarely mentioned women when complaining about their
worst-behaved slaves. Furthermore, black women's activities in the quarters
contributed to its stability. Women encouraged the strong family ties that
prevented men from running away or engaging in suicidal forms of rebellion.
For example, when Harriet Jacobs's uncle threatened to run away after being
punished, she "implored him not to go, but he paid no heed to my words. . . . I
reminded him of the poverty and hardships he must encounter among strang-
ers. I told him he might be caught and brought back; and that was terrible to
think of." Similarly, when safely in the North, she berated herself for having
fallen in love while still a slave: "Why does the slave ever love? Why allow
the tendrils of the heart to twine around objects which may at any moment
be wrenched away by the hand of violence? . . . I did not reason thus when I
was a young girl. Youth will be youth. I loved, and I indulged the hope that

the dark clouds around me would turn out a bright lining."[50] Like the efforts of white women, those of black women encouraged slaves to tolerate slavery, to make the best of a difficult situation. As a result, many of them can be viewed as a conservative force within the slave community.

Another view of women's behavior—one that sees women's activities and attitudes as having more radical consequences—also deserves consideration. In this view, the ideology of domesticity encouraged some plantation mistresses to deny or at least modify the teachings of their own culture about the depravity and dehumanization of slaves. Some white women made concerted efforts to enable slaves to live with a measure of human dignity. By expressing concern for the well-being of African Americans rather than simply the work that could be squeezed out of them, mistresses significantly limited the destructive possibilities of slavery. Their acceptance of the ideology of domesticity, while never carried to its logical end, still encouraged them to have sympathy for and identify with black women. In the antebellum South, even such a limited understanding was at least subversive, if not radical.

If the social role of plantation mistresses could be radical, then that of female slaves was even more so. By maintinaing values and preserving culture in the quarters, black women fought the dehumanization of slavery. Although they shared this responsibility with men, women were encouraged to see themselves as caretakers, with primary responsibilities for both the socialization of children and the preservation of family values and beliefs. While men were the leaders of the slave community, women performed the everyday functions that sustained life and spirit. Black women's pains to add dignity to slave life encouraged all African Americans to experience both an individual and a collective sense of self-worth. By thwarting dehumanization and encouraging self-respect, female slaves can be viewed as performing a radical social role.

Female slaves and plantation mistresses shared another dimension of radical behavior. By encouraging slaves to transcend degradation and preserve their culture, women of both groups helped all slaves to understand the conventions of nineteenth-century life. They helped to affirm the essential humanity of slaves and presented a muted but real challenge to the authority of white men. While their actions may not have led directly to the downfall of slavery, they unknowingly helped African Americans prepare for freedom.

Perhaps the interaction with the most potential for radical implications was women's recognition of their commonality. Halting, partial, and tentative as it was given the harshness of daily life on the plantation, it still was possible, even if it was rare. The ideology of domesticity as understood by women of both groups could allow them to question the cultural definitions of the two races. Even if only for brief moments, women forged bonds of sympathy and understanding across racial lines. Although tenuous, those ties represented a profound challenge to the assumptions underlying the institution of slavery and the authority of white men.[51]

The fragile bonds between women grew from a variety of common experiences and concerns. First, women shared fear-inducing biological experiences in the uncertain medical world of the nineteenth century. Women of both groups attended one another during pregnancy and childbirth, comforted one another's fear and pain, provided medical care, and tended one another through periods of ill health and recovery. In addition to the consequences of biology, female slaves and plantation mistresses shared values that placed concern for children and family at the center of their lives. Many were able to extend a degree of that concern to one another's children. As a result, children of each race could grow up with strong attachments to white and black women. The frequent use of the term "mammy" by whites and the large number of former slaves who remembered their mistresses as acting "just like a mammy" underscore the closeness of the emotional ties that sometimes developed. While the potential for rivalry for children's attention was real, the value all women placed on children could draw them together into a common understanding in spite of their differences.

Women in antebellum South Carolina also agreed on a definition of appropriate behavior for women and held a mutual desire to live up to its ideals. Although articulated differently by each group of women, the ideology of domesticity and the conventions of female behavior it implied led women to common assumptions about the world and a language with which to discuss them. Their shared experiences and perspective helped some women to recognize similar values in each other and thus develop a degree of sympathetic understanding. Female slaves couched their appeals to mistresses in language that reminded both of their common femaleness; mistresses claimed to understand female slaves and feel sympathy for them for much the same reason. Fanny Kemble perhaps expressed these common experiences most clearly, an insight made possible by her status as outsider and observer. While visiting the plantation her husband owned but did not live near or supervise closely, she kissed a black woman's baby: "The caress excited the irrepressible delight of all the women present—poor creatures! who seemed to forget that I was a woman, and had children myself, and bore a woman's and a mother's heart toward them and theirs; but, indeed, the Honorable Mr. Slumkey could not have achieved more popularity by his performances in that line than I by this exhibition of feeling."[52] While it is important to remember that the slaves Kemble describes had been without a mistress for some time and that she was not a southerner, this also helps to explain her ability to articulate what for others may well have been ordinary.

Although they were aware of their common bonds, southern women rarely, if ever, spoke directly about them. Certainly they did not adopt the sentimental language of female friendships used by northern women.[53] Plantation mistresses also did not wield the terms of racism in the same blunt way that many male slaveholders did.[54] Instead, women appealed to one another in language reminiscent of domesticity. They spoke to one another as women, assuming that because they were women they would understand one another. This is apparent in the appeals slave women threatened with rape made to mistresses, for example, and in the empathy at least some mistresses felt for the sorrows of slave life. Susan Witherspoon appealed to that sense of shared sympathy in the message she sent to a black woman she called Nurse, who was apparently reluctant to return from Witherspoon's daughter's home: "But tell Nurse if she knew how much I have been suffering and still suffer she would be glad to help me."[55] Born of perceptions of a mutual understanding, the language female slaves and plantation mistresses used reflected the significance of gender-defined experiences in their lives.

Gender-defined experiences certainly did not, however, always or even often transcend the other distinctions that separated black women from white women. Slavery created vast differences in the ways they viewed the world and one another. In spite of the many forces pulling mistresses and slave women together, their irresolvable inequality in status prevented them from full recognition of their similarities as women. Slave women in particular used their bonds with plantation mistresses as a means of aiding the slave community, which held their primary allegiance. Similarly, many plantation mistresses were unwilling to challenge the racist assumptions of their culture and could not imagine identifying with slaves. Plantation mistresses were inspired by the racism and paternalism of white men as well as by the ideology of domesticity in their thinking about slaves. The result of these conflicting motivations was a society in which differences of race and status easily overcame any tentative awareness of similarities based on gender.

For the most part, both slave and slaveholding men recognized that gender separated women's experiences from their own, but both failed to realize that gender had the potential to unite women. As a result, the bonds women did share were often rendered invisible, as was their role in shaping antebellum South Carolina society. Cornelius Holmes pointed to the significant role gender played in reinforcing other distinctions when he spoke to a WPA interviewer:

> Slavery did de white race a whole lot a good but it wasn't lastin' good. It did de Negro good, dat will be lastin' good forever. De Negro women protected de pure white women from enticement and seduction of de white man in slavery time. My grandpap says he never heard of a bad white woman befo freedom. I leave it wid you if

dere's any dese times? Dat was worth more to de South, my grandpap say, dis sanctification of de white women, than all de cotton and corn dat de Negroes ever makes, in all de years of slavery times. My grandpap say no race can rise higher than its women. De future of de Negro race, depends on its mothers.[56]

His views were shared by former Maryland slave Richard Macks: "Let me explain to you very plain without prejudice one way or the other. I have had many opportunities, a chance to watch white men and women in my long career, colored women have had many hard battles to fight to protect themselves from assault by employers, white male servants or by white men, many times not being able to protect, in fear of losing their positions. Then on the other hand they were subjected to many impositions by the women of the household through woman's jealousy."[57] Both of these men recognized that sexual tension divided slave women and plantation mistresses. Neither, however, seemed aware of the ways gender-based experiences might join women. As a result of this insensibility, assumptions about women as well as the forces that separated them were strengthened and the bonds between women consequently weakened. Male domination, racism, and slavery were simply too deeply entrenched to be overcome by the tenuous ties that united women.

 ~

Relationships between female slaves and plantation mistresses on large plantations originated in work patterns and the interactions they permitted among women. Work patterns for women who lived in South Carolina cities and on small plantations and farms, however, diverged, and as a result these women had distinct views of themselves and one another.[58]

    Female slaves in urban areas were for the most part highly skilled and often relatively autonomous house servants. Those who lived with wealthy families worked closely with their mistresses to maintain the elaborate homes and luxurious style of living characteristic of the urban elite. Wealthy white women, some of whom spent long periods living on plantations, viewed their city homes as relatively relaxed and comfortable. As a result, female slaves and wealthy mistresses in cities felt more goodwill for one another, although this was subject, as always, to the whims of circumstance, sexual jealousy, and personality. Wealthy white women found little in city life to prevent them from feeling sympathetic toward black women and acting on their impulses; they also knew that kindliness was more likely than harshness to elicit the cooperation they desired. These mistresses were fully aware of the ideology of domesticity and had fewer restrictions on their ability to put it into practice. Letitia Burwell acknowledged this behavior in her memoirs, in which she wrote of the urban families she knew and visited, "whose kindness to their slaves was unmistakable, and who, owning only a small number, could better afford to indulge them."[59] For wealthy mistresses in the cities, generosity toward trusted slaves was a relatively simple matter.

African-American women who worked closely with wealthy urban women were frequently aware of their value to their mistresses and the privileges they enjoyed. When compared with plantation slaves they were likely to agree with their mistresses' assessment of them as elite. Although the expectations for them were dissimilar, they were still demanding. In a letter to her sister, Fannie Colcock of Charleston acknowledged the harmony anticipated between mistress and slave in the city when she complained about her seamstress: "She has acted so badly that I am not willing to keep her about me. If we can't sell her, we will send her to the plantation. She would suit me exactly, if I lived in the country, but not so, in town."[60] A reciprocal relationship developed in which white women chose or retained slaves for their competence and the quality of their personal affinity with their mistresses and black women took pride in their long years of service to one family and the dependence whites claimed to have on them. As a result, the potential for women to share a common perspective was much greater in the city than on the plantation.

The harmonious quality of the relationships wealthy urban mistresses enjoyed with their female slaves can most easily be observed in the wills the white women wrote. Although most men and women did not write wills at all and in spite of the legal restrictions on married women's ownership of property, approximately one-quarter of the surviving antebellum wills in South Carolina were written by women. Some wealthy urban women wrote wills to arrange for the disposition of their material goods and the protection of their dependent children.[61] In addition, many tried to make arrangements for their slaves. Although partially obscured by legal jargon, the language they used reveals their sentiments toward their slaves and hints at the ways they believed slaves felt about them.

Many wealthy urban women chose to leave to their slaves a portion of their material goods, usually clothing and household items, or a small amount of money.[62] More frequently, the new owners of slaves were enjoined to treat them kindly, usually as a return for the kindness the will writers believed had been directed at them. Josephine Ferrette of Charleston gave a slave woman to a niece and her daughter, "trusting to their honor and tenderness to support her and consult her happiness." Jane O'Daniel willed a black woman to the daughter of a friend, stating, "It is my wish that my Negro woman Auber should be rewarded for her faithfulness to me [so she should] be treated with especial kindness and favor in token of her services to me."[63] Sometimes will writers made financial provisions for the care of the slaves they bequeathed. Mary Winthrop of Charleston willed her servant Clara and Clara's children to her sisters and "recommend[ed] her to their particular care on account of her long and faithful service to me." She directed that her executors apply "the three shares I have in the Planters and Mechanic's Bank" to care for Clara and her family. Elizabeth Lowndes's will gave her slave Maria to her daughter and directed her executors to pay the daughter seventy-five dollars a year "for the benefit of Maria."[64] Sometimes mistresses made stronger efforts to secure the financial and personal well-being of their slaves. Eliza Mackey willed two female slaves to a friend, but included a provision clearly designed to protect them: "John Cromer shall treat my said Negroes Nancy and Eve kindly but if he shall abuse and ill use them it is my will that they will be immediately taken away by my Executors."[65]

Although South Carolina law forbade willing money directly to slaves or setting them free, a few mistresses tried to make slaves as independent and as free as possible by the terms of their wills. Eliza Swinton arranged that her slave Rosella and family, "in reward of the great fidelity of my Said Servants and in testimony of my sense of their dutiful conduct," should be treated "with every degree of kindness and indulgence and [allowed] to dispose of their own time as far as the Laws of the State will permit so that without being free they may be spared as much as possible from the hardships of Servitude. If at any time it may be lawful so to do I request my said legatees . . . to emancipate Rosella and her family and their issue."[66] Margaret Laurens left a fifteen-year-old African-American woman money and requested her executors to serve as the slave's guardian while she worked out. Her will directed them to "aid and assist her in any way they can in her occupation and business and I further direct that her taxes, doctors bills and professional advice and council be paid out of my Estate. I direct that she be allowed to work out and the wages she makes be applied to her support and that of her children should she have any & that her children be placed under her care and the profits of their work be applied to their support . . . and they be allowed to move away from the State should it be for their advantage to do so."[67] Some will writers stipulated that slaves not be sold or families separated.[68] Women such as Laurens and Swinton who made elaborate arrangements for the protection of their slaves clearly viewed them with benevolence and respect and felt a moral obligation to ensure their well-being. Like other wealthy urban women, they had both the means and the desire to offer amenities to the female slaves they believed were so devoted to them.

Not all wealthy women were as generous with their emotions and money as Laurens and Swinton, nor were all slaves of such women recipients of their generosity. The slaves who were granted the nearest thing the law allowed to freedom were a privileged few who were often too old to enjoy their freedom for long. They had earned that privileged status by their years of devotion and were fortunate enough to have mistresses able to implement their ideals. Most wealthy urban mistresses were willing to allow only a small number of slaves such favor, usually those with whom they had worked and lived with mutual interdependence for a considerable period of time.

The attitudes of urban female slaves toward their mistresses are more difficult to determine. There were relatively few of them in South Carolina, and they left few records. Pauline Worth, whose mother, siblings, and one elderly man were the only slaves of a shopkeeper in Marion, remembered "old Missus provide good livin for us all de time. Wouldn' let nobody suffer for nothin be dat she know bout it."[69] Urban mistresses assumed that their feelings of affection were reciprocated, but occasionally experienced doubts.[70] Like many slaves, those with wealthy urban mistresses may have appeared devoted but for the most part kept their own counsel. Even so, their close interaction with their mistresses coupled with their mistresses' ability to make their lives in a relatively pleasant urban environment more comfortable made them likely to feel a degree of personal loyalty to the white women they knew so well.

Female slaves with less wealthy urban mistresses, as well as those on small plantations and farms, were not as privileged.[71] Their work lives were distinguished by the rigor and flexibility required when there were only a small number of slaves to do the necessary tasks. As a result, they worked even more closely with white women than other house servants did. For the most part, mistresses with only a few slaves did not have the means to treat them with the benevolence of wealthier women. Although these white women perhaps aspired to the ideology of domesticity, putting it into practice was only sometimes possible.

Less wealthy mistresses were probably not as aware of the ideology of domesticity and its implications because they were less likely to read the novels and magazines in which it was propounded. Not all women were literate, and even those who were did not necessarily have the leisure to read. They also may not have had the means or the time to function as benevolent mediators of slavery. With access to the labor of only a small number of slaves, these women assumed more housekeeping tasks themselves. While those tasks may not have been as extensive as in larger and wealthier households, domestic work was still rigorous enough to leave little time to attend to slaves' needs. Allowing a black woman even a brief respite required a white woman to find someone to do the extra work. When few slaves were present, that someone was more likely than not to be the mistress herself, who already considered herself overburdened. Also, extra goods and time away from the fields were resources few white men were willing to allow their wives to squander on slaves. Under such circumstances, few white women could afford the luxury of benevolence.

White women whose authority extended to only a small number of slaves were unable to offer them the same material and personal inducements to good behavior that wealthier women could and unfortunately the ideology of domesticity did not inspire in them the same sense of responsibility for slaves' well-being it did in wealthier women. David Gavin complained bitterly about his overseer's wife, who demanded that black women do her washing and other domestic work but was frequently brutal to them: "Mrs. Griffin has been cutting high capers this evening, as soon as I left the house or yard she fell aboard one of my little Negroes, Rachael and beat her unmercifully, with her feet and hands. She has been making a fuss on the place ever since she has been here, she commenced first with the large Negroes and now without any cause has beat this little Negro." Amos Gadsden, born a slave to a wealthy man in Charleston, claimed that neighbors who did not own slaves "hired negro help and ill-treated them—old mistress felt so bad about this."[72]

Being on a small plantation was not always harder, however, for sometimes black women turned the flexibility inherent in being part of a small number of slaves to their advantage. Former slave Sylvia Cannon, who served as a nurse, claimed her mistress had been good to her: "Many a time my Missus go work in de field en let me mind de chillun." Nancy Washington, her mother, and seven siblings were the only slaves belonging to a man who claimed not to want "no man colored peoples," according to Washington. When interviewed by the WPA, she was quick to point out that "my white folks hab uh nice plantation en dey keep uh nice house aw the time." When Washington was shifted from house work to field work, she "wuz shame" that her mistress had to suffer "cause I ne'er lak fa he to treat my Missus dat uh way." Washington was clearly aware of the consequences of being a small slaveholder not only for her mistress but for herself as well. She spoke of a neighbor who had "uh big ole plantation wha' been jes lak uh little town. He hab hundred colored peoples en dey is hab eve't'ing dere. Hab dey preachin' right dere on de plantation en aw dat."[73] For these slaves, as for their mistresses, financial limitations meant hard work and the possibility of deprivation. All women's lives were shaped not only by gender and race, but by class as well.

Part 3: The War and Its Aftermath

At the beginning of the Civil War, few South Carolina women could have imagined its outcome. Freedom, long dreamed about and prayed for by black women, had become a reality, shattering the expectations and security of white women. The war and its aftermath challenged the capacity of the ideology of domesticity to shape race relations and brought to the surface the hostilities separating slave women and mistresses. By shifting priorities and redirecting loyalties, the war years and the period of transition to freedom marked the ending of one pattern of race relations between women and the emergence of another.

The old pattern died slowly in most parts of South Carolina because the major disruptions of war remained at a distance. As their circumstances changed gradually over the four long years, women's behavior toward one another shifted in response. Despite their best efforts to hold onto the old South, the absence of white men, the difficulty of finding food and clothing, and, eventually, the presence of Sherman's army led white women to focus their attention first on the needs of the Confederate Army and then on their own survival instead of on the ideology of domesticity. African-American women, responding to the increasing laxity of white authority, found new ways of caring for their families and communities.

These new patterns of race relations emerged only gradually. Although emancipation and the end of the war arrived simultaneously in most parts of South Carolina, assessing what that would mean—and acting upon it—took months. Generations of precedent had to be replaced with novel ways of interacting, a process as eagerly insisted upon by black women as it was desperately resisted by white women. The negotiations transformed the work patterns, expectations, and interactions of the antebellum years. Black women's determination to make their freedom meaningful coupled with white women's reluctance to acknowledge the reality and implications of emancipation brought a new antagonism to their dealings with one another. Racial hostility, never far beneath the surface before the war, would replace tolerance based on shared gender expectations as the defining assumptions of women's interactions.

8

The Experience of War

The Civil War began in South Carolina when Fort Sumter was fired upon in April 1861. It ended four years later when Sherman cut a path of destruction through the state, burning cities and plantations alike. In between, after the fall of the Sea Islands, not much fighting occurred on South Carolina soil. But for all of their physical removal from the battlefields, people who lived in the state experienced the war in dramatic ways. For mistresses and female slaves, the conflict was a test of domestic production skills and southern assumptions about womanhood.[1]

Most South Carolinians believed the state could leave the Union peacefully. When that hope proved illusory, they assumed the conflict would be brief. The North's intransigence soon demonstrated that the war would be long and its costs high. For most of the men of the planter elite, the principles for which the war was being fought justified the necessary sacrifices. For their wives, however, the issues were more complex. While many were ardent southern patriots and shared their fathers' and husbands' faith in the justice of the southern cause, many simultaneously regretted the necessity of violence and dreaded its consequences.

The Civil War likewise created a certain ambivalence for South Carolina slave women. Although eager for freedom, without the presence of nearby Union troops most African-American women spent the war years waiting to see what would happen.[2] At the same time, the thought that freedom might be near led some of them to behave very differently than they had before the eruption of war. Their previous cooperativeness, though usually qualified, was tempered even further by their mistresses' inability to provide them with much in return as well as by the absence of white male authority.

Even so, without a place to go or assurances that they would find support for themselves and their children, most black women stayed put.

Plantation mistresses and female slaves in South Carolina, far from Union troops, were spared the worst horrors of the period for the most part.[3] Relatively few South Carolina mistresses were subjected to the experience of Kate Stone, who spent much of the war as a refugee because her family's plantation in northeastern Louisiana was in an area controlled by Union troops.[4] Except for those who fled the Sea Islands early in the war and others who were forced to leave Charleston after a fire destroyed parts of the city in December 1861, South Carolina's elite white women did not become refugees in large numbers until near the end of the war. Unlike slaves in occupied areas, with their legal status unclear and white authority over them uncertain, most black women in South Carolina remained tied to their obligations. Because southern white authority was not challenged by a northern military presence in South Carolina until the last months of the war, the conflict's immediate impact on women's relationships in South Carolina was comparatively slight.[5]

As the war stretched out, of course, with many white men in the army, life changed significantly for the black and white women left behind. The fighting disrupted normal economic arrangements and created major changes in the supply of food and material goods.[6] Perhaps most difficult of all was the emotional uncertainty the war created in the minds of mistresses and slaves alike. Yet despite deprivation, fears, and hopes for the future, work patterns in most cases remained undisturbed until anticipation of Sherman's arrival shook the state. Although the Civil War represented a turning point in southern life, the changes it wrought in the state that led the way developed gradually.

∾

To most political observers, war had seemed imminent for months: if not since the election of Lincoln in November 1860 then at least since South Carolina seceded from the Union that December. Stirred by these events, many members of the planter elite hoped independence would eliminate external challenges to slavery once and for all, and if war were necessary to achieve it, it would be brief and glorious. But for mistresses and slaves, who were excluded from direct participation, secession and the outbreak of fighting raised questions about the continuation of daily patterns of living.[7]

In the early months of the war, daily life for South Carolina's plantation mistresses and female slaves remained virtually unchanged. Although many

white men rushed to enlist in the army, enough remained on large plantations to ensure the continuity of work and discipline. As a result, the primary responsibilities of mistresses and slaves did not change, but their labors were intensified at the war's beginning by urgent need to supply soldiers
with clothing and blankets. Domestic production stepped up and continued
with decreasing intensity throughout the war, representing the first shift in
the activities of South Carolina women.

Increased domestic production for the war effort began quickly. In May
1861, Julia Cumming wrote to her daughter about plans to go to her summer home: "We had to again defer our move to the Hill. After the boys
determined to go [to war], I have been so busy making flannel shirts etc. for
them that I had not taken time to think scarcely of going." Elizabeth Allen
Coxe described the labors of Julius Porcher's wife and slaves when he raised
a company of soldiers early in the war: "She made the uniforms for the entire company of eighty men—she and her coloured seamstresses. The wool
from their own sheep was spun into yarn. . . . This was then woven by her
women on hand looms, cut out by her own hands, and made by her and her
seamstresses. She cut them all out herself, and the brass Confederate but-
tons were the only things bought." Catherine Edmondston put her slaves
to work making uniforms for the soldiers. Emma Holmes, whose Charleston home was one of those destroyed by the fire that swept the city in 1861,
noted an aunt's efforts to economize by improving her domestic production
efficiency: "She made Oliver, her little Negro boy about twelve years old,
whom she taught to work on the sewing machine and make all kinds of garments on it, as well as to spin—go every day to the depot and pick up the
loose cotton lying about and spin it—then ravel and card up scraps of red
flannel & other woolen which he also spun. Then she paid a woman ten cents
a yard to weave it and made 14 yards of stout warm cloth—enough to clothe
him for a year—and at the cost of $1.40 and some trouble and perseverance."[8]

While not all mistresses exhibited such industry and ingenuity, many
white women described the war years as an unrelenting round of sewing,
knitting, and other forms of domestic production. The white women who
contributed to the volume of wartime memories published by the South
Carolina United Daughters of the Confederacy mentioned this work as a
constant refrain. One woman was described as a beautiful knitter: She "spent
all of her spare moments in knitting socks, scarfs, and helmets. Weaving and
making all kinds of garments was carried on exclusively in her household,
for she had many capable house servants. Often these articles were given to
needy soldiers." Another mistress fled the coast early in the war, but still
contributed to the cause: "I learned to spin and weave, and having taught

several of the servants to do the same, we managed to make one suit of clothes a year for each Negro. One of my single sisters and I spun all of the thread, and knitted all of the stockings and gloves for the family." Yet another woman depicted what she considered the heroic efforts of women: "There was work for all. While the mothers were looking after the carding and spinning that had to be done, not only to supply the family with clothing, but to send to the soldiers . . . the young girls were busy knitting socks, and making garments to send to the loved ones in the camp." For some women, increased domestic production meant not only making clothing but also growing additional food for hungry soldiers. Ellen Elmore remembered working with slaves to accomplish both these activities: "My business, as general housekeeper and provider, was to see to the parching and grinding of coffee, making of crackers, and filling of haversacks, in which I was heartily aided by our faithful cook Cynthia; while the other girls, being clever workwomen, with Nellie, Phillis, Phoebe, and others, made up the flannel Garibaldis and gray wool hunting shirts, which were thought indispensable at that time."[9]

For many plantation mistresses, expanding domestic production was not simply an individual commitment: the war opened opportunities to do familiar tasks in new ways. Catherine Edmondston applauded "the universality & the eagerness with which the women entered into the struggle! They worked as many of them had never worked before, steadily & faithfully, to supply the soldiers with clothing & the Hospitals with comforts of various kinds. . . . The Ladies all over the country had formed themselves into Hospital associations & were at work on quilted comfortables, shirts, drawers, etc. for the sick & wounded." She was sure that the members of the Ladies Soldiers Aid Society were "heart and soul in the cause."[10] In many cities, white women gathered in churches and other public buildings to sew for soldiers.[11] The women in Mary Robarts's community formed "an organization—a committee to purchase, four to cut, and all the others to make garments. . . . We furnished three companies this week." She claimed "Action is the order of the day. I do not think there is a woman or child asleep in the Confederacy. Sometimes I have hardly time to eat."[12] Many erstwhile plantation mistresses volunteered their services as nurses; Louisa McCord organized nurses at the military hospital at Columbia as well as devoted her plantation to the production of food crops.[13] Women organized fairs to raise money, contributing food, jewelry, handmade luxuries, and carefully hoarded delicacies. In 1862, women throughout South Carolina campaigned to raise funds for a gunboat, eventually named the *Palmetto State*.[14] White women also debated about politics to a much greater extent than before the war and did not necessarily confide their opinions only in other women.[15]

White men were quick to applaud these patriotic activities, viewing them as part of the obligations of womanhood. Only a few months after the war began, a writer in *DeBow's Review* complimented women who "with a prescience and a zeal surpassing that of men, urged on the present revolution, and who are now devoting all their energies and industry to clothe the soldier, to heal his wounds, to tend on him in sickness, and to relieve the wants of his family." Women saw "that the time for secession had come, and, with courage and fortitude . . . prepared to meet and to bear up against all the privations, all the dangers, and all the sufferings that secession and war might bring on. Too many of the men lagged behind. They now say the women, from the first, were right." Although before the war women were not supposed to interfere in politics, now they showed "clearly enough that they fully understood and appreciated the consequences of war, and were prepared to meet them, without fear or trembling."[16] Another writer claimed that the Confederacy was the best place "to elevate woman and to mitigate the evil of the primal curse pronounced against her." Women anticipated that the Confederacy would be the "beginning of a nobler, loftier career for Southern women" that would bring "great advantages"; this helped to make them "such bold advocates of secession."[17] Although these wartime comments offered no direct challenge to the ideology of domesticity, they did legitimize an expanded sphere of activity for women.

Questioning the proper behavior of women naturally followed, although this opposition most often took the form of a defense of tradition. In spite of what might have been expected, Catherine Edmondston reported that southern women had "not the slightest approach to repining or even a desire for their friends return." After the fall of New Orleans, she claimed: "We women must show the men that we are their equals—nay their superiors." Female patriotism became more active than ever before. Judith McGuire claimed that women "must all work for our country. . . . While men are making a free-will offering of their life's blood on the alter of their country, women must not be idle. We must do what we can for the comfort of our brave men. We must sew for them, knit for them, nurse the sick, keep up the faint-hearted, give them a word of encouragement in season and out of season." Mary Tucker Magill believed women viewed the Confederacy as a child: "As a mother clasps in her loving embrace her new-born child, and rejoices in its perfection of life and limb and that it is all her own, so did they love the 'Cause' in its new birth."[18] By defining women as men's supporters, these women echoed socially acceptable views of womanhood but placed them in a new context.

Other white women attempted to move beyond the traditional female sphere and found cultural limitations on acceptable behavior a source of frustration. Very few challenged the ideology of domesticity directly, but many chafed under the limitations it imposed on their behavior. Sarah Dawson's frustration left her uncharacteristically speechless: "Coward, helpless woman that I am! If I was free—!" Julia LeGrand was more expressive: "I am like a pent-up volcano. I wish I had a field for my energies. I hate common life, a life of visiting, dressing and tattling, which seems to devolve on women, and now that there is better work to do, real tragedy, real romance and history weaving every day, I suffer, suffer, leading the life I do." Leora Sims wrote a friend in November 1861 from her home in Columbia: "The women are getting ready for any emergency. I am going to get me a bowie knife or look for some weapon of defense. We do not feel afraid of the Yankees but we must be ready for anything. . . . The women may expect no quarter, and if I ever fall into their hands, I earnestly pray I may be enabled to give them one 'fire eater' to deal with." Kate Stone wished to become a soldier. Her comment just after the war began is typical of her sentiments to the end: "Oh! to see and be in it all. I hate weary days of inaction. Yet what can women do but wait and suffer?"[19] As late as February 1865, just days before Sherman burned Columbia on his march northward, Malvina Black Gist wrote in her diary about her desire to remain in the city: "It is high time I was having some experiences out of the ordinary, and if anything remarkable is going to happen, I want to know about it. . . . It is frightfully monotonous, just because you are a woman, to be always tucked away in the safe places. I want to stay. I want to have a taste of danger."[20]

Other young women lamented the impact of war on their lives. Seventeen-year-old Emma LeConte complained to her diary in 1865: "No pleasure, no enjoyment—nothing but rigid economy and hard work—nothing but the stern realities of life. These which should come later are made familiar to us at an age when only gladness should surround us. . . . I have seen little of the light-heartedness and exuberant joy that people talk about as the natural heritage of youth." She asked, "Why does not the President call out the women if there are [not] enough men?"[21] Most of the elite women who expressed these views were young and frustrated by watching their brothers march off to glory while they remained home sewing and knitting. Because they did not share the increased responsibilities of their mothers even though they shared their work, these young women complained about inactivity rather than recognizing that white women's traditional role had been expanded by the war.

Other white women recognized the changes the war brought, not because of the boredom of sewing and a dull social life, but because they were forced to earn a living for themselves. Few South Carolina women were able to take advantage of opportunities for employment by the government open to women in Richmond.[22] Women desperate for income took in sewing, sold the products of their gardens and ingenuity, and became governesses and teachers. In part because the fighting remained at a distance for so long, relatively few women of the South Carolina elite were forced to such measures; most whose sources of economic support disappeared were able to depend on the assistance of others.

As the war went on and absences of husbands, sons, and overseers became prolonged, plantation mistresses found even familiar work expanding to include new tasks. To maintain their plantations as profitable or even self-supporting enterprises, white women adopted a wide variety of duties formerly the province of men. Catherine Edmondston, for example, noted in her journal in 1862: "Today for the first time in my life, I weighed out the plantation Allowance."[23] Meta Morris Grimball fretted in her diary about her inability to obtain corn or rice to feed her slaves. Other mistresses learned to economize—and the necessity for it—for the first time. For Grace Brown Elmore, this was familiar by 1864: "Our economies have become second nature. I am as careful of a lump of sugar as I used to be of a pound. In my dreams I am tantalized by seeing cake and candy, which I never taste."[24] Another mistress remembered white women's wartime improvisation: "The women of the household on every plantation were the power that evolved something out of nothing, and from the slimmest materials fashioned great comforts, rendering it possible for all the men to be away at the front while they ran the plantations, and raised the crops that fed the armies."[25] Elizabeth Pringle's mother began extensive domestic production early in the war but could not limit her activities to those associated with the female sphere. In July 1863 the family fled Charleston for the safety of Darlington County: "Mamma at once began to plant the farm and garden, with the house-servants, and made wonderful crops."[26]

Mistresses whose husbands and sons were killed, wounded, captured, or away in the army had no choice but to run plantations, either alone or with overseers. Adele Allston managed her family's plantation before and after her husband's death in the last year of the war; Ellen Elmore did the same as well as running a lumber mill that enabled her to supply the Confederacy with heavy timber.[27] Catherine Edmondston complained about the difficulties of supervising the slaves she assigned to sort and dry cotton that had mildewed: "It needs the closest attention. I find if I leave them a half hour they neglect it. . . . I wish Mr. E. was at home. Master's eye and voice are more potent than Mistress's." She was grateful when he provided "minute directions about his business & the management of the Plantation during his absence, so I hope I will be able to carry it on as it should be done whilst he is gone." Mack Taylor, born a slave on a low-country rice plantation, remembered one consequence of wartime disruptions: "Old marster got kilt in de last year of de war, and Miss Margaret, dat was our Mistress, run de place wid overseers dat would thrash you for all sorts of things."[28] In spite of deprivation and unaccustomed labor, plantation mistresses worked hard to maintain an image of normal life. When Josephine Clay Habersham's son arrived home unexpectedly with seven friends, she tried to show them that she was pleased: "Fortunately, I was nicely dressed in a Spring-like lilac muslin, and not some old country trim! It made all the difference in the world! I could receive them without having to rush off to make myself presentable."[29]

The appearance of a normal life eroded significantly as time wore on and the war caused greater disruption in daily life. Many white women found themselves refugees in unfamiliar surroundings or with less than a full complement of trained household slaves. As a result, mistresses did a good deal of unexpected domestic work. A refugee in Camden, Emma Holmes had many new experiences during the war. In July 1863 she noted in her diary some of her additional tasks: "During the past week I have tried several new trades, as Sarah was suddenly taken & Joe, after losing a pound of tea $12 worth, was afraid to come home & was finally brought back after two days absence. So I turned chamber maid & even laundress, as we found it difficult to procure a washerwoman & besides they charge so extravagantly." A year later she added several other skills to her repertoire: "For 5 days, Marcus, Patty & Julianne have been sick so I have taken some practical lessons in housekeeping & minding babies. How thankful I am that I am neither cook nor nurse."[30] Emily Hammond sympathized with the plight of a relative: "Kate's nurse left her last night, and she feels quite bowed down with care and responsibility." Mary Chesnut found herself in the same situation shortly after the fighting began: "Then Molly's baby is ill. . . . I had to see the cows fed in Molly's place." Late in the war, while a refugee in North Carolina, Chesnut again noted new domestic activities: "Today dirt has given me a black eye. I have fought a hard battle with that dread antagonist, and it is rather a drawn battle. Ellen has my washing to do, as well as my cooking. So I have elected to do some housework. I must needs make my own tea." A few days later she noted the results of her labors: "Ellen is a maid—comme il y en a peu—and if I do a little work it is quite enough to show me how dreadful it would be without her *if I should have to do it all.*"[31] Well within the boundaries of the female sphere, this work offered many mistresses their first glimpse of what life without slaves would be like.

To the extent possible, whites tried to enforce familiar work patterns on slaves during the fighting. Overseer's reports sent to Adele Allston throughout the war indicate that slaves worked according to typical prewar patterns.[32] Gordon Bluford, a black woman born in 1844, described her work during the war in terms that could easily describe a prewar experience: "At nights I carded and spinned on the mistress's wheels, helping my mammy. . . . I worked in the big house, washed, ironed, cleaned up, and was nurse in the house when the war was going on."[33] Manda Walker, born only a few years before the fighting erupted, was initiated into plantation labor in a way that was familiar to many older slaves: "I no work much 'til de end of de war. Then I pick cotton and peas and shell corn and peas. Most of de time I play and sometime be maid to my young misses."[34] But such familiar patterns masked a growing breakdown in work discipline.

Early in the war, when white women's enthusiasm was high and supplies plentiful, slave women were expected to sew for the soldiers. Kate Crawford remembered that even the youngest of her slaves made sand bags, while another mistress recalled the efforts of slave women for a wartime sewing circle: "Mine made fourteen pairs of drawers in a week for that association, and never seemed hurried."[35] No matter how they appeared to their mistresses, blacks were aware that they were sewing for the soldiers rather than themselves, which undoubtedly slowed their fingers.

Later, as the conflict raged on, mistresses' enthusiasm for domestic production, even for needy soldiers, waned along with reserves of necessary materials. With less cloth to sew and less food to preserve, many African-American women fell into inactivity. On at least two occasions in mid-1864, Adele Allston's overseer wrote to her about the enforced idleness of black women on her plantation: "Hagor & Sary is doing nothing if had some Cotton I would make them Spin." Field work also diminished in intensity. In 1863, Charles Colcock Jones Jr. reported that "the girls and women are succeeding very well in ploughing; Miley is preeminently successful," an apparently remarkable occurrence.[36] Whenever possible, slaves sought to take advantage of mistresses' growing difficulty in compelling their labor. When the consequences were not too severe, they accomplished less than before the war began.

Always hard workers, plantation mistresses found that the disruptions of war added significantly to both their responsibilities and the labor it was necessary to perform. Forced to fill in for absent men and increasingly un-reliable slaves, mistresses experienced the war years as a constant round of difficult and unaccustomed tasks. The increasing deprivation was difficult to manage or even understand, particularly when it meant not just doing without clothing or coffee, but outright hunger.

For slave women, to whom deprivation was all too familiar, the war brought unprecedented want and misery. Unlike mistresses, slaves worked and lived under circumstances rather similar to those of antebellum times, but with slaveholders distracted and slaves' hopes for freedom high, their daily experiences took on new meaning. Masters, the usual source of author-ity on the plantation, were often absent, and their replacements were fre-quently inexperienced and sometimes rather ineffective in imposing labor discipline. Although slave women were expected to perform more work than before, they could not always be made to do so, and much of it was sewing and other forms of domestic production. In other words, as the war went on slave women did the same sort of work they had always done—but less of it—while mistresses did not only more work, but also new kinds of work. That difference was crucial in shaping the changing relations between the two groups of women.

⌁

Even though sympathy based on gender—when it existed—did not disap-pear from the minds of plantation mistresses with the firing of the first shots at Fort Sumter, white women did begin to think carefully about the behav-ior of their slaves and their interactions with them. What many had taken for granted before the war was no longer possible. Some white women who previously believed they held common bonds with black women began to view them with trepidation. From the very beginning, the emotional dis-tance between mistresses and female slaves began to seem wider, if only because it was becoming more visible.

Ada Bacot sensed the disruptive consequences of the war on her dealings with her slaves two months before the fighting: "I find some of my young Negroes have been disobeying my orders, they were found away from home with out a pass. I hope I may be able to make them understand without much trouble, that I am Mistress & will be obeyed. I have never had any trouble with them until now. Even now I don't apprehend much." Bacot's hopes proved unfounded. A few days after the war began she punished a slave. Her comment in her journal is revealing: "My very soul revolted at the very idea, but I knew if I let it pass I would have more trouble so I thought the best way was to have a stop put to it at once. I hope I shall have nothing more of it." A few months later she was still complaining in frustrated tones about the behavior of her slaves. Only in September 1861 did she realize the war might change the way she interacted with her slaves, but even then she backed away from full acknowledgment of what could happen. Her reaction was provoked by reports that a neighbor woman had been smothered to death by blacks: "I can't get it out of my mind. We none of us know when we are safe. I have some [slaves] about me that I fear would take very little to make them put me out of the way. I don't mean any of my home servants for I think they are all very fond of me."[37] Although Bacot's fear subsided, events during the early months of the war challenged her belief in the possibility of harmonious relationships between mistresses and slaves.

Like Ada Bacot, Keziah Brevard was aware of changes in her associations with her slaves even before the fighting began. Believing that war would mean the end of slavery no matter who won, she agonized about the morality of slavery as well as her difficulty with individual slaves: "My God!! My God!! Save us from wars within. Oh our Negroes how much we have to bear with from them. I have some I scarce ever get a civil word from, no matter how kind and indulgent I am to them. . . . Sylvia if slavery continues I hope no relative of mine will keep you about them. Nothing on this earth can change your heart—it is a bad one. The truth is Sylvia hates a white face." As war became imminent, Brevard's panic mounted. Almost the last entry in her diary was written just days before the firing on Fort Sumter: "We know not what moment we may be hacked to death in the most cruel manner by our slaves. Oh god devise a way for us to get rid of them quietly & let us all be better Christians. . . . I think a desperate state of things wait at the South. Our Negroes are far more knowing than many will acknowledge. I had a little Negro girl about the house . . . [who] told me I did not know how my Negroes hated white folks & how they talked about me."[38]

A few mistresses did not acknowledge changes in the behavior of their slaves, at least at the beginning of the war. Six weeks after it began, Julia Cumming wrote to her daughter about the illness of her mammy. "The poor old soul looks most wretchedly but you cannot induce her to lie down or eschew action. Her cough is perfectly awful. Are these not dismal times in every way." When Catherine Edmondston's husband summoned his slaves before his departure for war, she noted that he "charged them in his absence to remember their duty to me and to give me no trouble. They were much affected. . . . They entreated me not to leave them & I have promised to remain at home & take what care I can of them."[39]

Far more common was the reaction of Mary Chesnut, who during the firing on Fort Sumter noticed both the appearance of harmony between mistresses and slaves and the uncertainty that lay beneath it: "Not by one word or look can we detect any change in the demeanor of these Negro servants. Lawrence sits at our door, as sleepy and as respectful and as profoundly indifferent. So are they all. They carry it too far. You could not tell that they hear even the awful row that is going on in the bay, though it is dinning in their ears night and day. And people talk before them as if they were chairs and tables. And they make no sign. Are they stolidly stupid or wiser than we are, silent and strong, biding their time?" Like Ada Bacot, Chesnut was stunned and horrified by the murder of her cousin Betsey Witherspoon in September 1861. Among other concerns, the murder forced her to worry about her own safety, although she struggled hard to recover her equilibrium and belief in the harmony between mistresses and slaves: "We ought to be grateful that any one of us is alive. But nobody is afraid of their own Negroes. These are horrid brutes—savages, monsters—but I find everyone like myself, ready to trust their own yard. I would go down on the plantation tomorrow and stay there, if there were no white person in twenty miles. My Molly and half a dozen others that I *know*—and all the rest I believe—would keep me as safe as I should be in the Tower of London." A month after the murder, she was critical of her mother-in-law's fear of being poisoned by slaves, although she and her sister "sat up and talked the long night through" when the murder was first discovered.[40] Chesnut could not detect any change in the behavior of her slaves or in her reactions to them after the fall of Port Royal in November 1861, but she felt her inability to read their minds:

> Their faces are as unreadable as the sphinx. Certainly they are unchanged in their good conduct. That is, they are placid, docile, kind, and obedient. Also as lazy and dirty as ever. . . . Mrs. Reynolds and Mrs. Withers, two of the very kindest and most considerate of slave-owners, aver that the joy of their Negroes at the fall of Port Royal is loud and open. . . . There is no change of any kind whatever with ours. The Chesnut Negroes are spoiled to a degree, but then, they have such good manners, they are so polite you forget everything else. And they make you so comfortable if you can afford ten to do the work of one servant.[41]

Mistresses who pretended not to see changes in their relationships with slaves early in the war frequently dismissed notions that their attitudes toward slavery had changed. Frightened by the war, they made elaborate efforts at denial so as to retain their emotional equilibrium. Ardent southern nationalism, doubts about some of the ramifications of slavery, and fears about their safety and the future combined in the minds of many plantation mistresses to produce intellectual and emotional confusion that began to be felt even before the outbreak of war. In August 1860, Lucilla McCorkle was inspired by political events to a defense of slavery in her diary: "Much excitement prevailing in reference to politics & insurrection. Black republicanism likely to give us much trouble. . . . As a class [slaves] are comparatively happy. No cares & no concern for the future." Susan Cornwall did not think slaves wanted freedom: "Not a single pulse among them throbs at the thought of freedom as offering them a wider sphere for the exercise of God-given faculties." As the war drew closer, Keziah Brevard wished for a peaceful end to slavery at the same time that she feared her slaves:

> [9 November 1860] I have never been opposed to giving up slavery if we could send them out of our country.

> [21 December 1860] How unhappy I feel about my country['s] rash move—my God let us get rid of slavery—this is my prayer.

> [22 December 1860] Can we doubt Gods protection. There have been several houses this week without a white gentleman at home & yet we are safe—has not our God been with us?

> [8 January 1861] Any Adams thinks our slaves will be faithful to us in the crisis should it come. . . . I have walked through the clearing twice today. I am not happy & can not think myself safe. Every time I wake in the night I think of my State being out of the Union. If my voice could have prevented—it would never have seceded alone.

These ambivalent sentiments were shared in large measure by Mary Chesnut, who recognized that war would mean an end to slavery no matter what its other outcomes. In April 1861 she consoled a maid upset with her husband with promises of freedom, but by June her feelings about slavery were more ambivalent: "Read Soulouque, the Haitian man. It has a wonderful interest just now. Slavery has to go, of course—and joy go with it. These Yankees may kill us and lay waste the land for a while, but conquer us? Never!" She pretended not to understand why slaves did not "all march over the border, where they would be received with open arms," to the evident dismay of the northern army:

> At any rate, they have found they cannot trust to help from the black brother. He will not rise and cut our throats in the rear. They are not really enemies of their masters—and yet I believe they are all spies for the other side. Inconsistent?
>   There is woman's logical, lucid talk for you—and yet it is all true, if a little confused.[42]

Chesnut's insistence on her own confused logic regarding slaves and slavery was unusual only because of her awareness of it. Her inconsistent sentiments were echoed by many other mistresses early in the war. As women, they were encouraged to sympathize with the slaves whose living conditions they tried to ameliorate; as southerners, they supported the Confederate cause with unquestioning enthusiasm. Their efforts at balancing these tendencies led them to the kind of "logical, lucid talk" Chesnut referred to so ironically.

Gradually, as the war lengthened from one year to two, then three, then four, plantation mistresses found their interactions with their slaves and their attitudes toward slavery changing. Even with reality staring them in the face a few continued to insist that nothing was different. In November 1862, Catherine Edmondston noted in her diary: "There is not a white soul within five miles of me & eighty-eight negroes immediately around me! What becomes of the dread of a servile insurrection in view of the fact that I have not a sensation of fear?"[43] As late as October 1863, Josephine Habersham could congratulate herself on the comfort and order her slaves created: "How little trouble I have, how little confusion, because of the good servants. My husband is very generous to me in this matter." In August of that year, Caroline Howard Gilman, who had fled Charleston for Greenville, reported "among the negroes, you would still not think of war. . . . The same merry laugh is heard, the same willing labor seen."[44]

Even if they wanted to, most white women could not remain blind to the changes in their relationships with their slaves. Mistresses experienced the shift most directly in their war-induced inability to act as mediators. As blockaded ports and the need to supply the army reduced the ability of even the most wealthy mistresses to provide comforts for African Americans, the plantation dynamic underwent a subtle conversion. With fewer amenities and burgeoning hope of freedom, black women grew bolder and less cooperative. As their behavior altered, fear of slaves began to intensify, although few rumors or actual incidents of rape, murder, or other violence ever surfaced. Fear mixed with anxieties about new wartime responsibilities, the fate of absent men, and the future of the Confederacy pushed many mistresses to modify their views and their actions.

One way this shift could be seen was in some mistresses' efforts to please their slaves. Once slaves had more reasons to escape and fewer to remain, some mistresses began to treat them in a conciliatory way. The consequences were significant for Fannie Page Hume in December 1862: "We adopted the *two meal system* today, in order to give the servants more time—had dinner & supper together just before dark."[45] When she fled Charleston, Meta Morris Grimball arranged for a housemaid to accompany her "to please her husband Adam." A year before the war ended, Grimball received through the blockade a precious box of shoes, cloth, pins, thread, and the like from a son in England. She gave each of her female slaves a yard of the cloth for an apron. Mary Chesnut sent her maid from Columbia to Camden in 1862 because her child was ill: "She is to come back or stay as she pleases, for though I cannot well do without her, she would be a nuisance if she were dissatisfied. Everything depends upon the health of that child, I daresay."[46] Although these mistresses maintained an attitude of benevolence toward slaves, there was a note of exasperation or reluctance in their words, as if they were loathe to offer blacks privileges that were either unheard of or not balked at before the fighting broke out.

Other white women were surprised by qualities in black women that earlier would not have seemed unusual. When Caroline Ravenel saw a friend's elderly mammy in Charleston midway through the war, she was pleased to be recognized and eager to inform her friend: "I think it would have been such a pleasure to her to see you, Bell. She seemed so glad to have someone to talk to."[47] Emma Holmes's family temporarily took in five children and their two servants six months before the war ended and were unusually impressed by their nurse: "We were quite taken by surprise, but they proved a most interesting and remarkably well behaved set. . . . Minta, their nurse [is] a perfect mint of comfort—more like a humble companion than servant yet never forgetting her place. She is really pretty. . . . She was dressed as neatly as any of us & was so thoughtful of everything."[48]

As the war dragged on and anxiety and responsibility took their toll, slaves and slavery became ever more unpleasant problems and were openly criticized. A year before peace was declared, one mistress found the jewelry she thought her slaves had stolen, but discovering their innocence did not prevent her from criticizing them:

> I do hope the Servts. are doing better. They will go on with their follies & sins until they suddenly find the balance so heavy against them that they will be ruined in character and position, whistled off as useless, got rid of as rats & cockroaches are by all sorts of means whenever they become unbearable. I hoped they would have come out well on this occasion. I think those missing broaches are in the middle drawer of grandms.'s dressing table. It flashed through me & was an immense relief as I thought on the peccadilloes of the establishment.

Close to the end of the war, the same woman considered selling some of her slaves: "As for Charlotte she will do as she chooses & if it proves very bad, as I daresay it will, [my daughter] Bell's heart will not break if I sell her. Sometimes I feel as if it would be wise to relieve oneself of a good many drags. But I am too sad & worried to think about it just now."[49] Others were convinced that slaves whom they had considered relatively honest were turning into thieves. Sarah Putnam reported that blacks in Richmond commonly stole valuables, then disappeared themselves; this was particularly distressing when the slave was one in whom the mistress "placed implicit confidence, whose honesty and fidelity had been tested by years of trial, and on whom the mistress relied perfectly." However, she consoled herself that "troubles from the demoralization of the negroes were of a character less remarkable, and by far less annoying than could have been reasonably expected."[50] Belle Kearney was grateful that her mother's slave woman Sally kept northern troops from stealing silver she had helped to hide, but her manner was hardly comforting to the white woman. Sally told the soldiers there was no silver: "'Dey am de *stingiest* white folks yo' ebber sot yo' two eyes on.'"[51]

On at least one occasion six months before Lee's surrender Gertrude Thomas was so upset by war news that she claimed to be unable to continue to work with her slaves: "I had also been superintending the cutting out of some clothes for the plantation but I concluded to go out and divert my mind." As the war progressed and the southern cause seemed more and more hopeless mistresses such as Thomas strengthened their antislavery sentiments. Even a good day could bring new convictions. On a morning when the news was tolerable, her slaves did their assigned tasks, and she was able to work, Thomas found herself writing more vehement antislavery sentiments than ever before:

> What troubles me more than any thing else is that I am not certain that *Slavery* is *right*. The doctrine of self government I suppose of course to be right and yet our Southern people do not appear to have learned the art, even if they had the right granted them. . . . But as to the doctrine of slavery altho I have read very few abolition books (Uncle Toms Cabin making the most impression) nor have I read many pro slavery books—yet the idea has gradually become more and more fixed in my mind that the institution of slavery is not right. . . . Owning a large number of slaves as we do I might be asked why I do not free them? This if I could, I would not do, but if Mr. Thomas would sell them to a man who would look after their temporal and *spiritual* interest I would gladly do so. Those house servants we have if Mr. Thomas would agree to it I would pay regular wages but this is a subject upon which I do not like to think and taking my stand upon the moral view of the subject, I can but think that to hold men and women in *perpetual* bondage is wrong.

Thomas retracted her statement a week later, claiming that she must have been "badly whipped" and her mind so preoccupied that she was "not able to reason calmly," although in fact her confusion was quite common. It was shared at about the same time by Grace Brown Elmore in her own diary: "If we lost everything I believe I'd prefer the servants leaving us. Being without money, we would find it impossible to provide for so many, and they would be a trouble and a care. Poor things, I am truly sorry for them. As a class, so ignorant, so confiding, so easily deceived. They have lost the bliss of ignorance, and are not capable of becoming wise." Mary Chesnut, who had questioned the morality of slavery from the beginning, became somewhat more ambivalent as time went on. She reminded herself about the advantages of the institution during a visit to Charleston: "Those old gray-haired darkies and their automatic noiseless perfection of training—one does miss that sort of thing. Your own servants think for you, they know your ways and your wants; they save you all responsibility, even in matters of your own ease and well-being. Eben the butler at Mulberry would be miserable and feel himself a ridiculous failure, were I ever forced to ask him for anything." On the same day, in August 1864, Chesnut both praised her servants and criticized them:

> I have excellent servants. No matter for shortcomings behind my back. They save me all thought as to household matters, and they are so kind and attentive and quiet.

> It takes these half-Africans but a moment to go back to their naked, savage animal nature.[52]

Such contradictory sentiments reflected white women's growing confusion as they struggled to reconcile their prewar concern for blacks and doubts about slavery, their commitment to the Confederacy, their fears for themselves and the future, and their anxiety about what they perceived as the growing recalcitrance of slaves.

Some mistresses reacted to worsening war news with increased commitment to the institution. When Catherine Edmondston heard of plans to offer slaves emancipation in return for enlisting in the army, she was horrified: "We give up a principle when we offer emancipation as a boon or reward, for we have hitherto contended that Slavery was Cuffee's normal condition, the very best position he could occupy, the one of all others in which he was the happiest, & to take him from that & give him what we think misery in the place of it, is to put ourselves in the wrong essentially. No! freedom for whites, slavery for negroes, God has so ordained it!"[53] Mary Jones, widow of Presbyterian minister Charles Colcock Jones, feared that with the emancipation of slaves "must come their extermination" because they were "incapable of self-government." Even in January 1865, she believed that "if ever we gain our independence there will be radical reforms in the system of slavery as it now exists. . . . We shall be free to make and enforce such rules and reformations as are just and right."[54] Like her husband, Jones believed the practice of slavery needed to be modified to bring it more into line with Christian principles.

In the winter of 1865, the armies drew closer to South Carolina. For the most part insulated from direct fighting until William T. Sherman extended his sweep through Georgia into their state, South Carolinians experienced in the last months of war the fear, confusion, and upheaval that had plagued others much earlier. For many mistresses, anticipation of the arrival of Sherman and Yankee troops could have only one consequence: flight. In the last four months of the fighting, many who could find the means to do so fled to whatever relative safety they could find. Many urban white women chose to spend most of the war years on their family-owned plantations; others, particularly those from Charleston, sought safety among family and friends. Emma Holmes, for example, fled Charleston for the Camden area after the devastating 1861 fire destroyed her home; Meta Morris Grimball left both her home in Charleston and her nearby plantation to live in rooms at St. Johns College in Spartanburg.[55] Once established in their temporary homes with a few slaves, these women lived out the war years quietly, at least until the anxious times inspired by Sherman. Flight suddenly clarified some mistresses' confused feelings about slaves and slavery. Facing danger and humiliation as a result of a war about slavery, they rapidly lost the remnants of their benevolence and the sense of shared femaleness that they had felt for black women.[56]

By the winter of 1865, many mistresses found their slaves' behavior as perplexing as the failure of the once glorious Confederate cause. Many slaves, who had appeared loyal for nearly four years, took advantage of the confusion caused by the proximity of Yankee troops and fled the plantations, leaving behind mistresses who felt betrayed and angry. By the end of February, Susan Jervey was terrified: "What I most fear is not the Yankees, but the Negroes, cut off from all help from across the river, and at their mercy, what will become of us? Disorder has already started. Aunt Nenna's people have all returned to their work, except Edward; the leader, I firmly believe. . . . When she sent word he must come, he decamped and has not been heard from since." Her friend Charlotte Ravenel shared her terror when Sherman invaded her area in early March: "The people about here would not have suffered near as much if it had not been for these Negroes, in every case they have told where things have been hidden and they did most of the stealing. The Negroes here have behaved worse than any I have heard of yet." Eliza Andrews, a Georgia woman who lived in an area devastated by Sherman on his way to South Carolina, recorded similar sentiments in her diary in January: "I wish sister would hurry home, on account of the servants. We can't take control over them, and they won't do anything except just what they please. . . . Harriet, Mrs. Green Butler's maid, is the most trifling of the lot, but I can stand anything from her because she refused to go off with the Yankees when Mrs. Butler had her in Marietta last summer."[57]

When the northern army marched near Elizabeth Coxe's home on the Santee River, the results were grim: "There was a general look of devastation and pillage, and, worst of all, the absence of many, many black faces, familiar to us from childhood . . . and considered our inseparable belongings." Mary Jones suffered similar distress, particularly about blacks: "Their condition is one of perfect anarchy and rebellion. They have placed themselves in perfect antagonism to their owners and to all government and control. We dare not predict the end of all this, if the Lord in mercy does not restrain the hearts and wills of this deluded people. . . . What we are to do becomes daily more and more perplexing." Catherine Edmondston was acquainted with one mistress who knew what to do. When Mrs. Tunis's slaves deserted her for the northern army, two small children were left behind. According to Edmondston, Tunis took the children to northern army headquarters, gained admittance to its commanding general, and "deposited the baby upon his table in the midst of his papers." She reportedly told him that since the children " 'have been deprived of their mother by your act I come here to surrender them to you.' " Most mistresses were neither so forthright nor so enterprising. As Sherman threatened, Mary Chesnut's slave Molly urged her to leave Columbia for the safety of one of the Chesnut family plantations near Camden. But Chesnut decided to ignore her maid's advice: "We thought if the Negroes were ever so loyal to us, they could not protect me from an army bent upon sweeping us from the face of the earth. And if they tried to do so—so much the worse for the poor things with their Yankee friends. So I left them to shift for themselves, as they are accustomed to do—and I took the same liberty."[58]

Other mistresses echoed Chesnut's sentiments. As terrifying as the behavior of slaves could be, Yankees could be worse—and slaves were often loyal.[59] Grace Brown Elmore's family made plans to flee Columbia in December 1864:

> I spoke seriously to Jane today, who came to see me. I told her we were making every arrangement for leaving Columbia, and 'twas time for intelligent servants to be told how matters stood, and what they were to expect from the Yankees, should they reach here and should the servants remain. She said she never thought of being anywhere but with me. I then told her I would not force any of mine to

go with me, but such as desired I would take if possible, but I did not know if I could take all of them. I tried to present as plainly as possible all the hardships we would have to undergo, that it would not be a life of ease to any.

Although most of the slaves chose to remain where they were, they helped with the packing; one slave woman made a cake to try to infuse some Christmas gaiety into the anxious whites.[60]

Susan Jervey, in spite of her fear of slaves, was well aware that they could remain steadfast in adversity. A friend's maid successfully prevented the Yankees from distributing the white family's clothing to slaves, and one of her own family's slaves later helped her father avoid the loyalty oath imposed by the northern soldiers. Emma Holmes worked as a governess near Camden during the last months of the war. When Sherman arrived, she relied on a black maid for comfort and protection: "For two or three nights, I did not undress completely, having no fancy to be caught completely unprepared, & got Liddy to sleep in my room. . . . I asked Liddy if she would like me to read the Bible to her at night, she said yes, &, when I had finished, she was very much obliged." Holmes also noted the behavior of her mother's slaves: "Mother's family fared remarkably well through the fidelity and good behavior of all the servants,—to my great surprise, for I did not trust Judy's family." Elizabeth Allston Pringle reported comparable preparations for Sherman and equal loyalty on the part of the African-Americans in her home: "We never went to bed or took off our clothes during that time. We sat fully dressed in the parlor, all night through, Phibby always sitting with us on the floor near the door, leaning straight up against the wall, her legs stretched out in front of her, nodding and praying. She was a great comfort."[61]

Mistresses who spoke of the loyalty of slaves referred primarily to those they knew best: permanent house servants whose devotion had always seemingly been without question. Now, with destruction pressing in, this faithfulness engendered congratulation and self-congratulation—proof that their assumptions about their ties with their female slaves had been correct. The vehemence with which so many white women insisted upon the loyalty of black women is testimony not only to the reality of that steadfastness but also to mistresses' need for the emotional rewards associated with their role. Desperate to preserve the world as they knew it, white women searched impatiently for examples of the continued faithfulness of African-American women even as Sherman's army destroyed the foundation of their expectation. By the end of the war they found themselves terrified by what they considered the unreliability of slaves and eager to seek out the emotional rewards of slaves' loyalty. Even so, mistresses who found instances of slaves' loyalty deceived themselves about its nature. Slaves' loyalty was a reflection of their feelings about a particular individual; it was not loyalty to slavery. White women never understood the distinction.[62]

∾

Slaves experienced and understood the war very differently from their mistresses, although the available source material leaves many questions unanswered. WPA interviewers did not necessarily ask former slaves about their wartime experiences, and most of those old enough to remember slavery in 1937 were young children when the war began. There can be no doubt, however, that slaves in South Carolina were well aware of its implications. Louis Manigault complained of their knowledge in his plantation journal during the first year of the war: "House servants, from their constant contact with the family, become more conversant with passing events and are often the first to have their minds polluted with evil thoughts." Blacks may have had their minds polluted but few changed their behavior significantly until the presence of Union soldiers offered them some protection. Alfred Sligh remembered that on the plantation where he lived as a child, slaves heard rumors of freedom in 1863 but continued to work until Sherman came through the area. Annie Harper observed that in the presence of federal troops, "the new order of things had asserted itself, elsewhere they were in the chaotic state so far as the negro was concerned." She thought "the first to leave were the pampered body servants of the wealthy planters," while "the slaves of the hardest masters remained at home longer than any other class." Catherine Edmondston agreed, complaining that "the indulged negroes, servants of widows & single Ladies who have not been kept in proper subordination, are terribly insolent. As a general rule the 'favourite' servants, who have had more liberty than their fellows are worse." Mary Mallard reported: "The people are all idle on the plantations, most of them seeking their own pleasure. Many servants have proven faithful, others false and rebellious against all authority or restraint."[63]

For some slaves, a willingness to work for whites throughout the war was inspired by loyalty and the desire to comfort their mistresses. Sarah Poindexter, who lived on a plantation near Columbia, remembered the faithfulness of other African Americans during the war: "De slaves work some, all durin' de war, sometimes I now 'spects it was for de sake of de missus. All of us loved her, 'cause she was so kind and good to us. She was cryin' and worryin' all de time 'bout her manfolks who was away fightin' damn Yankees, she say. She sho' had plenty of backbone or spunk, when stragglers show up, they always hungry and always ready to take what they want to eat, until the missus come on de scene with her trusty shotgun." Poindexter's testimony hints at what may have been an important motivation for blacks' loyalty: the material goods and protection mistresses could provide. However, this behavior was too widespread to be explained solely as prudence, particularly because as the war went on blacks—more than whites—experienced increasing deprivation, sometimes outright hunger.[64]

Former slave Houston Holloway observed the results of the Confederate draft of men aged sixteen to sixty. "This left the white women and girls at home with the Slaves and I have got to hear of the first one yet that betrade his or her Trust." Henry Jenkins was proud of the record of the slaves on the plantation where he was a slave. "Ours was a fine body of slaves and loyal to de mistress and her chillun." Loyalty to mistresses was sometimes reinforced by fear of Yankees. Fannie Page Hume noted the reactions of one slave woman who had chosen to become a refugee with her white family. "We had an entertaining conversation with the little nurse, Pleasanna, who seems to have a perfect horror of the Yankees."[65] For many slaves, the virtues of remaining with their mistresses and on the plantation far outweighed the dangers of seeking a dubious fate behind Yankee lines, particularly because masters were away and discipline informal. Slaves took pride in their loyalty to mistresses, but many also recognized that it was in their interest to remain where material goods and a degree of protection were available.

Before northern troops arrived in South Carolina, slave women and mistresses sought to protect their different interests while preserving a measure of familiarity and security in their daily lives. White women, burdened by unaccustomed work and anxieties about loved ones, their own safety, and the increasingly uncertain future, tried to maintain as many of the external circumstances of life as wartime conditions allowed. Black women were eager for freedom, but until northern troops offered aid, were reluctant to jeopardize their own well-being and that of their children by abandoning their homes and communities. Because the actual fighting remained at a distance from most of the state for nearly four years, these strategies were relatively successful, and the changes the war forced in daily life were ones of degree, not kind. Women's attitudes about one another did undergo a subtle shift during the four long years of fighting, but for the most part new attitudes were not acted upon until the arrival of northern troops marked the beginning of the transition to freedom.

The war's end signified nearly opposite outcomes to plantation mistresses and female slaves in South Carolina. For white women, the end of the war represented a glorious cause that failed; for black women, it brought the freedom about which they had been dreaming and for which they had been struggling for so long. For both the assumptions and understandings each group of women had about the other were challenged. Although the absence of Yankee troops made the war years appear relatively harmonious on the state's large plantations, in fact they were a period of testing and change. Unlike other states in which cataclysmic change was precipitated by Union troops, in most parts of South Carolina there was a slow erosion beneath a smooth-appearing surface.

For plantation mistresses, the war profoundly challenged the ideology of domesticity that had influenced their thoughts and behaviors in antebellum years. Before the war, when threats to the southern way of life did not take the form of guns and soldiers, some plantation mistresses were able to disagree with their husbands about slaves and slavery, albeit privately. Thanks to the ideology of domesticity, which taught women that they inhabited a distinct, morally superior sphere from men that was characterized by benevolence to dependents and selflessness, mistresses were encouraged to sympathize with at least their female slaves. Entrenched in the trappings of nineteenth-century ideal womanhood, a few mistresses recognized they were at odds with the dominant political ideology of their state.

At the same time, southern white women on the whole clashed strongly with northern abolitionists, whose goals they perceived as not only freeing slaves but also forcing social equality and humbling the South. No friend of slavery, Keziah Brevard made her hatred of abolitionists explicit in her journal shortly before the war began:

> That wretch John Brown—if he had come as one of Christs Apostoles & preached down sin he might have been the instrument of good. But he came down to cut our throats because we held property we would not do otherwise with, was preposterous. Did God set the children of Israel to cutting their Masters throats to free them from bondage—no—no—he brought them out of Egypt in his own peculiar way & he can send Africas sons & daughters back when he knows they are ready for their exode. . . . But I do hope & pray that every one will be made to suffer here on this earth who mars the peace of another. This is a dirty subject and had I not thought of those cruel abolitionists who wish to free such a people in our midst I would not have spoken this truth here.[66]

Hatred of northern interference and southern patriotism were stronger emotions than the tentative challenges to slavery that had been facilitated by the ideology of domesticity before the war.

Plantation mistresses' ability and willingness to implement the ideology of domesticity were altered by the war in other ways as well. Because the war modified or eliminated many of the preconditions for domesticity, mistresses were unable to treat slaves the way they thought they should. For example, implementing the ideology of domesticity required white women to have financial and material resources with which to improve the physical conditions of blacks' lives. They also needed enough free time to carry out their benevolent activity. Finally, mistresses had to be knowledgeable about a group of people that could be perceived of as sufficiently needy and grateful as to make helping them emotionally satisfying. By the end of the war, all three of these factors had been transformed.

The chief reason for this alteration was the emphasis mistresses placed on Confederate success, or more precisely, Confederate men. White women who before the war had made black women the objects of their benevolence now shifted their attention to soldiers. A good deal of energy and material goods once available for slaves was diverted to soldiers, who were deemed more worthy of care. As a result, although most mistresses continued to provide for slaves as best they could, they exhibited diminished willingness to implement domesticity for the benefit of their slaves even before their ability to do so was limited by the circumstances of war. Aware more than ever of their responsibility as slaveholders, and anxious to preserve the loyalty of slaves, some South Carolina mistresses attempted to maintain their prewar practices at least until the winter of 1865, when Sherman's troops made anything approaching normal life impossible.

By that time many wealthy white women who began the war years as mistresses of large plantations with many slaves had become virtual paupers. When emancipation canceled their investments in slaves, a considerable part of their family fortunes was wiped out. Further, many women's husbands invested heavily in the Confederacy; some had their homes and property looted or destroyed by soldiers. For those women with only a small number of slaves, the ramifications of the Confederate surrender were even more life-shattering. Because a larger proportion of their wealth was invested in their slaves, preventing African Americans from leaving was critical. Only white men who controlled the labor of large numbers of slaves were exempt from the Confederate draft, so the likelihood of less wealthy white women handling households alone was much higher and their comforts were nearly nonexistent. By the end of the war, few had the financial means to provide for themselves, let alone their slaves. Necessities were difficult and luxuries all but impossible to obtain. As the battle wore on, wealth lost some of its ability to determine the quality of life for all South Carolina women. By the last weeks of the war more than one mistress found herself the recipient of material favors from slaves.[67]

In addition, the war imposed new burdens on mistresses' time that made the leisure necessary for benevolence almost as scarce as material goods. Not only was the pace of domestic production stepped up to meet the needs of the army but mistresses also took on a variety of obligations that had previously fallen to men. This additional burden made the amount of attention focused on slaves in antebellum times impossible to sustain.

Because they spent less time with African Americans, white women gradually became alienated from them in ways that were unusual during the antebellum period. With threats of freedom and fighting endemic in the South, mistresses who had judged slaves appropriately grateful recipients of their benevolence before the war considered their behavior problematic during it. No longer could they assume the loyalty of black women without question. Instead, even mistresses who claimed not to detect a change in their behavior began to describe slaves as inscrutable. African Americans who had once been thought of in familial terms were now seen as potential killers.

Complicating this new outlook on blacks, which was fed by fear, was the more influential gratitude of soldiers. All plantation mistresses had male friends or relatives actively engaged in the fighting; women's efforts to provide comforts to the troops were inspired by the knowledge that what they produced might help those tied by love or family. Because they were fighting for the South, suffering for a just cause, and righting the wrongs inflicted by dreaded northerners, white men were regarded as more needy, more deserving, and more grateful for the clothing and food that white women offered them. Grace Brown Elmore, for example, worried about her ability to support her slaves and had economized for months before the Yankees approached her Columbia home. The night before they arrived, her male relatives fled with the Confederate army, but not before they ate the "good supper" she had prepared for them. Elmore and her mother spent the day cooking so they could fill the soldiers' knapsacks and, as the troops passed, stood at the gate and offered them drinks from their only bottle of wine and "all the blankets we could spare."[68]

In addition to changing views of blacks on an individual level, the war changed the way plantation mistresses thought about the institution of slavery itself. Witnesses to a war that everyone knew was being fought to save slavery, white women were directly confronted with the contradiction between their previous doubts about slavery and the cause for which the South was fighting. Just as their antebellum sentiments were diluted by the racism they were unable to overcome, so was their wartime ideology. In fact, that racism was strengthened by the war and the southern patriotism it encouraged. South Carolinians who hated Yankees and abolitionists found the experience of losing to them humiliating, especially because black troops were used as an occupying force in parts of the state.

Mistresses' doubts about slavery were based largely on the threat it posed to family life: slavery was evil because it separated families and encouraged miscegenation and other behaviors considered immoral. But once Union troops appeared in the state, white women learned that the evils they hated were not solely products of slavery: white Yankee troops also engaged in sexual activity with black women. Gertrude Thomas believed the outcome of the war would bring to northern white women "the bitter cup of humiliation which they will be compelled to drink to the dregs." In January 1865 she wrote to General Sherman's wife: "Rest satisfied Mrs. Sherman and quiet the apprehension of your Northern sisters with regard to the elevation of the Negroes—Your husbands are amongst a coloured race whose reputation for morality has never been of the highest order—and these gallant cavaliers are most of them provided with a 'companion du voyage.' . . . I will only add that intensely Southern woman as I am *I pity you.*"[69] Perhaps more generous than most with her pity, Thomas captured the sentiments of mistresses who by war's end were disgusted with slaves as well as Yankees and whose assumptions about racial differences were becoming harsher.

By the end of the war white women's sentiments about slavery were changing for yet another reason. Before the fighting their ambivalence about the institution was made possible in part by their comfortable style of living. Freed by slaves from the most onerous of domestic tasks, they enjoyed the benefits of the labor of slaves and thus felt encouraged to reward them and regret their oppression. When faced with the loss of those benefits, however, mistresses were quick to overcome their scruples. Even those who hated slavery were nevertheless unable to imagine an alternative fate for blacks or another labor system for the South. They certainly were not prepared to do their own domestic work. These sentiments added to the cauldron of resentment that mistresses were brewing against newly freed slaves.

The final ingredient in that cauldron was suspicion of disloyalty. Although the actions of black men and women bore witness to their continuing faithfulness long beyond the point when alternatives were possible, mistresses found that once the war began they could no longer assume that loyalty. Even if their own slaves remained docile, most knew that African Americans would ultimately prefer freedom, in spite of past kindnesses by mistresses. Under such circumstances, white women concluded that there was less reason to be sympathetic to black women than they had once thought. As the war was ending, Emma Holmes complained about the behavior of slaves who sympathized with Union soldiers: "Tremendous excitement prevailed, as they prayed their cause might prosper & their just freedom be obtained. Great numbers of servants went off from town really crazy from excitement. . . . I could fill this book with their fiendish deeds & the heroism & spirit of the Southern women under such calamities as have swept over our land—fragile women, left without a servant, as Mary Boone was, cooking & washing without a murmur."[70]

Slave women's questionable loyalty, like their unwillingness to continue working, caused many mistresses to doubt the wisdom of continuing to practice domesticity as they had before the war. Once viewed as pitiable and childlike, slave women had become guilty of being insufficiently grateful for the benevolence they had received for so long. Mistresses who found losing the war painful found it simple to turn their resentment against their slaves.

Although they were aware of this resentment, South Carolina's slaves chose to disguise their knowledge when dealing with their mistresses. They believed silence would be to their advantage because mistresses were most generous when told what they wanted to hear. African-American women, particularly those with children, knew that survival would be difficult without the food, clothing, and shelter mistresses provided. They also knew that the price of those goods was affection, gratitude, and loyalty. Given the lack of alternatives throughout the war years, most chose to pay the price. However real that loyalty may have appeared to mistresses who wanted to believe in it, slave women knew it was ambivalent at best. Some black women wanted to remain with the white women who offered them protection and kindness, while others were eager to alter their immediate circumstances. All wanted freedom, but until that freedom and alternate methods of survival became a reality, most slave women chose to remain where they were as the surest road to security for themselves and their children.

Although they shifted their efforts at domestic production from themselves to the soldiers as mistresses required and remained predominantly faithful until the raids of Sherman's men, their actions could not allay their mistresses' suspicions or halt the gradual erosion of white women's benevolence. As a result, by the end of the war newly freed slaves were beginning to question their previous willingness to appear loyal as they simultaneously sought to define the meaning of freedom for themselves. Although probably not intended to provoke white women, black women's new perspective further strained relations between the two groups until they had lost many of the ties that had bound them together for so long. In spite of protestations of loyalty on both sides, by the end of the war the common experience of gender that offered women a sense of shared values was disappearing. As slavery was replaced by freedom, women's shared work and relatively sympathetic attitudes were replaced by newly rigid racial perspectives. These new perspectives were still only apparent as outlines when the war ended in South Carolina, but they would rapidly become clearer as black and white women struggled to define the meaning of freedom.

9

The Transition to Freedom

By the time Sherman's men arrived in Columbia in February 1865, most people in the Confederacy recognized that the end of the war was very near. Those in South Carolina, who had anxiously waited to see whether Sherman would head toward Charleston or Columbia, knew that at last the fighting would be on their soil. The arrival of the fighting in South Carolina so late meant that relatively few in the state suffered the direct impact of the war. This did not provide much comfort for white women, who had to cope with losing their cause, their slaves, their livelihoods, and sometimes their homes all at once. Black women greeted the arrival of northern troops with jubilation: slavery was effectively over. The two groups of women, whose reactions to peace were so different, did share a degree of apprehension as they sought to restore security, guarantee their futures, and define the meaning of freedom. Their efforts to do so during the period of transition between the ending of the war and the resumption of established authority brought them into unprecedented conflict.

As Sherman's men poured through the state and customary sources of authority disappeared, black women who had earlier considered their loyalty a virtue began to behave in less constrained fashion. Some followed the lead and the logic of Mary Pope, interviewed by the *Freedman's Record* in January 1865: "Missus was very kind to us till after the war [started], when Massa went away. Den 'pears like she could not work us hard enough. I knowed something was up. She used to make us spin all day, and far into the night. She was a mighty weaver herself, and 'pears like she wanted to done get all de cloth she could. Ebery little while Missus tell me I better go to de Yankees; dey'd work me harder then she eber did, and I'd starve at that. I'se allus used to minding Missus, so ob course I did dis yer time."[1] Former slave Delia Thompson's family chose to wait for the arrival of the Union forces: "Yankees dat come to our house was gentlemen, they never took a thing, but left provisions for our women folks from their commissary."[2]

Other slaves reacted to the presence of Sherman's men with attitudes mistresses found far more pleasing. The immorality and brutality of some soldiers made a deep impression, causing many African-American women to view Yankees with horror. Emma Holmes noted such feelings in the last weeks of war: "In one instance, a servant sav[ed] her young mistress by taking her place, & another servant's death [was] caused by their brutality in her advanced pregnancy. I told Liddy of this, & she said that few know what had taken place at Dr. Milling's plantation, because the Negroes were so ashamed they could not bear to tell. The wretches staid there a week & gave themselves loose rein in the most indecent manner without the men daring to interfere to save their wives."[3] These were not the only slave women raped by northern troops. Mary Mallard worried about black women in her journal when "squads of Yankees came all day": "The women, finding it entirely unsafe for them to be out of the house at all, would run in and conceal themselves in our dwelling. . . . These men were so outrageous at the Negro houses that the Negro men were obliged to stay at their houses for the protection of their wives; and in some instances they rescued them from the hands of these infamous creatures."[4]

Eliza Hasty, who was a teenager during the war, apparently barely escaped being raped: "De Yankees come. They took notice of me! They was a bad lot dat disgrace Mr. Lincoln dat sent them here. They insult women both white and black, but de Lord was mindful of his own."[5] Northern whites were similarly horrified by what they saw. Esther Hawks, a New Hampshire physician sent to the Sea Islands as a teacher by the National Freedman's Relief Society, thought "no colored woman or girl was safe from the brutal lusts of the soldiers. . . . Mothers were brutally treated for trying to protect their daughters, and there are now several women in our little hospital who have been shot by soldiers for resisting their vile demands."[6] A northern soldier stationed in South Carolina observed several other soldiers rape a nine-year-old girl.[7] Northern troops were not immune from racism and had no particular incentive to respect African-American women. Like southern white men, northern servicemen allowed assumptions about race and gender to shape their interactions with slaves, who happily viewed them as liberators from the effects of such assumptions until direct experiences proved them wrong.

Federal soldiers were also not reluctant to compel the labor and loyalty of blacks in a manner southern white observers found quite brutal.[8] Northern troops bent on destroying southerners' property were also destroying the work of slaves, and many African Americans resented the callous disregard for their labor. Emma Coxe had a friend who reported that the fences on her plantation were set on fire by Yankee soldiers; the blaze was extinguished by white women and house servants. Coxe's own "Maumer" was horrified by the looting and destruction of the troops at her mistress's home: "Maumer went with my mother after them into the house and tried to stop their injuring things, continually reproaching them for their conduct." Grace Brown Elmore deplored the behavior of northern soldiers in the slave yard: "The servants cloths they stole, ripped open their boxes and trunks, took the best of what they had." For blacks who witnessed or heard about rape and destruction, Union soldiers were hardly welcome liberators. Instead, according to one slave, they were "a holy terror to dis part of de world, as naked and hungry as they left it."[9] Many black women found loyalty to white women, whose efforts to feed and clothe them were apparent, far preferable to the brutality and destructiveness of Yankee troops, who raped and ruined or stole provisions intended for slaves.

Although slaves had many pragmatic reasons to be loyal to mistresses and to dislike northern soldiers, Yankees had one redeeming quality: they brought freedom. Many African Americans took advantage of this proximity to flee to Union lines, in hopes of ensuring their freedom.[10] Others waited for their owners to release them. In a scene repeated thousands of times across the state, slaveholders gathered their slaves and informed them that they were free. An emotional event for both groups, the occasion coincided in South Carolina with the end of the war, marking the end of the Confederacy and the beginning of a whole new way of life. Slaves' jubilation was instantaneous, although blacks and whites only gradually understood the implications for their personal lives.

Many newly freed slaves' first response to freedom was to vow to remain where they were. Alfred Sligh, nearly twenty years old at the time, remembered the scene vividly: "We gang up at my grandmother's cabin and she tell us it am so. We look scared, lak mules in de midst of a hornet nest, as we stood dere. We didn't wait long, for old Mistress Sligh, she cam 'long and say: 'Sho' it am so, you am free.' Many of de slaves, cludin' me, tell her we love to stay on and work as usual 'til de big white folks come. She smile and say: 'All right, maybe we be able to feed and clothe you, and when your old master git back from Virginia, maybe he will hire you!'" Hester Hunter, a teenager in 1865, also decided to stay with "my white mammy en I stay dere long as she live too." Lila Rutherford made the same decision: "When freedom came, my mother moved away, but I stayed on." Jimmie Johnson reported: "Missus told me that I was free, but I told her I was going to stay on where I was and protect her until I died."[11] As late as May 1865, Mary Chesnut could not see the slightest change in the behavior of her former slaves: "Everyone has known he or she was free for months, and I do not see one particle of alteration. They are more circumspect, politic, quieter, that's all. All goes on—in status quo antebellum. Every day I expect to miss some familiar face. So far, I have been disappointed." She asked African Americans on her plantation when they were going to leave: "In their furious emotional way they swore devotion to us to their dying day. All the same, the minute they see an opening to better themselves they will move on."[12]

Unlike the Chesnuts' former slaves, some recognized an opening to better themselves once Union troops appeared. Aware that the soldiers could guarantee their freedom and eager to experience it, some newly freed men and women seized the first opportunity to leave. Gertrude Thomas wrote in her journal about her mother's slave Nancy: "Nancy was the first servant belonging to any of our family who left, and shows a more impertinent manner than any of the others." Nancy left, but returned to get her clothing—with a Union soldier as an escort: "Nancy evidently expected to produce a great sensation and awe Ma by the presence of Yankee majesty but she reckoned without her host, and left very differently from what she had expected."[13] Emma Holmes also knew slaves who fled to the safety proffered by northerners: "Louis & Joe went off from here, & we believe Mary & several others would have done so, save they got [started] too late & were turned back by our men. Chloe & Judy do not deny it, but the former said 'if she had known in time that her son Thomas was there, she would have gone.'"[14] Some black women used the presence of federal troops as an excuse to behave in ways they had previously considered too dangerous. Catherine Edmondston heard that Sally Harvey "was slapped in the face by one of their own servants because she tried to keep her from taking her dresses! The print of the negroe's hand was on my cousin's face for several days!" Grace Brown Elmore was as much upset at the loss of a mule one of her slaves took with him to freedom as she was by the loss of the slave: "For that I grieve, as the mule was my dependence to make my crop."[15]

Some former slaves reacted to the presence of Yankee troops and the news of freedom more pragmatically, choosing to observe unfolding events while securing the best possible situation for themselves. Although they remained on the plantation, some refused to work. Susan Jervey was aware of conflict among newly freed slaves about what sort of behavior to adopt: "Rius gave his wife (Ellen) a fearful beating because she came to wait on Aunt Nenna. Those who are faithful suffer so much from the rebellious ones, and we can do nothing to protect them." Charlotte Ravenel reported that blacks had taken most of the plantation's provisions: "The next morning everything looked so desolate that it made us feel sad, most of the house servants came in crying, and said they were willing to do for us, but were afraid. Of course we would not put them in any danger, so sent them all off." Her father reported the same events but interpreted them differently: "Since Thursday the Negroes have not been at work. Sandy comes in & does his work about the house as usual, & George partially. We have no cook or washer. . . . The Negroes are on a 'strike' for terms & until an agreement can be made matters will be no better." Eva Jones reported simply: "On our plantation everything is 'at sixes and sevens.' One day they work, and the next they come to town."[16]

Occasionally a newly freed slave would assert her independence, then retract under the pressure of circumstances. Elizabeth Pringle remembered such a confrontation between her mother and a black woman: "As [mother] was about to leave the corn barn a woman stretched her arms across the wide door so as to hold up the passageway. Mamma said, 'Sukey, let me pass,' but Sukey did not budge. Then mamma turned to Jacob. 'This woman has lost her hearing; you must make her move from the doorway.' Very gently Jacob pushed her aside and we went out and Jacob locked the door."[17] Mary Chesnut knew an elderly slave woman who had been a nurse on one of the Chesnut plantations. Myrtilla had run off with the Yankees, but was not happy: "And now from Orangeburg comes the most pathetic letters. Old Myrtilla begs to be sent for. She wants to come home." James Chesnut refused to pay for her transportation back to Camden: "And that ended the Myrtilla tragedy as far as we were concerned, but poor old Myrtilla, after the first natural frenzy of freedom subsided, knew too well on which side her bread was buttered—and knew too, or found out, where her real friends were. So in a short time old Myrtilla was on our hands to support once more. How she got back we did not inquire."[18]

For blacks such as Myrtilla, knowledge of freedom and the protection of Union forces were not sufficient inducements to leave the plantation, at least not for very long. Those who left learned quickly that the Union soldiers did not want them or treat them kindly. Although former slave men and women wanted desperately to enjoy their freedom, they also knew that the plantation provided the surest source of food and clothing. Esther Hawks observed the terrible conditions among blacks who fled to northern troops in Charleston at the very end of the war: "Dirty ragged, *starving* expresses their condition. . . . I never saw such misery and utter destitution as this. . . . The rations now allowed is not sufficient to sustain life."[19] Although newly freed slaves valued the plantation for pragmatic reasons during the transition to freedom, they frequently attributed their decision to remain to loyalty to mistresses. Although mistresses were the most likely source of both protection and material goods, the former slaves' professed loyalty nevertheless spoke to their expectation that mistresses would treat them kindly and fairly. Most blacks had little reason to think that white women would abandon their benevolence once slavery ended.

A few black women offered a very different form of tribute to their white mistresses. Instead of appearing to be loyal, these former slaves chose to demonstrate their freedom by imitating white women, a practice facilitated by the Yankee habit of distributing whatever clothing they could find on a plantation to its inhabitants. These women boldly defined their freedom by more consciously adopting the external trappings of the free women they knew best. Instead of feeling flattered by imitation, however, white women were enraged. Emma Holmes believed the best costume for a slave woman was "the respectable & becoming handkerchief turban, so familiar to low country eyes," and was critical of those who refused to wear it: "The other Negroes at church were all in the most ludicrous & disgustingly tawdry mixture of old finery, aping their betters most nauseatingly—round hats, gloves & even lace veils— the men alone looking respectable. How much better in every way a plain, neat dress for the working classes, as in other countries, & indeed among our country Negroes formerly. If I ever own Negroes, I shall carry out my father's plan & never allow them to indulge in dress. It is ruin body and soul to them."[20] Emulating white women took many forms. One black woman's chief impression of her encounter with a Yankee soldier was not the coin he gave her baby but his polite willingness to call her Mrs. Sparks.[21] When several soldiers visited Henry Ravenel's plantation, they told the African-American women they should not be toiling in the hot sun; the women apparently heeded the advice and stopped working. Even Elizabeth Botume, a northern white woman teaching for the New England Freedman's Aid Society at Beaufort, was aware of changes in the behavior of a black woman: "Our first cook . . . belonged to a wealthy planter and had been a field-hand. Before the war she was detailed to cook for the overseer. Now that she had been installed as cook and housekeeper, she was much set up, and put on many fine airs."[22] Black women who imitated white womanhood, while continuing a practice familiar from slavery, were experimenting with the meaning of freedom in a way that would soon become familiar as well.

While slave women learned of their freedom simultaneously with the arrival of federal troops and the end of the war, incorporating the meaning of that freedom into their daily lives took some time. Without an alternate means of support for themselves and their children, they relegated the expression of their freedom to symbolic ways at first, remaining for the most part on familiar plantation ground. The appearance of loyalty to mistresses was an important part of those customary surroundings, and so many newly freed slaves chose to pass the first weeks of freedom observing the conventions of that loyalty. Only after the first flash of freedom had been confirmed as reality did freed women began to change their behavior in ways that marked a major shift from antebellum times.

Like their slaves, plantation mistresses did not immediately comprehend the full consequences of surrender. Although many had doubts about slavery before the war, few shared Mary Chesnut's perception that the outcome could mean only the end of the institution. By early 1865, most finally recognized that slavery would cease with the Confederacy, although a few spoke of owning slaves even after its final days.[23] However, because of the confusion of the last days of the war and the apparent loyalty of slaves, most mistresses took some time to realize the consequences of their new status.

Most plantation mistresses reacted to the final days of the war with anxiety, uncertainty, and depression. Fearful of northern troops, they did not know what to think about their slaves or how to treat them. Grace Elmore objected to her mother's criticism of their cook, who did not prepare a turkey properly: "Mother is very cute, but some times, I think she is too suspicious just now about the servants. They are respectful enough, but evidently do not care to work." Kate Logan remembered that "all of the colored people behaved with great propriety, kept themselves in good order, and there was not the least trace of insubordination," even though federal soldiers were in the area. Even so, she claimed, "it was pathetic to see my mother slip around so briskly to prove to her old servants that she could be, if necessity arose, independent of them." Just days after the burning of Columbia, Emma LeConte feared that her family's slaves were planning to leave: "We ask as little as possible of them—such as cooking our little food and bringing water from the well. . . . If Jane offers to clean up our room, all very well—if not, we do it ourselves. This afternoon I washed the dinner things and put the room to rights. . . . This is my first experience in work of this kind and I find it better than doing nothing." Many white women found the uncertainty depressing. In mid-April, Sarah McIver found it paralyzing: "I feel very much depressed in spirit, hardly know what work to get at, but do very little of anything."[24] Sam Polite reported that "W'en Freedom come, Missis didn't say nutting, she jest cry."[25]

Although some mistresses' anxiety was alleviated by the loyal behavior of many newly freed slaves, only a few recognized the motivations behind it. Jane Pringle knew one of those who did: "Mrs. Read fears that after the 60 days during which planters were bound to feed the blacks all the servants in Plantersville will leave." Pringle warned Adele Allston not to leave her home: "If you come here all your servants who have not families so large as to burthen them and compel a veneering of fidelity, will immediately leave you. The others will be more or less impertinent as the humor takes them and in short will do as they choose." In March, most of Grace Brown Elmore's slaves remained faithful, although she noted "there is at times a difference in manner." She was convinced that "those who remain must understand they belong to me now as ever." She believed "the negroes idea of freedom goes not further than that he need not work" and thought they expected to live by plunder. Elmore complained "this doubt in our servants is very disagreeable, even the most faithful cannot be wholly trusted." She recognized that her attitudes were influenced by the behavior of former slaves: "I think a marked difference should be shown between those who act in a thoughtful and affectionate manner, and those who show no thought or care for you." She vowed to send away one woman who refused to work, and mentioned three others whose behavior she found comforting, adding, "to be able to assist them will give me pleasure."[26]

In May, Catherine Edmondston found "astounding" her brother's decision to free his slaves: "It seemed inexplicable to me & suicidal in the last degree." She feared that the men in her family were making a mistake when they tried to negotiate with slaves: "Make no promises, so as to have none to break, is a good rule in dealing with both children and negroes." Only a few days later, however, she admitted feeling sorry for them: "The poor creatures seem as usual, only terribly dejected, & are much more tender & affectionate in their manner to us than ever before. It is a terrible cruelty to them, this unexpected, unsolicited gift of freedom, & they are at their wits ends. Their old moorings are rudely & suddenly cut loose, & they drift without a rudder into the unknown sea of freedom." She complained that the black women and men "occupy themselves ceaselessly trying their new chains, seeing how little work they can accomplish & yet be fed and endeavouring to be both slave & free at the same moment—a slave on the food, shelter, & clothing question but free where labor is concerned."[27]

As the behavior of newly freed slaves became more erratic, mistresses began to realize the ramifications of peace. Some were shocked into comprehension the first time a servant refused to work. Forced to do the most unpleasant domestic tasks themselves, mistresses learned firsthand what they would have to give up. But because some African-American women began rebelling before the official end of the war, some white women were forced to take on domestic chores early. On 1 March 1865, Charlotte Ravenel was acutely aware of the consequences: "We sat down to breakfast to a plate of hominy and cold corn bread that had been cooked the day before for one of our soldiers. The very night before we had sat down to an elaborate supper—such are the fortunes of war! We cleaned up the house and cooked dinner." Some days later, the women of her family were still cooking: "We have to do our own cooking now, and you don't know how nicely we do it. We take it by turns to cook dinner in the pantry, two going together every day." By 11 March, however, life had returned to normal: "One item of news, which I must not forget to tell you, is that Newport has taken the cooking, and we are all ladies again."[28] Gertrude Thomas baked her first cake later that same month: "I went into the kitchen and made up the first cakes I ever accomplished. I remember trying once before to work up some flour without success—Today the dough would stick to my hands but with Tamahs advice I at length succeeded—The children stood around admiring 'Ma's performance' . . . but my back ached when I was through and I have seen things I liked to do better. Yet I intend hereafter to do more cooking—make up bread and ?—Once before I had a similar idea and tried to help Tamah in drawing some fish and it was about as hard work as I ever did."[29]

Sarah McIver, who had been paralyzed in April, was able to work again in May: "I have not felt quite so much depressed in spirit as I did last week. I suppose the reason is that I have found so much work to do." By mid-April, Charles Manigault wrote his son, all of their slaves had left, "but your two sisters, & Victoire do every thing, & do it extremely well, & cheerfully & we are really getting on comfortably, all things considered." Elizabeth Coxe also remembered the lessons of those weeks: "Except Maumer's family, there were few left but the old and incapacitated, although many of those who followed the troops wandered back by degrees. At first Mamma and I had to do what housework Maumer could not manage, and I became quite an expert ironer, also making all the bread and many other things."[30] The wife of one former planter remembered the hard work white women did as the war was ending and slaves went off with Yankee troops: "The Negroes came straggling back after some days; but they did not stay. There was no money to pay them regular wages. . . . Some very few were fond enough of their 'white people' to stay by the children they had helped raise; a good many lingered for a month or two, and then went off to some one who could pay them well."[31]

In contrast, for white women in the Sea Islands, containing some of the richest land for producing rice and valuable sea island cotton in the state and the highest concentration of slaves, the process of adjustment started early. When Union troops captured the islands early in the war, the wealthy owners of the land and slaves fled, setting the stage for what Willie Lee Rose called the "rehearsal for reconstruction."[32] Under the jurisdiction of the U.S. Army, the slaves in the Port Royal area were given land to work and the opportunity to live as free men and women. Northern abolitionists, eager to help black women and men prove their ability to survive without masters, were quick to offer assistance. Some female abolitionists helped open schools for the children and adults there; their papers provide a vivid outsider's account of the slaves' response to freedom. For all but a handful of African Americans, northern soldiers and teachers were the first representatives of the world beyond their local area.[33]

The experiment at Port Royal provided slaves their first opportunity to experience freedom, sometimes in dramatic ways. Susie King Taylor escaped from near Savannah to the Sea Islands, where she became a laundress for a regiment of black troops; she also learned to shoot, clean, and load muskets. Taylor was proud of the hundreds of black women "who assisted the Union soldiers by hiding them and helping them to escape. Many were punished for taking food to the prison stockades for the prisoners. . . . Others assisted in various ways in the Union army." Other black women devoted their energy to improving life for themselves and their families. Lucretia Heyward's mother earned enough by her work in a cotton gin run by the northerners to buy twenty acres of land on Parris Island. Although Heyward was unusually successful, Laura Towne, a northern woman teaching on St. Helena Island, also noted the energy and success of other African-American women in her diary in July 1862: "Pay-day for the Negroes. Nelly and Mr. Hooper paid them at the rate of $2 per acre. Most of the women had earned $5—the men, on an average, not so much."[34]

Towne, a committed abolitionist who made the Sea Islands her home for more than twenty years, unwittingly echoed many of the sentiments of plantation mistresses when she wrote about servants. Shortly after her arrival in 1862, she described the difficulties associated with training young servants and of their eagerness to work as domestic producers:

The servants [are] untrained field hands,—and worse, very young girls, except the cook—and so I shall have a time of it.

All who can be are kept busy with the cotton, but there are some women and young girls unfit for the field, and these are made to do their share in housework and washing, so that they may draw pay like the others—or rations—for government must support them all whether they work or not, for this summer. So far as I have seen, they are eager to get a chance to do housework or washing, because the Northerners can't help giving extra pay for service that is done them, even if it is paid for otherwise, or by policy.

What Towne attributed to northerners' generosity would have been familiar to every domestic producer who had ever asked for a favor and every mistress who had ever granted it. White women would have found Towne's complaints about black women's ineptness familiar as well. In 1864, she too experienced a disastrous dinner: "A hard working morning getting ready for our dinner this evening. The dinner was not ready at the right time, and I had to leave the guests . . . again and again, to see about it. Rina had in the kitchen Hastings, Brister, Lame John, and a boy helping her, but when dinner was at last on the table we found . . . [it] was a failure."[35]

Esther Hill Hawks was part of a group of whites trying to turn a ravaged Barnwell home into a hospital and similarly complained about African Americans: "It took so long to do the smallest job—that I would sometimes almost despair of ever having the house put into decent order for a hospital. . . . These negroes are like ignorant unformed children, and the difficulty of reasoning them out of an opinion or ideas when it once takes possession of them, can never be known 'till tried. You talk to willing listeners—they assent heartily to what you say but—they are of the same opinion still." Another woman complained that "the important operations of dish-washing and arranging the rooms upstairs take longer than you can imagine" and remarked: "H. begins to pity the Southern housekeepers."[36]

Black women might be difficult and childlike, but they could also be helpful, as plantation mistresses knew. When a nearby battle brought an influx of wounded men into the hospital, Hawks reported: "The colored people came promptly to our aid and almost before we knew what we needed they brought . . . everything needed for the immediate wants of the men." In spite of former slaves' often frustrating behavior, Hawks, Towne, and other white women discovered early that black women could be dependent on their mistresses. Towne observed: "We have been riding around all week to different plantations to cheer up and reassure the rather down-hearted Negroes, or rather the Negro women. It is not a cheering thing to do, except as it is gratifying to be so able to give comfort. They think a white lady a great safeguard from danger, and they say they are 'confused' if there are no ladies about. . . . The sight of ladies gives them a feeling of security that nothing else does."[37] While Towne's comments reflect her own racial biases and desire for good servants, they also help demonstrate how slowly black women's behavior and attitudes were changed by freedom. Because economic security was their first priority, they were willing to work hard, but they also wanted to assert their own autonomy. Towne, like plantation mistresses at the close of the war in the rest of the state, found herself in an ambivalent relation to newly freed slave women. Like black women elsewhere during the transition to freedom, those on the Sea Islands were neither willing to defer wholly to white women nor able to deny completely their authority.

ᵔᴗ

The war, which decided the fate of slavery and the Union, also helped to shape new relations between black and white women. By changing the basic labor system in the South, it altered the foundations of women's interactions with one another and consequently the way they behaved and thought. Because they depended upon slavery, the relations that characterized the prewar era could not long survive it. After the war ended, Union Army officers assumed political control of South Carolina for the federal government. The resulting confusion left all residents uncertain about their legal status, their economic situation, and their future. Many did not know how they could obtain food, clothing, and shelter. Certainly white women realized the trauma and disorientation of the times. As Elizabeth Allen Coxe said later: "It seemed like a frenzy of despair that had fallen upon the people." Aware of the political and personal decisions being made by and for South Carolinians in June 1865, Emma Holmes tried to assess what was happening in her journal: "Truly this revolution has been like a volcanic eruption, sudden and fierce . . . bearing all worthless things to the surface & burying all that made our goodly land fair to the heart & soul, as well as eye, beneath its streams of lava-blood and its ashes of desolation. The very foundations of society are uprooted."[38]

Black women were equally perceptive about the upheaval and uncertainty of the period. Rebecca Jane Grant, who had been a slave near Beaufort, described her mother's first experiences in a nearby but unfamiliar area: "My mother say she didn't know a soul. All de time she'd be prayin' to de Lord. She'd take us chillun to de woods to pick up firewood, and we'd turn around to see her down on her knees behind a stump, aprayin'. We'd see her wipin' her eyes wid de corner of her apron, first one eye, den de other, as we come along back. Den, back in de house, down on her knees, she'd be aprayin'." One night she had a vision of Jesus, who asked her what she was "frettin' bout." She told him: "Sir, I'm a stranger here, parted from my husband, with five little chillun and not a morsel of bread."[39] Her prayers and problems undoubtedly echoed those of other African-American women throughout the state. It was out of this despair, confusion, anxiety, uncertainty that black and white women would have to fashion not only new lives for themselves but also new ways of relating to one another.

The first priority of most women in South Carolina, once they accepted the war was really over, was restoring a measure of security to their lives. For former mistresses, security meant the comfortable lifestyle that slavery had made possible, including someone else to do the most unpleasant domestic tasks. For former slaves, security meant the ability to provide the necessities of life for themselves and their families. In the first year or so after the fighting ceased, women of both groups scrambled to obtain security and to adjust to postwar realities.

Former mistresses began this process of adjustment by attempting to restore their familiar domestic comforts. Many once wealthy plantation mistresses found themselves unable to command much labor or cash; although some would eventually recoup their wartime losses, many would not.[40] Blacks whose work had previously been taken for granted now had to be paid, and planters trying to restore their fortunes were not always able or willing to do so. Some previously wealthy planters could afford to hire only a cook or laundress to help their wives with the most burdensome household tasks. Black women took advantage of the opportunity to choose their labor by rejecting domestic work whenever possible—or insisting on high wages for it, knowing that white women could not pay them. Caroline Ravenel learned the meaning of defeat shortly after the war was over: "We are literally our own servants except for cooking. We make up our own rooms, & Mamma has been at the wash tub for two or three weeks. It almost makes me cry to see her. She tried to get a washer, but the woman said she would wash at the rate of 1 doz. clothes for 10 lbs of bacon, which, of course, we could not pay. . . . One of the hardest of my trials is to sit still & see my delicate Mother doing the hard work, & know that I am not able to assist her." Eliza Andrews learned a similar lesson in her home across the Savannah River in Georgia:

> Charity and Mammy both sick, and Emily preparing to leave. I don't think the poor darkey wants to go, but mother never liked to have her about the house, and father can't afford to keep such a big family on his hands when he has no use for them, though he says he will do all in his power to keep them from suffering. Our circumstances are so reduced that it is necessary to reduce our establishment and retrench our expensive manner of living. We have not even an errand boy now. . . . Sister and I do most of the housework while Mammy and Charity are laid up.[41]

Unable to afford to pay a servant's wages, Susan Dabney Smedes's father chose to do the hardest work himself: "He determined to spare his daughters all such labor as he could perform. General Sherman had said that he would like to bring every Southern woman to the wash-tub. 'He shall never bring my daughters to the wash-tub,' Thomas Dabney said. 'I will do the washing myself.' And he did it for two years."[42] Some formerly comfortable women had difficulty making ends meet at all, as one woman admitted in 1867: "I have never felt the pressure of money so much as at this time—I sent my watch by Mrs. D. C. Rowe to try to sell it for me—she was offered $6 or 8—I did not feel like sacrificing it for such a sum. We need dry goods so much—know not what we will do till fall—it is a constant struggle."[43]

For some former mistresses, the major difficulty was not paying servants, but finding someone willing to work. Emma Holmes at first believed that hiring help would be easy, as she noted in her journal in May 1865: "At any rate, like everyone else, we expect to have a great deal thrown upon us at first but will soon get servants. For, though no one has money, they will be glad to be taken for their food, provisions being so scarce." In June, she still believed black women would soon be desperate for jobs, even as she reported that several of their former slaves had departed: "We had been expecting it & were rather pleased, for we do not want unwilling, careless, neglectful servants about us, &, though the transition state will of course be trouble-some, we will soon be able to get others, and better, and at less cost to re-place them, for we won't have the children to support." But by early fall, she reported that she had been quite busy doing a variety of domestic chores because she had been unable to hire anyone to help: "We have a constant ebb & flow of servants, some staying only a few days, others a few hours, some thoroughly incompetent, others though satisfactory to us, preferring a plantation life."[44]

Gertrude Thomas confronted the problem of finding servants earlier than Holmes, in May 1865. She struggled for weeks to find someone to do the cooking and washing, but none of the servants she hired was willing to re-main for very long, even though Thomas did a portion of the work herself. By the end of the month she was in despair when yet another cook left: "I told Mr. Thomas that I did not know but what we were fighting shadows. I certainly sacrificed a good deal to principal for I lost an opportunity to get an excellent cook at $5 per month. . . . The fact is that all the best servants belonging to familys we know will be engaged by the low class of people and we will have to take inexperienced servants until we can supply ourselves with white servants."[45] One planter's wife confessed the strain caused by the con-tinuing uncertainty about servants in a letter to a friend: "I cannot help feel-ing depressed at times. The servants torment me, but I suppose they do the same to everybody. The man & woman I have, have quarrelled & the man leaves to-morrow & a stranger takes his place." Another's daughter was more explicit about the torments she considered her family to be suffering:

> I believe it was since I last wrote you that our serving girl, Fanny, asserted her rights to freedom, that is throw off every restraint, imposed by the laws of decency, and cast herself head long in the broad road. She got so unsatisfactory that Mamma dismissed her. . . .
>
> Having no servants is a great draw back—We have now a little stupid girl, for her food and clothes. I am obliged to holloa at her so, I am afraid my voice will lose its dulcet tones.[46]

Catherine Edmondston also struggled after a servant asserted her rights to freedom. Edmondston had been sick for three months, and Fanny had taken care of her "with the most earnest & tender solicitude. . . . Yet when I was scarce able to walk without assistance she left me without provocation or warning, left me in the night, and that too without the slightest notice." Fanny's replacement worked for a fortnight, then "announced that she was sick & retired from the house, her disease being cheifly intense 'Laziness.'" Edmondston blamed her difficulties with Fanny on the cessation of slavery: "With the ability to govern her firmly & consistently I have lost a very fair servant. No one could put up with her now." One woman celebrated another's good fortune in finding a white servant; she thought "they are greatly to be preferred." White men were similarly discomfited by the difficulty of finding household help after the war: "We are without servants and all of us have to do the work of servants. Fortunately, Jim the cook remained. Abby too stuck to us & Lewis 'for a while.' So you can imagine the state of things. A painful thing is that the only education the children are getting is that of being servants."[47] This man's letter pointed to what was perhaps the most difficult aspect of the transition period for many former mistresses: the prospect of permanently being responsible for keeping house.

Even though plantation mistresses had always performed a certain amount of domestic labor themselves, in the first months after the war ended white women routinely did far more domestic work than they had ever done before, and of a more physically demanding sort. Some, such as Emma Holmes, found the experience rewarding: "Lila & I determined to commence at once with our household duties, so take it by turn to knead biscuits & churn & attend to the drawing room. Yesterday 28th, I made my first batter, of which I felt rather proud. We succeed right well with our biscuits. . . . Of course it occupies a good deal of time, but the servants find we are by no means entirely dependent on them." Two weeks later she was still able to find virtue in doing domestic work, including laundry: "I was very tired yesterday after my various pieces of manual labor but hope they will drive off headache as medicine won't. . . . Though of course it was fatiguing, standing so long, it was not near as difficult nor as hard work as I fancied. Indeed, since our wardrobes have diminished, so has our washing list."[48]

At first Eliza Andrews enjoyed similar satisfaction in household chores. After dusting and sweeping the parlor, she was pleased with her accomplishments, in spite of the teasing of her friends: "I never saw the parlor and library so tidy. I was in high good humor at the result of my labors, and the gentlemen complimented me on them. I don't think I shall mind working at all when I get used to it. Everybody else is doing housework, and it is so funny to compare our experiences." She soon recognized how tiring housework could be, particularly for a young woman simultaneously trying to pursue an active social life. At a party, she found herself "too tired to enjoy the dancing as much as usual," and she complained more frequently in her journal: "My legs ached as if they had been in the stocks, but when I become more accustomed to hard work, I hope it won't be so bad. I think it is an advantage to clean up the house ourselves, sometimes, for we do it so much better than the Negroes." She quickly found even that consolation insufficient: "I worked very hard in the morning because I had a great deal to do. . . . I never was so tired in my life; every bone in my body felt as if it were ready to drop out, and my eyes were so heavy that I could hardly keep them open. I don't find doing housework quite so much of a joke as I imagine[d] it was going to be, especially when we have company to entertain at the same time, and want to make them enjoy themselves." That evening she and her sister went to a party, "though we would both a great deal rather have stayed at home. . . . I was so tired that I made Jim Bryan tell the boys not to ask me to dance."[49]

Emma Holmes also learned quite quickly that doing housework was not as rewarding as she had hoped when she started: "But I don't like cooking or washing. Even the doing up of muslins is a great annoyance to me, & I do miss the having [things] all ready prepared to my hand. I generally rise at five or before, though sometimes not till six when very tired, but often rouse servants & household by going to sweep the drawing room." Her complaints continued, as the servants came and went: "I am very weary, standing up washing all the breakfast & dinner china, bowls, kettles, pans, silver, etc. & minding Jims churning, washing stockings, etc.—a most miscellaneous list of duties, leaving no time for reading or exercise. . . . Last night I hemmed an apron in order to gain a little leisure today, for it has taken me three days to make one . . . so little time have I had. It is eight years since I've sewed at night."[50] Holmes and Andrews apparently continued to feel the pressure and fatigue of domestic work, for both stopped keeping diaries shortly after these comments were written.[51]

Another woman tried to make the best of unaccustomed and unpleasant duties: "Now I am better off, I have a washerwoman for her feed & lodging & a maid for the same, & tho' neither are very cleanly they seem willing & I get on. Of course they don't work very hard, but I do, & the children being so much older, even the baby nearly 3 years old, I get on better than I could expect, & am very thankful, & good health is a great blessing." After describing a variety of makeshift arrangements with servants, Adele Allston reported a bit of gossip that spoke volumes about the work former plantation mistresses were doing in the summer after the war ended: "We hear that Helen Alston has to cut wood and bring it in from the woods, cook and wash and labour in every way." Annie Harper summed up the situation by lamenting the time that "soon came in many homes, when mother alone was left to fill all the vacant places, and in the unaccustomed, unprovided for drudgery, many a mother sunk, or in the conflict with an impudent, thieving, presuming cook. It is hard to realize how helpless the mass of Southern women were—never a day in their lives had they ever had to work with their hands, and thro' most bitter experience did they learn."[52]

Recognizing how difficult and unpleasant housework was with their first encounters with dishpan and broom, other white women never bothered to convince themselves of the virtues of housework. By the end of June, Grace Elmore knew that the old way of life for wealthy white women in the South was over: "Now we can only deal with the hard realities of the present. We have truly said goodbye to being ladies of leisure, my time is fully occupied, often not having time to sleep. Rise at 5 o'clock, dress, come down to see after breakfast, then a multitude of small cares. . . . I don't like to live among the pots and kettles. I hate being always beset with small worries. . . . Never have I so longed to possess money and leave the country."[53]

For women unaccustomed to sustained physical labor, doing housework for the first time contributed significantly to the pain of losing the war. Women who were left to do their own domestic labor found sympathizing with former slaves nearly impossible. Grace Brown Elmore noted that indifference was common, while "in most instances there is . . . a bitter feeling & a sharp antagonism between the two races." She saw them as "natural enemies" now; before "only their relative positions bound them in affection as well as law together." She predicted only "starvation and suffering" for the future.[54]

Some former mistresses were spared a measure of the intensity of that pain because their former slaves did not leave them. This kind of loyalty, when sustained for more than a month or two after the war's end, was grat-ifying to white women who believed they had lost so much. Catherine Ham-mond's former slaves remained loyal as late as September 1865, which she considered cause for self-congratulation: "We have not lost many Negroes. . . . Thank God I find more to do every day than I can accomplish and I am able to interest myself in it. My children are very kind and my household cheerful and satisfied. My servants behave pretty well."[55] When Sally Taylor's mother became ill in October 1865, their former slaves worked hard to make her comfortable: "Penelope is a good sick room servant and Eva does very well. Phoebe too is great and willing to help.—The servants seem so anxious and gentle—Jack cutting wood late or early—Kit too try-ing by quickness to aid us."[56]

At least one family of Meta Grimball's former slaves remained with her as late as January 1866, which gave her great pleasure. Eliza Andrews wel-comed her mammy's loyalty but understood that it was limited by her de-sire to be with her family: "Mammy tells me all this gossip about the other Negroes. She is not going to leave us till she can hear from Jane and Char-lotte, who are supposed to be in Philadelphia. She says she will stay with us if she can't go to them, and more could not be expected of her. It is not in human nature that fidelity to a master should outweigh maternal affection, though mammy has always been more like a member of the white family than a Negro."[57]

In some instances, the faithfulness of former slaves could be unwelcome. Catherine Hammond, who congratulated herself on the behavior of her servants, still found their loyalty problematic: "I wish I could get rid of many of the useless ones. 300 mouths to feed is no small charge—meat and corn both low, but the new crop coming in." Many of the African Americans who had worked for Emma Holmes's family had not left by August 1865: "The Negroes are getting worse daily; in every direction we hear of families be-ing left without a single servant, or those who stay doing almost nothing. Mary Ann disappeared last evening, and our hired washer expressed great dissatisfaction because she had so much water to bring." Servants who did not leave could annoy mistresses unable to discipline them, as Gertrude Thomas discovered in May: "Yesterday numbers of the Negro women some of them quite *black* were promenading up the streets with black lace veil shading them from the embrowning rays of a sun, under whose influence they had worked all their lives."[58] Whether or not their former slaves con-tinued to work, the first year of emancipation was one of difficult readjust-ment and unfamiliar duties for former mistresses. Raised with the assump-tion that slaves would always be available to relieve them of the most taxing work, elite white women resented housework and the former slaves who refused to do it. Unaccustomed to physical labor, they undertook it with spirit and the belief that it would be a temporary measure. Although thwarted by unfamiliar poverty and the behavior of former slaves, white women spent the first year after the war trying to recreate a measure of domestic harmony. Their obvious goal was to fashion a world as much like the antebellum world as possible.

The last thing most black women wanted after emancipation was to live in the antebellum world. Jubilant at freedom, they nevertheless recognized the implications of self-support inherent in it. As a result, their actions during the first months after the war ended were motivated by two goals: to take advantage of freedom and to secure a means of support for themselves and their families. Their efforts brought them into frequent contact not only with the U.S. Army and Freedman's Bureau officials but also with the white women who had until recently been their mistresses.

Many black women took advantage of their first months of freedom to erase the consequences of slavery in their personal lives. Reuniting their families became a high priority for many ex-slaves, as did securing a legal marriage.[59] Women wanted to care for their families without interference. African Americans eagerly shed the bondage of slavery; some not only left hated plantations but also spoke bluntly to their former masters about their feelings. Despite limitations imposed by poverty and federal troops, recently freed slaves sought expression of their freedom by whatever means available.

Although rumors of land distribution were common, its failure to materialize forced African Americans to scramble for their own support. The army demanded that planters provide for their former slaves for an interim period, and government rations and private charity rescued the destitute. For the most part, however, blacks had no alternative but to provide for themselves. The mechanism devised by the Freedman's Bureau to help them do so was the labor contract, an agreement between planter and freedman designed to create a stable labor system and provide for the immediate needs of freed slaves.[60] Although the details could vary, most contracts stated that in return for the labor of the signer and his family, all would receive housing and food for the year as well as a portion of the crop. Because African Americans preferred women to care for homes and families, many black men tried to negotiate contracts that paid them enough to support their wives and children. However, planters' demands that the contract include the labor of an entire family were usually successful. These contracts, promoted and enforced by the army officials who staffed the Freedman's Bureau, imposed unwelcome values on former slaves and limited their ability to express their freedom.

For black women, the labor contract system meant continuing the same sorts of work they had done before the war. Most toiled in the fields along with their husbands, while some were hired to do domestic work.[61] Many black women remained with their former owners during that first year after emancipation, laboring just as they had before. The contracts agreed to by Mary Jones and her former slaves, for example, stipulated that women would work one acre in corn and cotton, men two acres. Sara Brown's family remained where they had been slaves, because their former mistress "was good to all her colored people en dey stay on dere for part of de crop. Give dem so much of de crop accordin to de chillun dey had to feed." Adele Frost had been purchased when she was twelve to work as a maid. She was twenty-one when the war ended, but her work did not change: "After de war I still work' as a maid for Mr. Mitchell." Violet Guntharpe remembered her mother made the same decision: "My mammy stay on wid de same marster 'til I was grown."[62]

Anne Rice, a child at the end of the war, remembered the first years of freedom in terms that were reminiscent of slavery: "When freedom come, my folks stayed on with Capt. Posey, and I washed and ironed with them later when I was big enough. I done some cooking, too. I could card and spin and make homespun dresses. My ma learned me." Both George McAlilley and Milton Marshall had mothers who stayed on as cooks for their former owners, as did Adeline Grey: "My Ma cooked for de white folks for one year after freedom." William Henry Davis, born in the closing weeks of the war, knew that his mother's job had made his childhood special: "My mamma, she do all de cooking to de big house en dere be a division in de Missus kitchen for de cook en she chillun to stay in." Lucy Gallman was employed to do slave women's work: "I worked hard, plowed, cut wheat, split cord wood, and other work just like a man."[63] For these women and others like them, the end of the war and the beginning of freedom did not bring substantial change in the daily pattern of work.

Some former slave women who remained with their former mistresses were expected to work harder than before. Eva Jones complained about the difficulties of finding and keeping servants in July, without considering the impact on the black women: "Our menage has been frightfully reduced; and of our numerous throng there remains a seamstress (who has had to lay aside her old calling to become cook, washer, and chambermaid) and one who attends to everything else about this unfortunate establishment." A few black women did not welcome even the appearance of change. Caroline Ravenel described the excitement of a family nurse when she was asked to sign a labor contract: "She did not know what was the matter, she had not done anything. Missis seemed to want her to go off the place. That was not the way to treat her; if Missis had taken her aside & told her, she would have given her opinion. The Yankees did not know her, but 'missis knows what I am.' And the tone of pride with which she said the last! After talking off her excitement, she made her sign."[64]

Some recently freed women were eager to escape as quickly as possible from the plantations. Some, like Catherine Edmondston's maid Fanny, were eager to join their husbands or fathers. Edmondston noted that Fanny's husband "has been trying to entice her off since the Proclamation of Freedom & that now taking advantage of a temporary indisposition of her child, he has promised that if she would go with him she should do naught but tend it whilst he would support her in idleness. She has at length succumbed and has gone off into the unknown future with only him to depend on. She actually left without bidding me good bye, altho she knew I neither would or could detain her."[65] Edmondston's assumption that Fanny had to be enticed to leave suggests how thoroughly the former mistress had come to believe that domesticity and family life had no meaning for black women. Grace Brown Elmore claimed the desire of black women to follow their spouses could not be explained "because they have investigated the matter and seen the right of the thing." Instead, she thought, "it suits present circumstances" since before the war slaves were so indifferent to "the sacredness of the marriage relation . . . that the owner would have to affix some penalty to the infringement" of it. A planter wrote to his aunt about his fears that two female servants would leave in November 1865: "Judy does more for me now than ever—& the girl—there is no better—they wish to stay another year but their fathers' say no."[66]

Unlike Fannie Griffin, remaining on the plantation was not an option for some blacks: "De massa and missus let all de slaves go 'cepting me; they kept me to work in de house and de garden." One planter believed one woman was expected to do all the work of a white family: "I think they will not keep her another year."[67]

As whites were forced to offer wages, many black women such as Emoline Wilson began to appreciate the value of their own work. Wilson chose to leave her former owners: "One time after de war, dey paid me only $5.00 and I quit 'em."[68] Rebecca Jane Grant's mother made her living doing laundry after the war and took every opportunity to increase her earnings: "Now my mother was an unusually good washer and ironer. De white folks had been sayin', 'Wonder who it is that's makin' de clothes look so good.' Well, bout dis time, dey found out; and dey would come bringin' her plenty of washin' to do. And when dey would come dey would bring her a pan full of food for us chilluns. Soon de other white folks from round about heard of her and she was gettin' all de washin' she needed."[69]

Free women who remained with former owners sometimes found their experiences all too similar to slavery. Solomon Caldwell reported that after freedom, his mother worked for her former master's son: "He was a purty good man, but my mammy was always careful. At night she say, 'Come in chilluns, I got to fasten de do' tight.' "[70] Another man tersely suggested that it made very little difference whether black women remained where they had been or moved away: "Moved right away soon as Freedom came. Women done cooking and washing same as now."[71]

The work may not have changed when peace came, but the basic labor system in the South did, and when it departed so did the foundations of women's interactions with one another and consequently the way they behaved and thought. Because they depended upon slavery, the relationships that characterized the prewar era could not long survive it. Both former mistresses and former slaves found the period of transition between slavery and freedom difficult. White women, eager to overcome the traumas of the war years, sought to restore stability and leisure to their lives. Black women, eager to enjoy freedom and the opportunity to devote themselves to their families it promised, were reluctant to continue old patterns. Because customary ways of thinking about one another no longer applied, women experimented with new work responsibilities and new ways of interacting. Old incentives for harmonious interaction died slowly but surely during the period of transition, exposing ever more plainly the differences in black and white women's interests and goals. For most former slaves and mistresses this was a gradual transition, worked out slowly as black women came and went as domestic servants and as white women vacillated between the responsibility of providing for former slaves and the unpleasantness of doing their own domestic chores. The decisions women made during the period of transition, seemingly a response to conditions prevailing at the moment, would have important implications for the future.

IO

Toward the Future

Once the roughly year-long transition between slave and free labor was effectively over, the work experiences of black and white women settled into a pattern that remained virtually unaltered throughout the Reconstruction period and for a long time thereafter. The new work patterns inherited some familiar parts of antebellum practices, but without slavery as a foundation, work relations between the two groups of women were markedly different. These changes would have profound implications for the meaning of freedom, racism, and race relations between women until at least the beginning of the twentieth century.

During the postwar period black women's work experiences bore a superficial similarity to those under slavery. They still labored in the fields and in the kitchens and laundries of white women. On some postwar plantations black women continued to work in gangs, sometimes at gender-specific tasks, sometimes separate from men. For example, in 1869 on the Keating S. Ball rice plantation on the Cooper River, women planted potatoes and rice just as men did, but in different locations. This way of organizing labor became increasingly unusual as more and more owners divided their plantations into small plots to be worked by families of freed blacks, who were paid a share of the crop. The experience of Adeline Grey's mother was typical: "After freedom, my Ma plow many a day, same as a man, for us chillun. She work for ole man Bill Mars. Den she marry again. Part of de time dey work for Mr. Benny Lawton, de one-arm man." Working on shares was no less backbreaking than working as a slave, but it did allow blacks to toil in family groups for what they believed would be their own profit. Frances Butler

Leigh described the result of planting on shares for freed slaves: "The con-sequence is that 'the crop,' being the only thing thought of, every able-bodied man, woman, and child is engaged on it." Adeline Grey's mother and step-father and the blacks Leigh knew were finally working for themselves, and many of them, especially women, found working in the fields alongside their family members far more rewarding and allowed far more personal auton-omy than slavery. Infused with a sense of the value of her labor, Emoline Wilson left her former owner shortly after the war because she was not paid enough. She then went to work for her mother, a seamstress, but that too was unsatisfactory. Her solution was to "get me a man of my own."[1] Nei-ther changing jobs nor relying on marriage to shape the quality of life would have been so simple before the war.

Working by contract for a share of the crop forced black men and wom-en to negotiate new ways of working together and occasionally pushed them into different roles. Elizabeth Botume, a white woman from the North who had gone to Beaufort to teach freed slaves, recognized the important dif-ferences in the behavior of men and women in 1869:

> Most of the field-work was done by the women and girls; their lords and masters were much interrupted in agricultural pursuits by their political and religious duties. When the days of "*conventions*" came, the men were rarely at home; but the women kept steadily at work in the fields. As we drove around, we saw them patiently "cleaning up their ground," "listing," "chopping down the old cotton stalks and hoeing them under," gathering "sedge" and "trash" from the river-side, which they carried in baskets on their heads, and spread over the land. And later, hoeing the crops and gathering them in.[2]

No longer hampered by slavery, African-American men began asserting their authority over family members. Mary Chesnut reported that the husband of one of her former slaves tried to negotiate a contract for his wife at the end of the war. He asked for high wages in addition to the room and board the woman and her children were receiving. When Chesnut told the woman she had no money to pay her, the woman was dismayed, but not because she would not be paid. She told Chesnut: "Claiborne is an old fool—always meddling."[3]

Black women had their own priorities, which led, in some cases, to petty conflicts, as Gertrude Thomas reported in her journal: "She (Mollie) wished her account separate from her husbands. . . . 'What's mine is mine, she said and whats tother folks is tother folks.' Robin (her husband) she said 'like to buy too much sweet things, too much sugar and such like to put in his belly and I likes to put on my back.' This she said and proved herself a true wom-an." Thomas knew that black women had more important priorities than clothing. She complained bitterly about white men who expected their sons to plow and considered them "indispensable in the field" because "the boys head suffers and he grows up an ignoramus." On the other hand, she said, black women "toil and strive, labour and endure in order that their children 'may have a schooling.'"[4] Sometimes the demands of earning a living could force black families to duplicate the social patterns of slavery. Charlie Meadow reported that the first year after the war ended his family stayed with their former owner, but after that things changed: "Next year maw and her maw went to de Mabry Thomas plantation in Santuc to work fer a fourth. My pa stayed at de Meadow plantation. I went wid my maw, but I also stayed wid my paw and his ma some. After dat, when ma's maw died she went back to pa and dey worked fer a fourth; and de older boys hired to de big house fer wages."[5]

Fieldwork, as in the prewar period, was not black women's sole occupation. While some were hired to do domestic work for whites, all had to do the domestic tasks necessary for the survival of their own families. Sabe Rutledge's mother spent winter evenings making clothing for her family: "Mudder spin you know. . . . We four chillun have to pick seed out the cotton. . . . When we gro bigger, Mudder make one card. One would spin and then Mudder go to knitting." Elizabeth Botume reported that the mothers of the children in her school as well as the boys and girls themselves enjoyed sewing and begged her for scraps to make into quilts. Black women's own domestic work did not change very much as a result of the war. As one man put it, "Women done cooking and washing same as now."[6]

Unlike before the Civil War, blacks were expected to produce their own food and clothing or purchase them from the many small shops springing up throughout the countryside. As a result, the only work for which white women hired black women was specific to the white household. With incomes reduced and entertainment curtailed, even that domestic work was far less elaborate than it had been before the war. Further, since slaves did not need to be cared for, much of the domestic production work that had been women's responsibility no longer needed to be done and some of what was left white women did themselves. Few white women, however, did *all* domestic work themselves. When it was possible they hired servants to do the most unpleasant and time-consuming tasks. Kate Stone, for example, noted in her journal in 1867 that in spite of a variety of economic difficulties her family was usually able to keep a cook, because they found cooking the most disagreeable sort of work.[7]

African-American women who worked as domestic servants did so under conditions that both parties to the agreement could find trying. One planter's wife hired a woman to cook, but expected her to attend "all my patches & my garden." Within eighteen months that cook had been replaced by another, whose responsibilities were even more extensive: "She washed & irons nicely [and is] a good plain cook. Scours—which Charlotte would not do—& I am going to have a cotton patch for her to work—we give her $3 a month." Gertrude Thomas also had difficulty limiting her expectations of servants' work. When the former slave who had been doing housework left in 1868, Thomas added her duties to those of another servant: "I have been giving her seven dollars to cook, wash and iron, and now she does the house work that Patsey did and the washing and ironing for the same price." Throughout 1869 and 1870 she hired and fired several cooks and other servants whose work she found unsatisfactory; several others agreed to work for her and then changed their minds:

> I hired an old woman a few days since to attend to my poultry and cows—When I sent for her she said she could not come in two weeks.

> My cook is called Cordelia Shelman and she is the most utterly worthless of all the indolent race—Since breakfast she has added the crowning annoyance of impertinence to her other aggravations and I have dismissed her. I have told her to go home two or three times before but this time I think I will insist upon her leaving.[8]

The experience of Cordelia Shelman and the large number of other African-American women named by Thomas points to the most significant difference between working for white women before and after the war. Before the war, women whose work as domestic producers or in the house was considered unsatisfactory were sent to the fields or sold when they could not be beaten into cooperation. After the war, they were out of a job. The lack of security in domestic service caused many black women to prefer work in the fields with their husbands, where they believed they had a better chance for success. Field work also allowed them to avoid white women, whose nagging and fault-finding were unpleasant and unwanted.

Black women with young children discovered that finding and keeping jobs as domestic servants was especially difficult and were reluctant to take those that were available because they were pressured to leave their children elsewhere. As hard a time as Gertrude Thomas had keeping servants, she was reluctant to hire women with children: "I have a girl Anna who cooks milks the cows & sweeps the yard whom I give four dollars to. She wished me to raise her wages this morning but I would not do it as she has a babe with no nurse who occupies a good deal of her time." Although Thomas found one woman "a very indifferent cook," she chose to keep her, at least temporarily: "She has no children which has been the one reason why I have tolerated her." One of her replacements was a better cook but not more fortunate: "We will have to dismiss her. I am sorry for her. She has a child two years old & expects soon to have another. Her old mistress has her eldest child. Diania went in town with me taking her little boy whom she leaves with a married coloured woman whom she calls Miss Green."[9]

Freed black women, with or without responsibility for young children, generally considered the drawbacks of domestic service not worth the limited benefits, preferring instead the uncertain profits of farming with their husbands. Although large numbers of them continued to work at domestic service throughout the state, their jobs were generally temporary and often less than satisfactory to both parties. This led to a shortage of African-American women willing to perform domestic services, as Frances Butler Leigh discovered in 1867: "My cook and his wife have departed altogether, and my washerwoman and seamstress 'are picking cotton seed' . . . leaving me Daphne, who is expecting her eleventh confinement in less than a month."[10] In 1867, one white woman reported success in finding a cook: "About a week ago we succeeded in hiring a cook, Father had been trying every where & finally concluded he would let them go, when to our surprise the one we have, came & applied for a situation." Six months later, however, she feared her domestic concerns were only temporarily settled: "The grief I have now is to know she will leave me another year—says she is weary of cooking—been at it all her life—I do not blame her—but I know I never can replace her." Eighteen months later another letter indicated that the cook had not lasted long, and a replacement was difficult to find: "It is a hard matter to get hands down here—ours have all left, except Tony—& he had a great desire to do so. . . . His lazy wife would not agree to work—& she only has 7 1/2 bushels corn to depend on for the long year—& nothing else." Emma Holmes complained about the same problem: "The Negroes are getting worse daily; in every direction we hear of families being left without a single servant, or those who stay doing almost nothing. . . . All have turned hoof together."[11] For those women willing to be domestic servants, work proved plentiful. Julia Woodberry reported that ever since she left the home of the woman who had been her mistress during slavery, "I been in white people house. If it ain' one class, it another. De very day dat Dr. Dibble been pronounce me to de hospital, dey come after me to wait on a woman."[12]

Although there were exceptions, remembered with great fondness by white women, most African-American women rarely spent time in white women's houses and those that did were usually trusted house servants who withstood the war's test of their loyalty. Far more typical was the experience of Dolly Haynes. The husband she married just after Lee surrendered wanted to be a preacher, so for three years she worked the farm while he went to school. Afterwards, she continued to farm: "De briars cut my legs an' de breshes tore my skirt, but I tuck up de skirt an' plow right on 'til I bought my little farm."[13] Although unusual for her ability to purchase land, Dolly Haynes was typical of black women in her commitment to doing farm labor for her family during Reconstruction and beyond. Although black men might have preferred to have their wives remain at home and women might have preferred not to do work that reminded them of slavery, both recognized the necessity of the economic contributions women made to their families.

White women's work was similarly transformed during Reconstruction. First, they no longer managed the production of large amounts of food and clothing for slaves, nor did they supervise the domestic producers who did most of the work. Without responsibility for the well-being of many slaves, the most complex and time-consuming of former mistresses' tasks disappeared. Second, many former plantation mistresses' style of living was dramatically reduced by the war's inroads on their wealth, which precluded not only lavish entertaining and extensive wardrobes but sometimes even basic comforts.[14] Most important, the difficulty of finding and the expense of keeping domestic servants forced women such as Fannie Caison to take on many household chores permanently: "I have gone to regular *hard* work. I am learning to do every thing, from making wine, preserves, pickles, & c, down to baking a hoe-cake. I think I *excell* in cooking: but poor little Floy often wishes 'we could get a good cooker.' The dear child *feels* the change, sensibly, though she is unconscious of the great loss she has sustained." Another woman apologized for her delay in writing, claiming the necessity of domestic chores and the inability to find a cook kept her busy. While complaints about the pressures of work were familiar from the prewar era, the content of the work was new: "For the last four months I have had our cooking to do & all of the house work with only the help of the little girls. It kept me very busy all of the time, I tell you I found little time for sewing, consequently my work has gotten a long ways a head of me." Mary Anderson Moore's diary for 1868 is filled with references to a variety of domestic pursuits. In March, her activities included the following:

> March 4, 1868: Performed my round of duties in the forenoon, cut Irish potatoes for planting in the evening. . . . Four of us spent the evening planting a small patch.
>
> March 7, 1868: Washed up the glass ware and cleaned about generally. Was busy with little matters all day.

March 11, 1868: Made preparation for scouring, finished in the forenoon. Sorted potatoes in the afternoon.

March 16, 1868: Began to clean up stairs, mended up the shades, made some new ones.

March 25, 1868: I was out most of the day attending to my soap. Succeeded in making some beautiful soap.

Her sentiments after one particularly busy day could easily have been echoed by many white women unaccustomed to such hard work: "Our slumbers were scarcely interrupted during the whole night. Truly sleep is sweet to the laboring man." Throughout this period Moore had at least one domestic servant to handle the laundry and cooking. Sarah Witherspoon McIver also considered domestic work worthy of note. "I have been in the garden almost all day. . . . L. & I and Eliza cooked & ate our dinner in less than an hour and a half."[15]

Sometimes white families were compelled to make uncomfortable arrangements. Henry Ravenel's 1871 decision had significant impact on several white and black women: "We have decided to make a change in our household arrangements. We have had Peggy cooking for us at $1.50 per week & Leah washing at $1.30 per week. We find it necessary to curtail these expenses, & tomorrow we will begin to do our own cooking in the house, & Leah, Rony & Peggy will each give us a days washing every week for house rent."[16] One white woman had both a cook and a cook stove, a useful device she refused to allow the cook to use for fear it would break and the cook would leave: "When one leaves us then I can go to my stove & find things as I left them."[17]

White women's new obligations sometimes included those that had previously been the domain of white men. Because the war created many widows and because newly impoverished men needed the active assistance of their wives, the practice of women doing men's work became even more widespread after the war. One planter's wife recalled the impact of dead and incapacitated husbands on the women of South Carolina: They "took upon themselves the duties of not only the servants of the family, while filling their own places, but they had to be the men of the household as well." Sarah Witherspoon McIver, widowed before the war, continued to run her plantation afterwards. She did not provide daily supervision, but arranged labor, labor contracts, and management herself:

Although the snow & sleet is still on the ground I went to the plantation to see the Negro laborers about making a crop this year.

I have been very much troubled about getting some one to live in my yard to take care of the place. J. has moved his family to R. Adams' but he is working here today.

She was actively concerned about the progress of her farms: "Went to the plantation crop very much injured by the rain." McIver was not the only white women to arrange labor contracts with former slaves. Frances Butler Leigh did so too, but not without some effort: "It seemed quite hopeless even to get the Negroes to settle down to steady work, and although they still professed the greatest affection for and faith in me, it certainly did not show itself in works." After persuading them to sign, she breathed a sigh of relief: "The backbone of the opposition thus broken, and the work started more or less steadily, I turned my thoughts to what I considered my principal work, and belonging more to my sphere than what I had been engaged in up to that time."[18] Even women who did not have primary responsibility for a plantation sometimes performed traditionally male tasks. When Elizabeth Allen Coxe's family returned to their plantation, they found a neighbor so poor that the plantation's flower garden and walks were "destroyed and dug up to plant a small ladies' crop of cotton."[19]

Some women were forced to become self-supporting as a result of the war, a horrifying situation for women of the planter class. A year after the fighting broke out, Mary Chesnut vowed she would never work for wages outside her home, a comment inspired by the Confederate government's practice of hiring women for routine tasks in the Treasury Department: "Mrs. Preston and I have determined. Coute que coute—or come what will, survive or perish—we will not go into one of the departments. We will not stand up all day at a table and cut notes apart, ordered round by a department clerk. We will live at home with our families and starve in a body. Any homework we will do. Any menial service—under the shadow of our own rooftree. Department—never!" Although Chesnut was poor for much of the last ten years of her life, she successfully avoided working outside her home. Instead, she managed the family plantation and business while her husband continued his involvement in politics.[20]

Many of the women forced to work for a living were young and unmarried. Raised to wed the men killed in the war, they had few options for employment. Emma Holmes worked as a governess during part of the war, but returned to her family before the fighting ceased. Afterward she was embarrassed to ask a former slave to help her find work sewing: "I told her I had resolved on taking in some plain work during my leisure this summer & asked her, if she heard of any, to take it for herself & turn it over to me, which she promised to do. . . . I could not help smiling to myself at the revolution of fortune which had made me apply to Keturiah Workman for work. . . . As

Nanna [Hughes] says, my pride is buried with the Confederacy, or at least all false pride." Several months later she was still sewing for money, but with less subterfuge: "Thursday I rested by spending the day with cousin Sallie [Boykin] & sewing for her. Miss Emma Holmes going out for days work at 50 cts—O tempora, O mores!!!!" She attempted to earn a living by writing and translating, but instead was a schoolteacher for most of the rest of her life.[21] Belle Kearney also "swallowed my pride and asked the negroes to bring their sewing to me." She was pleased that "none sat in our presence" or did anything else to make her unnecessarily uncomfortable with the arrangement. Grace Brown Elmore "knocked about" and feared "being in the way" as she sought to find a home and a living. She and a sister opened a school; she also left friends and family for a time to teach in North Carolina and even was offered a job by "Miss Beecher of Abolition notoriety" in a school she planned to open in the South.[22] For women left without any means of support after the war, working for money was an unanticipated necessity that was probably even more burdensome than the unfamiliar domestic responsibilities faced by most former plantation mistresses.

The end of slavery had a wide variety of implications for women's work in South Carolina. For black women, freedom meant doing the same kind of work they had done as slaves, but under very different circumstances. Prevented from working for the sole benefit of their families before the war, they made doing so their first priority afterward. For white women, the end of slavery meant losing some work responsibilities, as well as losing assistance with most types of domestic work. Primarily occupied by supervisory and managerial activities before the war, white women did many of the physical tasks necessary for family comfort and survival themselves after it was over. Both groups of women found the war a turning point not only because it brought freedom, but also because it changed the nature of their work. Changed work relations in the postwar period changed the way black and white women thought about one another and themselves. Before the war, the frequent interaction and mutual dependence of women, reinforced by white women's interpretation of the ideology of domesticity, could cause them to recognize similarities in spite of their differences. After the war, new work patterns caused both the frequent interaction and the mutual dependence that had brought them together to disappear. Much of the common ground they sometimes recognized would vanish as well.

~⁌~

In addition to labor patterns, the war's upheaval and the changes it brought to so many aspects of life in the South dramatically influenced the ideologies that helped women define proper behavior and, by extension, the way they thought about one another. For many elite whites, the most important goal of the postwar years was to restore their primary place in society in spite of what they considered humiliating defeat and the deprivation associated with poverty. Accomplishing this required reestablishing dominance over former slaves, which in turn required new race and gender distinctions. Although the ideology of domesticity that emerged after the war bore a superficial resemblance to that of the antebellum years, the differences were momentous.

During Reconstruction and beyond, expectations for white women echoed those from before the war. While women were periodically applauded for their wartime contributions, they were expected to behave in traditional ways. A writer in *DeBow's Review* proclaimed in 1866: "The girl is kind, merciful, gentle and humane. . . . Woman was sent into the world on a mission of mercy—to help and to comfort man; and nobly and devotedly does she perform her allotted task. . . . She has more of prudence and caution, nicer instincts, more intuitive sagacity, better judgement, and more wisdom than he." Women's work was defined in poetry:

> Darning little stockings-
>   For restless little feet,
> Washing little faces
>   To keep them clean and sweet
> Hearing Bible lessons,
>   Teaching Catechism,
> Praying for salvation,
>   From heresy and schism—
>   Woman's work!

And prose: "It is her bounden duty to be honest and earnest in every undertaking. Let thoroughness be her motto, truth her standard; and let her conscience be taught that truth consists of more than simply stating facts."[23]

However much white southerners wanted to believe statements like these, they knew that expectations for women and their work could never be the same. In 1876, Annie Harper lamented: "The old Southern gentleman is passing rapidly away. That courtly chivalrous dignity . . . —where shall we find it in a few more years? The coming woman will know nothing of that deferential gallantry which marked his treatment of women, and how much she will miss—Beautiful past with its weakness even its sins, the world will look in vain for anything that can compare socially with thee, Type of the

noblest in man. Farewell." Letitia Burwell compared the lives of antebellum girls to those she observed in 1895 and was astonished at the changes:
"At that day the parents of a girl would have shuddered at the thought of
her venturing for a day's journey without an escort on a railway car, being
jostled in a public crowd, or exposed in any way to indiscriminate contact
with the outside world." Grace Brown Elmore took a more cynical view.
Teaching at a boarding school in North Carolina, she resented being "de-
tained to listen to a harangue from every man present, on the duties and
charms of a woman, till I wished from the bottom of my heart they would
go home and speechify to their own women."[24] The real problem, as Elmore
knew, was not the demise of chivalry, apparent changes in morality, or even
the persistence of the ideology of domesticity, but rather postwar women's
need to contribute to their own and their families' support. The necessity
for self-support caused definitions of women's sphere to change even as
postwar writers tried to convince themselves that nothing was different.

In the years following the war, writers on women's education justified their
efforts with familiar rhetoric. In 1868, one argued: "The thorough training
of our girls is a matter of the most vital importance. Upon it depends the
happiness of home, the moral excellence of social life, the elevation or degradation of mankind." However, this writer went on to maintain that "girls
should, with regard to education be allowed every possible privilege" because
"they are not all sure of husbands." Although quick to disavow being "in the
least degree . . . an advocate for woman's rights," the writer thought "girls
should be educated to be independent of marriage. . . . To rear them to look
forward to matrimony as their sole aim and ambition is degrading." The
writer also suggested that it was "unfair" for "the husband and father to be
the sole producer in a large family of consumers" and that women should
prepare for widowhood. As the writer pointed out, in the postwar South
marriage was not possible for all women, and contributing to the economic
stability of a family was often crucial for survival. To compensate, this writer urged a practical education for women that would leave more than "only
the most menial and unremunerative resources to which to look for support."
Such an education, however, should not lead to an "unwomanly pursuit,"
but rather to one at which women could earn a living: "Without aiming to
be preachers, or degrading themselves by becoming politicians, stump speak-
ers or in any way overstepping the bounds of womanly delicacy and dignity,
there are numberless avenues of support for which women should be fitted
and which should be open to them."[25] Another writer was more specific: "If
then employment may be offered to women with which they are content and

which enables them to gain an independent subsistence, it is certainly the duty of society to provide such employment as will be acceptable to them. Among the lighter operations of manufacture appears the conversion of cotton into cloths and yarns. The education of female operatives would enable us to convert this vast and valuable product of our own soil, into fabrics worth three-fold more than the material."[26]

White women were indeed looking for remunerative work, although their idea of acceptable employment was different. In 1870, a group of women wrote a public letter outlining their difficulties: "The issue of the war has deprived thousands of us of our only means of support. Harder to bear than this, its terrible vicissitudes of slaughter and disease have taken away from many of us the strong arms and brave hearts of those who would have counted it all joy to labor for us." Women who were "suddenly thrown upon their own resources" asked only "the opportunity to help ourselves." They urged creation of an institution to teach women practical skills such as printing, wood engraving and carving, gardening, bookkeeping, and telegraph operating.[27]

Even though these writers and petitioners were recalling old definitions of white women's place and proper relationship to sources of power in the public world, all also recognized the changes brought by war. They urged a looser construction of the ideology of domesticity to make possible a degree of economic independence for those white women unfortunate enough to require it. Sally Elmore Taylor felt the power of the old ideology and new realities. She learned by experience "how much skill goes into coarse work . . . [and] nearly worked off my arms to do it." But Taylor continued to pretend she was an ideal woman, even in retrospect: "Such [menial] jobs were *sneaked* in by me when the lord of the Manor and manners was out of sight. . . . It was fun to hurry into a fresh gown and sit down in a rocker after meeting the master at the porch steps, and then let him put on the andirons the big wood because too heavy for his gentle lady, when she had toted it all into the house from the wood pile. Women are sweetly duplicitous."[28]

As the ideology of domesticity was reconstructed, so were ideas about the appropriate behavior of white women toward former slaves. As white southerners redefined their racial views to encompass emancipation, they extended the customary analogy comparing the proper relationship between whites and blacks to those between husbands and wives or parents and children. In each case, white writers argued that members of the subordinate group should not complain about their position: "Laws are necessarily general in their character, and work injustice in peculiar cases. Yet we must have laws however hardly they may sometimes operate. . . . Generally men are best qualified to be the heads of families, and the law is right that recognizes men as such." This writer made explicit the political connection between white women and blacks in the postwar South: "If the white woman can't complain, justly, that they are not put on an equality with the men, but really become, in legal contemplation, slaves, so soon as they are married, why should the negroes, male or female, complain that they are subordinate to the male whites. As a class are negro men superior to white women? Should not the right of suffrage be conferred on white women before it is given to negro men?" His comments were made in the context of the national debate about extending suffrage to black men and all women after the war. This writer further maintained that "immemorial usage, law, custom and divine injunction" led to the subordination of women, "inferior races," and those under twenty-one and concluded that all three groups needed "protection."[29]

Although this writer relegated white women to the same status as all blacks, most southerners continued to believe that blacks should be protected by white women. One writer knew that "ladies who had taught slave women to cut out and sew, to spin and weave, were conscious of the truth that to improve the mind, is to increase the capacity for usefulness and even for profit" and urged women to continue offering such training to freed blacks. Another also encouraged such activities and admired those who did them, but was more direct about his reasoning: "I know of instances now, where young women of the highest type of refinement and culture bestow a portion of their time daily in teaching the children of the field hands. It is an old custom. But prejudice has not destroyed it, and the colored parents will cling to the plantations, and sympathise with their employers, who thus manifest a regard for their offspring." Another writer warned about the apparent dangers of "contracted benevolence and philanthropy," which he thought were visible in "the condition of the freedmen of both sexes and of all ages, who, always accustomed to a state of pupilage, are not as well qualified in general to take care of themselves as a parcel of monkeys." He claimed that one consequence of previous kindness to slaves was that freed blacks "who can get places are all gradually going into service—that is, selecting masters and mistresses to take care of them and provide for them. The hire is a mere nominal affair."[30]

Without doubt, white women were still expected to behave benevolently toward all dependents, white and black, for reasons seemingly more urgent in the postwar period than ever before. White women's willingness and ability to live up to these expectations in the face of defeat and poverty were uncertain at best, but they were bombarded with direct incentives to do so.

However, as they found to their sorrow, even the best incentives did not stand up to black women's insistence on shaping their own lives.

Determined to implement their newfound freedom and devote themselves to their families, black women were reluctant to continue to work for white women as they had as slaves, but old habits died slowly. Some African-American women chose to remain with mistresses who were like mothers to them, as did Sylvia Cannon: "Miss Hatchel been so good to me dat I stay on dere wid her 8 years after freedom come. Miss Hatchel tell me I better stay on dere whe' I can get flour bread to eat. Yes, mam, never got a whippin in all my life. . . . Dat de reason, when my parents come after me, I hide under de bed." Julia Woodberry remained with her former mistress and took pride in the white woman's trust in her: "No, child, I ain' never think bout to lay no shame on dese hands. White folks been used to leave money all bout whe' I bresh (brush) en dust en I ain' never had no mind to touch it no time."[31]

Others, eager to enjoy the reversal of roles, went out of their way to be kind to their former mistresses. Daniel Huger Smith remembered their behavior long after peace came: "The Negroes continued to keep some touch with us for a long time, calling to see 'Ole Missis' on their rare visits to town, and there was the same interchange of small gifts of eggs or a chicken or two on the one side and perhaps an article of clothing on the other." Sometimes this aid was more necessary than white women preferred to admit, as a plantation superintendent from St. Helena reported to an official of the Freedman's Bureau in 1865:

> The thrift and success of the freedmen makes them objects of attention to their former masters who are returning every day to visit their plantations. Two young ladies went from house to house among their father's slaves, pleading their poverty and receiving from one some grits or potatoes, from others plates and spoons—or money. One woman took the shoes from her own feet and gave them to her former mistress. . . . One lady came from Beaufort a week or two ago and sent word that "she thought some of her Ma's niggers might come to wait upon her." None volunteered. Some went to see her, however, and from these she received food, money, and clothes. She offered to become a dressmaker for the Negroes and will probably get enough money for a support in that way.

Elizabeth Botume, a teacher at Beaufort for the New England Freedman's Aid Society, recorded the remarks of a black woman she knew: "'Us going to well fur water fur the lady what bring we up, an' was like a muther to we,' she said. 'Her is come back, an' is awful poor an' sick, an' us all say us can't stan' seein' her workin' fur herself, bringin' water, an' sich-like, fur she bin very kin' to we. . . . Massa set great store by my mudder, an' us mus' help them now.' " Sometimes helping former mistresses came at a high price, as Sally Taylor indicated in a letter to her sisters about their mother's serious illness: "Grace's Phillis stole away from Abram [her husband] to see mother yesterday. They say he won't allow her to come lest she'll offer to do something for the family—said she'd try and come today—but thought she could certainly Sunday."[32] As Taylor's comment indicates, black women, finally free, placed a higher priority on their relationships with their husbands than on their employers. As Phillis learned, the two impulses could generate conflict unless that priority were made explicit.

Black women were pressured from all sides to be submissive and subordinate to their husbands. Black men imposed their views on black women in a variety of ways, with mixed results. Ezra Adams, a former slave from the Columbia area, shared his beliefs about women and men's proper roles with a WPA interviewer:

> It is sho' worth somethin' to be boss, and, on de farm you can be boss all you want to, 'less de man 'low his wife to hold dat 'portant post. A man wid a good wife, one dat pulls wid him, can see and feel some pleasure and experience some independence. But, bless your soul, if he gits a woman what wants to be both husband and wife, fare-you-well and goodbye, too, to all love, pleasure, and independence; 'cause you sho' is gwine to ketch hell here and no mild climate whenever you goes 'way. A bad man is worse, but a bad woman is almost terrible.

The black woman who did not obey her husband suffered the consequences, as Frances Leigh recognized: "The good old law of female submission to the husband's will on all points held good, and I once found a woman sitting on the church steps, rocking herself backwards and forwards in great distress, and on inquiring the cause I was told she had been turned out of church because she refused to obey her husband in a small matter. So I had to intercede for her, and on making a public apology before the whole congregation she was re-admitted."[33]

According to Robert Smalls in his election speech in 1876 black men allowed women only one kind of power: "When John went to Massa [Wade] Hampton and pledged to vote for him his wife told him, 'She would not give him any of that thing if you vote for Hampton.' John gone back to Massa Hampton and said, 'Massa Hampton, I can't vote for you, for woman is too sweet, and my wife says if I vote for you she won't give me any.' And ladies, I think if you all do that we won't have a Democratic ticket polled on Parris Island." Mack Taylor recounted similar efforts by black preachers to convince men to vote for a particular candidate for governor: "De preachers sure got up de excitement 'mongst de colored women folks. Dey 'vised them to have nothin' to do wid their husbands if they didn't go to de 'lection box and vote for Moses. I didn't go, and my wife wouldn't sleep wid me for six months."[34]

Laura Towne described the activities of men who made women leave a political meeting called to form a Republican Party:

> It is too funny to see how much more jealous the men are of one kind of liberty they have achieved than of the other! Political freedom they are rather shy of, and ignorant of; but domestic freedom—the right, just found, to have their own way in their families and rule their wives—that is an inestimable privilege! . . . Several speakers have been here who have advised the people to get the women into their proper place—never to tell them anything of their concerns, etc., etc.; and the notion of being bigger than women generally, is just now inflating the conceit of the males to an amazing degree. When women get the vote, too, no people will be more indignant than these, I suppose.[35]

While Towne's assumptions about black men's response to women's suffrage ultimately proved incorrect, her assessment of men's attitudes during Reconstruction was echoed in a letter written by a former slave from Camden reporting on his remarriage: "I found her a girl of good character, well-behaved and sensible, so she and I talked the matter over and she told me she liked me well enough to try to take care of me, and I promised to do the same for her. So far I am very much pleased with her. She does as I direct. What is my pleasure seems to be hers. She listens to my counsels and I think strives to do right. . . . She is industrious as far as she knows and I think will learn very readily."[36]

In a discussion of the social equality preached by radical Republicans, Moses Lyles offered insight as to why black women would submit to their husbands: "Nigger men lak dat kinda talk, nigger women didn't lak it so much. They fear dat if nigger men have a chance to git a white wife, they would have no chance wid de nigger men. They was sure dat no white man would take a black wife, 'ceptin' it be a poor white trash man and then if they git one of them, him would beat her and work her harder than in slavery time." Charley Barber believed that after the war, a black woman, unlike a white woman, "ain't gonna have money in de back of her head when her pick out a man to marry. Her gonna want a man wid muscles on his arms and back." Ed Barber disagreed, claiming that when he attended St. Mark's Church in Charleston, "dat all de society folks of my color went to," the women "did carry on, bow and scrape and ape de white folks. I see some pretty feathers, pretty fans, and pretty women dere!" He reported feeling uncomfortable "'cause they was too 'hifalootin' in de ways, in de singin', and all sorts of carryin' ons." Black men were eager to take advantage of freedom by enjoying what they considered their masculine prerogatives. Some took these too far, as Millie Barber soon discovered: "Well, my husband die and I took a fool notion, lak most widows, and got into slavery again. I marry Prince Barber."[37]

In spite of the apparent wishes of black men, black women did not always submit. Gertrude Thomas knew one woman who insisted on a separate account from her husband, "so she would know how she stood."[38] Elizabeth Botume reported black women's reluctance to sell their land in the Sea Islands as their husbands asked: "From the friends of the freed people in town, who tried to shield them against sharpers and carpet-baggers, the women had learned that they too had independent rights in their ten-acre lots, most of which had been bought with their own money. Some of these women were firm in refusing to sign the papers which transferred their lands. The men, directed by their white leaders, used all sorts of ways to bring their wives into subjection." One man tricked his wife into signing away her land by telling her she was signing a receipt for medicine.[39]

Women able to stand up to their husbands were rare, as were husbands determined to dominate them. Instead, the vast majority of black women and men were committed to their families and eager to work together to improve their lives. Rather than viewing their society in gendered terms, they united for family and racial advancement. Most sought to keep wives and children at home under the watchful eyes of husbands and fathers as much as possible.

Protecting black women was not a high priority among whites, however. Instead, white men and women pressured black women to behave properly. White men used every method available to compel African-American women to obey. One of Catherine Edmondston's former slaves, who had been a foreman, tried to break his contract by demanding that his daughter be returned to him rather than work as a housemaid. When Edmondston's husband told the father "that if he persisted he would be forced to leave himself, he became overwhelmed with contrition & begged in the most abject manner that she & him be allowed to remain. . . . He claimed her, however, at Christmas when she was of course resigned to him." The father also lost his position, "made worthless by emancipation."[40] Other white men, when they felt it necessary, used force. In testimony about the Ku Klux Klan, Caroline Smith reported being beaten by a white man to ensure a submissive attitude: "He whipped me some. . . . He gave me fifty more and then

said, 'Don't let's hear any big talk from you, and don't sass any white ladies.'"[41] The pressure to submit to black men also came from the Freedman's
Bureau, which in arranging labor contracts and issuing rations assumed that
men were heads of households.[42] It also came from white women who urged
"morality," marriage, and recollection of past ties. One of Mary Jones's
former slave women chose to follow her husband, much to the white woman's sorrow. Jones reminded the black woman "of Sam's want of fidelity to
her, and the unjust and unkind manner in which he had often treated her.
She, however, decided to go; and I told her if so, I preferred she should go
at once; whereupon she withdrew Elizabeth. . . . I told Sue if she was ever
in want or ill-treated, she must return to me. She replied: 'No, ma'am, I'll
never come back, for you told me to go,' thus in a saucy way perverting my
remark." Another of Jones's former slaves was "influenced" by her mother
to leave, while a third "wants to be relieved of the heavy burden of cooking
for two and wait on her husband."[43]

Ties forged in slavery meant increasingly little as the Reconstruction years
continued. Eager to enjoy uninterrupted family life and to work for the benefit
of their children, black women placed a far higher priority on their own wishes
and those of their husbands than they did on what their former mistresses
wanted. Since even the appearance of devotion offered benefits for African-
American women when they were enslaved, many had been willing to allow
their mistresses a degree of intrusion into their personal lives and to offer them
loyalty. Once peace was declared, however, there were few advantages to be
gained. While relatively few former slaves were actively hostile to previous
mistresses, many resented what they perceived as changes in their mistresses'
attitudes toward them. No longer generous or benevolent, white women
seemed to be far less kindly and as a result black women were no longer willing to maintain even a facade of the loyalty expected by white women. Instead,
they chose to work for themselves and their families.

~

The new options available to black women directly influenced the way white
women viewed their former slaves. Although at first many plantation mistresses could take satisfaction from the apparent loyalty of their newly freed
slaves, they simultaneously ceased to believe very strongly in it. As Reconstruction made it increasingly apparent that black women would rather work
with their families on farms than for white women doing domestic work,
white women abandoned their former beliefs and looked at African Americans with increasing frustration and bitterness. Adele Allston's impressions
were typical: "The Negroes are as unsatisfactory as possible, the prospect

ahead discouraging. The poor nigs have certainly deteriorated very much in *appearance and manners* in the last year or 8 months. . . . I fear Milly is tired of being good and faithful. It seems to me she wants the whole of the stock, the profits of it at least." Gertrude Thomas shared her frustration and puzzlement: "I have had three of the most indolent and slovenly servants I have ever hired. Their principal recommendation being that they were quiet and not quarrelsome among themselves. Louisa and Harriet both could read well yet they evinced little interest in books." She was angered by her servants' inefficiency: "America . . . is cooking and attempting to carry on the washing and ironing but not successfully altho she has Fannie to assist her." Thomas also found them dishonest and unreliable. One morning she fired her cook: "That morning she broke open the potato house and took out a great many. . . . Tuesday I hired a woman by the name of Hannah. . . . This morning after breakfast I was in the yard—went into the kitchen to see if it had been cleaned up. None of the dishes had been washed and in front of the fire was my new cook fast asleep."[44]

While Thomas expressed her feelings more explicitly than some, her consternation with servants' behavior predominated. It was certainly shared by Grace Brown Elmore: "The cows have been giving nothing, so I took both cows and dairy woman in charge. She talked down Albert and the cowboy, but I've gotten her cows up to eight quarts at a milking. She is good natured, but the poultry woman is a perfect crab and brings in precious few eggs." Catherine Edmondston complained that the former slaves she encountered "are still respectful & even subservient, but O! how utterly worthless and Lazy!" She was frustrated by her dealings with them: "They admit that they do not know what is to become of them or where they are to go next year & yet they will not agree to work so as to secure their future from want. . . . They will do nothing but sleep & get wood for themselves." She was pleased by "the *only* instance of faithfulness which out of so large a number has fallen under my immediate notice," two former slaves who "have been unwaveringly true, faithful, cheerful, industrious, & grateful." She was especially pleased because "they have earnestly endeavoured to make others follow their example . . . in spite of opposing causes, temptation, & even threats."[45]

Eliza Andrews uttered one of the most extreme expressions of bitterness at black women's unwillingness to work for white women:

> It does seem to me a waste of time for people who are capable of doing something better to spend their time sweeping and dusting while scores of lazy Negroes that are fit for nothing else are lying around idle. Dr. Calhoun suggested it would be a good idea to import some of those man-apes from Africa and teach

them to take the place of the Negroes, but Henry said that just as soon as we had got them tame, and taught them to be of some use, those crazy fanatics of the North would insist on coming down here to emancipate them and give them universal suffrage.

Mary Jones articulated her sense of betrayal after emancipation: "I shall cease my anxieties for the race. My life long (I mean since I had a home) I have been laboring and caring for them, and since the war have labored with all my might to supply their wants, and expended everything I had upon their support, directly or indirectly; and this is their return." On another occasion she formulated her deep resentment: "My heart is pained and sickened with their vileness and falsehood in every way. I long to be delivered from the race."[46]

Some white women's ability to find and keep satisfactory servants mitigated the pain of losing the war, the humiliation brought on by Reconstruction, the shock of losing their wealth, and the unfamiliarity of their new position in southern society. Aware of how unusual they were, these women sought as much evidence of loyalty as they could find. They frequently found virtue in adversity, recognizing that their servants could disprove their optimism at any time. One woman reflected this mixture of hope and doubt when writing about her newly hired cook: "I like her first rate so far, the only objection (if it can be called one), is her talking a great deal but she is always in a fine humor & I can over look her gabs. . . . I only hope we can keep her & she will be as well satisfied as she is now." Meta Morris Grimball displayed the same mixed feelings when writing about the decision of several of her former slaves to leave early in 1866. Although they had all been quite generous to her, their departure still seemed something of a betrayal: "I am thankful amid the wreck of all to have this example of affection and duty to always remember. The old Mauma is living at Mrs. Hankels her own choice." Another woman was also thankful. "The Negroes are quiet I don't scold much now." Emma Holmes thought she knew why her brother's family was able to make satisfactory domestic arrangements. "Hannah, Maria's nurse, is cooking for them, made humble by starvation."[47] Suzanne Keitt's unqualified self-congratulation was quite rare—and unconvincing. "I can manage Negroes—all my father's old slaves will do just what I tell them to do, are attached and very respectful." Even loyal servants could be a mixed blessing, as Mary Chesnut suggested in an 1866 letter to a friend: "The coloured ones hang on. . . . We will have to run away from their persistent devotion. We are free to desert them now I hope. In point of fact their conduct to us has been beyond all praise."[48]

Most white women, even when their servants appeared loyal and satis-factory, remained skeptical of their good faith. One woman was suspicious of the work several of her ex-slaves did when assigned fall cleaning: "They have succeeded in obscuring the light of day by clouds of dust, and keep up such a 'jawing,' as to even render my retreat to the third story a vain attempt at quiet. I hope the result will be commensurate with the outlay of breath."[49] Women whose servants behaved badly or disappeared were convinced that freedom had transformed black women in unrecognizable ways. Few would have disagreed with the sentiment one white woman expressed years later: "'Tis sad to know that the mutual love of master and servant passed away with the Confederacy. Such devotion should never die." Another was con-vinced that past generations of mistresses should be venerated and eulogized for the loyal behavior they had elicited from slaves: "For what courage, what patience, what perseverance, what long suffering, what Christian forbear-ance, must it have cost our great-grandmothers to civilize, Christianize, and elevate the naked, savage Africans to the condition of good cooks and re-spectable maids!"[50]

Former mistresses who battled mightily to recreate the comforting pat-terns of slavery, expected in vain that old approaches would be met with the same response. They continued to interfere in the personal lives of the black women but were often rebuffed. Eliza Andrews feared this would happen shortly after the war ended: "There will soon be no more old mammies and daddies, no more old uncles and aunties. . . . The sweet ties that bound our old family servants to us will be broken and replaced with envy and ill-will. I am determined it shall not be so with ours, unless they do something to forfeit my respect." In 1867, Frances Butler Leigh made efforts to repair the homes and hospital building used by blacks and to open a school for them, but with little success: "The people did not seem to like either of my pro-posals too much; especially the old plantation midwife, who is indignant at her work being taken away from her. . . . I hoped by degrees to bring them to approve of my arrangements, by showing them how much more comfort-able they would be in my hospital, and by presenting the babies born there with some clothes, and the old women who lived there with blankets, to make them like it. (I never did succeed, however, and after several attempts, had to give it up.)" Leigh also tried to encourage "morality" among the African Americans she knew, but considered her efforts only partially successful: "We had a great many marriages this winter, and wishing to encourage the girls to become moral and chaste, we made the ceremony as important as possi-ble, that is, if a grand cake and white wreath and veil could make it so, for the ceremony, as performed by our old black minister, could hardly be said to be imposing, and I think I have gone through more painful agonies to keep from laughing at some of these weddings than from any physical suffering I ever experienced."[51]

Learning not to meddle in the personal lives of black women was a difficult lesson for white women. Some, such as Gertrude Thomas, claimed after the war that she had never interfered in the personal lives of her slaves:

> During my married life I have never been the confidant of our servants in their matrimonial and love affairs. Indeed I shrewdly suspected that they would have preferred almost any one else should have read their love letters and I am quite sure I had much preferred someone else should have answered them. When they belonged to us they all preferred having husbands off the plantations, thought that it was exceedingly hard if they could not marry away from home and yet I have known of a number of instances of men leaving now they are free the very women they were so anxious to have before and marrying some one else.

In spite of Thomas's claims, her diary from the antebellum years demonstrates how faulty her memory was; that from the postwar years shows how far from shrewd she was in her assessment of her own character and behavior. Other women had to be lectured, like this sister: "Will you let me tell you as plainly as I ever have talked, it is quite useless for you to trouble yourself about Henny's morals. It is no concern of yours. You could do nothing when you felt yourself in a measure responsible, & now it is not your responsibility. You had better take comfort in the fact that she still waits on you & leave the rest to her. There will be tares with the wheat, even in human motives."[52]

Blocked from meddling in the personal lives of black women, white women judged their behavior instead. White women suddenly found conduct shocking and immoral that was once tolerated. One white woman in Charleston dismissed a servant whose work was unsatisfactory and was even more critical of her subsequent activities: "Quash, who you know, was always known for his hospitality received her as an honored guest, in the ruins which he inhabits in Tradd Street—They live in a whirl of gayety, balls night and day, showing a capacity for the enjoyment of the present, and wonderful faith for the future—I consider them a damned race, and regard them with a *mingled* feeling of pity and disgust." Emma Holmes was also repulsed by blacks' behavior: "Two of the Brownfields' former Negroes have married Yankees—one a light colored mustee had property left her by some white man whose mistress she had been. She says she passed herself off for a Spaniard, & Mercier Green violated the sanctity of Grace Church by performing the ceremony. The other, a man, went north & married a Jewess—the idea is too revolting."[53]

Gertrude Thomas was upset by the conduct of a maid named Diania, whose marital and romantic entanglements she recorded at length in her diary. Her explanation reveals her awareness of a change in her own thinking about blacks:

> The moral character of our Negro is so low. Their standard of morality has always been low but that was not their fault. Some might say that the fault is with them *now* and not with us. Very true, but as we have assisted in retarding their moral development as a race heretofore, we ought now in justice to assist them in their efforts to do right. We show them so plainly we expect nothing from them. We place no high stand point for them and urge them to gain it. The majority of us expect no more virtue from our Negro men and women than we do from our horses and cows.

Thomas's son and husband stopped her impulse to meddle. Her son informed her how typical Diania's behavior was, and her husband argued: "I hope you won't interfere unless you wish to deprive me of two excellent hands." Frances Leigh also believed that African-American women's moral standards had declined since antebellum days: "Always inclined to be immoral, they have now thrown all semblance of chastity to the winds, and when I said to my old nurse how shocked and grieved I was to find how ill-conducted the young girls were, so much worse than they used to be, she said, 'Missus, dere not one decent gal left in de place.'"[54]

Faced with what they considered immoral and lazy African-American women, many white women found it easy to take the next step and condemn the entire race. Gertrude Thomas was upset by the need for laws forbidding blacks to marry whites: "We have the superiority of race by nature & education. Let us see that we maintain it and then all laws concerning marrying or giving in marriage will be useless. As it is the law is almost an insult to Southern women."[55] Refusing to recognize what women of the two races had in common before the war, Grace Elmore could see only the antagonism that separated them after it was over:

> What this miserable race is to do, is engaging much of the thoughts of their former owners. We have gone through so much, that this breaking of old ties has excited but little feeling, both parties are very indifferent, and the most that is felt is a polite and gentle interest in the affairs of each other. In most instances there is I believe a bitter feeling, and a sharp antagonism between the two races. I almost think they are natural enemies and that only their relative positions bound them together in affection, as well as by law.

Louise Wigfall Wright echoed her sentiments at the turn of the century: "The Negro in slavery, before and during the War, was lazy and idle—he will always be that—but he was simple, true and faithful. What he has become since his emancipation from servitude is a queer comment on the effect of the liberty bestowed upon him." Letitia Burwell believed "the problem of their race remains unresolved. . . . The tie which once bound the two races together is broken forever, and entire separation in churches and schools prevents mutual interest or intercourse." Since their work was no longer shared either, women had even fewer opportunities or reasons to try to get along.[56]

A few white women were willing to acknowledge benefits deriving from emancipation, even if they amounted to mere relief from the responsibilities of slavery. Catherine Edmondston was glad that she "had no longer negro children or babies to be responsible to God for" and her husband "need no longer trouble himself to make a parcel of lazy women support themselves. That care was henceforth their husbands." By 1876, Annie Harper believed blacks had "an advance on the old life, the idea of *home*, property rights, responsibility and independence is developing slowly in their breasts." She mourned the prosperity and freedom "from care and trouble" of the past, but did not wish to restore it: "With all that we have suffered I thank God that I have yet to hear the first voice wish that slavery might be restored. I also thank God that the future of my children is free from the plague spot of African Slavery." Letitia Burwell complimented those blacks who "have acquired independent homes, with the laudable purpose of becoming useful and respected citizens." However, she also believed that the "majority . . . are best pleased with itineracy."[57]

Like Burwell, Mary Jones exhibited wildly conflicting feelings. At the same time she told her son she could not "get over the feeling of confidence in those born and raised with us" she also considered herself "thoroughly disgusted with the whole race. . . . My heart sickens at . . . a prospect of dwelling with them." When some of her black laborers challenged their contract, she pushed the Freedman's Bureau agent to enforce it, then informed the laborers "that in doubting my word they offered me the greatest insult I ever received in my life; that I had considered them friends and treated them as such, . . . but that now they were only laborers under contract, and only the law would rule between us, and I would require every one of them to come up to the mark in their duty on the plantation. The effect has been decided, and I am not sorry for the position we hold mutually. They have relieved me of the constant desire and effort to do something to promote their comfort."[58]

Sentiments like those of Jones and Burwell indicate both ambivalence and how thoroughly white women believed their mutual experiences with black women had been destroyed. Once sympathetic ties had been replaced by hostility and contempt. Previously influenced by the ideology of domesticity to feel concern for slave women's lives, white women instead felt antagonism. No longer benevolent because they had nothing to give, no longer mediators of slavery because slavery was dead, white women after the war developed a virulent new form of racism. Fed by white women's decline in wealth and status and by their frustration with the difficulty of finding and keeping servants, this racism overpowered whatever remnants of goodwill existed after the war.

This harsher racism was a direct result of the new work patterns that had arisen. Instead of long-term relationships with large numbers of slaves, white women found their kitchens staffed by transient black women whose histories and families were unfamiliar. Feeling sympathy for black women they did not know and did not expect to stay was difficult, particularly because this absence of loyalty made their own duties so much more burdensome. Unable to concern themselves with the lives of blacks and unhappy with the changes in their personal circumstances, white women found newly virulent racist views a convenient outlet for their anger and confusion.

By reducing the interaction of black and white women, the work patterns of the Reconstruction period completed the transition in South Carolina life started by the Civil War. Changes in the work lives of both groups of women hardened their attitudes toward one another and eroded the influence of the ideology of domesticity in bringing them together. The increasing distance between the two groups of women made their views of one another far harsher than they ever had been. Whatever common ground women had disappeared as they identified their interests ever more closely with those of their husbands. South Carolina during Reconstruction became a place where the bonds of race proved more durable than the bonds of womanhood.

Changes in the ideology of domesticity as a force shaping white women's behavior also hardened racial lines after the war. Domesticity, an impossible luxury in the war-ravaged South, was replaced in large part by white women's belief in their own heroism and in the dead Confederacy. Instead of recognizing the harshness of black women's lives, white women bemoaned their own fate. Grace Elmore's views at the end of the war would have been familiar to many:

> O how different our feelings if we had won our "Cause." With what spirit and heart would we have gone to work, how willingly would loss of home and wealth have been borne for the sake of being free. But now we are forced to work; with-

out hope for our country,—but that we might obtain bread. Never have I so longed
to possess money and leave the country. . . . 'Tis inexpressibly mournful to feel
the necessity of giving up one's country, to feel that even should that land become
prosperous 'twould give no happiness to you, unless wholly free from the Yoke
of the Yankee.[59]

Although influenced by the frustration of losing the war, Elmore's statement
reflects the posture of white women during Reconstruction. In their hum-
bled situation, the only possible attitude toward the black women they had
previously seen as allies was anger. Benevolence was not possible for those
without the means to provide it, nor did it seem desirable to those who believed their humiliation had come at the price of freedom for slaves. Prac-
ticing domesticity's teachings regarding slaves was just as much a casualty
of the war as the luxurious style of life that made it possible. Ironically, the
teachings of the ideology of domesticity regarding the separation of spheres
and the subordinate position of women remained in force and may have even
grown stronger as whites and blacks sought to reduce the impact of slavery
and the war's damage on their lives.

The hardening of racial lines had profound consequences for the future
of the women of South Carolina. Once domesticity as a force encouraging
a degree of mutual understanding among women was destroyed, gender as
a category of social analysis became an anachronism. The demands of northern women for political, economic, and social equality horrified white wom-
en in the South, who associated them with abolitionism and the desire for
racial equality. Black women, excluded from political debate by their husbands but concerned with developing economic security for themselves,
mostly viewed such demands as irrelevant. With much dividing them and
no ideology suggesting they shared a common bond, black and white wom-
en widened the distance that separated them.

The failed effort for southern independence and the failed effort to effect
significant economic change after it was over brought real changes to race
and gender relations in South Carolina. Where before the war work patterns on large plantations reinforced the ideology of domesticity's teachings
to create a situation in which plantation mistresses were encouraged to feel
some measure of sympathy for female slaves, after the war no such sympathy existed. The destruction of the plantation economy and the disappearance of the ideology of domesticity's implications for race relations left white
women with little sense of responsibility toward or personal identification
with black women. Instead, they saw their former slaves as somehow hav-

ing failed them; their postwar feelings could perhaps best be characterized as disappointment, frustration, resentment—the bitterness associated with unpaid debts and insufficient gratitude.

If former mistresses viewed their former slaves as insufficiently grateful, black women saw no need for gratitude. Although some felt ties of personal loyalty and friendship for their former mistresses, all were eager to reap the rewards of freedom. One of the most eagerly pursued of these was the right to be wives and mothers without interference from whites—to work for their families instead of for whites. The breakdown of work ties between the two groups of women brought the breakdown of whatever tenuous feelings of sympathy or shared understanding those ties had created.

With women of both groups devoting themselves to their families, the ideology of domesticity was transformed. No longer did even the possibility of women recognizing a common gender experience exist. Instead, domesticity was privatized, and women believed that their only true calling was to their families. Whatever potential—and it was often only a potential—domesticity had had for transcending racial lines disappeared, and women now understood it to mean simply devotion to family. The impulse of plantation mistresses to practice domesticity beyond the walls of their own homes and the impulse of female slaves to use their sense of common womanhood with white women to aid themselves and their communities vanished. In their place stood a newly virulent racism on the part of white women and a renewed sense of being besieged on the part of black women. Both would last until the end of the century and beyond.

On a larger scale, the failed effort by southern states to achieve independence and effect significant economic change following the Civil War reformed race and gender relations in South Carolina, although some consequences would not be felt in significant ways until the next generation. Although gender differences continued to form the bedrock of southern society, the wartime experiences of women demonstrated that specific manifestations of those differences were not static. Women learned that expectations of acceptable behavior could be modified and that there were alternatives to traditional ways of relating to men and to one another. The effects of war and Reconstruction allowed women of both races to consider, perhaps for the first time, the possibility of questioning the ideology of domesticity as a social institution shaping their lives. Few did so, and even fewer did so in the name of feminism. But wartime modifications demonstrated that change was possible, and as memories faded and a new generation of women of both races reached adulthood, challenges to the ideology of domesticity would become more common in the South.

Notes

Introduction

1. Folklore materials are especially rich. See Edward C. L. Adams, *Tales of the Congaree* (Chapel Hill: University of North Carolina Press, 1987); A. M. H. Christensen, *Afro-American Folklore: Told Round Cabin Fires on the Sea Islands of South Carolina* (Boston: J. G. Cupples, 1892); Mason Crum, *Gullah: Negro Life in the Carolina Sea Islands* (Durham: Duke University Press, 1940); Savannah Unit, Georgia Writers Project, Works Progress Administration, *Drums and Shadows: Survival Studies among the Georgia Coastal Negroes* (Athens: University of Georgia Press, 1940, 1986); Ambrose E. Gonzales, *The Black Border: Gullah Stories of the Carolina Coast* (New York: Columbia University Press, 1922); Asa H. Gordon, *Sketches of Negro Life and History in South Carolina* (n.p., 1929); Guy Benton Johnson, *Folk Culture on St. Helena Island* (Chapel Hill: University of North Carolina Press, 1930); Elsie Clews Parsons, *Folk-Lore of the Sea Islands, South Carolina*, Memoirs of the American Folk-Lore Society 16 (Cambridge: American Folk-Lore Society, 1923); Society for the Preservation of Spirituals, *The Carolina Low-Country* (New York: Macmillan, 1931); Samuel Gaillard Stoney and Gertrude Mathews Shelby, *Black Genesis: A Chronicle* (New York: Macmillan, 1930).

2. Julia Cherry Spruill, *Women's Life and Work in the Southern Colonies* (Chapel Hill: University of North Carolina Press, 1938; New York: Norton, 1972); Guion Griffis Johnson, *A Social History of the Sea Islands: With Special Reference to St. Helena Island, South Carolina* (Chapel Hill: University of North Carolina Press, 1930); Mary Elizabeth Massey, *Bonnet Brigades* (New York: Knopf, 1966); Anne Firor Scott, *The Southern Lady: From Pedestal to Politics, 1830–1930* (Chicago: University of Chicago Press, 1970); Anne Firor Scott, *Making the Invisible Woman Visible* (Urbana: University of Illinois Press, 1984); Catherine Clinton, *The Plantation Mistress: Woman's World in the Old South* (New York: Pantheon, 1982); Suzanne Lebsock, *The Free Women of Petersburg: Status and Culture in a Southern Town, 1784–1860* (New York: Norton, 1984); Jacqueline Jones, *Labor of Love, Labor of Sorrow: Black Women, Work, and the Family from Slavery to the Present* (New York: Basic Books, 1985); Jean E. Friedman,

The Enclosed Garden: Women and Community in the Evangelical South, 1830–1900 (Chapel Hill: University of North Carolina Press, 1985); Deborah Gray White, *Ar'n't I a Woman?: Female Slaves in the Plantation South* (New York: Norton, 1985); Elizabeth Fox-Genovese, *Within the Plantation Household: Black and White Women of the Old South* (Chapel Hill: University of North Carolina Press, 1988); Jean E. Friedman, "Women's History and the Revision of Southern History," in *Sex, Race, and the Role of Women in the South*, ed. Joanne V. Hawks and Sheila L. Skemp (Jackson: University Press of Mississippi, 1983), 3–12.

3. Information about the number of slaves who were present is not always available in the narratives from former slaves collected by the WPA. For use of the narratives, see John W. Blassingame, "Using the Testimony of Ex-Slaves: Approaches and Problems," *Journal of Southern History* 41 (Nov. 1975): 473–92; B[enjamin] A. Botkin, "The Slave as His Own Interpreter," *Library of Congress Quarterly Journal of Current Acquisitions* 2 (Nov. 1944): 37–63; John B. Cade, "Out of the Mouths of Ex-Slaves," *Journal of Negro History* 20 (July 1935): 294–337; Paul Escott, *Slavery Remembered: A Record of Twentieth-Century Slave Narratives* (Chapel Hill: University of North Carolina Press, 1979); P. M. Mercer, "Tapping the Slave Narrative Collection for the Responses of Black South Carolinians to Emancipation and Reconstruction," *Australian Journal of Politics and History* 25, no. 3 (1979): 358–74; C. Vann Woodward, "History from Slave Sources: A Review Article," *American Historical Review* 7 (Apr. 1974): 470–81; Norman R. Yetman, "The Background of the Slave Narrative Collection," *American Quarterly* 19 (Fall 1967): 534–53.

Chapter 1: The Work Lives of Plantation Slave Women

1. On slave women's work, see White, *Ar'n't I a Woman?* esp. chap. 3; Jones, *Labor of Love*; Angela Y. Davis, *Women, Race, and Class* (New York: Random House, 1981), chap. 1; Jacqueline Jones, "'My Mother Was Much of a Woman': Black Women, Work, and the Family under Slavery," *Feminist Studies* 8 (Summer 1982): 235–69; Susan A. Mann, "Slavery, Sharecropping, and Sexual Inequality," *Signs* 14 (Summer 1989): 774–98; Fox-Genovese, *Plantation Household*, chap. 3. Much recent work illuminates the lives of African-American women. See, for example, Barbara Hilkert Andolsen, *"Daughters of Jefferson, Daughters of Bootblacks": Racism and American Feminism* (Macon: Mercer University Press, 1986); Bettina Aptheker, *Tapestries of Life: Women's Work, Women's Consciousness, and the Meaning of Daily Experience* (Amherst: University of Massachusetts Press, 1989); Bettina Aptheker, *Woman's Legacy: Essays on Race, Sex, and Class in American History* (Amherst: University of Massachusetts Press, 1982); Barbara Christian, *Black Feminist Criticism: Perspectives on Black Women Writers* (New York: Pergamon Press, 1985); Patricia Hill Collins, *Black Feminist Thought: Knowledge, Consciousness, and the Politics of Empowerment* (Boston: Unwin Hyman, 1990); Patricia Hill Collins, "The Social Construction of Black Feminist Thought," *Signs* 14 (Summer 1989): 745–73; Angela Davis, "Reflections on the Black Woman's Role in the Community of Slaves," *Black Scholar: Journal of Black Studies*

and Research 3 (Dec. 1971): 2–15; Paula Giddings, *When and Where I Enter: The Impact of Black Women on Race and Sex in America* (New York: William Morrow, 1984); Trudier Harris, *From Mammies to Militants: Domestics in Black American Literature* (Philadelphia: Temple University Press, 1982); Evelyn Brooks Higginbotham, "Beyond the Sound of Silence: Afro-American Women in History," *Gender and History* 1 (Spring 1989); Deborah K. King, "Multiple Jeopardy, Multiple Consciousness: The Context of a Black Feminist Ideology," *Signs* 14 (Autumn 1988): 42–72; Gerda Lerner, ed., *Black Women in White America: A Documentary Anthology* (New York: Random House, 1972); Ann Allen Shockley, *Afro-American Women Writers, 1746–1933: An Anthology and Critical Guide* (New York: New American Library, 1988); Dorothy Sterling, ed., *We Are Your Sisters: Black Women in the Nineteenth Century* (New York: Norton, 1984); Erlene Stetson, "Studying Slavery: Some Literary and Pedagogical Considerations on the Black Female Slave," in *All the Women Are White, All the Blacks Are Men, But Some of Us Are Brave: Black Women's Studies*, ed. Gloria T. Hull, Patricia Bell Scott, and Barbara Smith (Old Westbury, N.Y.: Feminist Press, 1982), 61–84.

2. References to children's work can be found throughout the slave narratives and plantation documents. Readers who wish specific references upon which this or other generalizations about women's work in this chapter are based should consult my dissertation, "Plantation Mistresses and Female Slaves: Gender, Race, and South Carolina Women, 1830–1880" (University of Rochester, 1986), chaps. 1 and 2.

3. Ella Kelly, in George P. Rawick, gen. ed., *The American Slave: A Composite Autobiography*, 19 vols. (Westport, Conn.: Greenwood Press, 1972), III, 3:80 (hereafter *AS*). Most of the volumes in this collection are divided into parts that are paginated independently. To make it easy for readers to find the material, I have used roman numerals in my citations to refer to the volume numbers and have included part numbers, or section descriptions when those were unavailable, as well as page numbers. Readers should also consult Rawick's *The American Slave: A Composite Autobiography, Supplement Series 1*, 12 vols. (Westport, Conn.: Greenwood Press, 1978) and *The American Slave: A Composite Autobiography, Supplement Series 2*, 10 vols. (Westport, Conn.: Greenwood Press, 1979).

4. White, *Ar'n't I a Woman?* 92–94.

5. Genia Woodbury, *AS*, III, 4:220. See also Maria Jenkins, *AS*, III, 3:27; Jessie Sparrow, *AS*, III, 4:123; Sylvia Cannon, *AS*, II, 1:188; Dinah Cunningham, *AS*, II, 1:234; Hector Godbold, *AS*, II, 2:144; John W. Blassingame, ed., *Slave Testimony: Two Centuries of Letters, Speeches, Interviews, and Autobiographies* (Baton Rouge: Louisiana State University Press, 1977), 564–65.

6. Mary Woodward, *AS*, III, 4:257.

7. Blassingame, *Slave Testimony*, 564–65.

8. For the experience of a male slave who served his mistress as a young boy and then became a field hand, see Melvin Smith, *AS*, XIII, 3:288.

9. Lucy Gallman, *AS*, II, 2:100. See also Duncan Clinch Heyward, *Seed from Madagascar* (Chapel Hill: University of North Carolina Press, 1937), 179.

10. Mary Johnson, *AS*, III, 3:56; Jane Hollins, *AS*, II, 2:292–93; Josephine Bristow, *AS*, II, 1:100; Gracie Gibson, *AS*, II, 2:114; Adeline Jackson, *AS*, III, 3:3; Margaret Hughes, *AS*, II, 2:327.

11. Sophia Watson to Henry Watson, 19 Apr. 1848, 8 Sept. 1848, Henry Watson Jr. Papers, Manuscript Department, William R. Perkins Library, Duke University, Durham, N.C. (hereafter Duke). The Watsons and their slaves lived in Greene County, Alabama, in the Black Belt; many of its residents in the late 1840s and 1850s were from the upper South and South Carolina. For more on the Watson slaves, see Herbert G. Gutman, *The Black Family in Slavery and Freedom, 1750–1925* (New York: Pantheon Books, 1976), 159–67.

12. Ella [Gertrude Clanton] Thomas Journal, Nov. 1857, Duke; Catherine Ann Devereux Edmondston, *"Journal of a Secesh Lady": The Diary of Catherine Ann Devereux Edmondston, 1860–1866*, ed. Beth G. Crabtree and James W. Patton (Raleigh: North Carolina Division of Archives and History, Department of Cultural Resources, 1979), 20.

13. Margaret Devereux, *Plantation Sketches* (Cambridge: by the author, 1906), 34, 22; Elizabeth W. Allston Pringle, *Chronicles of Chicora Wood* (New York: Charles Scribner's Sons, 1922), 90–91; Sarah Katherine Stone Holmes, *Brokenburn: The Journal of Kate Stone, 1861–1868*, ed. John Q. Anderson (Baton Rouge: Louisiana State University Press, 1955), quotations from 77, 88, see also 78–81, xi.

14. Henry William Ravenel, "Recollections of Southern Plantation Life," *Yale Review* 25 (1936): 763; Willie Lee Rose, ed., *A Documentary History of Slavery in North America* (New York: Oxford University Press, 1976), 293; "Agricultural Department: Management of Negroes," *DeBow's Review* (Mar. 1851): 326. See also N. B. P., "Treatment of Slaves in the Southern States," *Southern Quarterly Review* 21, n.s. 5 (Jan. 1852): 218.

15. For a rich description of field work performed by female slaves, see Jones, *Labor of Love*, 15–18. For work on rice plantations, see Charles Joyner, *Down by the Riverside: A South Carolina Slave Community* (Urbana: University of Illinois Press, 1984), chap. 2; Julia Floyd Smith, *Slavery and Rice Culture in Low Country Georgia, 1750–1860* (Knoxville: University of Tennessee Press, 1985), chap. 3.

16. Ulrich Bonnell Phillips, *Plantation and Frontier Documents: 1649–1863 Illustrative of Industrial History in the Colonial and Ante-Bellum South*, 2 vols. (Cleveland: Arthur H. Clark Co., 1909), 1:118–19, 122; Blassingame, *Slave Testimony*, 380; Thomas Journal, 18 Aug. 1856; Frances Anne Kemble, *Journal of a Residence on a Georgian Plantation in 1838–1839*, ed. John A. Scott (Athens: University of Georgia Press, 1984), 37.

17. These are, of course, subjective evaluations that cannot be judged accurately. See, for example, Blassingame, *Slave Testimony*, 380; Nancy Settles, *AS*, XIII, 3:233; Charlotte Foster, *AS*, II, 2:80; Lucy Gallman, *AS*, II, 2:100; Kemble, *Journal of Residence*, 66.

18. Hugh Fraser Grant, *Planter Management and Capitalism in Ante-Bellum Georgia: The Journal of Hugh Fraser Grant, Rice Grower*, ed. Albert Virgil House (New York:

Columbia University Press, 1954), 99, 159; Heyward, *Madagascar*, 28–29, 31; James Harold Easterby, *The South Carolina Rice Plantation as Revealed in the Papers of Robert F. W. Allston* (Chicago: University of Chicago Press, 1945), 270–73, 303, 316–27; James M. Clifton, ed., *Life and Labor on Argyle Island: Letters and Documents of a Savannah River Rice Plantation, 1833–1867* (Savannah: Beehive Press, 1978), 91, 142; Phillips, *Plantation and Frontier*, 1:30, 210, 213–14, 227, 229, 230, 242–44; Louis Hughes, *Thirty Years a Slave: From Bondage to Freedom* (n.p.: South Side Printing Co., 1897; reprint, New York: Negro Universities Press, 1969), 37; William Sparkman Plantation Record, 26 July 1844 and passim, Southern Historical Collection, Louis Round Wilson Library, University of North Carolina at Chapel Hill (hereafter UNC); John Edwin Fripp Diary, 24 Aug. 1857, 8 Sept. 1857, 4 Nov. 1857, 6 Nov. 1857, 7 Nov. 1857, 16 Nov. 1857, 28 Nov. 1857, 9 Dec. 1857, 23 Dec. 1857, 9 Jan. 1858, 29 Jan. 1858, 2 Feb. 1858, 17 May 1858, UNC; Peter Gaillard Stoney Diary, 10 Apr. 1824, 12 Apr. 1824, 13 Apr. 1824, Stoney and Porcher Family Papers, UNC; Frederick Law Olmsted, *The Cotton Kingdom: A Traveller's Observations on Cotton and Slavery in the American Slave States*, 2 vols. (New York: Mason Brothers, 1861), 1:243–45; John Berkley Grimball Diaries, 14 Oct. 1839, UNC; David Golightly Harris Farm Journal, 6 June 1859, UNC.

19. Heyward, *Madagascar*, 28–29, 31; David Doar, *Rice and Rice Planting in the South Carolina Low Country*, Contributions from the Charleston Museum 8 (Charleston: Charleston Museum, 1936), 30. Banks and trunks were part of the elaborate irrigation system necessary for periodic flooding and draining of the rice fields.

20. Clifton, *Life on Argyle Island*, 133; Pringle, *Chicora Wood*, 170–71; Susan D. Witherspoon to Susan McDowell, 24 Apr. 1837, 14 May 1837, Witherspoon-McDowell Family Papers, UNC; [Emma Holmes], *The Diary of Miss Emma Holmes, 1861–1866*, ed. John F. Marszalek (Baton Rouge: Louisiana State University Press, 1979), 215; Devereux, *Plantation Sketches*, 22, 25; Robert Manson Myers, ed., *The Children of Pride: A True Story of Georgia and the Civil War* (New Haven: Yale University Press, 1972), 248.

21. For a comparison of northern and southern domestic service, see Letitia M. Burwell, *A Girl's Life in Virginia before the War* (New York: Frederick A. Stokes Co., 1895), 42–43.

22. The mammy figure has generated significant controversy among historians. See White, *Ar'n't I a Woman?* 46–61; Clinton, *Plantation Mistress*, 201–2; Eugene D. Genovese, *Roll, Jordan, Roll: The World the Slaves Made* (New York: Random House, 1974), 353–61; Jesse W. Parkhurst, "The Role of the Black Mammy in the Plantation Household," *Journal of Negro History* 23 (July 1938): 349–69; Patricia Morton, "'My Ol' Black Mammy' in American Historiography," in *Southern Women*, ed. Caroline Matheny Dillman (New York: Hemisphere Co., 1988), 35–45; Harris, *Mammies to Militants*.

23. John Berkley Grimball Diaries, 13 May 1835; Katherine D. Meares to Eliza Jane DeRosset, 11 Sept. 1850, DeRosset Family Papers, UNC; Easterby, *South Carolina Rice Plantation*, 86; Daniel Elliott Huger Smith, *A Charlestonian's Recollections*,

1846–1913 (Charleston: Carolina Art Association, 1950), 65; Lucretia Heyward, *AS*, II, 2:279; Ned Walker, *AS*, III, 4:178; Elizabeth Allen Coxe, *Memories of a South Carolina Plantation during the War* (n.p.: by the author, 1912), 87; Frederick A. Ford Yearbooks, 18 Feb. 1828, 22 Oct. 1828, 7 May 1829, 27 May 1833, Ford Family Papers, South Caroliniana Library, University of South Carolina, Columbia (hereafter USCar); Mary Howard Schoolcraft, *The Black Gauntlet: A Tale of Plantation Life in South Carolina* (Philadelphia: J. B. Lippincott, 1860; Freeport, N.Y.: Books for Libraries Press, 1971), 147; Burwell, *Girl's Life*, 128–29.

24. Grace Brown Elmore Reminiscences, 13 Nov. 1860, USCar. See also Susan Dabney Smedes, *Memorials of a Southern Planter*, ed. Fletcher M. Green (Baltimore: Cushings and Bailey, 1887; New York: Knopf, 1965), 95; Holmes, *Brokenburn*, 9; Susan D. Witherspoon to Susan McDowell, 24 Apr. 1837, 14 May 1837, Witherspoon-McDowell Family Papers; Katherine D. Meares to Eliza Jane Lord DeRosset, 11 Sept. 1850, 29 Sept. 1850, DeRosset Family Papers; Eliza Ann DeRosset to Mary D. Curtis, 13 July 1841, 3 Mar. 1846, and Catherine Kennedy to Mary D. Curtis, 20 July 1837, all in Moses Ashley Curtis Family Papers, UNC; Ellen to Lotty, 27 July 1856, Wagner-Cheves Family Papers, UNC; Myers, *Children of Pride*, 486, 596; Claudia H. Means to Eugenia M. Means, 11 Apr. 1859, Mary Hart Means Papers, in *Records of Ante-Bellum Southern Plantations from the Revolution through the Civil War*, gen. ed. Kenneth M. Stampp (Frederick, Md.: University Publications of America, 1985), series A: Selections from the South Caroliniana Library, University of South Carolina, part 2: Miscellaneous Collections. Occasionally men were taught to do a variety of women's tasks as well. See Myers, *Children of Pride*, 248.

25. Eliza Ann DeRosset to Mary D. Curtis, 13 July 1841, Moses Ashley Curtis Family Papers; Katherine D. Meares to Eliza Jane Lord DeRosset, 29 Sept. 1850, DeRosset Family Papers.

26. The anonymous reviewer of Maria Sedgwick's *Live and Let Live*, which urged this sort of rotation, doubted whether it would produce good results: "It will strike many minds as a paper project, rather than a practical one; but it can never be a dangerous theory, for those who possess good cooks and chamber maids will rarely have the courage to transfer them to a different office, and teach them new details though it would be the very poetry of the kitchen if this height of benevolence could be attained." "Review of *Live and Let Live, or Domestic Service Illustrated*, by Miss Sedgwick," *Southern Rose* 6 (30 Sept. 1837): 41–42.

27. Elmore Reminiscences, 13 Nov. 1860; Natalie de DeLage Sumter Diary, 21 July 1840, USCar; Keziah G. H. Brevard Diary, 20 Jan. 1861, USCar; Susan D. Witherspoon to Susan McDowell, 27 Apr. 1837, 20 July 1841, Witherspoon-McDowell Family Papers; David Gavin Diary, 24 Feb. 1859, 6 May 1859, UNC; Sarah Witherspoon McIver Diary, Mar. 1857, USCar; John Berkley Grimball Diaries, 14 Aug. 1833, 24 Aug. 1833, UNC; Meta Morris Grimball Diary, 10 Dec. 1860, UNC; Sophia Watson to Henry Watson, 2 May 1848, 9 May 1848, 3 June 1848, 15 June 1848, 7 July 1848, 15 July 1848, 20 July 1848, Watson Papers; Thomas Journal, Sept. 1857, Nov. 1857, 26 Dec. 1858, 16 July 1864; Holmes, *Brokenburn*, 33, 77–78, 81;

Devereux, *Plantation Sketches*, 6–8; Holmes, *Diary*, 57; Caroline Howard Gilman, *Recollections of a Southern Matron* (New York: Harper, 1838), 141; Easterby, *South Carolina Rice Plantation*, 58, 86, 156, 163; Mary Raines, *AS*, III, 4:2; Mary Ross Banks, *Bright Days in the Old Plantation Time* (Boston: Lee and Shepard, 1882), 137–38; Schoolcraft, *Black Gauntlet*, 234; Burwell, *Girl's Life*, 4; Myers, *Children of Pride*, 486.

28. Elmore Reminiscences, 13 Nov. 1860; Meta Morris Grimball Diary, 10 Dec. 1860; Mary Raines, *AS*, III, 4:2.

29. Thomas Journal, 26 Dec. 1858, 16 July 1864. See also John Berkley Grimball Diaries, 21 May 1832; Clayton Holbert, *AS*, XVI, Kansas narratives:3; Smedes, *Memorials*, 70; Schoolcraft, *Black Gauntlet*, 191, 205; Clinton, *Plantation Mistress*, 155–56; Sally McMillen, "Mothers' Sacred Duty: Breast-Feeding Patterns among Middle- and Upper-Class Women in the Antebellum South," *Journal of Southern History* 51 (Aug. 1985): 333–56; Jane Turner Censer, *North Carolina Planters and Their Children, 1800–1860* (Baton Rouge: Louisiana State University Press, 1984), 35–36; Kemble, *Journal of a Residence*, 61; Theodore Rosengarten, *Tombee: Portrait of a Cotton Planter; with the Plantation Journal of Thomas B. Chaplin (1822–1890)* (New York: McGraw-Hill, 1987), 370; R[obert] Q. Mallard, *Plantation Life before Emancipation* (Richmond, Va.: Whittet and Shepperson, 1892; reprint, Detroit: Negro History Press, n.d.), 9; Elizabeth Avery Meriwether, *Recollections of Ninety-Two Years: 1824–1916* (Nashville: Tennessee Historical Commission, 1958), 114–15. For a white woman nursing a black infant, see Myers, *Children of Pride*, 415.

30. Thomas Journal, Nov. 1857, Sept. 1857.

31. Brevard Diary, 10 Oct. 1860; Fannie M. Colcock to Hattie, 7 Dec. 1854, Colcock-Hay Family Papers, USCar; Alexander J. Lawton Plantation Diary, 1816–28, UNC; John Berkley Grimball Diaries, 13 May 1835; Sophia Watson to Henry Watson, 9 May 1848, 3 June 1848, 15 June 1848, 7 July 1848, 20 July 1848, and Henry Watson to Sophia Watson, 18 July 1848, all in Watson Papers; Thomas Journal, Sept. 1857, Nov. 1858, 26 Dec. 1858; Holmes, *Brokenburn*, 33; Devereux, *Plantation Sketches*, 8–10; Clifton, *Life on Argyle Island*, 156, 267, 270, 291–93; Easterby, *South Carolina Rice Plantation*, 86, 156, 168; Adeline Jackson, *AS*, III, 3:2; Claude Augusta Wilson, *AS*, XVII, 356.

32. See John W. Blassingame, "Status and Social Structure in the Slave Community: Evidence from New Sources," in Harry P. Owens, ed., *Perspectives and Irony in American Slavery* (Jackson: University Press of Mississippi, 1976), 137–51.

33. Olmsted, *Cotton Kingdom*, 1:236–37.

34. Thomas Journal, Sept. 1857; Holmes, *Brokenburn*, 33.

35. Clifton, *Life on Argyle Island*, 183, see also 267.

36. John Berkley Grimball Diaries, 13 May 1835.

37. Sophia Watson to Henry Watson, 2 May 1848, 9 May 1848, 3 June 1848, 15 June 1848, 7 July 1848, 15 July 1848, 20 July 1848, 8 Sept. 1848, Watson Papers.

38. Clifton, *Life on Argyle Island*, 270, see also 267.

39. Caroline Elizabeth Merrick, *Old Times in Dixie Land: A Southern Matron's Memories* (New York: Grafton Press, 1901), 20–21.

40. Edmondston, *"Journal,"* 20; Brevard Diary, 10 Oct. 1860; Lawton Plantation Diary.

41. Brevard Diary, 11 Sept. 1860; Henry H. Cumming to Julia A. B. Cumming, 5 Oct. 1827, Hammond, Bryan, and Cumming Papers, USCar; Katherine D. Meares to Eliza Jane Lord DeRosset, 7 Oct. 1850, 23 July 1854, DeRosset Family Papers; Eliza Ann DeRosset to Mary D. Curtis, 26 Oct. 1841, 2 Aug. 1837, 3 Mar. 1846, 14 Apr. 1846, Armand John DeRosset to Mary Curtis, 27 Oct. 1837, Mary Curtis to Eliza Ann DeRosset, 5 Jan. 1842, Mary Curtis to Catherine Kennedy, 19 Mar. 1842, and Mary Curtis to Magdalen DeRosset, 14 Nov. 1842, all in Moses Ashley Curtis Family Papers; Susan Witherspoon to Susan McDowell, 24 Apr. 1840, Witherspoon-McDowell Family Papers; Clifton, *Life on Argyle Island,* 140, 144, 192, 291–93, 302; Phillips, *Plantation and Frontier,* 1:171; S. M. Stevens to Maria [Ravenel?], 20 Aug. 1828, Thomas Porcher Ravenel Papers, in *Records of Plantations,* series B: Selections from the South Carolina Historical Society; Claudia H. Means to Eugenia M. Means, 11 Apr. 1859, Means Papers, *Records of Plantations,* series A, part 2.

42. Mary D. Curtis to Catherine D. Kennedy, 19 Mar. 1842, Mary D. Curtis to Magdalen DeRosset, 14 Nov. 1842, Eliza Ann DeRosset to Mary D. Curtis, 2 Aug. 1837, Armand John DeRosset to Mary D. Curtis, 27 Oct. 1837, Catherine D. Kennedy to Mary D. Curtis, 27 Nov. 1837, and Mary D. Curtis to Catherine D. Kennedy, 9 Sept. 1844, all in Moses Ashley Curtis Family Papers.

43. Susan Witherspoon to Susan McDowell, 24 Apr. 1840, Witherspoon-McDowell Family Papers; Will of Elizabeth Ervin, Wills of Darlington County, S.C., vol. 2, Book 9, 1838–53, 4, South Carolina Department of Archives and History, Columbia, S.C. (hereafter cited as S.C. Archives); Clifton, *Life on Argyle Island,* 140, 155, 192, 291–93, 302.

44. Maria Jenkins, *AS,* III, 3:27; Ryer Emmanuel, *AS,* II 2:12–13; Amos Gadsden, *AS,* II, 2:92; Gus Feaster, *AS,* II, 2:67; Heyward, *Madagascar,* 105–6; Clifton, *Life on Argyle Island,* 72, 270; John Berkley Grimball Diaries, 6 Apr. 1836; [Mary Howard Schoolcraft], *Letters on the Condition of the African Race, by a Southern Lady* (Philadelphia: T. K. and P. G. Collins, 1852), 12; Schoolcraft, *Black Gauntlet,* 38–39; Annie Harper, *Annie Harper's Journal: A Southern Mother's Legacy,* ed. Jeannie Marie Dean (Denton, Miss.: Flower Mound Writing Co., 1983), 34–35; Edmondston, *"Journal,"* 45; N. B. P., "Treatment of Slaves," 218.

45. Schoolcraft, *Black Gauntlet,* 38; Maria Jenkins, *AS,* III, 3:27. Jenkins's use of the male pronoun to refer to Rachel is typical of the Gullah speech used by slaves on the rice-growing Sea Islands.

46. Heyward, *Madagascar,* 105.

47. Although women who tended young children were also called nurses, this paragraph refers only to those who cared for the sick. Of course, sometimes the two overlapped. Sophia Watson to Henry Watson, 19 June 1848, 15 July 1848, 17 July 1848, 20 July 1848, Watson Papers; Gus Feaster, *AS,* II, 2:55; Lila Rutherford, *AS,* III, 4:57; Lina Anne Pendergrass, *AS,* III, 3:249; Easterby, *South Carolina Rice Plantation,* 61; Clifton, *Life on Argyle Island,* 140, 302; Fripp Diary, 9 Apr. 1857, 18 Apr.

1857, 20 Apr. 1857, 21 Apr. 1857, 22 Apr. 1857, 23 Apr. 1857, 16 May 1857, 19 May 1857, 20 May 1857, 6 June 1857, 15 June 1857, 25 Nov. 1857, 16 Jan. 1858, 18 May 1858, 19 May 1858; Gavin Diary, 29 Aug. 1856, 9 Sept. 1856, 13 Sept. 1856, 25 May 1857, 17 Sept. 1857; Susan Witherspoon to Susan McDowell, 24 Apr. 1840, Witherspoon-McDowell Family Papers; John Berkley Grimball Diaries, 24 Aug. 1833, 6 Apr. 1835, 1836; "Management of a Southern Plantation," *DeBow's Review* 22, third series, 11 (Jan. 1857): 41; Schoolcraft, *Black Gauntlet*, 114.

48.   Fripp Diary, 9 Apr. 1857 and passim; Sophia Watson to Henry Watson, 20 July 1848, Watson Papers; Eliza Mims to Emily Jordan, 17 Sept. 1849, Daniel W. Jordan Papers, 1827–66, *Records of Plantations*, series F: Selections from the Manuscript Department, Duke University Library, part 2: South Carolina and Georgia.

49.   Lina Anne Pendergrass, *AS*, III, 3:249; Gus Feaster, *AS*, II, 2:55; Robert W. Gibbes, "Southern Slave Life," *DeBow's Review* 24, n.s. 4 (Apr. 1858): 321.

50.   Sophia Watson to Henry Watson, 19 June 1848, Watson Papers; Susan Witherspoon to Susan McDowell, 24 Apr. 1840, 2 July 1840, Witherspoon-McDowell Family Papers.

51.   Hughes, *Thirty Years a Slave*, 22; Ned Walker, *AS*, III, 4:177–78.

52.   Smedes, *Memorials*, 60, see also 75; Elmore Reminiscences, 13 Nov. 1860. See also Holmes, *Brokenburn*, 8, 33, 35; Charles L. Perdue Jr., Thomas E. Barden, and Robert K. Phillips, eds., *Weevils in the Wheat: Interviews with Virginia Ex-Slaves* (Charlottesville: University Press of Virginia, 1976), 88–89, 309; Sam Kilgore, *AS*, IV, 2:256; unidentified man, *AS*, XVIII:87; Ellen Belts, *AS*, IV, 1:75; John Smith, *AS*, XV:274; Shade Righards, *AS*, XIII, 3:200–201; Anna Parkes, *AS*, XIII, 3:156; Bob Mobley, *AS*, XIII, 3:137; Callie Elder, *AS*, XII, 1:312; Edward Alfred Pollard, *The Southern Spy; or, Curiosities of Negro Slavery in the South. Letters from a Southerner to a Northern Friend* (Washington: Henry Polkinghorn, 1859), 10; Anne Simons Deas, *Recollections of the Ball Family of South Carolina and the Comingtee Plantation* (n.p.: 1909), 166; White, *Ar'n't I a Woman?* 47–49; Jones, *Labor of Love*, 22. For male drivers, see Genovese, *Roll, Jordan, Roll*, 365–88. For a white woman weaver who most likely supervised slave spinners, see Evelyn D. Ward, *The Children of Bladensfield* (New York: Viking Press, 1978), 28–29.

53.   For an extended discussion of women's work in the quarters, see Jones, *Labor of Love*, 29–43.

54.   Adeline Jackson, *AS*, III, 3:3; Jane Johnson, *AS*, III, 3:49; Fred James, *AS*, III, 3:15; "Management of a Southern Plantation," 44; Easterby, *South Carolina Rice Plantation*, 347.

55.   Easterby, *South Carolina Rice Plantation*, 347. See also Clifton, *Life on Argyle Island*, 130; Ravenel, "Recollections," 753; Blassingame, *Slave Testimony*, 374–75; Moses Lyles, *AS*, III, 3:141; Benjamin Russell, *AS*, III, 4:53; Sally Banks Chambers, *AS*, IV, 1:215; Easter Huff, *AS*, XIII, 2:248; Amanda Jackson, *AS*, XIII, 2:289–90; John Jackson, *AS*, XV:2–3; Henry James Trentham, *AS*, XV:364; Mary Belle Dempsey, *AS*, XVI, Ohio narratives:33.

56.   Houston H. Holloway Autobiography, 49–52, Manuscript Division, Library

of Congress. See also Maggie Black, *AS*, II, 2:58–59; Charlie Grant, *AS*, II, 2:175; Genovese, *Roll, Jordan, Roll*, 315–20; Joyner, *Down by the Riverside*, 122–23. Even religious activity could be sex-segregated. See Coxe, *Memories*, 55. For more on corn shuckings, see Roger D. Abrahams, *Singing the Master: The Emergence of African-American Culture in the Plantation South* (New York: Penguin, 1992).

Chapter 2: The Work Lives of Plantation Mistresses

1. For a discussion of the work done by mistresses, see Clinton, *Plantation Mistress*, chap. 2; Scott, *Southern Lady*, 28–37; Friedman, *Enclosed Garden*, 21–32; Orville Vernon Burton, *In My Father's House Are Many Mansions: Family and Community in Edgefield, South Carolina* (Chapel Hill: University of North Carolina Press, 1985), 124–29; Fox-Genovese, *Plantation Household*, chap. 2. See also Rosser H. Taylor, *Ante-Bellum South Carolina: A Social and Cultural History* (Chapel Hill: University of North Carolina Press, 1942; reprint, New York: DaCapo Press, 1970), esp. chaps. 2 and 5.

2. John B. Irving, *A Day on Cooper River*, ed. Louisa Cheves Stoney, 2d ed. (Columbia: R. L. Bryan, 1932), xi.

3. Mary E. Herndon, *Louise Elton; or, Things Seen and Heard* (Philadelphia: Lippincott, Grambo, and Co., 1853), 87. See also [Caroline Howard Gilman], "Recollections of a Southern Matron, Chapter VI," *Southern Rose* 4 (5 Sept. 1835): 1.

4. Lucilla Gamble McCorkle Diary, 14 June 1846, 5 July 1846, May 1850, 26 July 1846, see also 14 June 1846, 21 June 1846, 19 July 1846, 26 Sept. 1846, 5 Apr. 1847, and passim, William Parsons McCorkle Papers, UNC.

5. Pringle, *Chicora Wood*, 78.

6. Eliza Ann DeRosset to Mary D. Curtis, 16 Aug. 1837, Moses Ashley Curtis Family Papers; Edmondston, *"Journal,"* 408; Meta Morris Grimball Diary, 11 July 1861.

7. Meta Morris Grimball Diary, 29 Dec. 1860; Elmore Reminiscences, 13 Nov. 1860. See also Mary Boykin Chesnut, *Mary Chesnut's Civil War*, ed. C. Vann Woodward (New Haven: Yale University Press, 1981), 202, 261; United Daughters of the Confederacy, *South Carolina Women in the Confederacy*, collected by Mrs. A. T. Smythe et al., 2 vols. (Columbia: State Committee Daughters of the Confederacy, 1903, 1907), 2:170 and passim.

8. "Advice from a Father to His Only Daughter, Written Immediately after Her Marriage," *Southern Literary Messenger* 1 (Dec. 1834): 188; James Petigru Carson, *Life, Letters, and Speeches of James Louis Petigru: The Union Man of South Carolina* (Washington, D.C.: W. H. Lowdermilk, 1920), 75.

9. Myers, *Children of Pride*, 526. Jones described his wife's activities in detail in a letter to a son at school. Ibid., 35–36. The Jones family held strong ideas about proper behavior. Before Charles Jr.'s marriage, his family had exerted a good deal of pressure on the young couple to begin housekeeping immediately rather than boarding. Charles Jr. claimed his only reluctance to do so stemmed from his desire to in-

dulge his future bride's preference "at least for a time." However, two months before the wedding, she reportedly wrote her fiance that he should "effect just such arrangements as I may deem best in regard to our future manner of life." Charles Jr. explained to his family that she "shrank a little from the responsibilities that would immediately attach so soon as she entered her own house." Ibid., 435–42. The Jones family had an unusual religious history. In addition to Myers's introduction to *Children of Pride*, see Erskine Clarke, *Wrestlin' Jacob* (Atlanta: John Knox Press, 1979).

10. J. Motte Alston, *Rice Planter and Sportsman: The Recollections of J. Motte Alston, 1821–1909*, ed. Arney R. Childs (Columbia: University of South Carolina Press, 1953), 10–11; Heyward, *Madagascar*, 178, see also 190. See also Gavin Diary, 31 May 1856.

11. Henry H. Cumming to Julia A. B. Cumming, 5 Oct. 1827, [Nov.] 1827, Hammond, Bryan, and Cumming Papers. See also David Wyatt Aiken to wife, 23 Apr. 1861, 22 Aug. 1863, 26 Aug. 1863, 8 July 1865, David Wyatt Aiken Papers, USCar; Isaac H. Dychee to wife, undated letters, Isaac H. Dychee Papers, USCar. See also "Country Life in South Carolina, no. 2," *Charleston Courier*, 28 Mar. 1851.

12. Chevillette E. Simms to Mrs. James Lawson, 3 Jan. 1844, William Gilmore Simms Papers, USCar.

13. For an overview of the tasks required for domestic work, see Susan Strasser, *Never Done: A History of American Housework* (New York: Pantheon, 1982).

14. Fredrika Bremer, *The Homes of the New World: Impressions of America*, trans. Mary Howitt, 2 vols. (New York: Harper and Brothers, 1853), 1:279–80. See also Gilman, *Recollections of a Southern Matron*, 50–51.

15. Caroline E. Rush, *The North and South; or, Slavery and Its Contrasts* (Philadelphia: Crissy and Markley, 1852; reprint, Freeport, N.Y.: Books for Libraries Press, 1971), 226.

16. [Caroline Howard Gilman], "Recollections of a Housekeeper, Chapter XIV," *Southern Rose Bud* 3 (15 Nov. 1834): 41. See also [Caroline Howard Gilman], "Domestic Tyranny," *The Lady's Annual Register, and Housewife's Almanac, for 1841* (Boston: William Crosby and Co., 1841), 48; Emily Burke, *Reminiscences of Georgia* (n.p.: James M. Fitch, 1850), 155; Caroline Lee Hentz, *The Planter's Northern Bride*, 2 vols. (Philadelphia: Perry and M'Millan, 1854), 1:174; Schoolcraft, *Black Gauntlet*, vi, 84; Mary Henderson Eastman, *Aunt Phillis's Cabin; or, Southern Life as It Is* (Philadelphia: Lippincott, Grambo, 1852; reprint, New York: Negro Universities Press, 1968), 73–74, 94, 111; L[ouisa] S. M[cCord], "Carey on the Slave Trade," *Southern Quarterly Review* 25, n.s. 9 (Jan. 1854): 168; Merrick, *Old Times in Dixie Land*, 17–18; William Howard Russell, *My Diary North and South* (New York: Knopf, 1988), 103. Antebellum men also made the analogy between mistresses and slaves on occasion. See Elihu Burritt, "The Drunkard's Wife," *Southern Literary Messenger* 7 (July–Aug. 1841): 578; "The Progress of the Republic," *DeBow's Review* 17 (Aug. 1854): 129; "Right of Property of Married Women," *Southern Ladies' Book* 1 (June 1840): 364; "Review of *Woman Physiologically Considered*," *Southern Quarterly Review* 2 (Oct. 1842): 305–9. The comparison was also made after the war. See "What's to Be Done with

the Negroes?" *DeBow's Review* 1, after the war series (June 1866): 579; "The Negro Problem," *DeBow's Review* 5, after the war series (Mar. 1868): 249. Catherine Clinton agrees with this analogy and goes so far as to argue that the plantation mistress was the "slave of slaves." This vastly understates the work of black women and its significance for reducing the physical labor of white women. She does, however, point effectively to the clash between the myth of the genteel southern lady and the reality of her daily existence. See Clinton, *Plantation Mistress*, chap. 2. See also White, *Ar'n't I a Woman?* 51–52; Scott, *Southern Lady*, 30, 50–51; Fox-Genovese, *Plantation Household*, 145.

17. Myers, *Children of Pride*, 121.

18. For a discussion of white women's education, see chap. 3.

19. Burwell, *Girl's Life*, 194; Coelebs, "On Female Education," *Gospel Messenger* 1 (Dec. 1824): 367; Coxe, *Memories*, 78–79. See also Smedes, *Memorials*, xii; Holmes, *Brokenburn*, 24; Sarah Morgan Dawson, *A Confederate Girl's Diary* (Boston: Houghton Mifflin, 1913), 89; Thomas Journal, 22 Mar. 1852, 13 June 1852, 30 June 1852, and passim.

20. Holmes, *Brokenburn*, 32, 88, 97.

21. [Franklin W. Elmore] to [Ellen Elmore], 9 June 1844, Franklin Harper Elmore Papers, *Records of Plantations*, series A, part 2; Smedes, *Memorials*, 180–81; Katherine D. Meares to Eliza Jane Lord DeRosset, 7 Oct. 1850, see also 11 Sept. 1850, 20 Sept. 1850, DeRosset Family Papers. See also McCorkle Diary, Jan. 1850.

22. Schoolcraft, *Black Gauntlet*, 115.

23. On the significance of marriage for the daughters of planters, see Clinton, *Plantation Mistress*, chap. 4; Scott, *Southern Lady*, 23–28; Censer, *North Carolina Planters*, chap. 4. On courtship and women's sphere, see Steven M. Stowe, "'The *Thing* Not Its Vision': A Woman's Courtship and Her Sphere in the Southern Planter Class," *Feminist Studies* 9 (Spring 1983): 113–30; Steven M. Stowe, *Intimacy and Power in the Old South: Ritual in the Lives of the Planters* (Baltimore: Johns Hopkins University Press, 1987), chap. 2 and passim; Taylor, *Ante-Bellum South Carolina*, 62–66. See also chap. 4.

24. Schoolcraft, *Black Gauntlet*, 115.

25. Myers, *Children of Pride*, 326–27. Her uncertainty may have been exacerbated by her husband's high standards and firm belief in the separation of spheres, as well as his conviction that women should have full authority over domestic slaves. See Mallard, *Plantation Life*, 39.

26. Devereaux, *Plantation Sketches*, 5, 6–10. In fact, the installation of a new mistress frequently caused female slaves to move between house and field. See Henry H. Cumming to Julia A. B. Cumming, 22 May 1834, Hammond, Bryan, and Cumming Papers; Semdes, *Memorials*, 181. See also Rebecca Latimer Felton, *Country Life in Georgia in the Days of My Youth* (Atlanta: Index Printing Co., 1919), 72; Sally Elmore Taylor Memoir, USCar, and Franklin Harper Elmore Papers, UNC.

27. Edmondston, *"Journal,"* 344–45.

28. Nearly every collection of plantation documents contains examples of business records and correspondence signed by men. The few examples of such correspondence signed by women almost always can be attributed to women acting on behalf of absent husbands. Some business correspondence, however, was written by the few widows and unmarried women who managed their own property, a situation discouraged by their friends and southern society.

29. Catherine D. Kennedy to Mary D. Curtis, 2 Nov. 1837, Moses Ashley Curtis Family Papers. Similar references can be found throughout women's personal letters.

30. Susan Witherspoon to Susan W. McDowell, 3 Mar. 1840, Witherspoon-McDowell Family Papers; C[atherine] F[itzsimons] Hammond to Marcellus Hammond, 14 Feb. 1835, James Henry Hammond Papers, *Records of Plantations*, series A, part 1: The Papers of James Henry Hammond, 1795–1865.

31. Bremer, *Homes of the New World*, 1:337; Pringle, *Chicora Wood*, 62–63; Myers, *Children of Pride*, 364. See also Kemble, *Journal of Residence*, 34, 61, 73, and passim.

32. Hester Hunter, *AS*, II, 2:334; Nancy Settles, *AS*, XIII, 3:234. See also United Daughters of the Confederacy, *South Carolina Women*, 2:34, 194, and passim.

33. Sophia Watson to Henry Watson, 9 May 1848, Watson Papers. See also Keziah G. H. Brevard's Diary, which is filled with references to handing out clothing and bedding; Pringle, *Chicora Wood*, 154; Myers, *Children of Pride*, 265; [Gilman], "Recollections of a Southern Matron, Chapter VI," 1.

34. Harriott Pinckney to Mr. Winningham, 8 Feb. 1855, Harriott Pinckney Papers, USCar.

35. Burke, *Reminiscences of Georgia*, 155; Edmondston, "*Journal*," 49.

36. Elmore Reminiscences, 13 Nov. 1860; Meta Morris Grimball Diary, 29 Dec. 1860; Sumter Diary.

37. Holmes, *Brokenburn*, 77–78.

38. Note that I am not now referring to the wives of small holders, for whom economic uncertainty could be a constant peril, but rather to wives of usually successful planters experiencing temporary setbacks. Women could also face economic uncertainty in the early years of their marriages, before their husbands were fully established planters.

39. Meta Morris Grimball Diary, 11 July 1861; Susan Witherspoon to Susan McDowell, 24 Apr. 1840, 2 July 1840, 20 July 1841, Witherspoon-McDowell Family Papers; Meriwether, *Recollections*, 37.

40. Chevillette E. Simms to Mrs. James Lawson, 4 May 1845, Simms Papers. See also Eliza Ann DeRosset to Mary D. Curtis, 30 Dec. 1841, Moses Ashley Curtis Family Papers.

41. Eliza Mims to Emily Jordan, 17 Sept. 1849, Jordan Papers, *Records of Plantations*, series F, part 2.

42. Watson Papers. See also Easterby, *South Carolina Rice Plantation*, 154, 156, and passim.

43. Sophia Watson to Henry Watson, 19 Apr. 1848, see also 21 Apr. 1848, 9 May 1848, 15 June 1848, 7 July 1848, 17 July 1848, 14 Aug. 1848, 31 Aug. 1848, Watson Papers.

44. Henry Watson to Sophia Watson, 11 May 1848, 21 May 1848, 18 July 1848, and passim, Watson Papers.

45. Mary Strother Means to Mary Hart Means, 17 Nov. 1858, Means Papers, *Records of Plantations,* series A, part 2.

46. While Emily's work was partly due to taking on her husband's tasks, she also told her husband: "I am heartily tired of so many children." Emily Jordan to Daniel Jordan, 26 Nov. 1851, see also 26 Dec. 1851, Jordan Papers, *Records of Plantations,* series F, part 2. See also Taylor, *Ante-Bellum South Carolina,* 67–68. White women's assumption of men's work would become more common during the Civil War. See chap. 8.

47. Pinckney Papers; Ada Bacot Diary, 20 Mar. 1861, USCar.

48. Brevard Diary. See also Easterby, *South Carolina Rice Plantation,* 51 and passim; Lawton Plantation Diary; Miller-Furman-Dabbs Family Papers, USCar; Banks, *Bright Days,* 11; Holmes, *Brokenburn;* Clinton, *Plantation Mistress,* 29–35, 74–78; Scott, *Southern Lady,* 34–35; James Oakes, *The Ruling Race: A History of American Slaveholders* (New York: Random House, 1982), 50.

49. Sumter Diary, 1 July 1840.

50. William Kauffman Scarborough, *The Overseer: Plantation Management in the Old South* (Baton Rouge: Louisiana State University Press, 1966), 16.

51. Sumter Diary, 24 Oct. 1840, 10 Dec. 1840.

52. Emily Hammond to Julia A. B. Cumming, 21 June 1861, Hammond, Bryan, and Cumming Papers; McCorkle Diary, 14 June 1846, 5 July 1846. See also United Daughters of the Confederacy, *South Carolina Women,* 2:170.

53. Susan Cornwall Journal, typescript pp. 46, 50, UNC; Caroline [Howard] Gilman, *The Lady's Annual Register and Housewife's Memorandum-Book, for 1838* (Boston: T. H. Carter; Philadelphia: Henry Perkins, 1837), 28; [Caroline Howard Gilman], "The Wife," *The Lady's Annual Register, and Housewife's Almanac, for 1843* (Boston: T. H. Carter, 1843), 65. Rev. R. Q. Mallard endorsed Gilman's work heartily to his future wife, claiming: "The pictures of Southern manners are drawn to the life." Myers, *Children of Pride,* 297.

54. Mary D. Curtis to Eliza Ann DeRosset, 5 Jan. 1842, Mary D. Curtis to Catherine D. Kennedy, 9 Sept. 1844, and Eliza Ann DeRosset to Mary D. Curtis, 3 Mar. 1846, 14 Apr. 1846, all in Moses Ashley Curtis Family Papers. See also Myers, *Children of Pride,* 278, 280, 327.

55. Sophia Watson to Henry Watson, 15 June 1848, Watson Papers; Flora Adams Darling, *Mrs. Darling's Letters; or, Memories of the Civil War* (New York: John W. Lovell Co., 1883), 17. See chap. 10 for a postwar woman who refused to allow black hired servants to use her cookstove.

56. Catherine D. Kennedy to Gaston Meares, 18 June 1855, DeRosset Family Papers. See also Heyward, *Madagascar,* 111–12; Smith, *A Charlestonian's Recollections,*

10–11; Malvina to Emily Jordan, 7 Apr. 1850, Jordan Papers, *Records of Plantations*, series F, part 2.

57. Edmondston, *"Journal,"* 166, see also 142; Henry H. Cumming to Julia A. B. Cumming, 22 May 1834, Hammond, Bryan, and Cumming Papers; Smedes, *Memorials*, 18–19.

58. Virginia Clay-Clopton, *A Belle of the Fifties: Memoirs of Mrs. Clay, of Alabama, Covering Social and Political Life in Washington and the South, 1853–1866*, ed. Ada Sterling (New York: Doubleday, Page, and Co., 1904), 215. See also Gilman, *Recollections of a Southern Matron*, 10–11; Kemble, *Journal of a Residence*, 50 and passim.

59. Myers, *Children of Pride*, 343.

60. White women wrote frequently about all aspects of their work. Their letters, diaries, and other personal papers are filled with accounts of the day-to-day responsibilities associated with supervising domestic producers and house slaves. They wrote even more frequently of the directly productive work they accomplished and of their activities caring for their own families and those of slaves. For additional details, see my dissertation, "Plantation Mistresses and Female Slaves."

61. For more information on this topic see chap. 6.

62. Coxe, *Memories*, 87; Holmes, *Brokenburn*, 7; Virginia T. J. Campbell to her uncle, 24 Mar. 1837, Campbell Family Papers, Duke; Hester Hunter, *AS*, II, 2:334; George Fleming, *AS*, suppl. 1, XI, South Carolina, 134.

63. Heyward, *Madagascar*, 190; Brevard Diary, 22 Sept. 1860, 30 Aug. 1860.

64. See, for example, Katherine Meares to Eliza Jane Lord DeRosset, 11 Sept. 1850, DeRosset Family Papers; Mary Curtis to Catherine Kennedy, 9 Sept. 1844, Moses Ashley Curtis Family Papers; McCorkle Diary, 5 July 1840, 11 July 1847, 10 Oct. 1847; Devereux, *Plantation Sketches*, 6–8, 9–10; Maria Bryan Harford to Julia Cumming, 20 Mar. 1833, and Emily C. Hammond to Julia Cumming, 21 June 1861, both in Hammond, Bryan, and Cumming Papers; Brevard Diary, 30 Aug. 1860 and passim; Sumter Diary, 7 Aug. 1840, 25 June 1841; Thomas Journal, Nov. 1857; Smedes, *Memorials*, 95–96.

65. McCorkle Diary, May 1850; Eliza Ann DeRosset to Mary Curtis, 14 Apr. 1846, Moses Ashley Curtis Family Papers.

66. Many of the 1848 letters between Sophia Watson and her absent husband address such issues. Watson Papers. See also chap. 1.

67. Sumter Diary, 21 July 1840, 22 July 1840; Catherine Kennedy to Mary Curtis, 2 Nov. 1837, Moses Ashley Curtis Family Papers. See also Chesnut, *Mary Chesnut's Civil War*, 202.

68. Myers, *Children of Pride*, 630, 604. Sewing machines were not widely available in the South until after the Civil War.

69. Anna W. King to [Fannie H. Manigault], 6 Aug. 1858, Louis Manigault Papers, 1776–1865, *Records of Plantations*, series F, part 2. Such sewing societies would become common among the white women of South Carolina during the Civil War as they sought to produce uniforms, bandages, flags, and even tents for soldiers. See chap. 8.

70. McCorkle Diary, Jan. 1850.

71. Sumter Diary, 15 Oct. 1840, 18 Oct. 1840, 6 Dec. 1840; Brevard Diary, 27 Dec. 1860; Meta Morris Grimball Diary, 29 Dec. 1860, May 1861; Eliza Ann DeRosset to Mary Curtis, 17 Dec. 1838, 17 Aug. 1841, and Catherine Kennedy to Mary Curtis, 10 Sept. 1836, 23 May 1839, all in Moses Ashley Curtis Family Papers; Holmes, *Diary*, 287, 364–65; Sophia Watson to Henry Watson, 31 Aug. 1848, 5 Sept. 1848, Watson Papers; Chesnut, *Mary Chesnut's Civil War*, 72.

72. Meta Morris Grimball Diary, May 1861; Sophia Watson to Henry Watson, 5 Sept. 1848, see also 31 Aug. 1848, Watson Papers; Sumter Diary, 15 Oct. 1840; Chesnut, *Mary Chesnut's Civil War*, 72.

73. Sam Mitchell, *AS*, III, 3:201; Sumter Diary, 14 Jan. 1841; Pringle, *Chicora Wood*, 91–93. Natalie de DeLage Sumter also taught slave children to pray and served them dinner afterward. Sumter Diary, 5 July 1840, 12 July 1840, 6 Aug. 1840, 10 Aug. 1840.

74. Sally G. McMillen, *Motherhood in the Old South: Pregnancy, Childbirth, and Infant Rearing* (Baton Rouge: Louisiana State University Press, 1990), 2 and passim. See also Bertram Wyatt-Brown, *Southern Honor: Ethics and Behavior in the Old South* (New York: Oxford University Press, 1982); Censer, *North Carolina Planters*; Joan E. Cashin, "The Structure of Antebellum Planter Families: 'The Ties That Bound Us Was Strong,'" *Journal of Southern History* 56 (Feb. 1990): 55–70; Chalmers Gaston Davidson, *The Last Foray: The South Carolina Planters of 1860: A Sociological Study* (Columbia: University of South Carolina Press, 1971).

75. See Clifton, *Life on Argyle Island*; Gavin Diary; John Salter to Daniel Jordan, 10 Nov. 1835, 12 Mar. 1836, Jordan Papers, *Records of Plantations*, series F, part 2.

76. Catherine Kennedy to Mary Curtis, 20 July 1837, Moses Ashley Curtis Family Papers.

77. By convention, small plantations are units with fewer than twenty slaves; slaveholding farms had five or fewer. In South Carolina in 1860, "nearly half of the white families" owned slaves, with a statewide average of fifteen slaves per owner. "The average slaveholding in the Low-Country was twenty-one; in the Up-Country, eleven." Taylor, *Ante-Bellum South Carolina*, 41. See also Sam Bowers Hilliard, *Atlas of Antebellum Southern Agriculture* (Baton Rouge: Louisiana State University Press, 1984), chaps. 3 and 4; Lewis Cecil Gray, *History of Agriculture in the Southern United States to 1860*, 2 vols. (Washington, D.C.: Carnegie Institute of Washington, 1933; Gloucester, Mass.: Peter Smith, 1958).

78. See, for example, George Woods, *AS*, III, 4:248, 251.

79. Lawton Plantation Diary; Gavin Diary, 31 May 1856.

80. Except for Charleston, South Carolina's cities were quite small, even by antebellum standards. Taylor provides the following populations for 1850: Charleston, 42,984; Columbia, 6,000; Beaufort, 897; Greenville, 1,305; Spartanburg, 1,176; Camden, 1,333; Hamburg, 1,070; Yorkville, 511. Taylor, *Ante-Bellum South Carolina*, 23.

81. Burwell, *Girl's Life*, 159, 161. During the war, Fanny's master proposed to pay her fifty dollars to discontinue making soap because he found paying for the wood to boil it prohibitive. Burwell reported she refused the offer and continued her soap-making enterprise while her owner "continued paying fabulous sums for wood." Ibid., 161–163, quotation from 162–63.

82. Jane H. Pease and William H. Pease, *Ladies, Women, and Wenches: Choice and Constraint in Antebellum Charleston and Boston* (Chapel Hill: University of North Carolina Press, 1990), esp. chap. 3; Richard C. Wade, *Slavery in the Cities: The South, 1820–1860* (New York: Oxford University Press, 1964); Ira Berlin, *Slaves without Masters: The Free Negro in the Antebellum South* (New York: Random House, 1974); Robert S. Starobin, *Industrial Slavery in the Old South* (New York: Oxford University Press, 1970); Lebsock, *Free Women of Petersburg*, esp. chap. 4; Michael P. Johnson and James L. Roark, *Black Masters: A Free Family of Color in the Old South* (New York: Norton, 1984); Fox-Genovese, *Plantation Household*, 70–80; Pauline Worth, *AS*, III, 4:261–63.

83. The differences in white women's lives in city and countryside are most clearly depicted in Chesnut, *Mary Chesnut's Civil War*. See also Scott, *Southern Lady*, 33–34, 43; Lebsock, *Free Women*, esp. chap. 6.

Chapter 3: Expectations for White Womanhood

1. The historical literature on domesticity is extensive. See, for example, Barbara Welter, "The Cult of True Womanhood: 1820–1860," *American Quarterly* 18 (Summer 1966): 151–74; Nancy F. Cott, *The Bonds of Womanhood: "Woman's Sphere" in New England, 1780–1835* (New Haven: Yale University Press, 1977); Carroll Smith-Rosenberg, *Disorderly Conduct: Visions of Gender in Victorian America* (New York: Knopf, 1985); Barbara Leslie Epstein, *The Politics of Domesticity: Women, Evangelism, and Temperance in Nineteenth-Century America* (Middletown, Conn.: Wesleyan University Press, 1981). The phrase "angel in the house" is from a poem by Owen Patmore.

2. For an alternative view of expectations of women of the yeoman class, see D. Harland Hagler, "The Ideal Woman in the Antebellum South: Lady or Farmwife?" *Journal of Southern History* 46 (Aug. 1980): 405–18. See also Virginia Kent Anderson Leslie, "A Myth of the Southern Lady: Antebellum Proslavery Rhetoric and the Proper Place of Woman," in *Southern Women*, ed. Dillman, 19–33.

3. Discussions of when—or whether—the South can be considered a distinct region of the nation have occupied southerners and historians for generations. What follows is an effort to add to that debate by including the experiences of white women. See Clinton, *Plantation Mistress*, xii–xvi and chap. 1; Scott, *Southern Lady*, 239–44; Stowe, *Intimacy and Power*, intro. and passim; Fox-Genovese, *Plantation Household*, chap. 1. There is also a long tradition of discussion among historians whose focus is not gender. See, for example, Eugene D. Genovese, *The World the Slaveholders Made:*

Two Essays in Interpretation (New York: Random House, 1969); Carl Degler, *Place over Time: The Continuity of Southern Distinctiveness* (Baton Rouge: Louisiana State University Press, 1977); Oakes, *Ruling Race*.

4. "The Women of the South," *DeBow's Review* 1, n.s. (Aug. 1861): 147.

5. [Thomas R. Dew], "Dissertation on the Characteristic Differences between the Sexes, and on the Position and Influence of Woman in Society," *Southern Literary Messenger* 1 (May 1835): 493. Dew wrote two additional installments of his "Dissertation," in which he continued his analyses of the consequences of women's physical inferiority and its implications for their position in society. See "Dissertation on the Characteristic Differences between the Sexes 2," *Southern Literary Messenger* 1 (July 1835): 621–32, and "Dissertation on the Characteristic Differences between the Sexes, and on the Position and Influence of Woman in Society, 3," 1 (Aug. 1835): 672–91. See also Scott, *Southern Lady*, 64–67; William R. Taylor, *Cavalier and Yankee: The Old South and American National Character* (New York: G. Braziller, 1961), 170–72.

6. [Dew], "Dissertation on Differences," 495–96, 511.

7. "Review of *Woman Physiologically Considered*," 281, 298; A. G. M., "The Condition of Woman," *Southern Quarterly Review* 10 (July 1846): 168–73, quotations from 168, 169, 170, 173; [Dew], "Dissertation on Differences, 2," 626.

8. "An Essay on the Moral and Political Effect of the Relation between the Caucasian Master and the African Slave," *Southern Literary Messenger* 10 (June 1844): 331. See also Pythion, "The Relative Moral and Social Status of the North and the South," *DeBow's Review* 22, third series, 2 (Mar. 1857): 225–48.

9. "Stowe's *Key to Uncle Tom's Cabin*," *Southern Quarterly Review* 24, n.s. 15 (July 1853): 231–32; George Fitzhugh, *Cannibals All! or, Slaves without Masters* (Richmond, 1857; reprint, Cambridge, Mass.: Belknap Press of Harvard University Press, 1960), 28, see also 66, 201, 204–6, and passim.

10. George Fitzhugh, *Sociology for the South; or, The Failure of Free Society* (Richmond: J. W. Randolph, 1854; reprint, New York: Burt Franklin, n.d.), 213, 246. For a rich analysis of Fitzhugh, see Genovese, *World Slaveholders Made*.

11. J. B. D., "Maria Edgeworth," *Southern Literary Messenger* 15 (Sept. 1849): 579; [Philip C. Pendleton and George F. Pierce], "Introduction," *Southern Ladies' Book* 1 (Jan. 1840): 2–3. See also "Mrs. DuPre's Female Academy," *Southern Quarterly Review* 3 (Apr. 1843): 532; [Dew], "Dissertation on Differences, 2," 630.

12. J. L. M., "The Women of France," *Southern Literary Messenger* 5 (May 1839): 297–98. The context makes it clear that the conclusions do not refer exclusively to France.

13. Maria J. McIntosh, *Woman in America: Her Work and Her Reward* (New York: D. Appleton and Co., 1850), 119–20. In contrast, William Porcher Miles argued that Charleston society had become far too domestic in nature because married women were expected to remain at home rather than participate in a rich social life. Miles attributed this deterioration in the social position of women to men's "earnest pursuit of money . . . for the mere pleasure of accumulation" and to women's fear of

slander. [William Porcher Miles], "American Literature and Charleston Society," *Southern Quarterly Review* 10 (Apr. 1853): 380–421, quote from 406. Attribution to Miles is by Stowe, "'*Thing* Not Its Vision,'" 130.

14. "A Few Thoughts on Slavery," *Southern Literary Messenger* 20 (Apr. 1854): 198. See also A. G. M., "The Condition of Woman"; "The Women of the South," 150–51 and passim; Fitzhugh, *Sociology for the South*, 213; White, *Ar'n't I a Woman?* 56–61.

15. "Northern and Southern Slavery," *Southern Literary Messenger* 7 (Apr. 1841): 314–15. See also "The Ills That Slavery Frees Us From," *DeBow's Review* 22, third series, 2 (Apr. 1857): 437–38; [William John] Grayson, "The Hireling and the Slave," *DeBow's Review* 21, third series, 1 (Sept. 1856): 250. Fitzhugh, of course, would have disagreed.

16. Eastman, *Aunt Phillis's Cabin*, 136. See also Edwin Herriott, "Wants of the South," *DeBow's Review* 29, o.s. (Aug. 1860): 221–22; Pythion, "Relative Moral and Social Status"; "The Women of the South"; M[aria] J[ane] McIntosh, *The Lofty and the Lowly; or, Good in All and None All-Good*, 2 vols. (New York: D. Appleton and Co., 1852), 1:183–84.

17. "Stowe's *Key to Uncle Tom's Cabin*," 231; B., "The New Social Propositions," *Southern Literary Messenger* 20 (May 1854): 300. See also Burwell, *Girl's Life*, 53; "The Domain of Fashion," *DeBow's Review* 4, enlarged series, 29 (Dec. 1860): 698.

18. [Sue Petigru Bowen], *Busy Moments of an Idle Woman* (New York: D. Appleton and Co., 1854), 253. For a review of this collection of stories, see "Review of *Busy Moments of an Idle Woman*," *Charleston Daily Courier*, 5 Jan. 1854 and 7 Jan. 1854.

19. "Mrs. DuPre's Female Academy," 532. See also "Popular Education," *Southern Literary Messenger* 2 (Jan. 1836): 90; [Pendleton and Pierce], "Introduction," 2. For historians' views of female education, see Clinton, *Plantation Mistress*, 12–14 and chap. 7; Scott, *Southern Lady*, 67–77; Lebsock, *Free Women*, 172–76; Burton, *Fathers' House*, 84–85; Censer, *North Carolina Planters*, chap. 3; Steven M. Stowe, "The Not-So-Cloistered Academy: Elite Women's Education and Family Feeling in the Old South," in *The Web of Southern Social Relations: Women, Family, and Education*, ed. Walter J. Fraser Jr., R. Frank Saunders Jr., and Jon L. Wakelyn (Athens: University of Georgia Press, 1985), 90–106; Taylor, *Ante-Bellum South Carolina*, 31–32, 111–13.

20. G. W., "Desultory Speculator; No. V: Thoughts on Female Education," *Southern Literary Messenger* 5 (Sept. 1839): 598.

21. Oliver Oldschool, "Odds and Ends," *Southern Literary Messenger* 4 (Oct. 1838): 640. See also "Female Education," *Southern Literary Messenger* 1 (May 1835): 519–20; "Education," *Southern Quarterly Review* 1 (Apr. 1842): 329; N. Carolina, "Female Education," *Southern Literary Messenger* 6 (June 1840): 452–53; S., "The New Constitution," *Southern Literary Messenger* 18 (Feb. 1852): 118; G. I. A. M., "Letter on Female Education," *Southern Rose* 7 (2 Feb. 1839): 183; "Mrs. DuPre's Female Academy," 532; [Caroline Howard Gilman?], "Education," *The Housekeeper's Annual, and Ladies' Register for 1844* (Boston: Redding and Co., 1843), 38–42; Bishop Horne, "Thoughts on the Importance of Forming the Female Character by

Education," *Gospel Messenger* 2 (July 1825): 207–9. A few southern writers argued that women made the best teachers for all children, or at least all daughters, not just their own. See E. T., "Female Education," *Southern Literary Messenger* 27, n.s. 6 (Sept. 1858): 218–19; J. B. D., "Maria Edgeworth," 579; Rev. L. Pierce, "The Education of the Poor," *Southern Ladies' Book* 1 (Apr. 1840): 222–23. Southern periodicals also sometimes reprinted such arguments made by northern writers. See Sarah J. Hale, "A Profession for Ladies," *Southern Literary Messenger* 2 (Aug. 1836): 571–72; [Lydia] Sigourney, "Duty of Mothers," *Southern Literary Messenger* 4 (Dec. 1838): 786.

22. "The Women of the South," 153.

23. Quoted in E. T., "Female Education," 221. See also Coelebs, "On Female Education," 368; Port Folio, "Untitled," *Gospel Messenger* 1 (Dec. 1824): 368–69; "Woman," *Southern Ladies' Book* 1 (Mar. 1840): 189; [Pendleton and Pierce], "Introduction," 2–3; "Editor's Table," *Southern Literary Messenger* 27, n.s. 6 (Oct. 1858): 310–11; S., "The New Constitution," 117; Hon. Eugenius A. Nisbet, "Views of Female Education and Character," *Southern Ladies' Book* 1 (June 1840): 331. At least one writer warned of the dangers inherent in too much education or ambition for women. See Augusta Jane Evans Wilson, *St. Elmo* (New York: Carleton, 1866), 259–62, 292–93, and passim.

24. "Education," 329; Nisbet, "Views of Female Education," 328; G. I. A. M., "Letter on Female Education," 183. The same point about internal improvements is made by N. Carolina in "Female Education," 454.

25. Alexander H. Sands, "Intellectual Culture of Woman," *Southern Literary Messenger* 28, n.s. 7 (May 1859): 325. See also Nisbet, "Views of Female Education," 326–27 and passim.

26. "Importance of Home Education," *Southern Ladies' Book* 2 (July 1840): 2, 4–5. At least one editor of the journal was interested in the Georgia Female College, which may have influenced his estimation of the evils of northern education.

27. S., "The New Constitution," 118.

28. "Education of Southern Women," *DeBow's Review* 31, enlarged series, 6 (Oct.–Nov. 1861): 383–84. *DeBow's* continued to emphasize the importance of southern education for women after the war. See "Southern Female Education—The Carnatz Institute," *DeBow's Review* 5, after the war series (Apr. 1868): 447.

29. "Importance of Home Education," 7.

30. Ibid., 3, 6. See also Clinton, *Plantation Mistress*, 135–36.

31. Myers, *Children of Pride*, 251. Some daughters were not so ambitious. When Cora Jordan's mother sent her to school in Charleston, "she left in tears as usual it seems that she never will get accustomed to going from home. . . . I do not think she will ever say that her school days were her happiest." Emily Jordan to her children, 11 Jan. 1861, Jordan Papers, *Records of Plantations*, series F, part 2. For the importance of school in one woman's life, see Stowe, "'*Thing* Not Its Vision.'"

32. G[eorge] F. P[ierce], "The Georgia Female College: Its Origin, Plan, and Prospects," *Southern Ladies' Book* 1 (Feb. 1840): 65–74; S., "The New Constitution," 118–19; "Mrs. DuPre's Female Academy," 533; "Female Education," 519–20; "Ed-

ucation of Southern Women," 381–90; "Southern Female Education—The Carnatz Institute," 447.

33. [Caroline Howard Gilman?], "Matrimonial Maxims for Married Ladies," *The Lady's Annual Register, and Housewife's Almanac, for 1842* (Boston: William Crosby and Co., 1842), 16. See also Carol K. Bleser, "The Perrys of Greenville: A Nineteenth-Century Marriage," in *Southern Social Relations*, ed. Fraser, Saunders, and Wakelyn, 72–89.

34. Dr. Balguy, "Balguy's Advice to an Unmarried Lady," *Gospel Messenger* 1 (Nov. 1824): 344–45. See also [Gilman], "Matrimonial Maxims," 16.

35. [Caroline Howard Gilman], "Recollections of a Housekeeper, Chap. XI," *Southern Rose Bud* 3 (4 Oct. 1834): 18; A. W. Habersham to [Fannie Manigault], 26 May 1858, Manigault Papers, *Records of Plantations*, series F, part 2. See also Myers, *Children of Pride*, 630.

36. [Caroline Howard Gilman], "Recollections of a Southern Matron, Chap. XXXIV: The Planter's Bride," *Southern Rose* 5 (18 Feb. 1837): 98. See also L. C. T., "A Mistake in Philosophy," *Southern Literary Messenger* 7 (May–June 1841): 382–84; Schoolcraft, *Black Gauntlet*, 54–55; "Advice from a Father," 187–88; Sands, "Intellectual Culture of Woman," 328; Wilson, *St. Elmo*, 193, 259–62, 291–92, and passim.

37. "Letter to a Young Friend," *Southern Rose Bud* 2 (22 Feb. 1834): 102; Port Folio, "Untitled," 369. See also "Get Married," *Southern Ladies' Book* 1 (June 1840): 342–43; "Review of *Busy Moments of an Idle Woman*."

38. E. B. C., "The Mothers and Children of the Present Day," *Southern Literary Messenger* 22, n.s. 1 (May 1856): 393. See also McMillen, *Motherhood in the Old South*.

39. Gilman, "Education," 39; "Review of *A Year of Consolation. By Mrs. Butler, Late Fanny Kemble*," *Southern Quarterly Review* 12 (July 1847): 205.

40. "Education," 329. The anonymous writer made no mention of the significance or rewards of the mother of daughters, although another writer claimed "the influence which a mother's care and a mother's love produces upon a girl, is much greater than that wrought on a boy." [Dew], "Dissertation on Differences," 504. See also Horne, "Thoughts on Importance," 207–9; Oldschool, "Odds and Ends," 640; [Caroline Howard Gilman], "A Mother's Love," *The Housekeeper's Annual, and Ladies' Register for 1844* (Boston: Redding and Co., 1843), 88.

41. Schoolcraft, *Black Gauntlet*, 456–57; "Stowe's *Key to Uncle Tom's Cabin*," 231; "Right of Property," 363. See also A. G. M., "The Condition of Woman," 169; "Review of *Woman Physiologically Considered*," 295–97; McIntosh, *Woman in America*, 22–25; M[aria] J[ane] McIntosh, *The Lofty and the Lowly; or, Good in All and None All-Good*, 2 vols. (New York: D. Appleton, 1852), 2:164–65; Wilson, *St. Elmo*, 392–97. One author took a somewhat more judicious view of the question, but concluded that men and women "can no more change their sexual relations than they can change their social and domestic relations." L., "Female Prose Writers of America," *Southern Quarterly Review* 21, n.s. 5 (Jan. 1852): 116. See also Anne Firor Scott, "Women's Perspective on the Patriarchy in the 1850s," *Journal of American History* 61 (June 1974): 52–64; Lebsock, *Free Women*, 240–44.

42. "Ellet's Women of the Revolution," *Southern Quarterly Review* 17, n.s. 1 (July 1850): 326–27. The author's assessment of women's political role in the Revolution is similar to Kerber's analysis of republican motherhood. See Linda K. Kerber, *Women of the Republic: Intellect and Ideology in Revolutionary America* (Chapel Hill: University of North Carolina Press, 1980). See also C[aroline Howard] G[ilman], "Isaac Hayne; or, The Patriot Martyr of Carolina," *Southern Rose* 5 (22 July 1837): 185; [Philip C. Pendleton and George F. Pierce], "Notes by the Editors: Woman's Influence," *Southern Ladies' Book* 1 (Apr. 1840): 256; Laura, "Responsibility of Females," *Gospel Messenger* 1 (Oct. 1825): 306–8.

43. See chap. 5.

44. Rebecca Felton believed that *Uncle Tom's Cabin*'s "unpopularity in the South was reflected, illogically and absurdly enough, in a bitter feeling against feminine authors in general." She claimed "it took years to break down this prejudice." Rebecca Latimer Felton, *The Romantic Story of Georgia's Women* ([Atlanta:] Atlanta Georgian and Sunday American, 1930), 38.

45. George Frederick Holmes, "Review of *Uncle Tom's Cabin*," *Southern Literary Messenger* 18 (Dec. 1852): 721–22. See also "Notices of New Books: Review of *Uncle Tom's Cabin*," *Southern Literary Messenger* 18 (Oct. 1852): 630–31; G[eorge] F[rederick] H[olmes], "Review of *A Key to Uncle Tom's Cabin*," *Southern Literary Messenger* 19 (June 1853): 321. Other women writers could be criticized for the same failings. See "Review of *Journal* by Frances Anne Butler," *Southern Literary Messenger* 1 (May 1835): 530–31.

46. Holmes, "Review of *Key to Uncle Tom*," 322–23.

47. E., "Woman's True Mission; or, 'The Noble Ladies of England,'" *Southern Literary Messenger* 19 (May 1853): 305–6.

48. "[Editor's Introduction to] Extract from the Abbe de la Mennais," *Gospel Messenger* 1 (Feb. 1824): 50. See also Barbara L. Bellows, *Benevolence among Slaveholders: Assisting the Poor in Charleston, 1670–1860* (Baton Rouge: Louisiana State University Press, 1993).

49. The Charleston Ladies' Benevolent Society was founded in 1813 and had a mostly continuous history until at least sometime after World War I. Its officers were from South Carolina's most elite families. See "Delicate Benevolence," *Southern Rose* 5 (4 Feb. 1837): 95; "Report of the Ladies' Garment Society," *Southern Rose* 5 (4 Mar. 1837): 111; "Ladies' Fair," *Southern Rose* 6 (11 Nov. 1837): 96; Schoolcraft, *Black Gauntlet*, 330–34; E. T. Campbell to Mary, 9 Feb. 1841, George Noble Jones Papers, *Records of Plantations*, series F, part 2; Lebsock, *Free Women*, chap. 7; Barbara L. Bellows, "'My Children, Gentlemen, Are My Own': Poor Women, the Urban Elite, and the Bonds of Obligation in Antebellum Charleston," in *Southern Social Relations*, ed. Fraser, Saunders, and Wakelyn, 52–71; Taylor, *Ante-Bellum South Carolina*, 32, 47–48; Johnson, *Social History of Sea Islands*, 122. Such activities would become far more common during the war, when women organized to provide for the needs of soldiers; see chap. 8. For a contrasting interpretation, see Friedman, *Enclosed Garden*.

50. Sands, "Intellectual Culture of Woman," 329; Mrs. S. A. Dinkins, "A Letter from a Village Bride to a Friend in the City, and the Reply Thereto," *Southern Literary Messenger* 33, n.s. 12 (Dec. 1861): 453.

51. The passage continues with a long list of charitable activities. W., "The Lyceum, No. II: Old Maids," *Southern Literary Messenger* 3 (Aug. 1837): 473–74.

52. E., "Woman's True Mission," 303. See also "A Prayer," *Gospel Messenger* 1 (July 1824): 198–99; "Address, by the President of the Georgia Female College, to the Graduating Class," *Southern Ladies' Book* 2 (Aug. 1840): 67–68; Sands, "Intellectual Culture of Woman," 329.

53. "Advice from a Father," 188; "Thoughts on Slavery, by a Southron," *Southern Literary Messenger* 4 (Dec. 1838): 745.

54. McIntosh, *Woman in America*, 118. See also W., "Old Maids," 474; "Few Thoughts on Slavery," 199.

55. McIntosh, *Woman in America*, 117; M., "The Selfish Girl," *Rose Bud, or Youth's Gazette* 1 (13 Apr. 1833): 129–30. See also William H. Holcombe, "Little Kindnesses," *Southern Literary Messenger* 34 (Apr. 1862): 256; Schoolcraft, *Black Gauntlet*, 113–15.

56. Eastman, *Aunt Phillis's Cabin*, 256, see also 28; Schoolcraft, *Black Gauntlet*, 548, see also 55.

57. Scott, *Invisible Woman*, 190, see also 191–211. See also Donald Mathews, *Religion in the Old South* (Chicago: University of Chicago Press, 1977); Kenneth K. Bailey, "Protestantism and Afro-Americans in the Old South: Another Look," *Journal of Southern History* 41 (Nov. 1975): 451–72; Alan Gallay, "The Origins of Slaveholders' Paternalism: George Whitefield, the Bryan Family, and the Great Awakening in the South," *Journal of Southern History* 53 (Aug. 1987): 369–94.

Chapter 4: Plantation Mistresses' Behavior toward Slave Women

1. Scott, *Southern Lady*, 8. See also Lebsock, *Free Women*, 232–36. See chap. 5 for the effects of sexual jealousy on the part of white women and chap. 7 for the views of slaves and for a consideration of the behavior of women in Charleston and among small slaveholders.

2. McCorkle Diary, undated materials, Monday after Fourth Sab., Nov. 1848, Jan. 1847.

3. Mary Hort Diary, 2 Aug. 1837, USCar; Brevard Diary, 14 Nov. 1860, 28 Nov. 1860; Sumter Diary; Thomas Journal; Holmes, *Brokenburn*; Edmondston, *"Journal"*; Chesnut, *Mary Chesnut's Civil War.*

4. Thomas Journal, 9 Feb. 1858, see also 11 Apr. 1855, 12 May 1856. Later in life Thomas would substantially revise her opinions about her husband.

5. Edmondston, *"Journal,"* 282, 302, 345. See also Darling, *Mrs. Darling's Letters*, 11.

6. Edmondston, *"Journal,"* 21–22, see also 270; Eastman, *Aunt Phillis's Cabin*, 55.

7. Note I am not discussing routine allotments of material goods granted to every slave, but rather extra allotments given to those perceived by the mistress to need them.

8. Sumter Diary, 11 July 1840, 12 July 1840, 22 July 1840, 26 Dec. 1840. See also Myers, *Children of Pride*, 179, 186; Sarah A. Brock Putnam, *Richmond during the War: Four Years of Personal Observation, by a Richmond Lady* (New York: G. W. Carleton and Co., 1867), 89; Edmondston, *"Journal,"* 141; Burwell, *Girl's Life*, 7, 24, 64; Eastman, *Aunt Phillis's Cabin*, 28; Schoolcraft, *Black Gauntlet*, 112–15; Martha Haines Butt, *Antifanaticism: A Tale of the South* (Philadelphia: Lippincott, Grambo, and Co., 1853), 63–66, 159.

9. Sophia Watson to Henry Watson, 15 July 1848, Watson Papers. See also [Gilman], "Recollections of a Southern Matron, Chap. VI," 1; [Caroline Howard Gilman], "Recollections of a Southern Matron, Chap. XI: Jacque's Funeral," *Southern Rose* 4 (14 Nov. 1835): 41; Myers, *Children of Pride*, 155; Kate Virginia Cox Logan, *My Confederate Girlhood: The Memoirs of Kate Virginia Cox Logan*, ed. Lily Logan Morril (Richmond, Va.: Garrett and Massie, 1932), 29; Burwell, *Girl's Life*, 129; Gibbes, "Southern Slave Life," 323.

10. Brevard Diary, 14 Nov. 1860, 6 Dec. 1860, 10 Nov. 1860. See also Myers, *Children of Pride*, 394.

11. Edmondston, *"Journal,"* 130, 132, see also 141.

12. Constance Cary [Mrs. Burton Harrison], *Recollections Grave and Gay* (New York: Scribners, 1912), 145; Smedes, *Memorials*, 42, 58; Smith, *A Charlestonian's Recollections*, 48; Easterby, *South Carolina Rice Plantation*, 153; Katherine D. Meares to Armand John DeRosset, 26 Sept. 1860, DeRosset Family Papers; Putnam, *Richmond during the War*, 89.

13. Gus Feaster, *AS*, II, 2:66; Sarah Poindexter, *AS*, III, 3:269; Genia Woodbury, *AS*, III, 4:221; Walter Long, *AS*, III, 3:119. For a telling example of the ways in which slave women could manipulate white women to provide such extras, see Friedman, *Enclosed Garden*, 80.

14. Perdue, *Weevils in the Wheat*, 257. Similarly, Catherine Hammond acknowledged her own inability to intervene in a quarrel between her sons and her husband: "I myself am utterly useless—helpless in my family—I don't know how to advise the boys, and to open my mouth is only to bring a storm on my own head that I often wish I could be dumb whenever the subject is mentioned." Carol Bleser, ed., *The Hammonds of Redcliffe* (New York: Oxford University Press, 1981), 70.

15. Fanny Cannady, *AS*, XIV, 1:162. See also Kemble, *Journal of a Residence*, 210–11.

16. Ben Horry, *AS*, II, 2:317. See also L[ouisa] S[usannah] M[cCord], "Woman and Her Needs," *DeBow's Review* 1 (Sept. 1852): 285–86; L[ouisa] S[usannah] M[cCord], "Enfranchisment of Women," *Southern Quarterly Review* 5 (Apr. 1852): 335–36.

17. Nelson Cameron, *AS*, II, 1:172.

18. George McAlilley, III, 3:143. See also Bill McNeil, *AS*, III, 3:165–66; Susan Nelson, *AS*, III, 3:214; Phillip Rice, *AS*, III, 4:17.

19. Adeline Hall, *AS*, III, 3:36.

20. [Gilman], "Recollections of a Southern Matron, Chap. XXXIV: The Planter's Bride," 98.

21. Hester Hunter, *AS*, II, 2:342–43. See also Louisa Gause, *AS*, III, 2:109; Emma Lowran, *AS*, III, 3:125.

22. For evidence from an earlier period, see Marylynn Salmon, *Women and the Law of Property in Early America* (Chapel Hill: University of North Carolina Press, 1986). See also Lebsock, *Free Women*.

23. Blassingame, *Slave Testimony*, 380. See also Kemble, *Journal of a Residence*, 214, 222–23, and passim; Thomas Journal, 18 Aug. 1856.

24. Junius Quattlebaum, *AS*, III, 3:284; John Berkley Grimball Diary, 14 Aug. 1833.

25. Eliza Ann DeRosset to Mary Curtis, 18 Sept. 1838, Armand John DeRosset to Mary Curtis, 23 Dec. 1841, and Eliza Ann DeRosset to Mary Curtis, 30 Dec. 1841, all in Moses Ashley Curtis Family Papers. See also Holloway Autobiography, 19.

26. Burwell, *Girl's Life*, 64; Lucy Gallman, *AS*, II, 2:100; United Daughters of the Confederacy, *South Carolina Women*, 2:124; Maria Bryan Harford to Julia A. B. Cumming, May 1838, Hammond, Bryan, and Cumming Papers.

27. Anne Broome, *AS*, II, 1:105; Will of Susannah Sutton, Wills of Barnwell County, S.C., vol. 2, Book C, 1826–56, 70, S.C. Archives; Holloway Autobiography, 19. See also Janet Cornelius, "Slave Marriages in a Georgia Congregation," in *Class, Conflict, and Consensus: Antebellum Southern Community Studies*, ed. Orville Vernon Burton and Robert C. McMath Jr. (Westport, Conn.: Greenwood Press, 1982), 128–45; Kemble, *Journal of a Residence*, 132–40; Rosengarten, *Tombee*, 347–48.

28. Gus Feaster, *AS*, II, 2:65; Andy Marion, *AS*, III, 3:168–69. See also Perdue, *Weevils in the Wheat*, 257; Jacob Manson, *AS*, XV, 2:97–98; Esther Hill Hawks, *A Woman Doctor's Civil War: Esther Hill Hawks' Diary*, ed. Gerald Schwartz (Columbia: University of South Carolina Press, 1984), 154–55.

29. For further information on this topic, see chap. 6.

30. Magdalen DeRosset to Mary Curtis, 24 Feb. 1841, Eliza Ann DeRosset to Mary Curtis, 26 June 1837, 2 Aug. 1837, Armand John DeRosset to Mary Curtis, 27 Oct. 1837, and Mary Curtis to Catherine D. Kennedy, 19 Mar. 1842, 9 Sept. 1844, all in Moses Ashley Curtis Family Papers. See also Burwell, *Girl's Life*, 128.

31. Eliza Jane Lord DeRosset to Katherine D. Meares, 10 June 1855, DeRosset Family Papers; Bacot Diary, 1 Apr. 1861; Sophia Watson to Henry Watson, 15 July 1848, Watson Papers. See also Edmondston, *"Journal,"* 11; Myers, *Children of Pride*, 679, 687–88.

32. Banks, *Bright Days*, 19–20; Susan Witherspoon to Susan McDowell, 25 Dec. 1840, Witherspoon-McDowell Family Papers; Myers, *Children of Pride*, 790, see also 1148.

33. Gibbes, "Southern Slave Life," 323. See also Christianus, "On the Religious Instruction of Slaves," *Gospel Messenger* 1 (Dec. 1825): 373.

34. Myers, *Children of Pride*, 132. See also Schoolcraft, *Black Gauntlet*, vii, 55; Edmondston, "*Journal*," 22; Kemble, *Journal of a Residence*.

35. Cary, *Recollections Grave*, 143–44; Fairy Elkins, *AS* suppl. 1, XI, South Carolina, 115; Nancy Settles, *AS*, XIII, 3:234. See also Sumter Diary; Brevard Diary; Charlie Grant, *AS*, II, 2:174; Benjamin Russell, *AS*, III, 4:54; Jessie Sparrow, *AS*, III, 4:129.

36. Walter Long, *AS*, III, 3:119. See also McIntosh, *Lofty and Lowly*, 1:205–9, 2:318–19; Eastman, *Aunt Phillis's Cabin*, 137; Kemble, *Journal of a Residence*, 262 and passim. Esther Hill Hawks reported on a slave woman in Charleston who was allowed to run a school for black children. Hawks, *Woman Doctor's Civil War*, 199. See also Massey, *Bonnet Brigades*, chap. 6.

37. Bremer, *Homes of the New World*, 2:448. See also Burwell, *Girl's Life*, 22.

38. John N. Davenport, *AS*, II, 1:241; Holloway Autobiography, 3–4. See also Caroline Farrow, *AS*, II, 2:39–40; Amos Gadsden, *AS*, II, 2:95; Thomas Goodwater, *AS*, II, 2:168; Sim Greeley, *AS*, II, 2:191; Jimmie Johnson, *AS*, III, 3:53; Joe Rutherford, *AS*, III, 4:56; Kemble, *Journal of a Residence*, 193, 271–72, 300, 302, 314.

39. Harriet Miller, *AS*, XIII, 3:127. See also Chesnut, *Mary Chesnut's Civil War*, 263, 464; Coxe, *Memories*, 73.

40. Burwell, *Girl's Life*, 34; Blassingame, *Slave Testimony*, 643; Maria Bryan Harford to Julia A. B. Cumming, 20 Mar. 1833, Hammond, Bryan, and Cumming Papers; Holmes, *Diary*, 76, see also 224; Eliza Frances Andrews, *The War-Time Journal of a Georgia Girl, 1864–1865* (New York: D. Appleton and Co., 1908), 320; Coxe, *Memories*, 25. See also Cary, *Recollections Grave*, 144–45.

41. Sumter Diary, 26 Dec. 1840; Smedes, *Memorials*, 42. See also Tom Singleton, *AS*, XIII, 3:270; Julia Woodbury, *AS*, III, 4:243; Felton, *Country Life*, 55–56.

42. Myers, *Children of Pride*, 645–46. For a male view of slaves' weddings— "tomfoolery . . . as if they were ladies of quality"—see Rosengarten, *Tombee*, 481.

43. Leon F. Litwack, *Been in the Storm So Long: The Aftermath of Slavery* (New York: Knopf, 1979), 235–36; Sylvia Cannon, *AS*, II, 1:181; Jimmie Johnson, *AS*, III, 3:53; Abbey Mishow, *AS*, III, 3:197. See also unidentified woman, *AS*, XVIII:61.

44. Myers, *Children of Pride*, 266, 265; Robert S. Starobin, ed., *Blacks in Bondage: Letters of American Slaves* (New York: New Viewpoints, 1974), 153; Melvin Smith, *AS*, XIII, 3:288. See also Eliza Scantling, *AS*, III, 4:80.

45. Smedes, *Memorials*, 58, 87. See also Taylor Memoir.

46. Clay-Clopton, *Belle of the Fifties*, 216; Myers, *Children of Pride*, 153. See also Kemble, *Journal of a Residence*, 77 and passim.

47. Burwell, *Girl's Life*, 4–5.

48. Thomas Journal, 26 July 1856. See also Burwell, *Girl's Life*, 26.

49. Pringle, *Chicora Wood*, 63, 90. See also Burwell, *Girl's Life*, 23.

50. Mary D. Curtis to Eliza Ann DeRosset, 15 Jan. 1842; see also Mary Curtis to Magdalen DeRosset, 14 Feb. 1842, 28 Feb. 1842, and Eliza Ann DeRosset to Mary Curtis, 26 Oct. 1841, all in Moses Ashley Curtis Family Papers.

51. Thomas Journal, Nov. 1857. In 1879, evidently when rereading the journal, Thomas added: "I wonder what ever became of Isabella. She was afterwards sold and I have never seen her since. She must be living somewhere in the world, and perhaps she may be suffering but I scarcely think so. I hope not." Nell Irvin Painter offers an interesting interpretation of Thomas's feelings for Isabella. See Nell Irvin Painter, "Introduction: The Journal of Ella Gertrude Clanton Thomas: An Educated White Woman in the Eras of Slavery, War, and Reconstruction," in Ella Gertrude Clanton Thomas, *The Secret Eye: The Journal of Ella Gertrude Clanton Thomas, 1848–1889*, ed. Virginia Ingraham Burr (Chapel Hill: University of North Carolina Press, 1990), 36–37.

52. Eliza Clitherall Autobiography and Diary, ms. vol. 4, p. 35, UNC. See also Susan Witherspoon to Susan McDowell, 14 May 1837, Witherspoon-McDowell Family Papers; Kemble, *Journal of Residence*, 41; Katherine Meares to Eliza Jane Lord DeRosset, 7 July 1854, 8 July 1855, DeRosset Family Papers; Brevard Diary, 10 Oct. 1860; Pringle, *Chicora Wood*, 61. Sentiments of affection for slaves are also frequently found in wills written by women, particularly those from Charleston. See chap. 7.

53. Rose, *Documentary History*, 436; Benjamin Russell, *AS*, III, 4:53. See also Ryer Emmanuel, *AS*, II, 2:23.

54. For more information on slave women's reactions, see chap. 6.

55. For more information on mistresses' violence, see chap. 6.

56. McCorkle Diary, 22 Nov. 1848, 5th Sab. May 1852, 1st Sab. June 1852; Edmondston, "*Journal*," 130.

57. Holmes, *Diary*, 237–39.

58. Bacot Diary, 16 Apr. 1861, 1 July 1861; Brevard Diary, 19 Sept. 1860, 9 Nov. 1860, 14 Nov. 1860, 16 Jan. 1861, 30 Jan. 1861, see also 5–9 Feb. 1861 and passim. See also Sumter Diary, 11 July 1840, 7 Sept. 1840, 25 June 1841; Holmes, *Brokenburn*, 35, 37; Easterby, *South Carolina Rice Plantation*, 292–93; Gavin Diary, 3 May 1859, 6 May 1859; Edmondston, "*Journal*," 20–22.

59. Chesnut, *Mary Chesnut's Civil War*, 199; Kemble, *Journal of a Residence*, 342, see also 213, 284, 311. See also Clinton, *Plantation Mistress*, 192–98.

60. See chap. 6.

Chapter 5: Plantation Mistresses' Attitudes toward Slavery

1. See Thomas F. Gossett's *Uncle Tom's Cabin and American Culture* (Dallas: Southern Methodist University Press, 1985) for a literary history of responses to Stowe's novel as well as a comprehensive bibliography of the anti–*Uncle Tom* literature discussed here. For the social and cultural significance of novels, see Barbara Bardes and Suzanne Gossett, *Declarations of Independence: Women and Political Power in Nineteenth-Century American Fiction* (New Brunswick: Rutgers University Press, 1990); Cathy N. Davidson, *Revolution and the Word: The Rise of the Novel in America* (New York: Oxford University Press, 1986); Mary Poovey, *Uneven Developments: The Ideological Work of Gender in Mid-Victorian England* (Chicago: University of Chicago Press,

1988); Mary P. Ryan, *The Empire of the Mother: American Writing about Domesticity, 1830–1860* (New York: Harrington Park Press, 1985); Jane Tompkins, *Sensational Designs: The Cultural Work of American Fiction, 1790–1860* (New York: Oxford University Press, 1985); Mary Kelley, *Private Woman, Public Stage: Literary Domesticity in Nineteenth-Century America* (New York: Oxford University Press, 1984).

2. Gerda Lerner, *The Grimké Sisters from South Carolina: Pioneers for Woman's Rights and Abolition* (New York: Schocken Books, 1967); Katharine DuPre Lumpkin, *The Emancipation of Angelina Grimké* (Chapel Hill: University of North Carolina Press, 1974); Scott, *Southern Lady*, 61–64.

3. Herndon, *Louise Elton*, 237, 239, 240. See also Schoolcraft, *Black Gauntlet*, iv–vii; Eastman, *Aunt Phillis's Cabin*, 11–18, 24, 134, 224.

4. Hentz, *Planter's Bride*, 1:v.

5. Butt, *Antifanaticism*, 267–68. See also Herndon, *Louise Elton*, 244; Hentz, *Planter's Bride*, 1:vi, 265, 2:chap. 4; McIntosh, *Lofty and Lowly*, 2:169; Eastman, *Aunt Phillis's Cabin*, 60, 66, 70–71, 93–96, 162, 277–79; Edmondston, *"Journal,"* 245; Merrick, *Old Times in Dixie Land*, 20.

6. Eastman, *Aunt Phillis's Cabin*, 279, see also 96.

7. Ibid., 277; Schoolcraft, *Black Gauntlet*, 49; Hentz, *Planter's Bride*, 1:204; Herndon, *Louise Elton*, 247–48, see also 238. See also Eastman, *Aunt Phillis's Cabin*, 256.

8. McIntosh, *Lofty and Lowly*, 2:318.

9. Butt, *Antifanaticism*, v.

10. Hentz, *Planter's Bride*, 1:265–67, 291, 294, 2:chap. 4; McIntosh, *Lofty and Lowly*, 2:169; Eastman, *Aunt Phillis's Cabin*, 57, 60, 66, 102–4, 257–59, 278–79.

11. Eastman, *Aunt Phillis's Cabin*, 258, see also 102–3.

12. Ibid., 233. Eastman was also critical of the African slave trade but would not accept responsibility for it: "As long as England needed the sons and daughters of Africa to do her bidding, she trafficked in the flesh and blood of her fellow-creatures; but our immortal fathers put an end to the disgraceful trade. . . . To England, not to the United States, belongs whatever odium may be attached to the introduction of slavery into our country." Ibid., 21–22, see also 24.

13. Herndon, *Louise Elton*, 245–46; McIntosh, *Lofty and Lowly*, 1:295. See also Eastman, *Aunt Phillis's Cabin*, 42–44.

14. "Southern Slavery and Its Assailants: *The Key to Uncle Tom's Cabin*," *DeBow's Review* 15 (Nov. 1853): 488, 491, 492. A similar argument is made by L[ouisa] S[usannah] M[cCord] in "Diversity of the Races: Its Bearing upon Negro Slavery," *Southern Quarterly Review* 19 (Apr. 1851): 392–419. See also the discussion of Schoolcraft and McCord later in this chapter.

15. "Southern Slavery and Its Assailants: *The Key to Uncle Tom's Cabin—Again*," *DeBow's Review* 16 (Jan. 1854): 55.

16. McCorkle Diary, 26 Aug. 1860; Cornwall Journal, 57, 58, 59.

17. Edmondston routinely used the term "Cuffy" to refer to slaves. Edmondston, *"Journal,"* 45, 418, and passim.

18. Bardes and Gossett, *Declarations of Independence*. See also Fox-Genovese, *Plantation Household*, chap. 5.

19. Scott, *Southern Lady*, 48–50, quote from 48. See also Scott, *Invisible Woman*, 182–84.

20. Lebsock, *Free Women*, 141–45, quote from 141; Suzanne Lebsock, "Complicity and Contention: Women in the Plantation South," *Georgia Historical Quarterly* 74 (Spring 1990): 75–76. George Rable disagrees: "In fact few white women could transcend barriers of race and class to develop a sympathetic understanding of the slave's plight. . . . Most women seemed simply to have accepted the institution without questioning its legitimacy." George C. Rable, *Civil Wars: Women and the Crisis of Southern Nationalism* (Urbana: University of Illinois Press, 1989), 31–32, see also 2.

21. Easterby, *South Carolina Rice Plantation*, 51; Eliza Ann DeRosset to Mary D. Curtis, 18 Sept. 1838, Moses Ashley Curtis Family Papers.

22. Amie Lumpkin, *AS*, III, 3:130–31. See also Susan Nelson, *AS*, III, 3:215–16.

23. Holmes, *Brokenburn*, 8, see also 84, 86.

24. Pringle, *Chicora Wood*, 74–75; H. R. Warren to John B. Miller, 22 Feb. 1849, Miller-Furman-Dabbs Family Papers. See also unidentified woman to "My dear sister," 4 Dec. 1856, Jordan Papers, *Records of Plantations*, series F, part 2.

25. Brevard Diary, 8 Jan. 1861.

26. Thomas Journal, 2 Jan. 1859. For Lurania Clanton, see Gutman, *Black Family*, 389. See also Felton, *Country Life*, 79.

27. Painter, "Introduction," 55–66. For Thomas's later life, see Mary Elizabeth Massey, "The Making of a Feminist," *Journal of Southern History* 39 (Feb. 1973): 3–22.

28. Thomas Journal, 18 Aug. 1856, 2 Jan. 1859, 12 Feb. 1858. See also Kemble, *Journal of Residence*, 275; Fox-Genovese, *Plantation Household*, 366–68.

29. The circumstances in which the diary was written, rewritten, and published are important for understanding it. See C. Vann Woodward, "Introduction," in *Mary Chesnut's Civil War*, xvi–xxvii. See also Mary Boykin Chesnut, *The Private Mary Chesnut: The Unpublished Civil War Diaries*, ed. C. Vann Woodward and Elisabeth Muhlenfeld (New York: Oxford University Press, 1984); Elisabeth Muhlenfeld, *Mary Boykin Chesnut: A Biography* (Baton Rouge: Louisiana State University Press, 1981); Drew Gilpin Faust, "In Search of the Real Mary Chesnut," *Reviews in American History* 10 (Mar. 1986): 54–59; Fox-Genovese, *Plantation Household*, chap. 7; C. Vann Woodward, "Slaves and Mistresses," *New York Review of Books* 35 (8 Dec. 1988): 3–6.

30. Woodward, "Introduction," xxx–xxxix.

31. Chesnut, *Mary Chesnut's Civil War*, 29–31, see also 168–70, 307. Harriet Jacobs denied that white women pretended not to know the fathers of mulatto children. See Linda Brent [Harriet Jacobs], *Incidents in the Life of a Slave Girl*, ed. Lydia Maria Child (Boston: by the author, 1861), 56–57.

32. Chesnut, *Mary Chesnut's Civil War*, 53, 31, 54.

33. Ibid., 15, see also 169, 729. See also McCord, "Carey on the Slave Trade," 168; Burke, *Reminiscences of Georgia*, 155; chap. 2.

34. Chesnut, *Mary Chesnut's Civil War,* 245, see also 248–49, 307, 718.

35. Ibid., 255, 357, 428.

36. Ibid., 718.

37. Thomas Journal, 2 Jan. 1859.

38. Chesnut, *Mary Chesnut's Civil War,* 169, 729, 307.

39. For information about and analysis of Gilman, see Edward T. James, Janet Wilson James, and Paul S. Boyer, eds., *Notable American Women: A Biographical Dictionary,* 3 vols. (Cambridge: Belknap Press of Harvard University Press, 1971), 2:37–39; Kelley, *Private Woman, Public Stage.*

40. Gilman, *Recollections of a Southern Matron,* vii; [Caroline Howard Gilman], "Recollections of a Housekeeper, Chap. III," *Southern Rose Bud* 2 (1 Feb. 1834): 90. The publication was also called *Southern Rose.*

41. Caroline [Howard] Gilman, "The Household Woman," *Lady's Annual Register, 1838,* 66.

42. [Gilman], *Housekeeper's Annual, 1844,* 88.

43. Gilman, "The Wife," 65; [Caroline Howard Gilman], "Feb.," *Lady's Annual Register, 1843,* 21.

44. At least one man endorsed Gilman's views—to his fiancée. Myers, *Children of Pride,* 297.

45. [Caroline Howard Gilman], "Recollections of a Southern Matron, Chapter III," *Southern Rose Bud* 3 (27 June 1835): 170; [Caroline Howard Gilman], "Recollections of a Southern Matron, Chap. VI," 1; [Caroline Howard Gilman], "Recollections of a Southern Matron, Chap. XXVIII," *Southern Rose* 5 (26 Nov. 1836): 49.

46. [Caroline Howard Gilman], "Recollections of a Southern Matron, Chap. XXXIII: Changes—White Servants," *Southern Rose* 5 (4 Feb. 1837): 89–92. For more on the difficulties associated with white servants, see Hentz, *Planter's Bride,* 1:265–67, 291, 294; Butt, *Antifanaticism,* vi, 268; Schoolcraft, *Black Gauntlet,* 506; Eastman, *Aunt Phillis's Cabin,* 162; Burwell, *Girl's Life,* 42–43, 57; Edmondston, *"Journal,"* 146; H. W., "Original Papers: Untitled," *Southern Rose Bud* 2 (11 Jan. 1834): 77; Meriwether, *Recollections,* 50; Merrick, *Old Times in Dixie Land,* 20; White, *Ar'n't I a Woman?* 54. For a postwar experience with a white servant, who turned out to be no more satisfactory to the mistress than her prewar counterparts, see Grace B. Elmore Diaries and Books, 14 July 1865, UNC. I have published an edition of Elmore's diary: Grace Brown Elmore, *A Heritage of Woe: The Civil War Diary of Grace Brown Elmore, 1861–1868,* ed. Marli F. Weiner (Athens: University of Georgia Press, 1997).

47. [Caroline Howard Gilman], "Recollections of a Southern Matron, Chap. XXXV: Local Attachments in Negroes—Trial of My Principle—My New Carriage—My Garden," *Southern Rose* 5 (4 Mar. 1837): 105.

48. Schoolcraft, *Black Gauntlet,* ix.

49. Ibid., v–vii.

50. Schoolcraft, *Letters,* 10, 15.

51. Schoolcraft, *Black Gauntlet,* 83. Schoolcraft's assessment was, of course, self-

serving and far from the truth. Slaves *were* murdered by whites, who escaped both the insane asylum and the legal system.

52. Schoolcraft, *Black Gauntlet*, 46–47; Schoolcraft, *Letters*, 8, 18, 21–22, and passim.

53. Schoolcraft, *Black Gauntlet*, 114–15.

54. Ibid., viii, 84, 238, see also 121–35, 159–60, 180, and passim.

55. Ibid., 546–48.

56. Ibid., 457–58, 179.

57. *Notable American Women*, 2:450–52. See Fox-Genovese, *Plantation Household*, chap. 5, and Manisha Sinha, "Louisa Susanna McCord: Spokeswoman of the Master Class in Antebellum South Carolina," in *Feminist Nightmares, Women at Odds: Feminism and the Problem of Sisterhood*, ed. Susan Ostrov Weisser and Jennifer Fleischner (New York: New York University Press, 1994), 62–87. McCord's essays have been colleced in Louisa S. McCord, *Louisa S. McCord: Political and Social Essays*, ed. Richard C. Lounsbury (Charlottesville: University Press of Virginia, 1995).

58. McCord, "Enfranchisement of Women," 331, 325–27, 335–36; L[ouisa] S[usannah] M[cCord], "Woman's Progress," *Southern Literary Messenger* 19 (Nov. 1853): 700.

59. Louisa S. McCord, *Caius Gracchus: A Tragedy in Five Acts* (New York: H. Kernot, 1851), 20, 21, 121. On the influence of the image of the Roman matron in the antebellum South, see Clinton, *Plantation Mistress*, 21–22; Rable, *Civil Wars*, chap. 7 and passim.

60. Interestingly, Caroline Howard Gilman came to a similar conclusion in her verse drama "Isaac Hayne; or, The Patriot Martyr of Carolina," set during the American Revolution. Gilman argued that given the threatening circumstances of war, women's behavior could change: "*Loveliness*, Anna, is a word for *peace*. / Stern deeds are beauty now.—Our land is rous'd, / And claims from woman's hand a nobler task." Gilman, "Isaac Hayne," 185.

61. L[ouisa] S[usannah] M[cCord], "Justice and Fraternity," *Southern Quarterly Review* 15 (July 1849): 357. See also L[ouisa] S[usannah] M[cCord], "The Right to Labor," *Southern Quarterly Review* 16 (Oct. 1849): 138–60.

62. L[ouisa] S[usannah] M[cCord], "*Uncle Tom's Cabin*: A Book Review," *Southern Quarterly Review*, n.s. 7 (Jan. 1853): 111, 118.

63. Ibid., 118–19, 109.

64. McCord, "*Uncle Tom's Cabin*," 94, 98. McCord often developed this theme in her criticisms of abolitionists, whom she accused of vastly underrating the sympathies of whites, particularly white women. See, for example, [Louisa Sussanah McCord], "British Philanthropy and American Slavery," *DeBow's Review* 14 (Feb. 1853): 279–80. See also McCord, "Diversity of the Races"; L[ouisa] S[usannah] M[cCord], "Negro and White Slavery—Wherein Do They Differ?" *Southern Quarterly Review* 20 (July 1851): 118–32.

65. McCord, "Woman and Her Needs," 285–86.

66. McCord, "British Philanthropy and American Slavery," 264. See also Mc-
Cord, "Enfranchisement of Woman," 334.

67. McCord, "Carey on the Slave Trade," 168–69.

Chapter 6: Slave Women Confront the Ideology of Domesticity

1. Maggie Black, *AS*, II, 1:58. See also Gus Feaster, *AS*, II, 2:47, 62; unidentified woman, *AS*, XVIII:205; Cora M. Taylor, *AS*, XVII:44; Salena Taswell, *AS*, XVII:306; Acie Thomas, *AS*, XVII:331; Emma Stone, *AS*, XV:325; Robert Shepherd, *AS*, XIII, 3:253; Delia Garlic, *AS*, VI, Alabama narratives:130.

2. Cary, *Recollections Grave*, 144–45. See also Hawks, *Woman Doctor's Civil War*, 184.

3. Blassingame, *Slave Testimony*, 643; unidentified woman, *AS*, XVIII:205. See also "A Northerner's Experiences in Regard to Southern Slavery," *DeBow's Review* o.s. 18, n.s. 1 (May 1855): 573–74; Burwell, *Girl's Life*, 6; Banks, *Bright Days*, 138; Edmondston, *"Journal,"* 129–30; B., "The New Social Propositions," 300; Hentz, *Planter's Bride*, 2:52; Fox-Genovese, *Plantation Household*, 215–24.

4. Amanda Styles, *AS*, XIII, 3:343; Lucy McCullough, *AS*, XIII, 3:69; Jane Johnson, *AS*, III, 3:49–50.

5. Phil Towns, *AS*, XIII, 4:40; Gus Feaster, *AS*, II, 2:61; W. M. Green, *AS*, II, 2:201. See also Charley Barber, *AS*, II, 1:31; Ed Barber, *AS*, II, 1:35–36; Henry Gladney, *AS*, II, 2:129–30; Mary Raines, *AS*, III, 4:2; Andy Marion, *AS*, III, 3:167; Neal Upson, *AS*, XIII, 4:50–51; George Taylor, *AS*, VI, Alabama narratives:372; Julia Branch, *AS*, XII, 1:158; Schoolcraft, *Letters*, 15; Eastman, *Aunt Phillis's Cabin*, 33; Logan, *Confederate Girlhood*, 28. Men's behavior toward women was also defined by the slave community. See Will Dill, *AS*, II, 1:323; Thomas Goodwater, *AS*, II, 2:166.

6. Unidentified man, *AS*, XVIII:307; Frank Menefee, *AS*, VI, Alabama narratives:280. See also Gutman, *Black Family*, chap. 2.

7. See White, *Ar'n't I a Woman?* 22, 158, and passim; Fox-Genovese, *Plantation Household*, 297, 299; Genovese, *Roll, Jordan, Roll*, 482–501.

8. "Management of a Southern Plantation," 44. See also "Rules in the Management of a Southern Estate (Conclusion)," *DeBow's Review* 22, third series, 2 (Apr. 1857): 378; Ulrich Bonnell Phillips, *American Negro Slavery: A Survey of the Supply, Employment, and Control of Negro Labor* (New York: D. Appleton, 1918; Baton Rouge: Louisiana State University Press, 1966), 276.

9. White, *Ar'n't I a Woman?* 16.

10. Judge [Chancellor] Harper, "Memoir on Slavery," *Southern Literary Messenger* 4 (Oct. 1838): 620. See also Myers, *Children of Pride*, 643–46; [Claudia H. Means to Mary H. Means], 4 Aug. 1859, Means Papers, *Records of Plantations*, series A, part 2.

11. Edward J. Pringle, "The People: Considerations on Some Recent Social Theories," *Southern Quarterly Review* 25, n.s. 9 (Jan. 1854): 54–55; [H. N. McTyeire], "Plantation Life—Duties and Responsibilities," *DeBow's Review* o.s. 29, n.s. 4 (Sept. 1860): 362. See also White, *Ar'n't I a Woman?* 98–101.

12. "Slave Marriages," *DeBow's Review* o.s. 19, n.s. 2 (Aug. 1855): 130. See also "Southern Slavery and Its Assailants—Again," 47; Butt, *Antifanaticism*, 159; McIntosh, *Lofty and Lowly*, 1:294–95; Eastman, *Aunt Phillis's Cabin*, 42–44. For the opposite view, which argued that slaves welcomed the changes associated with being sold and changing partners and that they were fundamentally polygamous, see "Stowe's *Key to Uncle Tom's Cabin*," 249; Schoolcraft, *Black Gauntlet*, 43. Others denied that families, or at least mothers and children, were separated. See Schoolcraft, *Letters*, 27; *Black Gauntlet*, 45. See also Genovese, *Roll, Jordan, Roll*, 52–53, 475–81.

13. Delia Thompson, *AS*, III, 4:160–61; Katie Sutton, *AS*, VI, Indiana narratives:195; Mary Raines, *AS*, III, 4:2. See also Edmundston, "*Journal*," 20.

14. Jessie Sparrow, *AS*, III, 4:126. See also Claude Augusta Raines, *AS*, XVII, 356.

15. Unidentified woman, *AS*, XVIII, 187.

16. See chap. 8.

17. Benjamin Russell, *AS*, III, 4:53; Elizabeth Hyde Botume, *First Days amongst the Contrabands* (Boston: Lee and Shepard, 1893), 6–7; Alice Green, *AS*, XII, 2:33–34; Tom Singleton, *AS*, XIII, 3:270.

18. Kemble, *Journal of a Residence*, 114, 210–11, 222–23, and passim, quotations from 108, 170.

19. Mack Taylor, *AS*, III, 4:158; Ben Horry, *AS*, II, 2:311, 317. See also Sam Polite, *AS*, III, 3:273–74.

20. Kemble, *Journal of a Residence*, 74. When confronted, the overseer claimed the woman was flogged for shamming illness and insubordination, 85–86; see also 154, 159–60.

21. Katherine Meares to Armand John DeRosset, 26 Sept. 1850, DeRosset Family Papers. See also Jessie Sparrow, *AS*, III, 4:123.

22. Eastman, *Aunt Phillis's Cabin*, 55, see also 104–5. See also Meriwether, *Recollections*, 22–24.

23. [Gilman], "Recollections of a Southern Matron, Chap. XXXIV: The Planter's Bride," 97; Edmondston, "*Journal*," 23. See also Schoolcraft, *Black Gauntlet*, 27, 148, 205–6; [Gilman], "Recollections of a Southern Matron, Chapter III," 170.

24. Caroline Richardson, *AS*, XV:199; Lila Nichols, *AS*, XV:149; Vermeille Bradford to John B. Miller, 5 Aug. 1839, Miller-Furman-Dabbs Family Papers.

25. Meriwether, *Recollections*, 55; Merrick, *Old Times in Dixie Land*, 17. For another interpretation of these women's interactions, see Fox-Genovese, *Plantation Household*, 142–44.

26. Blassingame, *Slave Testimony*, 262; Abbey Mishow, *AS*, III, 3:197; Hester Hunter, *AS*, II, 2:336, see also 340. See also Litwack, *Been in the Storm*, 235–37; Sylvia Cannon, *AS*, II, 1:181–89; Schoolcraft, *Black Gauntlet*, 508.

27. Granny Cain, *AS*, II, 1:166. See also Starobin, *Blacks in Bondage*, 153; unidentified woman, *AS*, XVIII:61; Dolly Haynes, *AS*, II, 2:259; Jimmie Johnson, *AS*, III, 3:53; Botume, *First Days*, 142; Gibbes, "Southern Slave Life," 323–24; Schoolcraft, *Letters*, 14; *Black Gauntlet*, 45; Hentz, *Planters' Bride*, 1:vii; Myers, *Children of*

Pride, 415. Deborah Gray White is one of the few to acknowledge the role of mistresses in caring for slave children. White, *Ar'n't I a Woman?* 53–54.

28. Benjamin Russell, *AS*, III, 4:51, see also 52–54; Starobin, *Blacks in Bondage*, 75. See also Blassingame, *Slave Testimony*, 107.

29. Walter Long, *AS*, III, 3:119; Andy Marion, *AS*, III, 3:168; Samuel Boulware, *AS*, II, 1:66; Sarah Poindexter, *AS*, III, 3:268–69. See also Anderson Bates, *AS*, II, 1:43; Mack Taylor, *AS*, III, 4:158; Delia Thompson, *AS*, III, 4:160–61; Jessie Sparrow, *AS*, III, 4:128; Mary Woodward, *AS*, III, 4:257; Junius Quattlebaum, *AS*, III, 3:285–86; Lucy Gallman, *AS*, II, 2:100; Schoolcraft, *Black Gauntlet*, 55.

30. Genia Woodbury, *AS*, III, 4:220; Mary Woodward, *AS*, III, 4:257; Pauline Worth, *AS*, III, 4:260; Emoline Glasgow, *AS*, II, 2:134. See also Margaret Hughes, *AS*, II, 1:327–28. Of course, as always with the WPA narratives, the possibility exists that at least some of these statements were motivated by the desire of elderly ex-slaves to please their white interviewers, in the hopes of receiving assistance or a government pension or for more personal reasons. Rebecca Jane Grant described her father's master's daughter, Mamie Willingham, as "a Christian lady. . . . She was sure a good woman. She'd fill her buggy with sugar, tea, coffee and tobacco, and go every Thursday to see the sick and old people. She'd give um de things; and she'd read de scriptures to um, and she'd kneel down and pray for um. . . . She wouldn't except none—white or colored. No'm she wouldn't except none!" Grant also identified the interviewer, Phoebe Faucette, as a granddaughter of Mamie Willingham, and added: "That's the kind of folks you sprung from. You's got a good heritage." Rebecca Jane Grant, *AS*, II, 2:179, 183. While Willingham may have behaved as Grant claimed, we have no way of knowing what she really thought or whether her description of the white woman as "good" and "Christian" was shared by the slaves who knew her directly. Grant may well have been flattering her interviewer in a manner similar to that of slave women talking to their mistresses.

31. Susan Hamlin, *AS*, II, 2:235–36.

32. Ibid., 234–35. See also Perdue, *Weevils in the Wheat*, 238.

33. Blassingame, *Slave Testimony*, 591, see also 118, 160. See also Rebecca Jane Grant, *AS*, II, 2:177–78. Sometimes women who owned slaves were able to provide protection for them based on property rights. See Emma Lowran, *AS*, III, 3:125; Botkin, *Lay My Burden Down*, 148–49.

34. Victoria Adams, *AS*, II, 1:10–11. See also Pauline Worth, *AS*, III, 4:260.

35. Unidentified woman, *AS*, XVIII:229; Dinah Cunningham, *AS*, II, 1:234. See also Hector Godbold, *AS*, II, 2:144; Fannie Griffin, *AS*, II, 2:210.

36. Jacob Branch, *AS*, IV, 1:139; Rebecca Jane Grant, *AS*, II, 2:177–78. See also [illegible] to "My Dear Mistress," [1863?], Jordan Papers, *Records of Plantations*, series F, part 2.

37. Norman R. Yetman, *Life under the "Peculiar Institution": Selections from the Slave Narrative Collection* (New York: Holt, Rinehart, and Winston, 1970), 226, 297, 298, 296, 225, 117; Austin Steward quoted in Genovese, *Roll, Jordan, Roll*, 333–34. See

also Ryer Emmanuel, *AS*, II, 2:25; Ephriam Lawrence, *AS*, III, 3:94; Jake McLeod, *AS*, III, 3:161.

38. John Boyd, *AS*, II, 1:72. See also Ephriam Lawrence, *AS*, III, 3:94; Jake McLeod, *AS*, III, 3:161. For more on control of slaves, see Drew Gilpin Faust, "Culture, Conflict, and Community: The Meaning of Power on an Ante-Bellum Plantation," *Journal of Social History* 14 (Fall 1980): 83–97; H. M. Henry, *The Police Control of the Slave in South Carolina* (Emory, Va., 1914; New York: Negro Universities Press, 1968); Norrece T. Jones Jr., *Born a Child of Freedom Yet a Slave: Mechanisms of Control and Strategies of Resistance in Antebellum South Carolina* (Hanover, N.H.: Wesleyan University Press/University Press of New England, 1990).

39. Fannie Griffin, *AS*, II, 2:209; Peggy Grigsby, *AS*, II, 2:215; Isaiah (Solbert) Butler, *AS*, II, 1:157. See also Lucretia Heyward, *AS*, II, 2:279; John Boyd, *AS*, II, 1:72; Emma Lowran, *AS*, III, 3:125; William Pratt, *AS*, III, 3:277; Alexander Scaife, *AS*, III, 4:76; Yetman, *Life under the "Peculiar Institution,"* 117, 225.

40. Mary Frances Brown, *AS*, II, 1:131, 134; Josephine Bacchus, *AS*, II, 1:22; Louisa Gause, *AS*, II, 2:109. See also Botkin, *Lay My Burden Down,* 148–49.

41. See chap. 7.

Chapter 7: Slave Women and the Meaning of Womanhood

1. Mrs. Sutton, *AS*, XVIII:30. See also Green Wilbanks, *AS*, XIII, 4:139; Harrison Wilbanks, *AS*, IV, 1:54; Henry James Trentham, *AS*, XV:364; Schoolcraft, *Black Gauntlet,* 240.

2. Sarah Benjamin, *AS*, IV, 1:71.

3. Emanuel Elmore, *AS*, II, 2:8–10.

4. Unidentified man, *AS*, XIX:148, 161; Unidentified woman, *AS*, XIX:19. See also Fereby Rogers, *AS*, XIII, 1:213; Meriwether, *Recollections,* 60.

5. Millie Barber, *AS*, II, 1:39; Sylvia Durant, *AS*, II, 1:344.

6. D., "Old Stephen," *Southern Rose* 7 (29 Sept. 1838): 35–36. For a discussion of shame among slaves, see Genovese, *Roll, Jordan, Roll,* 113–23. See also Christie Farnham, "Sapphire?: The Issue of Dominance in the Slave Family, 1830–1865," in *"To Toil the Livelong Day": America's Women at Work, 1780–1980,* ed. Carol Groneman and Mary Beth Norton (Ithaca: Cornell University Press, 1987), 68–83.

7. Fannie Moore, *AS*, XV:130; David Goodman Gullins, *AS*, XII, 2:81–82; Charlie Pye, *AS*, XIII, 3:187. See also Martha Spence Bunton, *AS*, IV, 1:174–75; Margaret Bryant, *AS*, II, 1:147.

8. Unidentified man, *AS*, XIX:146–47; Ben Leitner, *AS*, III, 3:101; Bill Young, *AS*, III, 4:271.

9. Unidentified woman, *AS*, XVIII:65; Brent, *Incidents in Life,* 119. See also Myers, *Children of Pride,* 532–33, 544; Ryer Emmanuel, *AS*, II, 2:25; Clarence L. Mohr, *On the Threshold of Freedom: Masters and Slaves in Civil War Georgia* (Athens: University of Georgia Press, 1986), 12; Mary Ames, *From a New England Woman's*

Diary in Dixie in 1865 (Springfield: Plimpton Press, 1906), 64–65. For slave women's practice of birth control, infanticide, and abortion, see White, *Ar'n't I a Woman?* 84–98; Gutman, *Black Family*, 80–83; Genovese, *Roll, Jordan, Roll*, 496–97.

   10. Blassingame, *Slave Testimony*, 374–75.

   11. Everett Ingram, *AS*, VI, Alabama narratives:216.

   12. Unidentified woman, *AS*, XVIII:277–78. See also Nicey Kinney, *AS*, XIII, 3:32.

   13. Unidentified former slave, *AS*, XVIII:9; Mary Smith, *AS*, III, 4:112–13.

   14. I refer to coerced sexual activity rather than rape deliberately so as to include behaviors ranging from what would today be called sexual harassment to rape. *Coerced sexual activity* is not intended to diminish in any way the violence of white men's behavior; rather, it is to acknowledge that threats of sexual violence were as important in their impact as rape itself. The term *miscegenation* has been used to refer to any interracial sexual activity and, more specifically, to interracial sexual activity resulting in offspring; it will be used here only in that narrow sense. See also Thelma Jennings, "'Us Colored Women Had to Go through a Plenty': Sexual Exploitation of African-American Slave Women," *Journal of Women's History* 1 (Winter 1990): 60–66; Catherine Clinton, "Caught in the Web of the Big House: Women and Slavery," in *Southern Social Relations*, ed. Fraser, Saunders, and Wakelyn, 19–34; Darlene Clark Hine, "Rape and the Inner Lives of Black Women," *Signs* 14 (Summer 1989): 912–20.

   15. Sexual relations between white women and slave men occurred in the antebellum South but were quite rare. Inpressionistic evidence suggests they may have been more common in colonial times than they were in the midnineteenth century. See Peter H. Wood, *Black Majority: Negroes in Colonial South Carolina from 1670 through the Stono Rebellion* (New York: Norton, 1974); Winthrop D. Jordan, *White over Black: American Attitudes toward the Negro, 1550–1812* (Baltimore: Pelican, 1968); Edmund S. Morgan, *American Slavery, American Freedom: The Ordeal of Colonial Virginia* (New York: Norton, 1975). Evidence from the antebellum years suggests that the white women were poor, often from the up country, and not members of the plantation elite. See, for example, Anthony Ransome, *AS*, XV:197; Harriet Miller, *AS*, XIII, 3:127; Sam T. Thomas, *AS*, XV:319–20; Thomas Journal, 12 Feb. 1858; Blassingame, *Slave Community*, 84–85; James Hugo Johnston, *Race Relations in Virginia and Miscegenation in the South, 1776–1860* (Amherst: University of Massachusetts Press, 1970), 250–68. An exception to this pattern is provided in the testimony of former North Carolina slave Adora Reinshaw:

> My pappy wuz borned free, case his mammy wuz a white 'oman an' his pappy wuz a coal-black nigger man. Hit happened in Mississippi, do' I doan know her name 'cept dat she wuz a Perry.
>
> She wuz de wife of grandfather's marster an' dey said dat he wuz mean ter her. Grandfather wuz her coachman an' he often seed her cry, an' he'd talk ter her an' try ter comfort her in her troubles, an' dat's de way dat she come ter fall in love wid him.

One day, he said, she axed him ter stop de carriage an' come back dar an' talk ter her. When he wuz back dar wid her she starts to cry an' she puts her purtty gold haid on his shoulder, an' she tells him dat he am her only friend, an' dat her husban' won't eben let her have a chile.

Adora Reinshaw, *AS*, XV:213. See also Brent, *Incidents in Life*, 80–81; Clinton, *Plantation Mistress*, 209–10. In a culture that defined the norm for wealthy white women as assexual purity and black men's punishment for engaging in sex with white women as death, such occurrences could not have been frequent.

16. Sena Moore, *AS*, III, 3:211.

17. Relatively few of the former slaves interviewed by the WPA had experienced interracial sex directly, although some were the mulatto offspring of it. Most WPA informants were still children just before and during the Civil War. However, many were aware of interracial sex during the period and spoke about it openly. See, for example, Thomas Goodwater, *AS*, II, 2:167; Carrie Mason, *AS*, XIII, 3:112; Willie McCullough, *AS*, XV:78; Fannie Moore, *AS*, XV:132; Jacob Manson, *AS*, XV:97–98; John Smith, *AS*, XV:270–71; Amy Chapman, *AS*, VI, Alabama narratives:59; Martha Bradley, *AS*, VI, Alabama narratives:46; Auntie Thomas Johns, *AS*, IV, 2:205; Anne Clark, *AS*, IV, 1:224; unidentified woman, *AS*, XVIII:1–2, 8; unidentified woman, *AS*, XVIII:298; Lizzie Williams, *AS*, XV:396–97; Charity Grigsby, *AS*, VI, Alabama narratives:173; Martha Jackson, *AS*, VI, Alabama narratives:221; Sarah Ross, *AS*, XVII:168; Sam T. Thomas, *AS*, XV:319–20; unidentified former slave, *AS*, XVIII:34; Fred Brown, *AS*, IV, 1:157–58; Young Winston David, *AS*, XVII:89–90; Savilla Burrell, *AS*, II, 1:150; Ryer Emmanuel, *AS*, II, 2:14; Gus Feaster, *AS*, II, 2:65–66; Ben Horry, *AS*, II, 2:304–5, 310–11; Perdue, *Weevils in the Wheat*, 36, 84, 117, 202, 207, 251, 257, 300–301; Blassingame, *Slave Testimony*, 540; Weld, *American Slavery*, 11, 16; Brent, *Incidents in Life*, 44–57 and passim. See also Thomas Journal, 2 Jan. 1858, 12 Feb. 1858; Rev. George Bourne, *Picture of Slavery in the United States of America* (Middletown, Conn.: Edwin Hunt, 1834); Edward Byron Reuter, *Race Mixture: Studies in Intermarriage and Miscegenation* (New York: McGraw-Hill, 1931); Johnston, *Race Relations in Virginia*; Joel Williamson, *New People: Miscegenation and Mulattoes in the United States* (New York: Free Press, 1980).

18. Carrie Mason, *AS*, XIII, 3:112; Perdue, *Weevils in the Wheat*, 207; Lizzie Williams, *AS*, XV:397.

19. Mrs. Sutton, *AS*, XVIII:34; unidentified woman, *AS*, XVIII:2; Perdue, *Weevils in the Wheat*, 84; Kemble, *Journal of a Residence*, 270.

20. Josephine Bacchus, *AS*, II, 1:22; Nelson Cameron, *AS*, II, 1:173; Hector Godbold, *AS*, II, 2:145. See also Sallie Paul, *AS*, III, 3:235. The question of whether slaves were bred, or forced to marry spouses chosen by the master, is controversial among historians. See, for example, White, *Ar'n't I a Woman?* 68–70, 100–105; Jones, *Labor of Love*, 34–35; Jennings, "'Us Colored Women,'" 46–52; Escott, *Slavery Remembered*, 43–45; Robert William Fogel and Stanley Engerman, *Time on the Cross: The Economics of American Negro Slavery*, 2 vols. (Boston: Little, Brown,

1974), 1:78–86; Phillips, *American Negro Slavery*; Clinton, "Caught in the Web," 23–24.

21. Perdue, *Weevils in the Wheat*, 84; Brent, *Incidents in Life*, 55 and passim; Martha Bradley, *AS*, VI, Alabama narratives:46.

22. See chap. 4; Perdue, *Weevils in the Wheat*, 257; Jacob Manson, *AS*, XV:97–98; Brent, *Incidents in Life*, 60.

23. Brent, *Incidents in Life*, 49, 53, 51, 57; Hawks, *Woman Doctor's Civil War*, 154–55.

24. Perdue, *Weevils in the Wheat*, 202, see also 250. See also Auntie Thomas Johns, *AS*, IV, 2:205.

25. Willie McCullough, *AS*, XV:78. See also Martha Jackson, *AS*, VI, Alabama narratives:221; White, *Ar'n't I a Woman?* 41–43.

26. Perdue, *Weevils in the Wheat*, 207. See also Bourne, *Picture of Slavery*, 124–25.

27. Lizzie Williams, *AS*, XV:397; Auntie Thomas Johns, *AS*, IV, 2:205. See also Brent, *Incidents in Life*, 55.

28. Unidentified woman, *AS*, XVIII:298. See also Brent, *Incidents in Life*, 57.

29. Lizzie Williams, *AS*, XV:397. See also Auntie Thomas Johns, *AS*, IV, 2:205; Fred Brown, *AS*, IV, 1:158; Anne Clark, *AS*, IV, 1:224; unidentified former slave, *AS*, XVIII:34.

30. Martha Jackson, *AS*, VI, Alabama narratives:221. See also Perdue, *Weevils in the Wheat*, 250; unidentified former slave, *AS*, XVIII:34; White, *Ar'n't I a Woman?* 31, 40–41.

31. Perdue, *Weevils in the Wheat*, 207, 117. See also Winston Davis, *AS*, XVII:89–90; Charity Grigsby, *AS*, VI, Alabama narratives:173.

32. Harper, "Memoir on Slavery," 620–21. See White, *Ar'n't I a Woman?* 29–46 for a discussion of the myth of the slave woman as Jezebel.

33. A few white women reacted to their husbands' sexual relations with slave women by initiating divorce suits, a clear rejection of the behaviors expected of white women. Such suits were rare, especially given the pervasiveness of interracial sexual activity, probably because the economic and personal consequences for the woman were severe and the outcomes were generally unfavorable. See Johnston, *Race Relations*, 237–50; Lebsock, *Free Women*, 69–72.

34. Willie McCullough, *AS*, XV:78; unidentified woman, *AS*, XVIII:298; unidentified woman, *AS*, XVIII:1; Jacobs, *Incidents in Life*, 45–53. See also Blassingame, *Slave Testimony*, 540; Ryer Emmanuel, *AS*, II, 2:14; Jones, *Labor of Love*, 26–27; Cornwall Journal, typescript p. 56.

35. Delia Garlic, *AS*, VI, Alabama narratives:130; Perdue, *Weevils in the Wheat*, 190; Blassingame, *Slave Testimony*, 540.

36. Jacob Manson, *AS*, XV:97–98; Savilla Burrell, *AS*, II, 1:150. See also Lizzie Williams, *AS*, XV:396–97.

37. See chap. 5.

38. Both women based their opposition to slavery on these grounds. See chap. 5. For alternate views, see Edmondston, *"Journal,"* 552; "Few Thoughts on Slavery," 198.

39. Chesnut, *Mary Chesnut's Civil War*, 29, 31.

40. By contrast, in the antebellum North opposition to prostitution and venereal disease as well as male tyranny could help to unite women across class lines. See Smith-Rosenberg, "Beauty, the Beast, and the Militant Woman," in *Disorderly Conduct*, 109–28, 318–22.

41. Mary D. Curtis to Magadalen DeRosset, 14 Nov. 1842, and Catherine Kennedy to Mary D. Curtis, 25 May 1839, both in Moses Ashley Curtis Family Papers. See also Katherine D. Meares to Eliza Jane Lord DeRosset, 7 July 1854, DeRosset Family Papers.

42. The rest of her letter suggests that she rarely chose the latter course. Maria Davis to Mr. and Mrs. Ezra Goddard, 5 Feb. 1843, James S. M. Davis Papers, US-Car.

43. Maria Davis to Emily Knowlton, 24 Mar. 1841, Davis Papers; Meta Morris Grimball Diary, 12 Jan. 1861; Will of Eliza Hannah Simkins, Wills of Edgefield County, S.C., Book D, vol. 1, 1836–53, 57, S.C. Archives.

44. W. H. Scarborough to John B. Miller, 30 May 1846, Miller-Furman-Dabbs Family Papers. See, for example, Benjamin Russell, *AS*, III, 4:53; Holloway Autobiography, 10; Chesnut, *Mary Chesnut's Civil War*.

45. Holloway Autobiography, 10; Henry James Trentham, *AS*, XV:364. See also Green Wilbanks, *AS*, XIII, 4:139; Ezra Adams, *AS*, II, 1:6; Frank Adamson, *AS*, II, 1:16; Charles Ball, *Slavery in the United States: A Narrative of the Life and Adventures of Charles Ball* (Lewiston, Penn: 1836), 1–13, quoted in Blassingame, *The Slave Community*, 25.

46. Ed McCrorey, *AS*, III, 3:146.

47. Although it was not legally possible to free slaves in South Carolina in this period except by special legislation, some slaveholders wrote wills in which they contrived to make slaves "as free as the law allows" or expressed their desire to have their slaves freed when the laws of the state made that possible.

48. Escott, *Slavery Remembered*, 90–93.

49. Harriet Tubman was the notable exception. Eugene D. Genovese, *From Rebellion to Revolution: Afro-American Slave Revolts in the Making of the Modern World* (Baton Rouge: Louisiana State University Press, 1979); Herbert Aptheker, *American Negro Slave Revolts* (New York: International, 1952).

50. Jacobs, *Incidents in Life*, 33–34, 58.

51. Since the early 1970s, historians have been asking whether women have a distinct culture from that of men. In fact, feminist scholars in a variety of disciplines have been asking not only how women are different from men but also what has been the experience of women from their own perspective. In examining the past, scholars have discussed what they have variously called the female world (Smith-Rosenberg, "Female World," *Disorderly Conduct*; Jessie Bernard, *The Female World* [New York: Free Press, 1981]), the female experience (Gerda Lerner, ed., *The Female Experience: An American Documentary* [Indianapolis: Bobbs-Merrill, 1977]), female per-

sonalism (Lebsock, *Free Women*, intro. and chap. 5), or the bonds of womanhood (Cott, *Bonds of Womanhood*). Most of these studies focus on the nineteenth-century Northeast. They draw for evidence upon the cluster of experiences peculiar to women (menstruation, pregnancy, childbirth, lactation, menopause), and the emotions, attitudes, and behaviors ascribed to women because of them. Thus, although the justification for women's culture is rooted in biology, its substance in history derives from what is considered appropriate behavior for women. Scholars in other disciplines have examined the notions of women's culture with respect to the patterns of language used by women, the art and literature produced by women, women's learning, and women's achievements in various endeavors. In recent years debate has also focused on whether women's experiences are rooted in biology (essentialism) or in cultural constructs such as language. Unfortunately, much of this debate has been profoundly ahistorical. See also Friedman, *Enclosed Garden;* Joan Renzer Gunderson, "The Double Bonds of Race and Sex: Black and White Women in a Colonial Virginia Parish," *Journal of Southern History* 52 (Aug. 1986): 351–72; Bonnie Thornton Dill, "Race, Class, and Gender: Prospects for an All-Inclusive Sisterhood," *Feminist Studies* 9 (Spring 1983): 131–50.

52. Kemble, *Journal of Residence*, 78.

53. See, for example, Smith-Rosenberg, "Female World."

54. This point is made dramatically apparent when reading collections of letters written by men and women from the same family. Fox-Genovese reaches the opposite conclusion. See *Plantation Household*, 349.

55. Susan Witherspoon to Susan McDowell, 24 Apr. 1840, Witherspoon-McDowell Family Papers.

56. Cornelius Holmes, *AS*, II, 2:296–97. See also Clifton, *Life on Argyle Island*, 251; Moses Lyles, *AS*, III, 3:141.

57. Richard Macks, *AS*, XVI, Maryland narratives:55.

58. Suzanne Lebsock's *The Free Women of Petersburg* is a rich and pathbreaking account of women in that Virginia city. The kinds of questions she asked could easily be raised about Charleston or other South Carolina cities; no attempt has been made to do so here. See also William H. Pease and Jane H. Pease, *The Web of Progress: Private Values and Public Styles in Boston and Charleston, 1828–1843* (New York: Oxford University Press, 1985); Pease and Pease, *Ladies, Women, and Wenches.*

59. Burwell, *Girl's Life*, 158.

60. Fannie M. Colcock to her sister Hattie, 7 Dec. 1854, Colcock-Hay Families, USCar.

61.

Years	County	Number of Wills by Women	Total Number of Wills	Percent by Women
1839–55	Abbeville	71	323	22
1826–56	Barnwell	41	239	16
1845–51	Charleston	93	204	46

1856–62	Charleston	88	239	37
1862–68	Charleston	93	238	39
1833–53	Chester	57	216	26
1827–53	Darlington	19	96	20
1836–53	Edgefield	53	281	19
1840–57	Fairfield	54	217	25
1823–53	Kershaw	27	112	24
1854–64	Richland	46	152	30
1840–58	Spartanburg	33	244	14
TOTAL		675	2,571	26

Source: Will Books, S.C. Archives.
Note: Not all wills for each county survive in the typescript volumes of wills prepared by the WPA, nor did all wills survive to be placed in the South Carolina Department of Archives. There are no surviving antebellum wills at all for Georgetown County. Some of the women who wrote wills were married; many more had either never married or were widowed. All obviously held disposable property in their own names; many who wrote wills were quite wealthy.

On the uses of wills as a source, see Lebsock, *Free Women,* 35–48, 77–79, 130–42, and passim.

62. See, for example, Will of Sarah F. Waring, Wills of Charleston County, S.C., vol. 39, Book C, 1826–34, 842–43, 846, S.C. Archives; Will of Eliza Swinton, Wills of Charleston County, vol. 44, Book A, 1845–51, 317; Will of Elizabeth Corbett, Wills of Charleston County, vol. 44, Book A, 1845–51, 319; Will of Mary Manson, Wills of Charleston County, vol. 46A, Book M, 1856–62, 237; Will of Margaret Harleston Laurens, Wills of Charleston County, vol. 48A, Book M, 1856–62, 272; Will of Elizabeth F. Greenhill, Wills of Charleston County, vol. 48A, Book M, 1856–62, 397; Will of Martha Ann Mathews, Wills of Charleston County, vol. 50A, Book N, 1862–68, 59; Will of Joanna C. Saltar, Wills of Charleston County, vol. 50A, Book N, 1862–68, 79–80; Will of Charlotte Griffin, Wills of Richland County, S.C., vol. 4, Book L, pt. 2, 1854–64, 187; Will of Elizabeth W. Green, Wills of Richland County, vol. 4, Book L, pt. 2, 1854–64, 198. Willing money to slaves was illegal under South Carolina law, but was seldom challenged when the amount was small.

63. Will of Josephine Ferrette, Wills of Charleston County, vol. 48A, Book M, 1856–62, 53; Will of Jane E. O'Daniel, Wills of Charleston County, vol. 48A, Book M, 1856–62, 104. See also Will of Caroline Francisco, Wills of Charleston County, vol. 44, Book A, 1845–51, 62; Will of Henrietta Edwards, Wills of Charleston County, vol. 44, Book A, 1845–51, 414; Will of Mary C. Boyle, Wills of Charleston County, vol. 48A, Book M, 1856–62, 244; Will of Jane Ladson Waring, Wills of Charleston County, vol. 48A, Book M, 1856–62, 259; Will of Mary Chapeau, Wills of Charleston County, vol. 48A, Book M, 1856–62, 301; Will of Mary Jones Morris, Wills of Charleston County, vol. 50A, Book N, 1862–68, 302; Will of Joanna C. Saltar, Wills of Charleston County, vol. 50A, Book N, 1862–68, 97; Will of Elizabeth Smith, Wills of Charleston County, vol. 50A, Book N, 1862–68, 205; Will of

Jane Findley, Wills of Abbeville County, S.C., vol. 3, 1839–55, 166; Will of Theresa Taylor, Wills of Richland County, vol. 4, Book L, pt. 2, 1854–64, 26; Will of Frances Edgar, Wills of Richland County, vol. 4, Book L, pt. 2, 1854–64, 278; Will of Priscilla Terry, Wills of Chester County, S.C., vol. 3, Book A-1, 1833–53, 217. On the emancipation of female slaves by men's wills, see Clinton, *Plantation Mistress*, 213–14.

64. Will of Mary Winthrop, Wills of Charleston County, vol. 44, Book A, 1845–51, 84; Will of Elizabeth Brewton Lowndes, Wills of Charleston County, vol 48A, Book M, 1856–62, 122. See also Will of Sarah Parker, Wills of Charleston County, vol. 44, Book A, 1845–51, 184; Will of Eliza Swinton, Wills of Charleston County, vol. 44, Book A, 1845–51, 317; Will of M. V. de Michel, Wills of Charleston County, vol. 44, Book A, 1845–51, 221–222; Will of Elizabeth Corbett, Wills of Charleston County, vol. 44, Book A, 1845–51, 319; Will of Mary Manson, Wills of Charleston County, vol. 48A, Book M, 1856–62, 237; Will of Margaret Harleston Laurens, Wills of Charleston County, vol. 48A, Book M, 1856–62, 272; Will of Elizabeth P. Greenhill, Wills of Charleston County, vol. 48A, Book M, 1856–62, 397; Will of Martha Ann Mathews, Wills of Charleston County, vol. 50A, Book N, 1862–68, 58–59; Will of Joanna C. Saltar, Wills of Charleston County, vol. 50A, Book N, 1862–68, 80; Will of Charlotte Griffin, Wills of Richland County, vol. 4, Book L, pt. 2, 1854–64, 187; Will of Elizabeth W. Green, Wills of Richland County, vol. 4, Book L, pt. 2, 1854–64, 198–201; Will of Elizabeth A. Clarke, Wills of Fairfield County, S.C., vol. 3, Book 9, 1840–57, 78–79. Sarah Waring willed not only material goods and money to Diana Wells, whom she had previously emancipated, but also a slave woman and her family. See Will of Sarah F. Waring, Wills of Charleston County, vol. 39, Book C, 1826–34, 842–46. See also Will of Diana Wells, Wills of Charleston County, vol. 44, Book A, 1845–51, 17.

65. Will of Eliza Mackey, Wills of Charleston County, vol. 44, Book A, 1845–51, 149–50.

66. Will of Eliza Swinton, Wills of Charleston County, vol. 44, Book A, 1845–51, 316. For the dangers of emancipating female slaves, see "Essay on the Moral and Political Effect," 338–39; Hentz, *Planter's Bride*, 1:265–67, 291, 294. For some of the consequences of emancipation, see Lebsock, *Free Women*, chap. 4; for white women's provisions regarding slaves, including emancipation, see 137–42.

67. Will of Margaret Harleston Laurens, Wills of Charleston County, vol. 48A, Book M, 1856–62, 272. See also Will of Sarah F. Waring, Wills of Charleston County, vol. 39, Book C, 1826–34, 842–46; Will of Rebecca E. Gough, Wills of Charleston County, vol. 44, Book A, 1845–51, 39–40; Will of Eliza Mackey, Wills of Charleston County, vol. 44, Book A, 1845–51, 149–50; Will of Jane MacIntosh Fisher, Wills of Charleston County, vol. 44, Book A, 1845–51, 432; Will of M. V. de Michel, Wills of Charleston County, vol. 44, Book A, 1845–51, 221–22; Will of Elizabeth Corbett, Wills of Charleston County, vol. 44, Book A, 1845–51, 319; Will of Harriet C. O'Driscoll, Wills of Charleston County, vol. 48A, Book M, 1856–62, 35; Will of

Martha Ann Mathews, Wills of Charleston County, vol. 50A, Book N, 1862–68, 58; Will of Alice J. Heyward, Wills of Charleston County, vol. 50A, Book N, 1862–68, 170; Will of Mary G. Keeley, Wills of Charleston County, vol. 50A, Book N, 1862–68, 212; Will of Nancy Tait, Wills of Abbeville County, vol. 3, 1839–55, 71; Will of Bella Cohen, Wills of Richland County, vol. 4, Book L, pt. 2, 1854–64, 327; Will of Martha Tinkler, Wills of Fairfield County, vol. 3, Book 9, 1840–57, 455; Will of Isabella Jane Belk, Wills of Kershaw County, S.C., vol. 3, 1823–53, 173; McIntosh, *Lofty and Lowly*, 2:5; Eastman, *Aunt Phillis's Cabin*, 259.

68. See Will of Elizabeth Mathews Hamilton, Wills of Charleston County, vol. 50A, Book N, 1862–68, 29; Will of Maria Mathews, Wills of Charleston County, vol. 50A, Book N, 1862–68, 32; Will of Rebecca B. Hayne, Wills of Charleston County, vol. 50A, Book M, 1862–68, 77; Will of Susannah Sutton, Wills of Barnwell County, vol. 2, Book C, 1826–56, 70; Will of Nancy Boyd, Wills of Fairfield County, vol. 3, Book 9, 1840–57, 43; Will of Rachel Griffin, Wills of Fairfield County, vol. 3, Book 9, 1840–57, 197.

69. Pauline Worth, *AS*, III, 4:261–63. See also Johnson and Roark, *Black Masters*; Michael P. Johnson and James L. Roark, eds., *No Chariot Let Down: Charleston's Free People of Color on the Eve of the Civil War* (New York: Norton, 1984); Wade, *Slavery in the Cities*.

70. Chesnut, *Mary Chesnut's Civil War*, 199.

71. Like other historians writing the history of slavery and race relations, I have been hampered by the paucity of sources addressing the lives of small slaveholders. What follows is tentative at best.

72. Gavin Diary, 3 May 1859, see also 24 Feb. 1869, 4 May 1869, 6 May 1869; Amos Gadsden, *AS*, II, 2:92.

73. Sylvia Cannon, *AS*, II, 1:189; Nancy Washington, *AS*, III, 4:184–85.

Chapter 8: The Experience of War

1. The impact of war on women has been a continuing subject of debate among historians of women. Some have argued that war loosens restrictions on women's behavior and opens new opportunities. See, for example, William H. Chafe, *The American Woman: Her Changing Social, Economic, and Political Roles, 1920–1970* (New York: Oxford University Press, 1972). Others suggest that any wartime advances are illusory. See, for example, Joan Hoff Wilson, "The Illusion of Change: Women and the American Revolution," in *The American Revolution: Explorations in the History of American Radicalism*, ed. Alfred F. Young (DeKalb: Northern Illinois University Press, 1976), 383–445. No matter what historians may argue about the implications of war, the women who lived through the Civil War in the Confederacy believed it had a dramatic impact on their lives. Some white women likened themselves to their grandmothers and self-consciously patterned themselves after the heroines of the American Revolution. Southern white women also liked to think of their experiences as

unique and rarely considered the impact of the war on northern women. Black women had no doubts about the significant effects of the war although, as will become clear, many wished its outcome made an even more dramatic impact on their lives.

2. The phrase *wait and see* is Litwack's: "While military fortunes fluctuated with every skirmish and battle, so did the slaves' responses to the war, with many of them adopting a 'wait and see' attitude and refusing to commit themselves irretrievably to either side." Litwack, *Been in the Storm,* 20.

3. Port Royal and other Sea Islands and coastal areas were an important exception and are discussed in chap. 9.

4. Holmes, *Brokenburn.* See also Katharine M. Jones, ed., *Heroines of Dixie: Confederate Women Tell Their Story of the War* (Indianapolis: Bobbs-Merrill, 1955); Mary Elizabeth Massey, *Refugee Life in the Confederacy* (Baton Rouge: Louisiana State University Press, 1964); James L. Roark, *Masters without Slaves: Southern Planters in the Civil War and Reconstruction* (New York: Norton, 1977); Massey, *Bonnet Brigades;* Bell Irvin Wiley, *Confederate Women* (Westport, Conn.: Greenwood Press, 1975); Rable, *Civil Wars;* Drew Gilpin Faust, "Alters of Sacrifice: Confederate Women and the Narratives of War," *Journal of American History* 76 (Mar. 1990): 1200–1228.

5. From the beginning, the war created significant conflict for the northern-born wives of southern planters. For them, the question of loyalty was a thorny one that had to be confronted daily. See Darling, *Mrs. Darling's Letters;* Katharine H. Cumming, *A Northern Daughter and a Southern Wife: The Civil War Reminiscences and Letters of Katharine H. Cumming, 1860–1865,* ed. W. Kirk Wood (Augusta: Richmond County Historical Society, 1976).

6. Mary Elizabeth Massey, *Ersatz in the Confederacy* (Columbia: University of South Carolina Press, 1952).

7. Slaves' experience of war is documented most fully in Litwack, *Been in the Storm.* Planters' experience is discussed in Roark, *Masters without Slaves,* and Rable, *Civil Wars.* Race relations (among men) are the primary concern in Mohr, *Threshold of Freedom.*

8. Bleser, *Hammonds of Redcliffe,* 94; Coxe, *Memories,* 12–13; Edmondston, "*Journal,*" 57, 60, see also 268, 282, and passim; Holmes, *Diary,* 215.

9. United Daughters of the Confederacy, *South Carolina Women,* 1:29, 194, 228–29, 2:196–97, see also 1:161–63, 233, 361, 2:34, 217–18. See also Pringle, *Chicora Wood,* 195; Holmes, *Brokenburn,* 146–47, 256, 286; Meta Morris Grimball Diary, 24 Oct. 1862; Emma to Fannie H. Manigault, 16 Jan. 1861, Manigault Papers, *Records of Plantations,* series F, part 2; Putnam, *Richmond during the War,* 250–51, 254; Myers, *Children of Pride,* 984, 999, 1004, 1006; Emma LeConte, *When the World Ended: The Diary of Emma LeConte,* ed. Earl Schenck Miers (New York: Oxford University Press, 1957; Lincoln: University of Nebraska Press, 1987), 8–9, 12–13.

10. Edmondston, "*Journal,*" 87–88, 112, see also 154–55.

11. Judith White Brockenbrough McGuire, *Diary of a Southern Refugee during the War* (New York: E. J. Hale and Son, 1867; New York: Arno Press, 1972), 12, 26, and passim; Putnam, *Richmond during the War,* 39–40, 58–59; Caroline Howard Gil-

man, "Letters of a Confederate Mother: Charleston in the Sixties," *Atlantic Month-ly*, Apr. 1926, 504, 507, 508, 509; Harper, *Annie Harper's Journal*, 11–12.

12. Myers, *Children of Pride*, 688, 989. See also Ward, *Children of Bladensfield*, 74; Cora, "Virginia's Tribute to Her Daughters," *Southern Literary Messenger* 37 (Mar. 1863): 169–70; Rable, *Civil Wars*, 138–44. Women's wartime contributions are celebrated in "Memories of the War: Women of the Confederacy," *DeBow's Review* 3, after the war series (Feb. 1867): 144–45.

13. *Notable American Women*, 2:452. On nursing, see Rable, *Civil Wars*, 121–28; Massey, *Bonnet Brigades*, chap. 3.

14. Elise Rutledge Scrapbook, UNC; United Daughters of the Confederacy, *South Carolina Women*, 1:127–35, 150–52, and passim.

15. Putnam, *Richmond during the War*, 17; Edmondston, "*Journal*," 16–17 and passim. See also Rable, *Civil Wars*, 144–51.

16. "The Women of the South," 147, 150, 151. See also "Memories of the War," 144–45.

17. "Education of Southern Women," 390.

18. Edmondston, "*Journal*," 155, 167; McGuire, *Diary of a Southern Refugee*, 12–13; Mary Tucker Magill, *Women; or, Chronicles of the Late War* (Baltimore: Turnbull Brothers, 1871), x.

19. Dawson, *Confederate Girl's Diary*, 81, also 92; Julia Ellen LeGrand Waitz, *The Journal of Julia LeGrand, New Orleans 1862–1863*, ed. Kate Mason Rowland and Mrs. Morris L. Croxall (Richmond: Everett Waddey Co., 1911), 52–53; Jones, *Heroines of Dixie*, 70; Holmes, *Brokenburn*, 24. See also Chesnut, *Mary Chesnut's Civil War*; Edmondston, "*Journal*," 567.

20. Jones, *Heroines of Dixie*, 359. Gist's life was anything but ordinary. She worked for the Treasury Department in Columbia, and just days after writing about her monotonous life, followed the department's operations to Richmond, where she lived independently with several other women employees. See also Elmore Diaries and Books, 21 Feb. 1865, 12 Mar. 1865.

21. LeConte, *When the World Ended*, 21–22, 90. On wartime pressure to marry, see Rable, *Civil Wars*, 51–54. For women who did flout expectations and take up arms or serve as spies or soldiers, see Rose O'Neal Greenhow, *My Imprisonment and the First Year of Abolition Rule in Washington* (London: Richard Bentley, 1863); Belle Boyd, *Belle Boyd: In Camp and Prison* (London: Saunders, Otley, and Co., 1865); Rable, *Civil Wars*, 151–53.

22. See, for example, McGuire, *Diary of a Southern Refugee*, 238–39, 244, 250–53; Putnam, *Richmond during the War*, 174–75, 273; Magill, *Women*, 328–29; Rable, *Civil Wars*, 131–35; Massey, *Bonnet Brigades*, chap. 7; Jones, *Heroines of Dixie*, 356–60, 376–83.

23. Edmondston, "*Journal*," 186. She prided herself on her new knowledge: "This war is teaching us many things." Among them she listed making yeast, malting corn, dying, spinning, and weaving. Ibid., 654.

24. Meta Morris Grimball Diary, 24 Oct. 1862; Elmore Reminiscences, 20 Nov.

1864. See also Josephine Clay Habersham, *Ebb Tide: As Seen through the Diary of Josephine Clay Habersham, 1863*, ed. Spencer Bidwell King Jr. (Athens: University of Georgia Press, 1958), 35, 94.

25. United Daughters of the Confederacy, *South Carolina Women*, 1:162–63, see also 1:196–97, 228–29, 233, 262–63, 2:34, 217–18. See also Massey, *Ersatz in the Confederacy;* Jones, *Heroines of Dixie*, 260–65, 276–77; LeConte, *When the World Ended*, 16–17, 84; Rable, *Civil Wars*, chap. 5; Mohr, *Threshold of Freedom*, 221–32. Perhaps the best account of the domestic ingenuity demanded by the scarcity of material goods during the war is Parthenia A. Hague, *A Blockaded Family: Life in Southern Alabama during the Civil War* (Boston: Houghton, Mifflin, 1888; reprint, Freeport, N.Y.: Books for Libraries Press, 1971).

26. Pringle, *Chicora Wood*, 189, quotation from 194. See also Edmondston, *"Journal,"* 215.

27. Easterby, *South Carolina Rice Plantation*, 292–93, 212–13; United Daughters of the Confederacy, *South Carolina Women*, 1:198. See also Bacot Diary, 16 Apr. 1861, 28 Sept. 1861; Ward, *Children of Bladensfield*, 74; Litwack, *Been in the Storm*, 11–14; Rable, *Civil Wars*, chap. 6, esp. 128–35.

28. Edmondston, *"Journal,"* 240, 649, see also 643, 658; Mack Taylor, *AS*, III, 4:158.

29. Habersham, *Ebb Tide*, 35, see also 63, 74, 102–3. See also McGuire, *Diary of a Southern Refugee*, 82, 185–86, 197; Putnam, *Richmond during the War*, 194, 252.

30. Holmes, *Diary*, 287, 364–65. See also Edmondston, *"Journal."*

31. Bleser, *Hammonds of Redcliffe*, 108; Chesnut, *Mary Chesnut's Civil War*, 72, 721, 733, see also 261. See also Fannie Page Hume Diary, 22 Apr. 1862, 25 Apr. 1862, 7 May 1862, 18 May 1862, 19 May 1862, Manuscripts Division, Library of Congress.

32. Easterby, *South Carolina Rice Plantation*, 270–73, 300, 303, 316–20, 323–27.

33. Gordon Bluford, *AS*, II, 1:62. See also Alfred Sligh, *AS*, III, 4:92; Sarah Poindexter, *AS*, III, 3:268; Blassingame, *Slave Testimony*, 456; Holloway Autobiography, 60; Holmes, *Brokenburn*, 25, 29, 31, 32, and passim; Bleser, *Hammonds of Redcliffe*, 95; Jones, *Labor of Love*, 48–49 and passim. Work in the Big House could take on added significance during the war because of the importance of the information it was possible to learn there. See Litwack, *Been in the Storm*, 20–22.

34. Manda Walker, *AS*, III, 4:170.

35. United Daughters of the Confederacy, *South Carolina Women*, 1:99, 79. See also Harper, *Annie Harper's Journal*, 12, 14; Edmondston, *"Journal,"* 57–58.

36. Easterby, *South Carolina Rice Plantation*, 284, 294; Myers, *Children of Pride*, 1015. See also Holmes, *Brokenburn*, 258–59.

37. Bacot Diary, 11 Feb. 1861, 16 Apr. 1861, 1 July 1861, 21 Sept. 1861. It is very likely that the murdered woman was Elizabeth Boykin Witherspoon, a cousin of Mary Chesnut. See Chesnut, *Mary Chesnut's Civil War*, 198–219, 226.

38. Brevard Diary, 30 Jan. 1861, 4 Apr. 1861; See also William Howard Russell, *My Diary North and South* (New York: Knopf, 1988), 98; Litwack, *Been in the Storm*, 15–18, 59–63, and passim.

39. Bleser, *Hammonds of Redcliffe*, 95; Edmondston, "*Journal*," 115; also 74. See also McGuire, *Diary of a Southern Refugee*, 12–14, 19.

40. Chesnut, *Mary Chesnut's Civil War*, 48, 211, 212, 199, see also 60. See also Holmes, *Diary*, 63–64.

41. Chesnut, *Mary Chesnut's Civil War*, 233–35. See also Burwell, *Girl's Life*, 181–83; Darling, *Mrs. Darling's Letters*, 109–10.

42. McCorkle Diary, 26 Aug. 1860; Cornwall Journal, typescript p. 54; Brevard Diary, 21 Dec. 1860, 22 Dec. 1860, 8 Jan. 1861, see also 29 Dec. 1860; Chesnut, *Mary Chesnut's Civil War*, 53, 88, 113–14, 153.

43. Edmondston, "*Journal*," 301. Edmondston may have protested too much. She said essentially the same thing on three other occasions: see 270, 306, 673. See also Myers, *Children of Pride*, 1068.

44. Habersham, *Ebb Tide*, 102–3; Gilman, "Letters of a Confederate Mother," 509. See also Magill, *Women*, 329; Putnam, *Richmond during the War*, 177–79; Hermine, "The Old Mammy's Lament for Her Young Master," *Southern Literary Messenger* 37 (Nov.–Dec. 1863): 732–33.

45. Hume Diary, 27 Dec. 1862. See also Hawks, *Woman Doctor's Civil War*, 145.

46. Meta Morris Grimball Diary, 23 July 1862, 15 May 1864; Chesnut, *Mary Chesnut's Civil War*, 353. See also Merrick, *Old Times in Dixie Land*, 48–50.

47. Daniel E. Huger Smith, Alice R. Huger Smith, and Arney R. Childs, *Mason Smith Family Letters, 1860–1868* (Columbia: University of South Carolina Press, 1950), 27. See also Andrews, *War-Time Journal*, 320.

48. Holmes, *Diary*, 388. See also Darling, *Mrs. Darling's Letters*, 109–10; Logan, *Confederate Girlhood*, 87–88.

49. Smith, *Mason Smith Family Letters*, 83, 150. Ironically, white women's postwar reminiscences are filled with tributes to trusted slaves who hid their valuables during the war and refused to divulge their whereabouts to Yankees.

50. Putnam, *Richmond during the War*, 264–66, quotes from 266. See also Merrick, *Old Times in Dixie Land*, 77–78, 80–81.

51. Belle Kearney, *A Slaveholder's Daughter*, 2d ed. (St. Louis: St. Louis Christian Advocate Co., 1900), 13–14.

52. Thomas Journal, 21 Nov. 1864, 23 Sept. 1864, 30 Sept. 1864; Elmore Reminiscences, 25 Dec. 1864; Chesnut, *Mary Chesnut's Civil War*, 488, 641–42.

53. Edmondston, "*Journal*," 651, see also 272, 638–39, 650, 652, 669, 676, 686. See also Darling, *Mrs. Darling's Letters*, 110–11; Litwack, *Been in the Storm*, 41–45; Elmore Diaries and Books, 12 Mar. 1865.

54. Myers, *Children of Pride*, 1244.

55. Holmes, *Diary*, xix and passim; Meta Morris Grimball Diary.

56. Rable, *Civil Wars*, chaps. 8, 9; Jane E. Schultz, "Mute Fury: Southern Women's Diaries of Sherman's March to the Sea, 1864–1865," in *Arms and the Woman: War, Gender, and Literary Representation*, ed. Helen M. Cooper, Adrienne Auslander Munich, and Susan Merrill Squier (Chapel Hill: University of North Carolina Press, 1989), 59–79; Faust, "Alters of Sacrifice."

57. Susan R. Jervey and Charlotte St. J. Ravenel, *Two Diaries from Middle St. John's, Berkeley, South Carolina, Feb.–May, 1865* (n.p.: St. John's Hunting Club, 1921), 7, 36; Andrews, *War-Time Journal*, 69.

58. Coxe, *Memories*, 48; Myers, *Children of Pride*, 1247; Edmondston, *"Journal,"* 421, see also 670; Chesnut, *Mary Chesnut's Civil War*, 715–16. See also Waitz, *Journal of Julia LeGrand*, 262–63.

59. There is, of course, no way to estimate how many slaves fled to the protection of northern troops and how many remained loyal to their owners, or at least stayed on the plantation. The situation was too flexible and the records too fragmented to offer guidance beyond the subjective accounts of slaveholders. The evidence for "loyalty" is strongest for house slaves, perhaps because they continued to enjoy better material conditions than field slaves. This may also simply be a reflection of the sources: white women were perhaps more likely to write about the slaves they knew best, whose loyalty they wanted to assume and whose activities directly influenced their daily lives. See also Litwack, *Been in the Storm*, chap. 1.

60. Elmore Reminiscences, 27 Dec. 1864. See also Elmore Diaries and Books, 12 Feb. 1865.

61. Jervey and Ravenel, *Two Diaries*, 11, 22; Holmes, *Diary*, 404, 413, 415; Pringle, *Chicora Wood*, 234. See also United Daughters of the Confederacy, *South Carolina Women*, 1:79, 216, 350, 2:124–27, 173; Coxe, *Memories*, 35–36, 54–55; Louise Wigfall Wright, *A Southern Girl in '61: The War-Time Memories of a Confederate Senator's Daughter* (New York: Doubleday, Page, and Co., 1905), 16–18; Devereux, "Mammy" in *Plantation Sketches*; Smith, *Mason Smith Family Letters*, 161–62; Grace Pierson (James) Beard Reminiscences, UNC; Elizabeth Ware Pearson, ed., *Letters from Port Royal, 1862–1868* (Boston: W. B. Clarke, 1906; New York: Arno Press and the New York Times, 1969), 206–7.

62. Many expressions of slaves' loyalty can be found in the postwar memoirs, reminiscences, and autobiographies written by white southerners. These expressions usually bear the stamp of hindsight and cannot be considered reliable accounts of white women's feelings during the war itself. They do, however, form the core of a powerful myth about race relations that shaped southern experience in the later nineteenth century and well into the twentieth.

63. Clifton, *Life on Argyle Island*, 320; Alfred Sligh, *AS*, III, 4:92; Harper, *Annie Harper's Journal*, 30; Edmondston, *"Journal,"* 173; Myers, *Children of Pride*, 1241. See also Coxe, *Memories*, 35–36.

64. Sarah Poindexter, *AS*, III, 3:268–69. See also Litwack, *Been in the Storm*, chaps. 1 and 3.

65. Holloway Autobiography, 60; Henry D. Jenkins, *AS*, III, 3:24; Hume Diary, 14 Mar. 1862.

66. Brevard Diary, 13 Oct. 1860, see also 24 Oct. 1860, 9 Nov. 1860, 14 Nov. 1860, 10 Dec. 1860, 16 Jan. 1861, 21 Jan. 1861.

67. See, for example, Dawson, *Confederate Girl's Diary*, 60; Elmore Reminiscences, 20 Nov. 1864; Chesnut, *Mary Chesnut's Civil War*, 699; Andrews, *War-Time Journal*, 272.

68. Giving the last of the wine to passing soldiers to fortify their courage was significant because of the important medical uses to which it could be put. Elmore Diaries and Books, 21 Feb. 1865.

69. Thomas Journal, 3 Jan. 1865. Thomas did not send the letter. See also Chesnut, *Mary Chesnut's Civil War,* 248.

70. Holmes, *Diary,* 434–35.

Chapter 9: The Transition to Freedom

1. Blassingame, *Slave Testimony,* 456. See also Holmes, *Brokenburn,* 128, 171, 175; Edmondston, *"Journal,"* 273, 306. For Reconstruction in South Carolina, see Martin Abbott, *The Freedman's Bureau in South Carolina, 1865–1872* (Chapel Hill: University of North Carolina Press, 1967); Carol K. Rothrock Bleser, *The Promised Land: The History of the South Carolina Land Commission, 1869–1890* (Columbia: University of South Carolina Press, 1969); Thomas Holt, *Black over White: Negro Political Leadership in South Carolina during Reconstruction* (Urbana: University of Illinois Press, 1977); Howard N. Rabinowitz, *Race Relations in the Urban South, 1865–1890* (Urbana: University of Illinois Press, 1980); John S. Reynolds, *Reconstruction in South Carolina, 1865–1877* (Columbia: State Co., 1905); Francis B. Simkins and Robert H. Woody, *South Carolina during Reconstruction* (Chapel Hill: University of North Carolina Press, 1932); Alrutheus Ambush Taylor, *The Negro in South Carolina during Reconstruction* (Washington: n.p., 1924); Joel Williamson, *After Slavery: The Negro in South Carolina during Reconstruction, 1861–1877* (Chapel Hill: University of North Carolina Press, 1965).

2. Delia Thompson, *AS,* III, 4:161. Complaints from whites about the destruction inflicted by Sherman's men are ubiquitous.

3. Holmes, *Diary,* 430, see also 102, 435, 441. See also LeConte, *When the World Ended,* 51–54.

4. Myers, *Children of Pride,* 1230.

5. Eliza Hasty, *AS,* II, 2:256. See also Genovese, *Roll, Jordan, Roll,* 153; Jones, *Labor of Love,* 50–51; Meriwether, *Recollections,* 164, 203, for rape of black women by Confederate soldiers, 178–80. For rape of white women by northern soldiers, see Rable, *Civil Wars,* 158–62. A few black women welcomed the attentions of northern soldiers, to the dismay of their husbands. See Meriwether, *Recollections,* 65–66.

6. Hawks, *Woman Doctor's Civil War,* 35. Hawks also reported the execution of three soldiers from Massachusetts who had "committed an outrage on a white woman." She noted that this measure would not have prevented "the same offense towards black women." Ibid., 61.

7. Litwack, *Been in the Storm,* 130. See also Waitz, *Journal of Julia LeGrand,* 228–30; Dawson, *Confederate Girl's Diary,* 211–12; Edmondston, *"Journal,"* 711.

8. Edmondston, *"Journal,"* 710, 713; Myers, *Children of Pride,* 1241; LeConte, *When the World Ended,* 53–54, 56–57.

9. Coxe, *Memories*, 61, 44; Elmore Diaries and Books, 21 Feb. 1865; Litwack, *Been in the Storm*, 123.

10. See Litwack, *Been in the Storm*, 52–59.

11. Alfred Sligh, *AS*, III, 4:93; Hester Hunter, *AS*, 2:340; Lila Rutherford, *AS*, III, 4:58; Jimmie Johnson, *AS*, III, 3:54. See also Amie Lumpkin, *AS*, III, 3:131.

12. Chesnut, *Mary Chesnut's Civil War*, 818, 821, see also 760. See also Elmore Diaries and Books, 31 May 1865.

13. Thomas Journal, 29 May 1865. For more on the disappearance of the Thomas family's slaves, see Litwack, *Been in the Storm*, 293–96. See also Edmondston, *"Journal,"* 510.

14. Holmes, *Diary*, 435. See also Hawks, *Woman Doctor's Civil War*, 69–70.

15. Edmondston, *"Journal,"* 520, see also 521; Elmore Diaries and Books, 24 May 1865.

16. Jervey and Ravenel, *Two Diaries*, 13, 33; Henry William Ravenel, *The Private Journal of Henry William Ravenel, 1859–1887*, ed. Arney Robinson Childs (Columbia: University of South Carolina Press, 1947), 217; Myers, *Children of Pride*, 1274; See also Waitz, *Journal of Julia LeGrand*, 262.

17. Pringle, *Chicora Wood*, 270, see also 266–67.

18. Chesnut, *Mary Chesnut's Civil War*, 805–6. See also Edmondston, *"Journal,"* 306; Elmore Diaries and Books, 1 Oct. 1865.

19. Hawks, *Woman Doctor's Civil War*, 141. See also Harper, *Annie Harper's Journal*, 31; Edmondston, *"Journal,"* 273, 306; Pearson, *Letters from Port Royal*, 293–94.

20. Holmes, *Diary*, 428. See also Dawson, *Confederate Girl's Diary*, 178; Holmes, *Brokenburn*, 175; United Daughters of the Confederacy, *South Carolina Women*, 1:330; Thomas Journal, 29 May 1865, 17 Sept. 1866; Meriwether, *Recollections*, 167; Jones, *Labor of Love*, 68–71.

21. Litwack, *Been in the Storm*, 121. See also LeConte, *When the World Ended*, 102.

22. Ravenel, *Private Journal*, 247; Botume, *First Days*, 128–29.

23. Thomas Journal, 9 Oct. 1865; Holmes, *Diary*, 428; Elmore Reminiscences, 17 May 1865. A few white women claimed to be glad slavery was over, although they spoke with the benefit of hindsight. See, for example, Merrick, *Old Times in Dixie Land*, 19.

24. Elmore Reminiscences, 6 Mar. 1865; Logan, *Confederate Girlhood*, 87–88; LeConte, *When the World Ended*, 54; McIver Diary, 17 Apr. 1865. See also Elmore Reminiscences, 27 Dec. 1864, 28 Dec. 1864, 4 Mar. 1865.

25. Sam Polite, *AS*, III, 3:275. See also William Pratt, *AS*, III, 3:278; Benjamin Russell, *AS*, III, 4:54; Silas Smith, *AS*, III, 4:120.

26. Easterby, *South Carolina Rice Plantation*, 211, 210; Elmore Diaries and Books, 6 Mar. 1865, 4 Mar. 1865, 12 Mar. 1865, 31 May 1865, see also 24 May 1865.

27. Edmondston, *"Journal,"* 709, 711, 713. See also Rable, *Civil Wars*, 252–64; Litwack, *Been in the Storm*, esp. 346–51.

28. Jervey and Ravenel, *Two Diaries*, 33, 36, 37. Ravenel's diary is in the form of

a letter to her friend Meta Heyward, the "you" of the entries. See also Ravenel, *Private Journal*, 217.

29. Thomas Journal, 29 Mar. 1865. See also Chesnut, *Mary Chesnut's Civil War*, 682; Jones, *Heroines of Dixie*, 379.

30. McIver Diary, 2 May 1865; Clifton, *Life on Argyle Island*, 351, see also 353; Coxe, *Memories*, 48. See also Elmore Reminiscences, 24 May 1865; Magill, *Women*, 144–45; Harper, *Annie Harper's Journal*, 30–31; LeConte, *When the World Ended*, 112.

31. United Daughters of the Confederacy, *South Carolina Women*, 1:167.

32. Willie Lee Rose, *Rehearsal for Reconstruction: The Port Royal Experiment* (New York: Vintage, 1964).

33. Ibid.; Jacqueline Jones, *Soldiers of Light and Love: Northern Teachers and Georgia Blacks, 1865–1873* (Chapel Hill: University of North Carolina Press, 1980); Carolyn E. Wedin, "The Civil War and Black Women on the Sea Islands," in *Southern Women*, ed. Dillman, 71–80; Mohr, *Threshold of Freedom*, chap. 3; Litwack, *Been in the Storm*, chap. 9.

34. Taylor, *Black Woman's Civil War*, 61, 141–42; Lucretia Heyward, *AS*, II, 2:280; Laura M. Towne, *Letters and Diary of Laura M. Towne: Written from the Sea Islands of South Carolina, 1862–1884*, ed. Rupert Sargent Holland (Cambridge, Mass.: Riverside Press, 1912; New York: Negro University Press, 1969), 83. See also Pearson, *Letters from Port Royal*, 14.

35. Towne, *Letters and Diary*, 13, 133–34, see also 149, 209–10, 213, 246, 267, 275. See also Botume, *First Days*, 128–29.

36. Hawks, *Woman Doctor's Civil War*, 48–49; Pearson, *Letters from Port Royal*, 23, see also 24–25, 144, 169, 213–14, 287–88.

37. Hawks, *Woman Doctor's Civil War*, 50; Towne, *Letters and Diary*, 21. See also Pearson, *Letters from Port Royal*, 216–18.

38. Coxe, *Memories*, 72; Holmes, *Diary*, 456.

39. Rebecca Jane Grant, *AS*, II, 2:180.

40. For a discussion of the persistence rates of wealthy planters in Alabama, see Jonathan Wiener, *Social Origins of the New South: Alabama, 1860–1885* (Baton Rouge: Louisiana State University Press, 1978). See also C. Vann Woodward, *Origins of the New South, 1877–1913* (Baton Rouge: Louisiana State University Press, 1951; reprint, Baton Rouge: Louisiana State University Press, 1971); Steven Hahn, *The Roots of Southern Populism: Yeomen Farmers and the Transformation of the Georgia Upcountry, 1850–1890* (New York: Oxford University Press, 1983).

41. Smith, *Mason Smith Family Letters*, 213; Andrews, *War-Time Journal*, 373. See also Coxe, *Memories*, 70–72; Myers, *Children of Pride*, 1280.

42. Smedes, *Memorials*, 223. See also Kearney, *Slaveholder's Daughter*, 28.

43. Unidentified woman to aunt, 25 June 1867, Bruce, Jones, and Murchison Family Papers, USCar. See also Elmore Reminiscences, 25 June 1865, 1 July 1865.

44. Holmes, *Diary*, 445, 453, 471. See also Litwack, *Been in the Storm*, chap. 7, esp. 354–58.

45. Thomas Journal, 27 May 1865 and passim. The desire for white servants was

not unique to Thomas; see Clifton, *Life on Argyle Island*, 353; Holmes, *Diary*, 466; Litwack, *Been in the Storm*, 351–54.

46. Smith, *Mason Smith Family Letters*, 248; unidentified woman to Anne, 10 Oct. 1865, Frederick Adolphus Porcher Papers, USCar.

47. Edmondston, "*Journal*," 717–18; Myers, *Children of Pride*, 1287, 1408–9; Smith, *Mason Smith Family Letters*, 218–19.

48. Holmes, *Diary*, 445, 454, 456.

49. Andrews, *War-Time Journal*, 374–76, 378.

50. Holmes, *Diary*, 467, 469–70.

51. Andrews, like many other women whose youth coincided with the war, became self-supporting, working as a teacher, novelist, and author of botany textbooks. She never married.

52. Smith, *Mason Smith Family Letters*, 223; Easterby, *South Carolina Rice Plantation*, 212; Harper, *Annie Harper's Journal*, 31. See also Kearney, *Slaveholder's Daughter*, 23.

53. Elmore Reminiscences, 25 June 1865. See also Elmore Diaries and Books, 13 July 1865.

54. Elmore Diaries and Books, 25 June 1865, 6 July 1865.

55. Bleser, *Hammonds of Redcliffe*, 144–45. See also Chesnut, *Mary Chesnut's Civil War*, 833–34; unidentified man to daughters, 5 May 1865, Elias Horry Deas Papers, USCar.

56. Sally Elmore Taylor to sisters, 7 Oct. 1865, Franklin Harper Elmore Papers, USCar. One of her sisters was Grace Brown Elmore.

57. Meta Morris Grimball Diary, 20 Feb. 1866; Andrews, *War-Time Journal*, 320.

58. Bleser, *Hammonds of Redcliffe*, 144; Holmes, *Diary*, 468; Thomas Journal, 29 May 1865, see also 17 Sept. 1866. See also Myers, *Children of Pride*, 1308; Ed Barber, *AS*, II, 1:36; Jones, *Labor of Love*, 68–71.

59. For reuniting families see Litwack, *Been in the Storm*, 229–36; for legalizing marriages, 239–44.

60. For the views of one white woman on the Freedman's Bureau, see Edmondston, "*Journal*," 718–19, 726–27, and passim.

61. Historians debate the extent to which freedwomen worked in the fields after emancipation. Evidence from South Carolina suggests that they had few options other than working in the fields, although they probably did not work the same number of hours or with the same intensity that they were forced to before. See Roger L. Ransom and Richard Sutch, *One Kind of Freedom: The Economic Consequences of Emancipation* (New York: Cambridge University Press, 1977). Part of the confusion may stem from the practice of requiring only male heads of household to sign labor contracts, although expectations of the labor of women and children were often specified in them. In addition, witnesses to the contracts were often wives of the freedmen named in them. See Records Relating to Contracts, Records of the Assistant Commissioner for the State of South Carolina, Bureau of Refugees, Freedmen, and Abandoned Lands, 1865–1870, National Archives, Washington, D.C. Historians

generally agree that the productivity of southern farms and plantations decreased in the years after emancipation, in part because of the reduction in labor by women and children. An author in *DeBow's Review* was aware of this in 1868: "The women and children of the colored race are no longer field producers to the extent they were formerly." He urged southern whites to use the labor of black women and children more "advantageously" by opening textile mills. "Exodus," *DeBow's Review* 5, after the war series (Nov. 1868): 982. See also W. M. Burwell, "Our Black Peasantry," *DeBow's Review* (June 1880): 9–10, 37. See also Genovese, *Roll, Jordan, Roll*, 490, 501; Gutman, *Black Family*, 167–68; Eric Foner, *Reconstruction: America's Unfinished Revolution, 1863–1877* (New York: Harper and Row, 1988), 85–88, 200–201, 400, 405; Jones, *Labor of Love*, chap. 2, esp. 45–46, 58–68; Litwack, *Been in the Storm*, 244–47. On restoring labor discipline, see Litwack, *Been in the Storm*, chap. 7.

62. Myers, *Children of Pride*, 1374; Sara Brown, *AS*, II, 1:142–43; Adele Frost, *AS*, II, 2:88–89; Violet Guntharpe, *AS*, II, 2:217.

63. Anne Rice, *AS*, III, 4:11; George McAlilley, *AS*, III, 3:144; Milton Marshall, *AS*, III, 3:172; Adeline Grey, *AS*, II, 2:205; William Henry Davis, *AS*, II, 1:308; Lucy Gallman, *AS*, II, 2:101. See also Sylvia Duralt, *AS*, II, 1:337; Fannie Griffin, *AS*, II, 2:211; Hester Hunter, *AS*, II, 2:340; Easter Lockhart, *AS*, III, 3:108; Charlie Meadow, *AS*, III, 3:178; Emoline Satterwhite, *AS*, III, 4:75; Victoria Adams, *AS*, II, 1:12; Julia Woodbury, *AS*, III, 4:244.

64. Myers, *Children of Pride*, 1280; Smith, *Mason Smith Family Letters*, 226.

65. Edmondston, *"Journal,"* 717–18. See also Ames, *New England Woman's Diary*, 14–16.

66. Elmore Diaries and Books, 4 Mar. 1865; A. R. Salley to aunt, 13 Nov. 1865, Bruce, Jones, and Murchison Family Papers.

67. Fannie Griffin, *AS*, II, 2:211; A. R. Salley to aunt, 13 Nov. 1865, Bruce, Jones, and Murchison Family Papers.

68. Emoline Wilson, *AS*, III, 4:213. Complaints about pay were common. See Pearson, *Letters from Port Royal*, 250, 303–4; Foner, *Reconstruction*, 57; Jones, *Labor of Love*, 54–55, 62.

69. Rebecca Jane Grant, *AS*, II, 2:181.

70. Solomon Caldwell, *AS*, II, 1:170. For postwar rape of black women by white men, see Gutman, *Black Family*, 23–28, 386–402; Litwack, *Been in the Storm*, 265–68.

71. William Oliver, *AS*, III, 3:218. See also Bouregard Corry, *AS*, II, 1:228.

Chapter 10: Toward the Future

1. John and Keating S. Ball Plantation Daybook, 5 Apr. 1869, 7 Apr. 1869, 21 Apr. 1869, 24 Apr. 1869, UNC; Adeline Grey, *AS*, II, 2:207–8; Frances Butler Leigh, *Ten Years on a Georgia Plantation since the War* (London: Richard Bentley and Son, 1883), 51; Emoline Wilson, *AS*, III, 4:213. See also Elizabeth Watris Allston Pringle [Patience Pennington], *A Woman Rice Planter*, ed. Cornelius O. Cathey (New York:

Macmillan, 1913; Cambridge, Mass.: Belknap Press of Harvard University Press, 1961).

2. Botume's conclusion reflected her liberal New England background: "We could not help wishing that since so much of the work was done by the colored women,—raising the provisions for their families, besides making and selling their own cotton, they might also hold some of the offices held by the men. I am confident they would despatch business if allowed to go to the polls; instead of listening and hanging around all day, discussing matters of which they knew so little, they would exclaim,—'Let me vote and go; I've got work to do.'" Botume, *First Days*, 273.

3. Chesnut, *Mary Chesnut's Civil War*, 830.

4. Thomas Journal, 19 June 1869, 26 June 1869. See also Botume, *First Days*, 277–78.

5. Charlie Meadow, *AS*, III, 3:178.

6. Sabe Rutledge, *AS*, III, 4:67–68; Botume, *First Days*, 276; William Oliver, *AS*, III, 3:218. See also Adeline Grey, *AS*, II, 2:206–7; Jones, *Labor of Love*, 63–65.

7. Holmes, *Brokenburn*, 373.

8. Unidentified woman to aunt, 25 June 1867, 10 Jan. 1869, Bruce, Jones, and Murchison Family Papers; Thomas Journal, 3 Dec. 1868, 12 Feb. 1869, 7 May 1869, and passim.

9. Thomas Journal, 3 Dec. 1868, 7 May 1869, 20 June 1869, and passim.

10. Leigh, *Georgia Plantation*, 52. See also McIver Diary, 4 Jan. 1867, 22 Jan. 1880, 30 Jan. 1880.

11. Unidentified woman to aunt, 31 Jan. 1867, 25 June 1867, 10 Jan. 1869, Bruce, Jones, and Murchison Family Papers; Holmes, *Diary*, 468, see also 488. See also Leigh, *Georgia Plantation*, 56–59, 83; Holmes, *Brokenburn*, 362; Myers, *Children of Pride*, 1405; Elmore Diaries and Books, 29 Nov. 1867, 30 Nov. 1867.

12. Julia Woodberry, *AS*, III, 4:244.

13. Dolly Haynes, *AS*, II, 2:259.

14. Few previously wealthy women were willing to admit the degree of want they suffered. Grace Brown Elmore confided to her journal that she could not afford firewood and was forced to get into bed for warmth. She was so eager for "the prospect of a good dinner" that she left her company one evening to barter with a black man. Elmore Diaries and Books, 21 Nov. 1867, see also 22 Nov. 1867. Her sister Sally left Columbia with her husband for a plantation in the country, to Sally's regret: "I had no enthusiasm in these lines, but with tribulation, persistence and beating out all that was dormant to meet opportunity," managed to survive. Taylor Memoir. One of the most detailed accounts of financial difficulties is in the Thomas Journal; see also Thomas, *Secret Eye*.

15. [Fannie Caison] to M. B. Murchison, 23 Nov. 1866, and unidentified woman to Aunt, 31 Jan. 1867, both in Bruce, Jones, and Murchison Family Papers; Mary Elizabeth Anderson Moore Diary, USCar; McIver Diary, 3 Feb. 1870.

16. Ravenel, *Private Journal*, 355. See also Leigh, *Georgia Plantation*, 37, 52.

17. Unidentified woman to aunt, 31 Jan. 1867, see also Eliza to Mrs. E. C.

Murchison, 26 July 1868, both in Bruce, Jones, and Murchison Family Papers. See also Darling, *Letters*, 17; Myers, *Children of Pride*, 1318, 1365.

18. United Daughters of the Confederacy, *South Carolina Women*, 1:167; McIver Diary, 1 Jan. 1867, 22 Jan. 1880, 1 July 1867; Leigh, *Georgia Plantation*, 83, 91. See also Pringle, *Chicora Wood*, 266–67, 270; Chesnut, *Mary Chesnut's Civil War*, xiii; Myers, *Children of Pride*, 1340–41, 1365–66, 1369–70, 1374.

19. Coxe, *Memories*, 71–72. See also unidentified woman to aunt, 10 Jan. 1869, Bruce, Jones, and Murchison Family Papers; Elmore Diaries and Books, 4 Dec. 1867.

20. Chesnut, *Mary Chesnut's Civil War*, xvi–xvii, quotation from 350; Muhlenfeld, *Mary Boykin Chesnut*.

21. Holmes, *Diary*, 471, xxii, quotations from 460, 469. See also Smedes, *Memorials*, xiv–xv; Dorothy Sterling, ed., *The Trouble They Seen: Black People Tell the Story of Reconstruction* (Garden City, N.Y.: Doubleday, 1976), 59.

22. Kearney, *Slaveholder's Daughter*, 55–57; Elmore Diaries and Books, 1 Apr. 1867, 12 June–29 Sept. 1867, 27 Oct. 1867, 29 Apr. 1868.

23. "Boys," *DeBow's Review* 1, after the war series (Apr. 1866): 369–70; "Review of Xariffa's Poems," *DeBow's Review* (Mar. 1870): 301; "Our Boys and Girls," *DeBow's Review* 5, after the war series (Sept. 1868): 856–57.

24. Harper, *Annie Harper's Journal*, 48; Burwell, *Girl's Life*, 195; Elmore Diaries and Books, 16 June 1867.

25. "Our Boys and Girls," 862–65. See also "Southern Female Education—The Carnatz Institute," 447.

26. Burwell, "Our Black Peasantry," 10. In context, Burwell is clearly talking about women of both races.

27. "Letter of the Women of the South to Mr. Peabody," *DeBow's Review* (Feb. 1870): 200–201.

28. Taylor Memoir.

29. "What's to Be Done with the Negroes?" 579–80. See also "The Negro Problem," 249–50.

30. Burwell, "Our Black Peasantry," 8; "Department of Freedmen: Education of the Freedmen," *DeBow's Review* 3, after the war series (Mar. 1867): 311; "Old Maids and Old Bachelors," *DeBow's Review* 2, after the war series (Sept. 1866): 289–90.

31. Sylvia Cannon, *AS*, II, 1:181; Julia Woodberry, *AS*, III, 4:244. See also Granny Cain, *AS*, II, 1:167; Caroline Farrow, *AS*, II, 2:40; Hester Hunter, *AS*, II, 2:340; Julia Woodbury, *AS*, III, 4:243; Litwack, *Been in the Storm*, 236–37.

32. Smith, *A Charlestonian's Recollections*, 127; Sterling, *The Trouble They Seen*, 58–59; Botume, *First Days*, 142; Sally Elmore Taylor to sisters, 7 Oct. 1865, Franklin Harper Elmore Papers, USCar. See also Towne, *Letters and Diary*, 131.

33. Ezra Adams, *AS*, II, 1:6; Leigh, *Georgia Plantation*, 164.

34. Sterling, *The Trouble They Seen*, 197–98; Mack Taylor, *AS*, III, 4:159.

35. Towne, *Letters and Diary*, 183–84. See also Ames, *New England Woman's Diary*, 92; Botume, *First Days*, 273; Foner, *Reconstruction*, 290–91, 574; Jones, *Labor of Love*, 66–67; Johnson, *Sea Islands*, 208. One black man even claimed political au-

thority over Mary Ames, a white teacher employed by the Freedman's Bureau. When she "ventured a remark" at a meeting, she "was quickly told by Ishmael, their leader, that I had 'Better go into the house and attend to study,' thus showing early in his life as freedman, that he had learned the proper sphere of woman." Ames never considered the possibility that Ishmael objected to her participation because she was white. Ames, *New England Woman's Diary*, 121.

36. Sterling, *The Trouble They Seen*, 218.

37. Moses Lyles, *AS*, III, 3:141; Charley Barber, *AS*, II, 1:32; Ed Barber, *AS*, II, 1:36; Millie Barber, *AS*, II, 1:40. On white women marrying for money, see Felton, *Country Life*, 63.

38. Thomas Journal, 18 June 1869. See also Sally Elmore Taylor to sisters, 7 Oct. 1865, Franklin Harper Elmore Papers, USCar; Chesnut, *Mary Chesnut's Civil War*, 830.

39. Botume, *First Days*, 277–78. See also Myers, *Children of Pride*, 1310.

40. Edmondston, "*Journal*," 723–24, see also 717–18.

41. Sterling, *The Trouble They Seen*, 392–93. Violence of all sorts against black women was common in the postwar years, as it had been before. See Jones, *Labor of Love*, 71–72; Litwack, *Been in the Storm*, 275–82 and passim.

42. Records of the Assistant Commissioner for the State of South Carolina, 1865–70, Bureau of Refugees, Freedmen, and Abandoned Lands, National Archives, Washington, D.C.; Litwack, *Been in the Storm*, 245–46; Towne, *Letters and Diary*, 183–84; Joel Williamson, *The Crucible of Race: Black-White Relations in the American South since Emancipation* (New York: Oxford University Press, 1984), 46–47.

43. Myers, *Children of Pride*, 1303, 1319, 1370. See also Ward, *Children of Bladensfield*, 110

44. Easterby, *South Carolina Rice Plantation*, 215; Thomas Journal, 7 Feb. 1870, 30 July 1870, 14 May 1869, see also 1 June 1869 and passim. See also Taylor Memoir.

45. Elmore Reminiscences, 5 Oct. 1865; Edmondston, "*Journal*," 719, 722, see also 721, 726, and passim. See also Myers, *Children of Pride*, 1341, 1391.

46. Andrews, *War-Time Journal*, 374–75; Myers, *Children of Pride*, 1308, 1313.

47. Unidentified woman to aunt, 31 Jan. 1867, Bruce, Jones, and Murchison Family Papers; Meta Morris Grimball Diary, 20 Feb. 1866; G. W. McDonald to Moses [McDonald], 7 Feb. 1866, Bruce, Jones, and Murchison Family Papers; Holmes, *Diary*, 488. See also McIver Diary, 4 Jan. 1867.

48. Suzanne S. Keitt to Mr. Carrigan, 20 Nov. 1879, Suzanne Mandeville Sparks Keitt Papers, USCar; Bleser, *Hammonds of Redcliffe*, 136.

49. Unidentified woman to Anne, 10 Oct. 1865, Frederick Adolphus Porcher Papers. See also Leigh, *Georgia Plantation*, 216; Bleser, *Hammonds of Redcliffe*, 262, 264; Eliza to Mrs. E. C. Murchison, 25 June 1867, Bruce, Jones, and Murchison Family Papers; Sally Elmore Taylor to sisters, 7 Oct. 1865, Franklin Harper Elmore Papers, USCar; Thomas Journal, 29 May 1865, 3 Dec. 1868, 30 July 1879; Andrews, *War-Time Journal*, 320, 344, 347; Chesnut, *Mary Chesnut's Civil War*, 833; William Pratt, *AS*, III, 3:279.

50. United Daughters of the Confederacy, *South Carolina Women*, 1:181; Burwell, *Girl's Life*, 44, see also 45–46, 208. See also McGuire, *Diary of a Southern Refugee*, 7.

51. Andrews, *War-Time Journal*, 347; Leigh, *Georgia Plantation*, 92–93, 161, see also 160, 164–66, 238–40. See also Andrews, *War-Time Journal*, 344–45; Coxe, *Memories*, 73; Maggie Black, *AS*, II, 1:59.

52. Thomas Journal, 16 Sept. 1866 and passim; Smith, *Mason Smith Family Letters*, 260.

53. Unidentified woman to Anne, 10 Oct. 1865, Frederick Adolphus Porcher Papers; Holmes, *Diary*, 466. See also Leigh, *Georgia Plantation*, 191; Thomas Journal, 26 June 1869.

54. Thomas Journal, 7 May 1869; Leigh, *Georgia Plantation*, 238–39. See also Myers, *Children of Pride*, 1382; Meriwether, *Recollections*, 174–75.

55. Thomas Journal, 26 June 1869. See also Meriwether, *Recollections*, 152–53. White women also supported the campaign of terror by the Ku Klux Klan and others. See Meriwether, *Recollections*, 204–9.

56. Elmore Reminiscences, 25 June 1865; Wright, *Southern Girl*, 18; Burwell, *Girl's Life*, 185–86, see also 188, 207–8. See also Chesnut, *Mary Chesnut's Civil War*, 821.

57. Edmondston, "*Journal*," 727; Harper, *Annie Harper's Journal*, 37, 32, see also 36, 38; Burwell, *Girl's Life*, 185–86, see also 188, 207–8.

58. Myers, *Children of Pride*, 1341, 1304. See also Putnam, *Richmond during the War*, 179–80.

59. Elmore Reminiscences, 25 June 1865.

Index

MARLI F. WEINER has published numerous articles on southern women and slavery as well as *A Heritage of Woe: The Civil War Diary of Grace Brown Elmore, 1861–1868*. She is an associate professor of history at the University of Maine.

Books in the Series Women in American History